W9-AMA-056

The Human Tradition around the World

Series Editors

WILLIAM H. BEEZLEY, Professor of History, University of Arizona
COLIN M. MACLACHLAN, John Christy Barr Distinguished
Professor of History, Tulane University

Each volume in this series is devoted to providing minibiographies of "real people" who, with their idiosyncratic behavior, personalize the collective experience of grand themes, national myths, ethnic stereotypes, and gender relationships. In some cases, their stories reveal the irrelevance of national events, global processes, and cultural encounters for men and women engaged in everyday life. The personal dimension gives perspective to history, which of necessity is a sketch of past experience.
The authors of each volume in this historical series are determined to make the past literal. They write accounts that identify the essential character of everyday lives of individuals. In doing so, these historians allow us to share the human traditions that find expression in these lives.

Volumes in The Human Tradition around the World Series

William B. Husband, ed. *The Human Tradition in Modern Russia* (2000). Cloth ISBN 0-8420-2856-0   Paper ISBN 0-8420-2857-9

K. Steven Vincent and Alison Klairmont-Lingo, eds. *The Human Tradition in Modern France* (2000). Cloth ISBN 0-8420-2804-8 Paper ISBN 0-8420-2805-6

Anne Walthall, ed. *The Human Tradition in Modern Japan* (2001). Cloth ISBN 0-8420-2911-7   Paper ISBN 0-8420-2912-5

Kenneth J. Hammond, ed. *The Human Tradition in Premodern China* (2002). Cloth ISBN 0-8420-2958-3   Paper ISBN 0-8420-2959-1

Kenneth J. Andrien, ed. *The Human Tradition in Colonial Latin America* (2002). Cloth ISBN 0-8420-2887-0   Paper ISBN 0-8420-2888-9

THE HUMAN TRADITION IN

COLONIAL
LATIN AMERICA

THE HUMAN TRADITION IN
COLONIAL LATIN AMERICA

EDITED BY
KENNETH J. ANDRIEN

NUMBER 5

SR BOOKS

Lanham • Boulder • New York • Toronto • Oxford

Published by SR Books
An imprint of Rowman & Littlefield Publishers, Inc.
A wholly owned subsidary of The Rowman & Littlefield Publishing Group, Inc.
4501 Forbes Boulevard, Suite 200
Lanham, MD 20706

PO Box 317
Oxford
OX2 9RU, UK

Copyright © 2002 by Scholarly Resources, Inc.
First SR Book edition 2004

Library of Congress Cataloging-in-Publication Data

The human tradition in Colonial Latin America / edited by Kenneth J.
Andrien.
    p. cm. — (The human tradition around the world ; v. 5)
    Includes bibliographical references and index.
    ISBN 0-8420-2887-0 (cloth : alk. paper) — ISBN 0-8420-2888-9
(pbk. : alk. paper)
    1. Latin America—History—To 1830—Biography. 2. Social
conflict—Latin America—History. 3. Latin America—Social
conditions. 4. Latin America—Biography. I. Andrien, Kenneth J.,
1951–   II. Human tradition around the world ; no. 5

F1412 .H76 2002
980".01—dc21   2002018763

∞ The paper used in this publication meets the minimum requirements
of the American National Standard for permanence of paper for printed
library materials, Z39.48, 1984.

To Jonathan and Elizabeth

About the Author

Kenneth J. Andrien is professor of history at The Ohio State University, Columbus. He is the author of *Crisis and Decline: The Viceroyalty of Peru in the Seventeenth Century* (1985); *The Kingdom of Quito, 1690–1830: The State and Regional Development* (1995); and *Andean Worlds: Indigenous History, Culture, and Consciousness under Spanish Rule, 1532–1825* (2001). He has also co-edited (with Rolena Adorno) *Transatlantic Encounters: Europeans and Andeans in the Sixteenth Century* (1991) and (with Lyman Johnson) *The Political Economy of Spanish America in the Age of Revolution, 1750–1850* (1994). Professor Andrien has published numerous scholarly articles in *Past and Present, Hispanic American Historical Review, The Americas, Journal of Latin American Studies, Colonial Latin American Review,* and in various books, encyclopedias, and research guides.

I believe in aristocracy, though—if that is the right word, and if a democrat may use it. Not an aristocracy of power, based upon rank and influence, but an aristocracy of the sensitive, the considerate and the plucky. Its members are to be found in all nations and classes, and all through the ages, and there is a secret understanding between them when they meet. They represent the true human tradition, the one permanent victory of our queer race over cruelty and chaos. Thousands of them perish in obscurity, a few are great names. They are sensitive for others as well as for themselves, they are considerate without being fussy, their pluck is not swankiness but the power to endure, and they can take a joke.

—E. M. Forster, *Two Cheers for Democracy* (1951)

Acknowledgments

This book has emerged from my experiences both as a research scholar and as a teacher. While administrators in higher education often explain that scholarship and classroom teaching reinforce each other, too often they do not. Preparing and teaching a class, grading papers, and spending time with students often takes hours away from conducting research and writing. In the case of this volume, however, that synergism between scholarship and teaching did occur. For over twenty-five years I have listened to my colleagues in various restaurants, bars, and cafés in Spain, Latin America, and the United States recount fascinating stories about the life histories of individuals, which they had uncovered during their archival research. During my time teaching at The Ohio State University, my own students also have found the real lives of historical figures one of the most interesting aspects of history classes. As a result, I have called on my colleagues to contribute some of the more "colorful" stories of ordinary people in colonial Latin America to this volume. I sincerely hope that students at Ohio State and elsewhere will find them an interesting and useful way to understand the past.

In the process of editing this collection, I have accumulated many debts. The History Department at Ohio State provided two dedicated research assistants, Sherwin Bryant and Andrea Smidt, who helped in innumerable ways to bring this volume to completion. Richard Hopper of Scholarly Resources gave me the opportunity to undertake the project and waited patiently for me to conclude it. I would like to thank the many students who took my classes at Ohio State; the joys and occasional frustrations of teaching those courses have inspired this book. As always, my wife, Anne, and our children, Jonathan and Elizabeth, have given me the love and emotional support that sustained my efforts. Indeed, I am dedicating this book to Jonathan and Elizabeth because being a father and watching my own children's efforts to learn about the past have taught me invaluable lessons, which I hope will make me a more sensitive, caring teacher. I trust that they will also make this collection a better and more useful book.

Contents

Introduction
Kenneth J. Andrien   xiii

**I New World Beginnings and Efforts to Create a
   Colonial Social Order, 1492–1610**   1

1 Gaspar Antonio Chi: Bridging the Conquest of Yucatán   6
   Matthew Restall

2 Don Melchior Caruarayco: A *Kuraka* of Cajamarca
   in Sixteenth-Century Peru   22
   Susan E. Ramírez

3 Doña Isabel Sisa: A Sixteenth-Century Indian Woman
   Resisting Gender Inequalities   35
   Ana María Presta

4 Domingos Fernandes Nobre: "Tomacauna," a Go-Between
   in Sixteenth-Century Brazil   51
   Alida C. Metcalf

5 The Mysterious Catalina: Indian or Spaniard?   64
   Noble David Cook

II The Mature Colonial Order, 1610–1740   85

6 Ursula de Jesús: A Seventeenth-Century
   Afro-Peruvian Mystic   88
   Nancy E. van Deusen

7 Zumbi of Palmares: Challenging the Portuguese
   Colonial Order   104
   Mary Karasch

8 Diego de Ocaña: Holy Wanderer   121
   Kenneth Mills

9 Felipe Guaman Poma de Ayala: Native Writer and
   Litigant in Early Colonial Peru   140
   Rolena Adorno

10 AhChan: The Conquest of the Itza Maya Kingdom   164
    Grant D. Jones

III Reform, Resistance, and Rebellion, 1740–1825   **189**

11 Pedro de Ayarza: The Purchase of Whiteness   **194**
    Ann Twinam

12 Victorina Loza: Quiteña Merchant in the Second Half of
    the Eighteenth Century   **211**
    Christiana Borchart de Moreno

13 José Antonio da Silva: Marriage and Concubinage in
    Colonial Brazil   **229**
    Muriel S. Nazzari

14 Eugenio Sinanyuca: Militant, Nonrevolutionary *Kuraka*, and
    Community Defender   **241**
    Ward Stavig

15 Juan Barbarín: The 1795 French Conspiracy in Buenos Aires   **259**
    Lyman L. Johnson

16 Miguel García: Black Soldier in the Wars of Independence   **278**
    Peter Blanchard

17 Angela Batallas: A Fight for Freedom in Guayaquil   **293**
    Camilla Townsend

Index   **309**

Introduction

KENNETH J. ANDRIEN

𝒜 major challenge in teaching colonial Latin American history is conveying to students the ways in which major historical events influenced the daily life experiences of common people. All of the essays in this volume address this problem by providing life histories, which show real people in colonial Spanish and Portuguese America adjusting to the large, impersonal historical forces that helped shape their lives. These personal stories seldom deal with momentous historical events, yet each one offers a glimpse into important aspects of everyday life in colonial Latin America. After all, history is never only the affairs of kings, noblemen, and generals; it is also those of more ordinary men and women who cope with daily challenges. At the same time, each of the personal histories contained in this book illustrates a recurring theme in Spanish and Portuguese colonial societies: the enduring social tensions that emerged when the political, social, religious, and economic ideals of the state and the Roman Catholic Church conflicted with the realities of colonial life. These societal tensions could arise from squabbles over a wide range of disparate issues—gender roles, racial and ethnic identities, or religious orthodoxy. Some could be resolved, while others reflected deep sources of discontent that exploded into violence and rebellion. In all cases, these daily "lived" experiences of people in colonial Latin America reveal how men and women dealt with the contradictions between elite notions of order and stability and the more disorderly and uncertain realities of everyday life.

ORDER AND DISORDER

Spanish and Portuguese settlers in the New World (then called the Indies) shared many basic assumptions about social stratification, religious orthodoxy, and entrepreneurship. The conquistadors and those who followed them wanted to establish a new colonial order that guaranteed their own preeminence and also maintained political, social, economic, cultural, and religious ties to their homelands in the Iberian peninsula. These new colonial societies would be rigidly hierarchical, with only limited social mobility, particularly for Amerindians, people of mixed racial ancestry, and persons of African descent. Church officials decided to incorporate the large Amerindian population into the social order by converting them to the "true faith." After all, the Iberian invaders had justified their overthrow of indigenous polities and subsequent colonization projects by vowing to reap a bountiful harvest of indigenous souls for the Catholic faith—a new crusade. And finally, the settlers went to the Americas to get rich. Most came from the middle classes in Spain and Portugal and had only limited prospects of rising in wealth and status at home. The New World offered rich deposits of gold and silver, abundant land, and many exotic products not available in Europe. As Bernal Díaz del Castillo, a Spanish conquistador in Mexico explained, the invaders acted "in the service of God and of His Majesty, and to give light to those in darkness, and to acquire that gold which most men covet."[1]

To these Spanish and Portuguese settlers, social status, honor, and wealth were assigned at birth; changing them threatened God's natural order. For most elites, however, social mobility signaled disorder—not a valuable way to ensure that society rewarded merit. In Spain, for example, gaining admission to a university, holding a government job, or entering the clergy required proof of "purity of the blood" (*limpieza de sangre*)—that is, an ancestry untainted by blood ties to Judaism, Islam, or social inferiors. Sumptuary legislation (laws limiting the consumption of luxury items) forbade commoners from carrying swords or from dressing above their social station. Honorific titles such as "don" and "doña" conveyed honor, status, and real privileges: freedom from judicial torture, certain exemptions from taxation, and the right to wear a sword. Iberian towns usually were constructed according to a grid pattern, with a central plaza surrounded by the church, municipal government buildings, the houses of some prominent citizens, and perhaps a monastery or convent. Where citizens resided in the city also reflected their social class and standing. In short, social hierarchies remained deeply rooted in the Iberian mentality.

Religion had become a key ingredient in enforcing unity in the Iberian peninsula, particularly in the Spanish kingdoms. While Portugal was a relatively united polity, Spain was a loose dynastic union of the crowns of Castile and Aragon (until the eighteenth century), with separate currencies, laws, customs, and several commonly spoken languages. During most of the Medieval period, Jews suffered from bigotry but also continued to exercise their faith, as Christians and Moors (Muslims) competed for control of the peninsula during the seven-hundred-year Reconquista. Given this heritage, Iberia remained a political and cultural polyglot, forcing the kings of both Spain and Portugal to rely on the Catholic Church as a key unifying institution. As a result, with the fall of the last Muslim kingdom of Granada in 1492, King Ferdinand and Queen Isabel of Spain reinforced the Church's power by ending the long era of religious coexistence and expelling all Jews who did not accept conversion to Christianity. After consolidating control in formerly Moorish regions, the Spanish crown issued a similar edict in 1502 that ordered the expulsion of any Muslims who refused conversion to Catholicism.[2] The task of enforcing religious orthodoxy in their kingdoms fell to the Holy Office of the Inquisition, a Church council designed to police the purity of the faith. The intermittent 700 years of warfare during the Reconquista had convinced Iberians that whenever different faiths existed side by side, disorder, conflict, and bloodshed inevitably followed.

Despite these shared ideals, most Spanish and Portuguese settlers found it difficult to impose European political, social, economic, and religious hierarchies in the New World. Resources were more open and difficult to control and maintain. Land became more readily available, particularly after European epidemic diseases decimated indigenous populations. Even the large deposits of gold and silver could be mined by anyone with both luck and an entrepreneurial spirit, regardless of a person's social class upon arrival. The invasion, conquest, and settlement of the Americas was essentially a middle-class enterprise; the wealthy had little incentive to risk their lives and fortunes, and the poor lacked the money to pay for passage to the Indies. Over time, men of new wealth and status claimed the title of "don," whether or not their birthright justified it. Sumptuary laws were more difficult to enforce. Spanish and Portuguese officials in the Indies, for example, continually railed against the lowborn and even slaves who dressed above their station in silks and satins. Even religious unity proved troublesome. Although the crown had founded a Holy Office of the Inquisition in both Mexico City and Lima by 1569, it had no jurisdiction over Amerindians. At first, conversion efforts proceeded smoothly, but later it became clear that many indigenous communities still clung to their traditional religious beliefs, often merging them with Christianity in ways that horrified members of the Church hierarchy. In short, the Spanish and Portuguese overseas possessions were truly a "New World" that mixed European, Amerindian, and African societal values.

European colonizers' attempts to control the large Amerindian population and the growing numbers of African slave laborers hardly created the more "orderly" societies of Iberia. In the Spanish Indies, for example, authorities attempted to enforce a legal separation of the races, establishing a corporate status for Amerindians, the Republica de Indios. The indigenous peoples had to pay a head tax, serve periodic terms of forced labor, and remain in Spanish-style towns (called *reducciones* in Peru). The failure of this policy of separation became apparent with the rise of a racially diverse population. Clerical and state authorities struggled to impose order by establishing categories for every possible mixture, as this partial list from New Spain demonstrates:

1) Spaniard and Indian beget *mestizo*
2) Mestizo and Spanish woman beget *castizo*
3) Castizo woman and Spaniard beget Spaniard
4) Spanish woman and Negro beget mulatto
5) Spaniard and mulatto woman beget *morisco*
6) Morisco woman and Spaniard beget *albino*
7) Spaniard and albino woman beget *torna atrás*
8) Indian and torna atrás beget *lobo*.[3]

Fixing social categories for the infinite number of racial combinations was clearly a futile exercise.

Over time the Spanish and Portuguese possessions in the Americas developed more stable, diverse economies, but signs of instability and disorder persisted. In the vast Spanish possessions in North and South America, European settlers established a network of regional markets initially based on the extraction of gold and silver deposits, which they exchanged for European imports. By the seventeenth century, however, these market exchanges expanded as several other viable economic activities emerged: agro-pastoral enterprises, manufacturing, and artisan production. In Portuguese Brazil, settlers initially bartered with Amerindian groups for brazilwood, a tree that yielded a red dye used by European textile producers. The success of coastal sugar cultivation, particularly in the northeastern provinces of Bahia and Pernambuco, laid the foundation for a prosperous colonial economy tied to Europe, the principal market for Brazilian sugar. The discovery of gold in the interior provinces of Minas Gerais, Mato Grosso, and Goiás also prompted a move to settle these remote frontier zones. Nevertheless, the expansion of these colonial economies provided both pitfalls and opportunities for European settlers, not the more stable socioeconomic order that prevailed in their homelands. Wealth could be made and squandered in a single generation, and social controls over access to wealth and status often proved difficult to enforce. A poor mulatto in the gold-mining zones of Minas Gerais, for example, might make a fortune that eclipsed the assets of a successful coastal sugar planter.

By the seventeenth century, social hierarchies and religious orthodoxy became more entrenched in the Spanish and Portuguese possessions. Colonial elites maintained control over society by inculcating the belief that all social classes and both sexes were connected in a hierarchical pattern established by God, with each member of society having certain responsibilities and rights. According to the Italian Marxist, Antonio Gramsci,[4] this represented a form of cultural "hegemony," which involved acceptance by all members of society. It also united people more effectively than brute force. Widespread belief that inequality represented the "natural order" allowed elites to dominate the lower classes and men to dominate women. The power of the Catholic Church also gave this hegemonic social ideal greater legitimacy by linking prevailing social attitudes to the "will of God." Ordinary people often internalized these values of European cultural superiority and the subordination of women to men.[5]

Despite the overall prevalence of this colonial worldview, individuals and groups contested inequalities and attempted to negotiate a better position for themselves. Sometimes, these everyday forms of resistance turned violent, and full-scale revolts against the colonial order erupted, such as the rebellion of Túpac Amaru in 1781. Nonetheless, full-blown rebellions were rare, and individuals most often resisted or contested their status in more limited, personal ways—by practicing indigenous religious rituals, resisting an employer's sexual advances, or promoting new ideas that challenged the prevailing order.

THE HUMAN TRADITION

The lives of the men and women that fill this volume epitomize what E. M. Forster has called the "true human tradition." According to Forster, such ordinary people represent "not an aristocracy of power, based upon rank and influence, but an aristocracy of the sensitive, the considerate, the plucky."[6] Their stories often challenged the prevailing colonial social, economic, and religious order. These biographies are not a representative sample of larger historical trends but instead give a single profile that opens a window onto colonial society. Each individual history also epitomizes what cultural critic Walter Mignolo calls "border thinking." These people did not always accept the hegemonic colonial order but viewed life from the borders or margins of society, which gave them a different perspective about the prevailing societal norms.[7] As a result, their lives demonstrate graphically how social tensions and disorder emerged when individuals attempted to cope with the demands of the values of colonial society as well as with the challenges of everyday life.

The life stories presented in this volume span the chronological divisions of the colonial era in Spanish America and Brazil. The selections in Part I illustrate the conflicting attitudes over efforts to create the new colonial social order. The selections in Part II deal with the struggles of a diverse group of individuals who were attempting to cope with prevailing hegemonic colonial social values. Part III presents the attitudes and realities of individuals dealing with the changes prompted by imperial reforms, rebellions against the colonial regime, and the turbulent wars of independence. Although very different from each other, the lives depicted here demonstrate the continual social tensions that emerged when ordinary people, in large and small ways, attempted to carve out a place for themselves despite the constraints that society imposed on them. From the turbulent years following the Spanish invasion in the sixteenth century to the long, slow-motion collapse of the colonial order between 1808 and 1825, these individuals dealt with life's many challenges, using a wide variety of strategies that ranged from reaching an accommodation with the hegemonic social order to violent rebellion. While their histories may not always be noble or dramatic, they afford insights into the lives of ordinary people, the true human tradition in colonial Latin America.

NOTES

1. Bernal Díaz del Castillo, *The Conquest of New Spain*, trans. J. M. Cohen (London, 1963), 9.

2. J. H. Elliott, *Imperial Spain, 1469–1716* (New York, 1963), 46–52.

3. Magnus Morner, *Race Mixture in Colonial Latin America* (Boston, 1967), 58.

4. Antonio Gramsci, *Selections from the Prison Notebooks of Antonio Gramsci*, ed. and trans. Quinto Hoare and Geoffrey Nowell Smith (New York, 1971), 12–13, 416–19.

5. David G. Sweet and Gary B. Nash, eds., *Struggle and Survival in Colonial America* (Berkeley, 1981), 6.

6. E. M. Forster, *Two Cheers for Democracy* (New York, 1951), 26.

7. Walter B. Mignolo, *Local Histories/Global Designs: Coloniality, Subaltern Knowledges, and Border Thinking* (Princeton, NJ, 2000), passim.

PART I

NEW WORLD BEGINNINGS AND EFFORTS TO CREATE A COLONIAL SOCIAL ORDER, 1492–1610

𝒯ollowing the first voyage of Christopher Columbus in 1492, the Spanish American empire expanded dramatically during the sixteenth century. Spanish colonists fanned out from a few isolated Caribbean outposts to include Mexico, as the armies of Hernán Cortés and his followers overthrew the Aztec empire and later moved southward to annex the Maya domains in southern Mexico and Central America. By 1533 equally spectacular victories by Francisco Pizarro in the Andes brought down the Inca empire (Tawantinsuyu), giving the Castilians control over vast human and mineral resources in South America. The conquistadors tried to ensure their wealth and status by making grants of *encomienda*, which allowed them to collect taxes and labor services from a defined group of indigenous towns in return for military protection and religious instruction. These grants gave the holders of an encomienda (called *encomenderos*) social status and economic power—a source of capital and labor that could be used to buy property, engage in mining, or pursue a wide range of commercial activities. By midcentury, however, squabbles among the fractious conquistadors had undermined the encomienda system, along with the omnipresent epidemics that dramatically reduced the Amerindian population in the wealthy central areas of the Spanish Indies. Moreover, crown authorities wanted to limit the political and economic power of the unruly encomenderos, while many Churchmen wanted to gain complete control over converting the indigenous peoples.

Over time the power of the Spanish conquistadors waned as crown bureaucrats, Churchmen, and other settlers from Castile came to rule, convert, and populate the newly acquired lands and to benefit from its fabled riches. The crown established an extensive bureaucracy to rule in the Indies, headed by one viceroy in each of the two major political units, New Spain and Peru. The Madrid government also established a network of high courts (*audiencias*) to hear civil and criminal cases, and the justices worked with the viceroys to enforce legislation sent from Spain and also to issue any laws needed to handle local matters (see Maps 1, 2). To limit the local powers of the encomenderos, authorities in Spain also created a network of rural magistrates (*corregidores de indios*) to regulate contact between Spanish settlers and Amerindians, to collect the head tax or tribute, and to assign *corvée* (forced) labor service. Magistrates (*corregidores de españoles*) also served in most important municipalities to

1

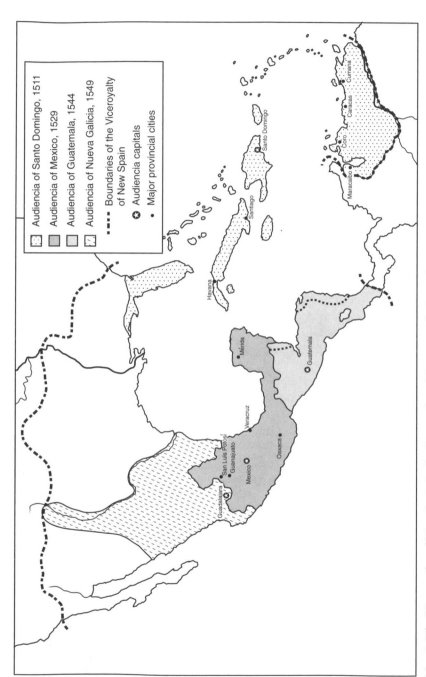

Map 1. The Viceroyalty of New Spain in the Sixteenth and Seventeenth Centuries

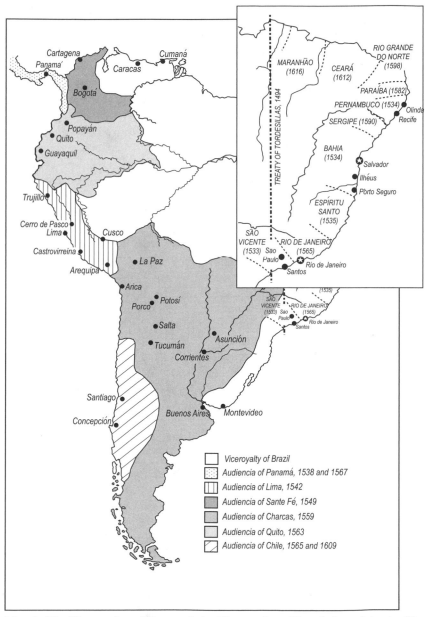

Map 2. The Viceroyalty of Peru and the Viceroyalty of Brazil (insert) in the Sixteenth and Seventeenth Centuries

hear court cases and to regulate local affairs in conjunction with the city council (*cabildo*). Colonial commerce was also strictly regulated through Spain's Atlantic port of Seville and a series of licensed ports in the Indies. From 1561 all trade went in legally sanctioned convoys dispatched from Seville to designated locations, where trade fairs (at Veracruz, Cartagena, and Portobelo) were held to exchange European wares for colonial products. The Church also took firm control of the evangelization of the Amerindians in the viceroyalties. At first the religious orders played a leading role, but then members of the secular clergy established parishes under the overall supervision of a series of bishoprics (seven in New Spain and eight in Peru). In short, by the first decade of the seventeenth century, the turbulent early years of the Spanish invasion and conquest of the New World gave way to a more stable colonial political and religious order.

The Portuguese exploration and settlement of Brazil proceeded more slowly, as the crown concentrated its resources on expanding trade links in the Far East and later in Africa. After the initial explorations of Pedro Alvares Cabral in 1500, small coastal settlements slowly appeared by the 1530s and engaged in a profitable trade with the local Tupi-Guarani peoples for brazilwood. Within a few decades this barter system began to break down as many Amerindian groups began to balk at cutting dyewoods for the Europeans. The economic success of Portuguese Brazil was not ensured until profitable sugar plantations emerged in the Northeast, around Olinda and Salvador da Bahia, by the second half of the sixteenth century. This only intensified the demand for labor, which the Portuguese met by enslaving Amerindians to work in the cane fields. Nevertheless, the Portuguese had founded stable coastal colonies; the only successful inland settlement was established at São Paulo in 1565.

In both Spanish America and Brazil the era of conquest and pillage had receded, but many troublesome problems emerged as Europeans, Amerindians, imported African slaves, and peoples of mixed racial ancestry all struggled to find a place in the new colonial order. Many of the stories in Part I deal with the efforts of indigenous people to accommodate themselves to this often unstable society. The Maya nobleman, Gaspar Antonio Chi, belonged to the Xiu clan, who had allied themselves with the Spaniards against competing Maya groups. Chi received his education from the Franciscans, serving as a translator for the order and for local political leaders, and he used his position as an intermediary between the Spaniards and the Maya to advance his own career and the interests of the Xiu. The northern Andean ethnic leader, Melchior Caruarayco, attempted with less success to meet Spanish demands for taxes and labor while still carrying out traditional leadership tasks—providing for the sick, poor, and disadvantaged of his community. Some indigenous leaders, such as Caruarayco, lost the respect of their people. Too often they failed to protect their communities from excessive Spanish demands. Over time, however, many Andeans learned to manipulate colonial law to their own advantage. The legal struggles between doña Isabel Sisa and her husband, don Domingo Inquilla, over the disposition of their joint assets illustrate just how skillful indigenous people had become in using the Castilian legal code to advance their own agendas.

Questions about racial and ethnic identities also disrupted the colonial social order in the formative years of the sixteenth century. In Brazil, people of mixed indigenous and Portuguese ancestry often served as go-betweens, mediating between the Portuguese coastal settlements and the Amerindians of the wilderness interior. Domingos Fernandes Nobre, known by his indigenous kinsmen and followers as Tomacauna, was a successful slave trader whose unorthodox life style and religious practices led local officials in Bahia to denounce him before the Inquisition in 1591. Although he escaped the most severe forms of punishment, Fernandes Nobre's life demonstrates the tensions between European notions of social hierarchy and the actual wilderness society in Brazil's interior. In a similar fashion, the controversy surrounding the racial identity of the servant girl, Catalina, in the Caribbean port of Havana, offers insights into the problems of assigning fixed, unambiguous identities in the racially mixed world of the Spanish Indies. Each life story, in its own way, illustrates the ambiguities, difficulties, and tensions that arose in attempting to impose European ideas about social order in the more disorderly environment of the New World.

CHAPTER 1

Gaspar Antonio Chi

Bridging the Conquest of Yucatán

MATTHEW RESTALL

Long after the Spanish conquest of the Yucatán peninsula by the armies of Francisco de Montejo in 1535, many crucial aspects of Maya civilization endured. Although the first Spanish settlers divided Maya towns into grants of encomienda, founded the colonial capital of Mérida, and established Franciscan missions in the province, the Maya attempted to control and incorporate these changes into their own social, cultural, and religious framework. Maya society continued to revolve around two central institutions: the cah *(plural* cahob), *a community with a defined geographical territory; and the* chibal *(plural* chibalbob), *a patrilineal descent group identified by a common surname. Class divisions also endured within the* cahob, *as some* chibalbob *apparently maintained prominent political and social roles from the pre-Conquest era onward. On the other hand, political battles revolved around local municipal councils imposed by the Spaniards. Over time, various Maya elite factions continued to vie for control of important municipal offices that regulated local affairs within the* cah *as well as relations with outsiders, especially the Spaniards.*

Preexisting political divisions often set the context for Maya accommodation or resistance to the Spaniards, and some prominent chibal, *such as the Xiu, made common cause with the invaders from the outset. For this reason, the lives of many important sixteenth-century Xiu noblemen, such as Gaspar Antonio Chi, were closely intertwined with those of the European invaders. After the assassination of his father by the rival Cocom* chibal, *for example, the family of Gaspar Antonio Chi wanted to have him schooled in the ways of the Europeans and put the young nobleman under the care of the Franciscans. The friars were a powerful political and religious force in the early years of Spanish rule, and they taught the young Maya lord Latin and Castilian and saw to his instruction in Roman Catholicism. For their part, the Spanish political and religious leaders in Yucatán enthusiastically embraced young, well-connected Maya boys such as Chi, who could help to forge alliances with influential* chibalbob. *Such connections would promote the spread of Roman Catholicism among the Maya and consolidate Spanish power in the Yucatán peninsula. The first generation of Spanish rule in any region of the empire usually involved such strategic alliances.*

6

This selection on Gaspar Antonio Chi begins with the venerable leader near death in 1610 and proceeds to his birth in 1530, reversing the usual chronology. This approach allows for a fuller elaboration of the eventful life of the Xiu leader, who worked as a translator and a notary for the leading Spanish bishops and politicos in the Yucatán peninsula. Chi even served the two powerful rivals for leadership among the Franciscans in the sixteenth century, fray Francisco Toral and firebrand fray Diego de Landa. While these two men vied for control over the evangelization process, Chi wisely withdrew from the whirlwind of Spanish politics to serve as a local leader of the Tizimin cah, far from the capital at Mérida. Later he moved closer to the center of Spanish power, but he still remained in the Maya world, taking up the post of notary and community leader (batab) *in his hometown of Mani. Throughout his adulthood, Chi used his position between the Spaniards and the Maya to advance his own career and the interests of his chibal, the Xiu. The life of Chi literally spanned two ages, linking what he described as an era of prosperity and abundance before the Spanish invasion with the years of disease, tumult, and religious discord that followed it. Although Chi became closely associated with the Spanish legal system and Christian evangelization, he remained deeply rooted in his heritage as both a Xiu and a nobleman of the old Maya order.*

Matthew Restall is associate professor of history at Pennsylvania State University. His pioneering analysis of Maya-language documentation has enabled him to offer new insights into the internal workings of indigenous communities in colonial Yucatán. This work falls squarely within the parameters of the "new philology" pioneered by his graduate school mentor, James Lockhart, at UCLA. Professor Restall has edited Life and Death in a Maya Community: The Ixil Testaments of the 1760s *(1995) and (with Susan Kellog)* Dead Giveaways: Indigenous Testaments of Colonial Mesoamerica and the Andes *(1999). He is the author of numerous articles as well as two books:* Maya Conquistador *(1998), and the work for which he is best known,* The Maya World: Yucatec Culture and Society, 1550–1850 *(1997).*

Gaspar Antonio Chi was a Maya nobleman whose eighty years spanned some of the most turbulent and remarkable decades in the history of the Yucatán peninsula (in what is today southwest Mexico). Chi was born before the Spanish invasion of Yucatán and died early in the seventeenth century when a Spanish colony had been firmly established, one that had employed Chi himself for much of his life. His longevity and career give us invaluable insights into the ways in which the Conquest affected native noblemen in the Americas and, equally important, the ways in which the native elite contributed to the course of the Conquest and the construction of the colony. In this chapter I shall trace Chi's life in reverse, from his death to his birth. The unconventional approach emphasizes the apparent riddle of his status and identity in old age. This "backwards" biography demonstrates who Chi became and then explores how he got there—and thereby we can see what Yucatán became and how it got there.

TWILIGHT (1610)

It was to be the final year of his life. Perhaps Gaspar Antonio Chi knew this as he stood by the baptismal font in the cathedral of Mérida, the capital of the Spanish colonial province of Yucatán. Perhaps he knew in that spring of 1610 that the christening of his great-grandson with Chi's own name of Gaspar Antonio would presage his own death before the baby would take his first steps, and with that passing would die the last member of his family to remember the age before the Conquest—the violent years when Spaniards first marched along the forested trails of Chi's Maya ancestors.

The Yucatán into which Gaspar Antonio Chi was laid to rest was a very different world from the one into which he had been born eighty years earlier, or even the one in which he had striven with considerable success to build a career. His great-grandson's baptism was a symbol of such change. In addition to Chi's Christian names the boy was also given the surname of his Spanish father, del Castillo. Thus the permanence of the Spanish presence in Yucatán was reflected not only in the baptismal ceremony, and the building and city in which it took place, but also in the very blood of Chi's descendants.

Chi participated in another event in 1610 that also can be seen as symbolic of the changes that had accompanied his life's passage as well as of the hybrid nature of his own identity. In what may have been his last professional deed, Chi acted as interpreter and notary during the trial of the so-called rebels of Tekax—the Maya men accused of inciting a riot and leading a revolt in that town during that year's February Carnival. The intended target of the rioters had been the town's native governor, or *batab*, don Pedro Xiu (pronounced "shoe"). The Xiu were one of the most prominent dynastic families in the peninsula, ruling before and after the conquest an important central region that included Tekax. The capital of Xiu territory was Mani, Chi's hometown, and Chi's mother had been a Xiu. As don Pedro was thus a kinsman of his, it must have been with a certain partisan satisfaction that Chi recorded on paper the damning testimony about—and official condemnation of—don Pedro's rival, don Fernando Uz, and his allies.[1]

It was not the Xiu dynasty that Chi represented, but rather the Spanish provincial authorities—colonists who had sought to manipulate political factionalism among the noble families of Tekax in the years before 1610 and then condemned its riotous expression as "rebellious." By and large, after the Conquest the Maya elite received confirmation of social status and local political office by being left to govern their own municipal communities, or *cahob*. But in the decades after the founding of Mérida in 1542, the growing Spanish community increasingly asserted its claim to monopolies on regional authority and political (and religious) violence, including the right to interfere with politics in the cahob should it serve Spanish interests. Chi was intimately acquainted with this pattern of colonial assertion; indeed, he had worked for its architects on and off for one-half century. His identity as an important instrument of the colonial Spanish legal system was thus as deeply rooted as his identity as a Xiu and a Maya nobleman.

SENIOR YEARS (1578–1610)

Chi, in fact, may have viewed himself as a key contributor to the development and maintenance of the colony and its legal system in Yucatán. Certainly he claimed as much in a brief autobiography that formed part of a petition to the king of Spain sent in 1580 and again, in revised form, in 1593. This petition was drawn up in a genre of letter that Spaniards called a *probanza de mérito*, or proof of merit, one that conventionally accompanied requests for royal rewards and pensions.

The king recognized the cogency of Chi's claims, albeit belatedly and not in the form of the coveted annual pension. Instead, he granted him lump-sum payments of 200 pesos in 1593 and in 1599 (the latter probably in response to a third petition). These grants were a recognition, at long last, of "the many merits and services performed, for which," as Chi wrote in 1580, "he had received neither remuneration nor help nor support, despite being poor and in need and weighed down by debt and the costs of keeping his wife and children and family, and being a noble and virtuous person, a good Christian of good repute." By 1593, Chi had served the colony still further and his burdens had increased too, for now, he wrote, "an ulcer on his leg caused him much pain and necessitated him going about on horseback."[2]

These letters to the king were by no means the sole writings of Chi's advanced years. During the long final decades of his career he lived and worked as a notary in Mérida, holding the post of the colony's Interpreter General beginning in the late 1570s. Thus, during this period, Gaspar Antonio Chi's handwriting and signature, the latter an elegant rendering of his Christian names sandwiched between a pair of tightly styled rubrics, are frequently found on the written records of colonial business. Such records were varied in nature, but three examples may suffice.

In the summer of 1600 the Spanish governor of Yucatán, in response to a minor land dispute among Maya communities to the colony's east, ordered three of these cahob to submit land titles. Chi wrote a translation of the order into Maya and signed his name to it before it was sent out from Mérida. The following month, he translated into Spanish the splendid record, written in Maya with an alphabet adapted from Spanish, of a territorial treaty made in 1545 and confirmed in 1600 between a half-dozen cahob and dozens of Maya batabob (governors) and nobles from the region. As "Interpreter General of the high court of this government for the king our lord,"[3] Gaspar Antonio was simply doing his job. But in doing so, he was a witness to (and a recorded participant in) the adaptation of the Maya nobility to the demands and opportunities of the new colonial system—its legal culture of writing, its self-interested concern for local political stability, and its willingness to allow (or failure to observe) various forms of continuity.

Just as we have imagined Chi's reaction to seeing colonial justice rescue the Xiu lord of Tekax in 1610, so we might imagine the Interpreter General's wry observation in 1600 of the dominant role played by Nachi Cocom in the 1545 land treaty. The Cocom, the traditional enemies of the Xiu, ruled the small region of Sotuta, which lay to the north of Mani. Nachi Cocom, the regional ruler, was able to survive the Spanish invasion, be confirmed in office as don Juan Cocom, and even win the friendship of Chi's own sometime mentor, the Franciscan friar Diego de Landa—all this despite his resistance to Spanish demands into the late 1540s (he is still styled as Nachi Cocom in the 1545 treaty), a resistance motivated in part by the early Xiu collaboration with the invaders.

The sight of Nachi Cocom's name thus probably prompted memories in the elderly Chi of the Xiu-Cocom feud, of its fifteenth-century roots, and of its pursuit in the sixteenth century through the complex machinations of Xiu, Cocom, and Spanish lords that culminated in the summer of 1562, when both Xiu and Cocom nobles were tortured by Inquisition officials and Nachi Cocom himself was condemned posthumously as an idolater. Almost certainly, Nachi Cocom's name would have reminded Chi of his own family and his own loss: when Chi was a boy of six, his father was murdered at the order of Nachi Cocom.

The second example of Chi's work goes back a couple of decades closer to these Conquest-era events, to the beginning of this long, final phase of his career in 1578. In that year he translated into Spanish the testimony of a Maya woman claiming to have been sexually abused by a Spanish priest named Andrés Mexia. In this instance, Chi sat with the woman and the priest and orally translated her replies to his questions; a Spanish notary wrote down Chi's translations, to which Chi signed his name. As Church officials under Bishop Landa built a case against Mexia during 1578, Chi translated other testimony, both oral verbal and written, including shocking and well-substantiated accusations of rape.[4] Unfortunately, while the case accounts record the voices of Maya parishioners, the outraged responses of the bishop and other Spaniards, and Mexia's own protestations, we can only imagine Chi's reactions. Perhaps he was not as appalled as might be imagined. After all, as we shall see, he had seen worse manifestations of the dark side of colonial relations; moreover, he had witnessed them firsthand.

In contrast, the third example of Chi's writing does give some insight into his perceptions of the early colonial Yucatec world. In 1577, Yucatán received its copies of a set of royal questionnaires sent from Spain as part of an ambitious campaign to gather detailed information on all the colonies of the empire. Every Spanish *encomendero* (recipient of a grant of native labor and tribute) was to answer all fifty questions; few did so, and in Yucatán at least a dozen sought out Gaspar Antonio Chi for assistance in responding to the two questions on pre-Conquest native religion, politics, and economics. Chi appears to have written replies for these Spaniards in 1579 and 1581 and to have done so with some relish. Rather than translating the words of others, he was here given a chance to express his own views.

Chi wrote wistfully of Yucatán before the Conquest as a land of great prosperity and abundance, governed well and densely populated. He lamented the decline of that population and, rather pointedly, blamed the loss not only on "the war of the conquest with the Spaniards" but also on misguided colonial policies of resettlement and the banning of native drinks (replaced by the pernicious wine of the Spaniards). He wrote too of the feud that had so touched his own life and of the death of his father, Ah Kulel Chi:

> The province of Mani was always at war with that of Sotuta—[particularly] with a lord of the ancients of the land named Nachi Cocom—because of an ancient enmity which the said Cocom had against the Xiu. . . . Thus after the initial invasion of the first conquerors, whom the lords of Mani received in peace, without any resistance, giving obedience to His Majesty, the aforementioned Nachi Cocom treacherously killed more than forty lords of the said province of Mani, who were passing through his province on a pilgrimage, unarmed and under safe passage—beheading and putting out the eyes of Ah Kulel Chi, who was the most senior of them.[5]

It is easy to dismiss as self-serving Chi's claims in his petitions to the king (mentioned above) that it was the Xiu's warm embrace of the Spaniards that provoked Cocom violence. Likewise, in another version of his account of Yucatán's past, written for the king in 1582 at the request of the provincial governor, Chi unabashedly promotes the Xiu dynasty as lords of "this province of Yucatán."[6] And even though many of his answers to the royal questionnaires were anonymous, his partisanship is clear. Nevertheless, he was surely telling it the way he saw it: the Xiu legacy was a supremely noble one. His father had died for the cause of the Xiu policy of peace and accommodation toward the Spaniards, a cause to which Chi himself had dedicated his life.

MATURITY (1561–1578)

One of the conquistadors whom Chi had helped in 1581 with his royal questionnaire, Pedro de Santillana, gratefully acknowledged Chi's role in a succinct hagiography:

> Usually called Gaspar Antonio among the Spaniards, his age is fifty years, a little more or less, and he is a man of many abilities, a scholar, a *ladino* [Hispanized, cultured] well versed in the Castilian language, the Mexican [Nahuatl] and Maya language [*mayathan*], which is his mother tongue. And he is a person who knows well all the local peculiarities . . . as he was born in this country and was taken as companion of the bishops here, which were fray Francisco Toral, glory be to his memory, and fray Diego de Landa, glory be to his memory, as they thought him a truthful man. And through him they learned about the peculiarities and customs that the natives used to have, and still have at present. And as a man of character these bishops relied upon the things that were investigated and understood, in the language of this country, by this Gaspar Antonio.[7]

The conquistador's ready association of Chi with the colony's first two bishops, Toral and Landa, evokes the significant roles that these two Franciscans played in Chi's life in his twenties, thirties, and forties. But it barely begins to convey the complexity of the relationships between the three of them, particularly the bitter rivalry between the obsessively driven and often irascible Landa and the mild-mannered Toral. Both men may have trusted Chi as "a man of character" and "a truthful man." But because they did not view each other in this light, Chi found himself caught between them, an uncomfortable position from which he sought escape. For over a decade, from the mid-1560s to the late-1570s, Chi pursued a career outside of Mérida and the immediate circle of the Franciscans. Although Toral was bishop until his death in 1571, and Landa, appointed as his replacement, returned from Spain in 1573, Chi worked for neither of them during these years.

Instead, around 1565, he took up a post as choirmaster and school-teacher in a Maya community, a role that was in a sense as close as a colonial Maya man could legally get to the position of a traditional Maya priest—the *ah kin* that Chi's father had been. The community was Tizimin, a cah with few Spanish residents far from Mérida and on the northeast margins of the colony. One imagines that here Chi found refuge from the Spanish world in which he had spent almost two decades of his young adulthood.

In 1572 he moved back into the center of things, but still very much within the Maya world, taking up the post of batab of his hometown; Mani's continued importance as a regional capital made its governorship one of the highest ranking Maya offices in colonial Yucatán. Although he was only batab for a year or two, he had succeeded in taking up the political legacy of his maternal ancestry, and it was in Mani that he remained for most of the 1570s, enjoying his status as a former batab and a high-ranking notary. When he moved to Mérida in the late 1570s as Interpreter General, it is not clear whether this was seen either by him or the colonial authorities as a permanent post. Surely neither anticipated that Chi would live and work a decade into the next century. Significantly, he did not go to work directly for the bishop. Moreover, Landa was ailing; not long (possibly months) after Chi's return, the bishop was dead.

The riddle remains: why, if Chi was so close to the bishops, did he escape their employ and pursue a career in Maya politics? The response that he sought to regain contact with his native roots and with his family is surely too facile, although this may have been part of it. A more compelling answer, however, lies in Chi's experience of the turbulent early 1560s. In 1561, Chi had recently turned thirty, had married not long before, and by now was probably a father. He and his new family were living in Mérida, where Landa, already famous throughout the colony as a Franciscan firebrand, moved that year to take up his new appointment as *provincial*, or head of this religious order in the province. Chi seems to have begun working for the provincial as notary, interpreter, and assistant almost immediately. His tasks were relatively routine, but that would all change the following spring. In retrospect, Chi's first year as Landa's assistant in Mérida must have seemed mercifully mundane.

In May 1562, Pedro de Ciudad Rodrigo, the Franciscan friar in charge of the monastery in Chi's hometown of Mani, received reports of the practice of "idolatry" in a sacred cave on the edge of town. Finding "idols" or non-Christian religious images in the cave, Ciudad Rodrigo initiated a sequence of events that would be repeated many times in this and other colonies of Spanish America: prominent locals were interrogated, some were tortured, confessions were made, and the transgressors were lectured, fined, and ritually humiliated in the town plaza. However, what made these events unique in Yucatán, and to some extent in Spanish America, was that in this case they were merely the beginning. Having read a full report of the matter, Landa decided to travel to Mani and investigate further. He took Chi with him.

Landa's investigation immediately took the form of a large-scale version of Ciudad Rodrigo's, with not dozens but hundreds, and then thousands, of Mayas arrested, jailed, and systematically tortured. Landa started in Mani and then moved north to Sotuta. He targeted women as well as men. Many were permanently maimed, some committed suicide, and some 5 percent of the 4,500 victims died under torture. Even for the sixteenth century this extraordinary campaign of extirpation was an excessively violent expression of colonialist frustration.

It culminated in the Mani plaza on July 12, 1562, at the ritual of public punishment and humiliation called an auto-da-fé. The Franciscans sentenced the condemned to having their heads shaved, or to wearing the yellow red-crossed robes of shame called *sanbenitos*, or to paying heavy fines, or to serving a Spaniard for up to ten years, or to suffering further torture (and possibly death) in the form of two hundred lashes. The representative of colonial government, the *alcalde mayor* (mayor) Diego de Quijada, repeated the sentences, which were then read out in Maya by a native interpreter to the gathering of condemned Mayas and their families. The interpreter was Gaspar Antonio Chi.

The assembled Mayas thus learned of their fate from the lips of one of their own—a Chi-Xiu nobleman from Mani, to whom many of them were related. It was surely difficult for Chi to participate in this Conquest ritual in this way—and to witness the brutal floggings and burning of religious images and objects that immediately followed his reading of the sentences. As much is suggested by the fact that when the procedure was repeated in Sotuta the following month, Chi was not present as interpreter. The arrests, tortures, suicides, and killings continued for weeks as the campaign spread through the Sotuta region and into neighboring Hocaba and Homun. But Chi was back in Mérida. He was there in late August when the colony's first bishop, Francisco Toral, arrived in the city and immediately summoned Landa to account for his actions.

Chi must have been relieved. He had watched his mentor wreak havoc on his hometown and neighboring communities for three months, learned how many of his relatives had been tortured to death, and found himself a party to a horrific ceremony of humiliation. He had also witnessed or learned of Landa's mass burning of "a great number of books in their letters [hieroglyphs],"[8] an act of vandalism that must have shocked a learned and literate Maya such as Chi. To be sure, he was the product of a Franciscan education, but his father had been one of the priests and scribes who had written and kept hieroglyphic manuscripts. The destruction of pre-Conquest Maya literature underscored the fact that, although Chi in many ways symbolized the continuity into colonial times of the Maya tradition of literacy, he and other native notaries would write only in the alphabet borrowed from the invaders as well as in the genres and formats set by them.

If Chi's absence at the August 1562 auto-da-fé in Sotuta can be taken as a sign of his feelings about Landa's campaign against "idolatry," further indication of his discomfort lies in the fact that shortly after Toral's arrival in Mérida, Chi began working for the new bishop. Toral knew Nahuatl and Popoloca but not Yucatec Maya, so he greatly needed a skilled interpreter such as Chi; for Chi, the job was a prestigious one. But Toral and Landa had almost immediately become bitter enemies, and Chi knew only too well the violent forms that Landa's disappointment and retribution could take.

Despite these risks, Chi accepted the position. Perhaps he viewed his new tasks as some kind of recompense for his work in the summer of 1562, for he now set about drawing up documents for Toral: a summons to Landa to justify certain aspects of his campaign, the translations of new Maya testimony asserting that earlier confessions had been false and forced under threat of torture, and the papers releasing still-imprisoned Mayas—including the lord of Mani, don Francisco de Montejo, who later wrote a bitter letter about "the great persecution" to the King of Spain.[9] The ubiquity of Chi's signature on the records of this power struggle between the two Franciscans reflects his role as an eye-witness to the battle for the soul of the new colony. The conflict was not solely over control but was about competing visions of the nature of native culture and the entire grand scheme of colonization.

If Chi's experience of the summer of 1562 turned him sour on Landa's vision of Yucatán's future, he was not alone. Spanish colonists and Maya leaders alike breathed collective sighs of relief as Toral continued to pursue his investigation into Landa's activities through the autumn of 1562, inexorably tipping the balance of power in the bishop's favor and, in January 1563, prompting Landa's sudden return to Spain. There, Landa spent the next decade defending his record of service in Yucatán, in 1566 writing his famous *Relación*, or "Account of the Things of Yucatán," which is part narrative of Yucatec history and the Conquest and part ethnography of the Maya.

There can be little doubt that Chi contributed to the book. The two men worked closely together when Landa was presumably making notes on Maya matters, and some passages in the *Relación* are very similar to Chi's own writings. Yet the only Maya informant given credit is the man whom Chi believed responsible for his father's murder, as Landa well knew—Nachi Cocom. Chi is not mentioned. In the end the retribution that one imagines that Chi feared from Landa uncharacteristically took the form of silence.[10]

YOUTH (1536–1560)

Landa's book was written as part of his defense, which culminated in his appointment as Toral's successor and his return to Yucatán as bishop in 1573. As we have seen, Chi stayed away, only returning to work in Mérida when Landa was subdued by age and illness and, it would turn out, was in his last year of life. The *Relación* then gathered dust in Madrid for three centuries before being discovered and published. It was just as well that Chi never saw the book—with its mention of Nachi Cocom and not Chi himself—for he had once been devoted to Landa, and the Franciscan had played something of the role of mentor to the Maya nobleman, although there were only seven years between them. While Chi does not seem to have begun working permanently with Landa until 1561, their paths almost certainly crossed repeatedly in the 1550s, and Spanish colonists later saw the two as having been closely associated, to the extent that Dr. Pedro Sánchez de Aguilar could claim erroneously that Chi "was raised from childhood by the lord bishop don Diego de Landa."[11]

Chi's youth, the time from his father's murder when he was six, to his turning thirty, was dramatically divided into two halves by the arrival of the Franciscans in his hometown when Chi was in his teens. In 1547 the friars began the construction of the convent church in Mani and also set up a small school. Based on a model established in Mérida a few years earlier—and in Mexico City a couple of decades before that—the school's purpose was for Franciscans to educate the sons of local nobles, native boys who would go on to be assistants, interpreters, and agents for the friars.

As Landa later put it, "These children, once they had been instructed, took care to inform the friars of any idolatries and drunkenness and to destroy any idols, even if they belonged to their parents." Landa claimed that parents soon got over their initial opposition to Franciscan schools such as the one in Mani, and they began sending their boys to live and study there while continuing to visit them and "bring them food." In turn, the friars "learned to read and write in the language of the Indians, which was so reduced to an art [that is, a grammar book] that it could be studied like Latin."[12]

Latin, in fact, was one of the languages that the young Chi soon learned in Mani, along with Spanish and Nahuatl. The Franciscan chronicler Diego López de Cogolludo, writing forty years after Chi's death, stated that "he knew Latin grammar very well."[13] Sánchez de Aguilar, who in the seventeenth century became dean of Mérida cathedral and a chronicler of the spiritual conquest of Yucatán, spent part of his childhood in Tizimin, where his elder brother was encomendero. There he got to know Chi—"everybody in that era knew him," the Spaniard later wrote—as he was the town's schoolmaster and choirmaster in the 1570s. Chi "knew grammar reasonably well," reminisced Sánchez de Aguilar, "and in my childhood it was he who placed its art in my hands. . . . He was as *ladino* as any Spaniard, sang plainsong [*canto llano*] and sang to the organ with great skill, and could play the keyboards. I knew him as organist of this holy church and later as Interpreter General to the governor."[14] According to Chi himself, he was

> the first native to learn the Castilian and Latin languages; and being of great ability and understanding, performed great services for God and Your Majesty in order to bring about the conversion of the natives of this province, which is of much concern to Your Majesty; and, as requested by the said friars [*religiosos*], translated and wrote sermons in the Indians' language in order to preach to them . . . the word of God and the Christian doctrine . . . and was always at the service of the friars, teaching them the language and interpreting for them.[15]

Chi must certainly have been a star pupil in the small school in Mani, where his Franciscan education began around 1548 and where he remained based for most of the 1550s. He almost immediately would have learned of the energetic and already somewhat controversial Diego de Landa; and, as a shining example of the efficacy of Franciscan policies, Chi would also have come to Landa's attention. Before long, the two men would have met. At this time, Landa was based in Izamal, where from 1553 to 1561 an impressive convent was constructed on the base of one vast Maya pyramid, adjacent to a sibling pyramid. The church was a monument to Landa's ambitions (and later denounced as such by Toral)— ambitions that frequently took him to Mérida and other parts of the colony. Similarly Chi's budding career as a notary of rare skill and learning took him often out of Mani. In 1557 he served as interpreter and chief notary to the Spanish judge commissioned to ratify the land boundaries within the Xiu domain centered on Mani and between it and the Cocom region of Sotuta. Chi participated in the summit at Uxmal, the great border walk, and the writing of the treaty—which was intended to impose the *pax colonial* on the feuding Xiu and Cocom but instead was used by both dynasties to consolidate their respective territorial and political authority.

The 1557 treaty contains the first example of Chi's signature. The treaty is also the earliest surviving example of the Maya language written alphabetically. It is thus a landmark, as it were, in both Chi's professional life and the early development of the colony, the two being as intertwined as the Spanish and Maya cultures represented in the treaty and its written records. This was not the first time, of course, that Chi had written his name or that Maya had been written alphabetically. Indeed, it is Chi's fully developed professional skills as well as the fully fledged nature of alphabetic Maya in these documents that indicates the effectiveness of Maya-Franciscan educational collaboration in the decade before 1557.

That the collaboration served Maya purposes as much as Franciscan ones is illustrated by Chi and other native notaries using literacy in contexts such as the 1557 treaty; as Sánchez de Aguilar would later write, Chi "defended the Indians in their lawsuits and presented or composed their petitions for them."[16] It was also about this time that Chi probably created an extraordinary drawing known to us as the Xiu Family Tree. It depicts members of the Xiu lineage descended from a pre-Conquest dynastic founder and including Chi himself and his mother, Ix Kukil Xiu. Its iconography mixes Christian, Maya, and native central Mexican elements in a way that reflects the unique Franciscan-Maya context of Chi's education—only the Tree was drawn not for Franciscans but for Chi's Xiu relatives and descendants, who jealously guarded it for centuries.[17]

This was not exactly the intention of the Franciscans when boys such as Chi had been brought into the Church and the order's schools in the late 1540s—even if the friars had to accept the fact that their students would become co-opted by the broader needs of Maya and Spanish provincial government, where in a sense they continued to serve the colony. This reality was foreshadowed by the symbolism of Chi's baptism in Mani. Although the young Maya nobleman, as an orphan, thereby acquired several new fathers in the faith—the Franciscan *padres*—it was to the father figure of civil rule that Chi was most explicitly linked. His full name became Gaspar Antonio de Herrera Chi, after his godmother doña Beatriz de Herrera, the wife of Yucatán's conquistador and governor, don Francisco de Montejo.

This complex new paternity of Chi's brought to an end a period of his life about which little is known but which must have been a difficult one for two reasons. First, he had spent these dozen years of childhood and adolescence without a father. When Chi was six, Ah Kulel Chi, a prominent priest, scribe, and government officer in Mani, had been murdered as a member of an embassy and pilgrimage from Mani to Chichen Itzá. To reach the sacred site, where rites were to be performed to bring rain to end a drought, the group of Xiu and related lords had to cross the territory of their Cocom enemies. In view of the peaceful nature of their mission, they were granted safe passage by Nachi Cocom, who then ordered the pilgrims massacred at the village of Otzmal. The event would live in infamy; as the annals of one Xiu town, Oxkutzcab, declared, "May it be remembered!"[18]

Chi certainly remembered. As quoted above, he detailed his father's mutilation in his contribution to the encomendero reports of 1581, later claiming in his petitions to the king that "they also cut out his tongue."[19] Indeed, Chi made his father's murder central to his argument that his life from the earliest age had consisted of service and sacrifice for the sake of the king and his officers. According to Chi, the motive for the Otzmal massacre was the Cocom desire to punish the Xiu for appeasing the Spaniards during the second unsuccessful Montejo invasion of the early 1530s. In support of this view, Chi was able to enlist the testimony of some twenty Spaniards that this was common knowledge.

Second, Chi's childhood and adolescence were lived against the backdrop of civil war, famine and epidemic disease, and a brutal war of invasion and conquest. The Otzmal massacre set off a series of hostilities between Xiu and Cocom. The drought that had necessitated the pilgrimage to Chichen Itzá persisted. Disease brought by earlier Spanish expeditions continued to ravage the Maya population. And then a few years after Ah Kulel Chi's death, the Spaniards returned in greater force and with unknown numbers of African slaves and Nahuas as auxiliaries. Within a couple of years the Spaniards had established a capital at the Maya site of Tiho, which the invaders called Mérida; from this and a number of other bases, the Spaniards carved out a colony in the northwestern portion of the peninsula. Chi's hometown of Mani was spared violence in its streets, but only by sending its men to fight for the Spaniards elsewhere. Throughout these years of Chi's youth, there was no peace in Yucatán.

DAWN (1530–1535)

Chi's dawning years were the twilight of pre-Conquest Yucatán. In 1530, the year of his birth, Yucatán was virtually free of Spaniards. By the time he was five, there was not a Spaniard for hundreds of miles from his hometown of Mani, where he lived with his father, the priest and nobleman Ah Kulel Chi, and his mother, Ix Kukil Xiu, of the region's ruling dynasty.

Not that the peninsula had avoided all contact with the foreigners. Spaniards were shipwrecked on its coasts in 1511, and perhaps even before then. Expeditions from Cuba in 1517 and 1518 landed at various points on the long Yucatec coast and engaged Maya warriors in brief but bloody battles. In 1519 the soon-to-be-famous Hernán Cortés landed at Cozumel and six years later passed along the peninsula's base. Then, for over two years in the late 1520s a fullscale campaign of conquest in Yucatán was undertaken by the family and allies of Francisco de Montejo. But it failed, as did a second campaign, begun in 1529 and abandoned after five years. In 1535, Chi's father, Ah Kulel, might have reasonably assumed, as he watched his young son playing on the family patio, that the threat of foreign invasion finally had passed and that his boy would grow up in a world much like that of Ah Kulel's own youth.

Ah Kulel could not have anticipated his own death just a year later, or the third invasion of Spaniards a few years after that, or their subsequent permanent settlement. He could hardly have foreseen that the priests who would educate his son would not be *ah kinob* like him, but foreigners who would teach him a new faith, foreign tongues, and a strange new way of writing. He could not possibly have imagined all that his son would witness and record on paper. But had he been able to witness, seventy-five years later, his great-great-grandson's strange initiation into colonial Yucatán's brave new world, his heart would have been warmed and his mind reassured by the persistence of family life—his family.

NOTES

1. Archivo General de las Indias, Seville (hereafter AGI), *Escribanía* 305a.

2. AGI, *México* 105, 4a/b (quotes my translations from 4a, f.3 and 4b, f.5).

3. Ralph L. Roys, *The Titles of Ebtun* (Washington, DC, 1933), 432; the Appendix contains the entire treaty record.

4. Archivo General de la Nación, Mexico City, *Inquisición* 69, 5.

5. Translation from Matthew Restall, *Maya Conquistador* (Boston, 1998), 149.

6. Chi's original 1582 *relación* went to Spain, was preserved in the AGI, and is reproduced in Alfred Tozzer, *Landa's Relación de las cosas de Yucatán* (Cambridge, 1941), Appendix C; a copy stayed in Mérida and was acquired by fray Diego López de Cogolludo, who worked it into his *Historia de la provincia de Yucathan* [1654] (Madrid, 1688), 233–38 (Book 4, Chapters III–IV).

7. *Relaciones de Yucatán*, 2 vols. (Madrid, 1898; Mexico City, 1983), 1:251.

8. Quote by Landa himself, who adds that the book burning "greatly amazed them [the Mayas] and caused them much pain"; my translations from Diego de Landa, *Relación de las cosas de Yucatán* [1566] (Mexico City, 1959), 105.

9. From my translation of the whole letter in *Maya Conquistador*, 165–68.

10. There is an element of speculation here on my part, as Landa did not actually write his *Relación* as we know it; the surviving text is a compilation made at least a century later from various of Landa's writings. See Matthew Restall and John F. Chuchiak, "A Reevaluation of the Authenticity of Fray Diego de Landa's *Relación de las cosas de Yucatán*," in *Ethnohistory* 49:1 (2001).

11. Pedro Sánchez de Aguilar, *Informe contra Idolorum Cultores del Obispado de Yucatán* [1639] (Madrid, 1892), reprinted in *El Alma Encantada: Anales del Museo Nacional de México* (Mexico City, 1987); quote my translation from p. 96.

12. Landa, *Relación*, 31–32.

13. López de Cogolludo, *Historia*, 238 (Book 4, Chapter IV).

14. Sánchez de Aguilar, *Informe*, 96.

15. AGI, *México* 105, 4a, f.3 et al.

16. Sánchez de Aguilar, *Informe*, 96.

17. The tree is reproduced in various places; for example, see *Maya Conquistador*, 145.

18. Taken from my translation of the annals in *Maya Conquistador*, 81.

19. AGI, *México* 105, 4b, f.2.

SUGGESTED READINGS

In addition to the primary sources cited in the notes, two previous Chi biographies contributed much to this chapter—a brief summary in my *Maya Conquistador* (Boston, 1998) that focuses on Chi's *relaciones* contributions; and a far more substantial account by Frances Karttunen in *Between Worlds: Interpreters, Guides, and Survivors* (New Brunswick, 1994), which also places Chi in the context of other native interpreters, most notably La Malinche and Guaman Poma.

For more on the conquest of Yucatán and on Diego de Landa, see *Maya Conquistador* and Inga Clendinnen's *Ambivalent Conquests: Maya and Spaniard in Yucatán, 1517–1570* (Cambridge, 1987). Also of interest is Landa's *Relación de las cosas de Yucatán*, of which the Alfred Tozzer edition is the most useful (Cambridge, 1941), although one by William Gates (New York, 1978) is the easiest to find. On the Mexia case, see my "The Telling of Tales: Six Yucatec Maya Communities and Their Spanish Priest," in Geof Spurling and Richard Boyer, eds., *Colonial Lives: Documents on Latin American History, 1550–1850* (New York, 2000). On the Mayas after the conquest, see my *The Maya World: Yucatec Culture and Society, 1550–1850* (Stanford, 1997). On other aspects of colonial Yucatec history, see the books and articles of Grant D. Jones and Robert W. Patch.

CHAPTER 2

Don Melchior Caruarayco

A *Kuraka* of Cajamarca in Sixteenth-Century Peru

Susan E. Ramírez

Although the victorious armies of Tawintinsuyu spread the official impe-rial religion, more localized Andean religious practices endured alongside these state cults of the Inca. The Andean peoples believed that the sacred permeated every aspect of their world and deeply influenced everyday life. Inanimate natural objects such as mountains or trees represented or evoked divine ancestors, known as huacas, *who had founded extended human kinship groupings or lineages called* ayllu. *Within these communities, tra-ditional leaders (*kurakas*) traced their ancestry back to these divine per-sonages and served as an essential link between the huacas and the more mundane world of the ayllu. Powerful kurakas served as political leaders, but they also performed a multiplicity of important tasks—assigning la-bor, confirming land usage, mediating community disputes, and punish-ing lawbreakers. These Andean lords even dispatched community members to live on and cultivate lands at different ecological levels, providing the ayllus with a range of goods (in the absence of formal market exchanges) that they could not secure where they lived. By linking divine powers with everyday events in the material world, the kurakas allowed Andean men and women to forge a profound spiritual link to their gods, who protected them from human enemies and arbitrary forces of nature.*

After the Spanish invasion and conquest of the Inca empire, the po-litical, social, and religious roles of the kurakas began to change in funda-mental ways. The conquistadors divided the Andean ethnicities among themselves into encomiendas, *which forced the kurakas to serve as inter-mediaries between the Spaniards and their kinsmen. Kurakas now allo-cated the tax and labor burdens demanded by Spanish* encomenderos *instead of exercising these powers in the name of local divinities. Later in the sixteenth century, crown bureaucrats (*corregidores de indios*) re-placed the encomenderos in administering these tax and labor assignments, as the crown slowly began to ease from power the fractious conquistadors to gain greater political control over the Andes. Nevertheless, too often kurakas had to deal with the exploitative demands of the Spaniards, who were interested only in draining human and material wealth from indigenous communities at a time when devastating epidemics spread throughout the Andean cordillera. These demands severely undermined the moral and* *political authority of the kurakas while, at the same time, Roman Catholic priests undercut their religious powers by spreading Christianity and suppressing Andean religious rites.*

Don Melchior Caruarayco, a leading kuraka of the Cajamarca region (Northern Peru), lived in this turbulent post-Conquest era. He came from an ancient line, yet his traditional powers slowly eroded under Spanish rule. Nevertheless, as his last will and testament indicates, don Melchior still retained many Andean notions of wealth and power, measuring his fortune by the numbers of his retainers. With Spanish rule, however, came new laws and customs, which emboldened rival claimants to ethnic leadership in Cajamarca. They finally managed to unseat the venerable don Melchior. Indeed, the life and travails of don Melchior were in many ways typical of the traditional kurakas, who found it harder and harder to meet escalating Spanish demands for tribute and labor. These ethnic lords were often forced either to exploit their kinsmen or to meet these quotas by depleting their personal resources. Like other lords, called dueños de indios, *don Melchior began to lose the respect of his own people for failing to protect them from Spanish depredations. These leaders also found it harder to fulfill traditional religious obligations and Andean notions of reciprocity— providing feasts and other largesse to validate their power, status, and authority in the community. Indeed, these old-style kurakas were slowly replaced often by handpicked cronies of local Spanish overlords who had no traditional claim to community leadership.*

Susan E. Ramírez is professor of history at DePaul University and a leading authority on Andean colonial history. Her early work concerned the growth of Spanish landed estates in Northern Peru, which culminated in the publication of Provincial Patriarchs: Land Tenure and the Economics of Power in Colonial Peru *(1986). She then turned her attention to the study of Peru's indigenous peoples in the sixteenth century, with the publication of numerous articles and her prize-winning book,* The World Upside Down: Cross-Cultural Contact and Conflict in Sixteenth-Century Peru *(1996).*

$\mathscr{B}$efore the Spanish invasion, the Andean peoples believed that the sacred penetrated every aspect of their world, profoundly influencing daily life experiences. The Sun and the Moon, the stars, and planets were all considered gods and ancestors who had given birth to human lineages. Moreover, divine power could manifest itself in mountains, streams, trees, boulders, and even mundane objects such as small stones. Places evoked stories of the origin of lineages where the founder first emerged or settled, of a past hero who turned to stone and became immortal, and of ancestor-gods and their forces who fought and won important battles. Indigenous leaders, called *kurakas* (or *caciques* by the Spaniards), traced their lineage back to these forefathers and led lives surrounded by public ritual. Within Andean communities, these chiefs represented more than just political leaders; they served as the living personification of divine forces. The kuraka was also responsible for the well-being of his people—coordinating work parties, redistributing crops from community fields (to care for the orphans, the widows, and the poor), and even dispatching community members to distant places to gain access to important products at different ecological levels. Products gained from these vertical exchanges between the colonists formed a portion of the goods that the kuraka dispensed among his people, since in Andean societies there were no markets, merchants, or money. Ethnic leaders also resolved disputes within the community or with outsiders, even meting out punishment when necessary, but the wise leader used this power sparingly. After all, the chief's status was measured by the number of his followers—the larger the population of faithful devotees, the higher a headman's position among his neighbors and peers. Thus, the chief was a central figure, serving as mediator between the living and the dead as well as between mere mortals and the gods, and as benefactor to all his devotees. These relationships gave nobles and peasants alike a sense of their common history, celebrated and taught in annual rituals and festivals. Such religious occasions also reinforced the social and ideological ties that kept local society cooperating, functioning, and viable.

These social and religious relationships changed dramatically in 1532 when the Spanish invaders arrived in the Andes. Some native leaders were not totally surprised and unprepared for the appearance of the Spaniards. Even before their boats anchored off the western shores of South America, there were signs that the gods were displeased with native leaders and society. During the reign of Guayna Capac, the last Inca king to rule a united empire that extended from what today is Chile to Colombia and inland into Bolivia and Argentina, omens appeared that foretold impending doom. A great condor, which might have a wingspan of ten feet or so, was attacked by less powerful and smaller hawks. It fell dead in the plaza of the ceremonial center, called the City of the Sun, after the main Inca deity. Other sky signs indicated that blood would spill. Guayna Capac dreamed about a plague during which thousands of his people would perish. He, himself, died of a strange disease (c. 1524–1526), a few years before the Spanish arrival. Neither of the persons he designated as his successors was favored in divinations meant to find out who the Sun god chose to be the next king. In this context of disease and impending gloom, a civil war between two half-brothers (Atahualpa and Huascar) broke out to see whom the gods would favor on the field of battle. A victory would mark one brother as the next king. In this conjuncture of events, the Spaniards sailed into view and began their own war of conquest against the massive Inca empire (called Tawantinsuyu), capturing the ceremonial center of Cusco in less than one year.

After the Spanish invasion, local kurakas served as mediators between their communities and their new European overlords, who were entrusted by the Spanish crown to supervise and indoctrinate them in return for labor services and tribute. The Spaniards called these chiefs *caciques*, using a term that they imported from the Caribbean. To survive colonial exploitation and abuse, the kurakas quickly learned to protect their followers, maintain their community's socioeconomic order, and celebrate religious rituals. At the same time, a paramount lord (*cacique principal*) had to meet Spanish labor and tribute levies. This task involved assigning men as bearers (in places where the numbers of llamas, horses, and mules were insufficient to transport needed supplies) and women as cooks and laundresses. The kuraka also delegated ever larger numbers of his followers to produce food, to spin and weave tribute cloth, to pan for gold in local rivers, or to dig for silver ore in highland mines. Thus, the kuraka became a go-between, linking native society and the emerging Spanish colonial order. In playing this uncertain and difficult role, the kuraka had to please the Spaniards, a task that often meant organizing, manipulating, cajoling, and even exploiting his own people.

The kuraka, don Melchior Caruarayco, found himself thrust into this rapidly changing era of invasion, conquest, and social upheaval. Indeed, his life story epitomizes how the local native social organization was turned upside down, or what the Andean peoples in the provinces termed a *pachacuti*, an inversion of their world of transcendental dimensions. In the first generation after initial encounter with the Europeans, native religious and political structures were discredited and simplified, thus reducing the number of indigenous authorities. Moreover, Andeans continued to sicken from European epidemic diseases and die in alarming numbers. Some native peoples left their communities to serve the Spaniards, thinking that the Christian god was more powerful than their own or trying to evade mounting tribute exactions. Others fled into remote areas to escape the Spaniards' demands for goods and labor and their wrath when quotas were not met. In the process, many commoners lost respect for their native authorities, as it became more evident that their ancestral gods either were not powerful enough to protect them against the Christians or had abandoned them. Worse, when the natives tried to worship their own gods and feed them to give the lineage renewed strength, they were condemned by omnipresent Roman Catholic priests. It seemed to many Andeans that the Spanish god and the Christian saints only helped the Europeans. Nonetheless, the Andeans often found ways to continue worshipping their ancestral deities in clandestine religious ceremonies. These traditional religious practices became one means, short of open rebellion, to resist the unreasonable demands of their Spanish overlords.

DON MELCHIOR CARUARAYCO

Descended from a long line of native leaders, don Melchior Caruarayco and his ancestors had been headmen of a large group in the sierras of northern Peru. Oral tradition records their title, *Guzmango Capac*— Guzmango being the name of the ethnic group or polity, while Capac signified a divine ruler whose forefathers displayed a special force, energy, and wisdom in ruling. By the time the Spaniards began to ask about their history, residents of this polity (called Cajamarquinos today) could only remember the names of two brothers who had served as Guzmango Capac under the Incas. The first was called Concacax, who was followed by Cosatongo.

After Concacax died, his son, Chuptongo, was sent south to serve the emperor, Túpac Inca Yupanqui. There he received an education at court and, as a young adult, became the tutor of one of Inca Yupanqui's sons, Guayna Capac. Oral history records that "he gained great fame and reputation in all the kingdom for his quality and admirable customs." It was also said that Guayna Capac respected him as he would a father. Eventually, Túpac Inca Yupanqui named Chuptongo a governor of the empire. When Guayna Capac succeeded his father, Chuptongo accompanied the new sovereign to Quito. After years of service, he asked Guayna Capac to allow him to return to his native people. His wish was granted; and, as a sign of his esteem, Guayna Capac made him a gift of one hundred women, one of the highest rewards possible in the Inca empire. In this way, Chuptongo established his house and lineage in the old town of Guzmango, fathered many children, and served as paramount lord until his death.

The struggle for the throne between the two half-brothers Huascar and Atahualpa, sons of Guayna Capac, also divided the sons of Chuptongo. During the civil war that broke out after Guayna Capac's death, Caruatongo, the oldest of Chuptongo's sons, sided with the northern forces of Atahualpa, while another son, Caruarayco, allied with Huascar, who led the forces from the south. Caruatongo, who was privileged enough to have been carried into the plaza of Cajamarca on a litter, a sure sign of the Inca's favor, died there on November 16, 1532, when Francisco Pizarro and his followers ambushed and killed many of the emperor's retainers and captured the Inca, Atahualpa.

Although Caruatongo left an heir (named Alonso Chuplingón, after his Christian baptism), his brother, Caruarayco, succeeded him as headman following local customs. Pizarro himself recognized Caruarayco and confirmed his right to assume the authority of his father. Caruarayco took the name Felipe at his baptism, becoming the first Christian kuraka of Cajamarca. He remained a steadfast ally of the Spaniards during his lifetime, helping to convince the lords of the Chachapoyas people to submit to Spanish rule. Felipe Caruarayco was paramount lord of the people of Guzmango, in the province of Cajamarca, under the authority of the Spaniard, Melchior Verdugo. Pizarro had awarded Verdugo an encomienda in the region in 1535. Documention from that year described Felipe as the *cacique principal* of the province of Cajamarca and lord of Chuquimango, one of seven large lineages or *guarangas* (an administrative unit of 1,000 households) that made up the polity. By 1543, however, Felipe was old and sick. His son, don Melchior Caruarayco, whom he favored to succeed him, was still too young to rule, so two relatives were designated as interim governors or regents: don Diego Zublián and don Pedro Angasnapon. Zublián kept this position until his death in 1560, and then don Pedro appropriated for himself the title "cacique principal of the seven guarangas of Cajamarca," remaining in office until his death two years later. After his death, the people of Cajamarca asked the *corregidor*, don Pedro Juáres de Illanez, to name don Melchior as their kuraka. After soliciting information from community elders, Illanez named him "natural lord and cacique principal of the seven guarangas of Cajamarca."

As the paramount Andean lord of Cajamarca, don Melchior was responsible for the guaranga of Guzmango and two more *parcialidades* (lineages or other groupings of a larger community): Colquemarca (later Espiritu Santo de Chuquimango) and Malcaden (later San Lorenzo de Malcadan). This charge involved approximately 5,000 adult males, under various lesser caciques; and, counting their families, the total population that he ruled approached 50,000. Most of these mountain people, who lived dispersed in more than 500 small settlements, subsisted by farming and by herding llamas. Their tribute responsibilities included rotating labor service at the nearby silver mines of Chilete.

During one of his many long trips down from the highlands to visit the nearest Spanish city, Trujillo, don Melchior was stricken by a serious illness. He prudently dictated his last will and testament before the local Spanish notary, Juan de Mata, on June 20, 1565. Coming as he did from a relatively remote area where very few Spaniards resided, his will reflects traditional Andean conceptions of society and values before they were fundamentally and forever changed. This is evident in the care he took to list all of his retainers. He claimed ten potters in the place or hamlet of Cajamarca, a mayordomo or overseer from the parcialidad of Lord Santiago, a retainer from the parcialidad of don Francisco

Angasnapon, and a beekeeper who lived near a river. In the town of Chulaquys, his followers included a lesser lord (*mandoncillo*) with jurisdiction over seven native families. At the mines of Chilete, he listed twenty workers who served him. Don Melchior also claimed six servants with no specific residence and at least twenty-four corn farmers and twenty-two pages in the town of Contumasá. Nine different subjects cared for his chili peppers and corn either in Cascas or near the town of Junba (now Santa Ana de Cimba?). He also listed the towns of Gironbi and Guaento, whose inhabitants guarded his coca and chili peppers; Cunchamalca, whose householders took care of his corn; and another town called Churcan de Cayanbi. Finally, he mentioned two towns that he was disputing with a native lord whose Christian name was don Pedro. In total, don Melchior claimed jurisdiction over a minimum of 102 followers and six towns, including the two in dispute.

This preoccupation of don Melchior with listing all of his retainers shows how strong Andean traditions remained in the Cajamarca region, even thirty years after the Spanish invasion. Among the indigenous peoples, numbers of followers denoted tangible wealth and power. An Andean chronicler, Felipe Guamán Poma de Ayala, wrote that lords "will gain rank if the numbers [of their subjects] multiply according to the law of the dominion over Indians. And, if their numbers decline, they too lose [status]." This concept of status was the same one held in the Inca system. The *hatun curaca* or *huno apo*, lord of 10,000 households, ranked higher than a *guaranga curaca*, the lord of 1,000. The latter dominated the lord of 100 Indians, a *pachaca camachicoc*, who in turn was superior to the overseers (*mandones* and mandoncillos) with responsibility for as few as five households. Don Melchior, as a chief of seven guarangas, had jurisdiction over other lesser lords, who themselves ruled individual lineages.

In several clauses of his testament, don Melchior reflected his concern for the poor and disadvantaged among his subjects, leaving them food and other items. He left a total of 15 fanegas (each approximately 1.5 bushels) of chili peppers, 5 fanegas of peanuts, 20 fanegas of corn, 10 fanegas of potatoes, 8 fanegas of yuca, three goats, and one *oveja* (a Castilian sheep or an Andean llama?) to the needy in Cajamarca, Contumasá, Chilete, and Cascas. The will also listed a number of items, all of them of Andean origin. They included five houses in Cajamarca, Guzmango, or Chilete, and fifteen planted pieces of land, noted as *chac[a]ras y tierras* (planted fields and ground). Land, like the air don Melchior breathed, was an open resource, available to anyone willing to work it while it remained fertile. The cacique did not claim ownership of these fields; he owned only the plants, which presumably had been sown by his retainers with seed that he had provided them. Other notable objects were all ceremonial items: the litter in which the Inca and presumably he himself was carried, a trumpet, and four large *cocos*, or ceremonial serving vessels, for drinking *chicha* (maize beer used in Andean religious ceremonies). Don Melchior listed only two items of European provenance: two mares. From his testament, it seems that people, more than material possessions, were the source of status and power.

Don Melchior did not die from the sickness that afflicted him in Trujillo but recovered to face many other challenges during his tenure in office. He returned to Cajamarca, the territory occupied by the people of the kingdom of Guzmango, to coordinate the activities of some 5,000 tribute payers (males, aged 18–50) and heads of household and a total population that was dying off rapidly but which still totaled between 25,000 and 30,000 individuals (see table). This population continued to pay the tribute required first by the encomendero, Melchior Verdugo, and then after his death in 1567 by his widow, doña Jordana Mexia. Although tribute assessments had been reduced over the years to reflect the precipitous decline of the indigenous population, they remained onerous and burdensome. Native shepherds guarded Verdugo's large herds of animals; other Cajamarquinos made cloth; many also served his household. Verdugo, notoriously cruel, ruled with an iron hand. The memory of his hunting dogs, which had once ripped apart the son of the lord of Bambamarca when his father had failed to meet his quota of gold, remained fresh in the minds of residents of Cajamarca.

Population of Cajamarca, 1570s

Guarangas	Pachacas*	Population
Bambamarca	9	3,511
Pomamarca	7	2,246
Chondal	4	5,207
Caxamarca	10	2,497
Guzmango	6	5,631
Chuquimango	4	2,435
Mitimaes	4	1,697
Parcialidades		
Colquemarca	4	2,219
Malcaden	4	2,395
	Total	27,838

Source: María del Pilar Remy Simatovic and María Rostworowksi de Diez Canseco, *Las visitas a Cajamarca, 1571–72/1578*. Lima: Instituto de Estudios Peruanos, 1992, Appendix 1.
*Units of 100 Indians

Dr. Gregorio González de Cuenca, a supreme court judge in the Spanish capital of Lima, visited the Cajamarquinos during the tenure of don Melchior to conduct a census of the indigenous tributaries. Cuenca counted 3,823 married and 1,346 single men eligible for tribute service. During this census, don Melchior negotiated new tribute allocations with Cuenca to reflect the declining Andean population. Cajamarquinos at midcentury delivered annually hundreds of lengths of fine woven cloth; thousands of fanegas of corn, baskets of chili peppers, chickens, and game birds; unnumbered pairs of sandals, and innumerable llamas, besides providing unpaid personal services. After 1567, however, each married male head of household was required to deliver 2.5 *pesos de plata corriente* (3 *patacones* or pieces of eight [reales]), one fanega of corn, and one chicken. Some of these goods could be delivered in silver. Thus, the Cajamarquinos paid 14,780 pesos de plata corriente (17,605 patacones and 5 reales), 3,823 birds, and 2,584 fanegas of corn in 1567.

As the population continued its decline, don Melchior still had to deliver the same amount of tribute as if all the persons counted by Cuenca were still alive or living in their natal communities. Either he could track down everyone who had left the polity to make them contribute what they owed or make those who remained each pay more to make up the deficit. If these two strategies failed, don Melchior then was obliged to make up the difference from his own resources, which he found increasingly difficult to do.

Don Melchior also had to adapt to profound religious changes brought about by the colonizers' introduction of Christianity. The Franciscans had established a monastery in the area in 1549. They and the Augustinians, who lived nearby in Guamachuco, insisted on baptizing the indigenous peoples and giving them Christian names. They also curtailed both the worship of Catequil, a famed local diety and oracle, and the ancestors of the Cajamarquinos. Andeans did not understand why they should forgo worshipping powerful spirits who had granted them fertility and life-giving rain for generations and who could talk and answer the questions of their devotees. How could these forces be replaced with a single god who had died far away and who did not speak? The coming of the missionaries also meant abandoning the practice of polygyny and adopting the notion of legitimate and illegitimate offspring.[1] Ancestor cults survived underground, however, with the connivance of don Melchior and other lords, but superficial repudiation of ancestor worship undermined the ancient mechanisms related to succession, whereby community leadership passed to brothers of the same generation. Instead, European ideas about primogeniture gained currency in the Andean provinces, and positions of power passed directly to the oldest (and usually male) child.

As Andeans began to realize that Spaniards neither understood nor respected traditional succession practices, many claimants came forward to challenge don Melchior's charge and mandate. Two cousins, don Sancho and don Cristóbal Xulcapoma, declared that they had rights to the position of kuraka and brought their claim to the Spanish magistrate, Juan de Fuentes. He ruled in favor of don Melchior's claim, but the cousins then appealed the ruling to Dr. Cuenca. At this point, more alternative candidates came forward to present their claims. It was clear that the Spaniards did not respect native succession rights. In pre-Hispanic times, the general pattern was for one brother to succeed another, and only after the death of all able sons of one generation did leadership pass to a son of the next generation. After having heard testimony by the interested parties, Dr. Cuenca settled the dispute by naming Alonso Chuplingón, a son of Caruatongo, as lord. At the investiture all the other lords accepted Chuplingón, making gestures of veneration to him once he had been seated on the *duho* (stool of office): "each one of the said nobles came up to the said don Alonso Chuplingón who was seated on the said stool [and] they worshipped him in recognition of and as a sign of [his status] as cacique and natural lord." All participated except don Melchior, who remained at a distance, obstinate and convinced that his legitimate, ancestor-given rights had been usurped in 1568.

Don Melchior was not the only headman to face such difficulties. In the late 1560s and early 1570s, there were various indications that the old-style kurakas, called *dueños de indios*,[2] were dying off and not being replaced by individuals who were respected and feared like those of the past. It became harder for these new kurakas to mobilize labor and convince their Andean followers to obey. Therefore, the colonial state, which relied on their assistance and mediation, began to recognize them officially, issuing written titles to the positions they held and granting them privileges to bolster their faltering image. When royal officials traveled through the area, they gave the lords coveted licenses to ride horses with saddle and bridle, to own *arcabuces* (matchlock guns), to be carried on a litter, to wear Spanish clothing, and to have trumpets. But these privileges did little to maintain the general esteem that kurakas of old had enjoyed.

The absurdity of installing Alonso Chuplingón soon became obvious, even to Spanish authorities. He was described as "an incapable Indian because of his innate rudeness and little intelligence." As a result, a regent or governor, Juan Bautista, assumed his responsibilities. When Bautista died soon thereafter, the corregidor, Diego de Salazar, named a new governor, don Pablo Malcaden, even though he was a lord of a guaranga and not of the Guzmango lineage. Once again, Spanish authorities allowed ethnic leadership to pass to an illegitimate candidate who in pre-Hispanic times might not have been considered.

Despite lacking any legitimacy, don Pablo Malcaden served as governor after the death of Alonso Chuplingón, who died without children. There was a general consensus that the lordship should revert to a Caruarayco. Since don Pablo had outlived don Melchior, he declared Luis Caruarayco, the son of don Melchior, his successor as kuraka. In the end, Luis won back the title and position of kuraka of the people of Cajamarca, but only after a court case involving another pretender, Sebastián Ninalingón (of questionable parentage and a distant relative of Alonso Chuplingón). Viceroy Conde de Chinchon installed Luis Caruarayco as cacique principal in 1635.

EPILOGUE: THE TRANSITION FROM ANDEAN TO SPANISH VALUES

These struggles over local power illustrate how Andean values, practices, customs, and beliefs were subverted and changed under the Spaniards during the first half-century of colonial rule. Indigenous concepts of legitimacy were based on the supernatural powers and special ties to the ancestor gods, which the Conquest had undermined. As ethnic leaders and their people converted (at least outwardly) to Catholicism, accepted baptism, and took Christian names, divination rituals and native religion in general were prohibited and usually driven underground. Although many lords continued to pray and sacrifice to the ancestors for wisdom to rule, other aspects of pre-Hispanic practices declined. Moreover, traditional ideas about legitimacy and succession also suffered by the imposition of Spanish ideas regarding primogeniture, which destroyed the custom of one generation of brothers ruling before their sons.

The imposition of Christianity brought many new rules and values, particularly monogamy. Don Melchior could not live as his ancestor, Chuptongo, taking 100 wives. Instead, don Melchior remained legally married to only one woman, but, as he noted in his will, he had taken several mistresses and sired many illegitimate children. Old customs such as these were hard to eradicate. The imposition of Catholicism also began to destroy the basis of an individual's identity. Before the Spanish invasion, individuals worshipped many gods—from the Sun and the Moon to notable ancestors. In this way every person felt part of a divine kin network and an extended ethnic community. It was not until the seventeenth century, and in some places the eighteenth, that the natives began to identify themselves as Christians. Likewise, the term "Indian" was a new one for Andeans; they had, of course, never heard the term *indio* before the arrival of the Spaniards. Indigenous leaders lobbying in Lima for colonial reforms in the mid- and late seventeenth century were the first to use the term to underscore their demands to the Spanish authorities for change.

Some aspects of communal life survived, but only for a few more years. The redistributive economy continued to function, though weakened, as the colonists demanded more and more silver or gold as tribute instead of products and services. To get these metals, tribute payers had to work for the Spaniards to earn cash wages, to sell surpluses in the Spanish market, or to travel to the mines or rivers in search of specie. In fact, parallel and overlapping economic systems were operative for many years. Natives traded, exchanged, and gave gifts among themselves to obtain commodities that they could not produce or procure on their own. They used the market to obtain cash and European goods.

Change would become even more pronounced when Spanish authorities began to consolidate the scattered settlements of don Melchior's time into only forty-three villages, called *reducciones*, to facilitate religious conversion, tribute collection, and overall Spanish control. These were later further consolidated into only seventeen towns by the 1570s. The problem faced by don Melchior's successors was how to satisfy the Spaniards without exploiting their own kin to the point that they would either sicken and die or flee to areas of the Andes beyond Spanish reach. Others chose to leave their communities and become the retainer of a Spanish master, which could take them into the city and eventually merge them and their descendants with the growing class of cultural and biological half-breeds or *mestizos*. Any of these alternatives weakened native polities and drove some to the point of extinction.

NOTES

1. According to European customs, a man could only have one wife, and any offspring of that relationship were legitimate. Any other children sired with any other women were illegitimate. Under Andean traditions, however, a man could have multiple spouses, and any children that resulted from such unions were considered legitimate, not just the offspring of the principal or first wife.

2. *Dueño de indio* means "owner of Indians" when translated literally. It was not meant to indicate slavery, but rather an administrator who managed people.

SUGGESTED READINGS

The best general work on the history of Cajamarca is a three-volume set compiled by Fernando Silva Santisteban, Waldemar Espinoza Soriano, and Rogger Ravines, entitled *Historia de Cajamarca* (Cajamarca: Instituto Nacional de Cultura, 1986). Another work worthy of mention is José Dammert Bellido, *Cajamarca en el siglo XVI* (Lima: Pontificia Universidad Católica del Perú, 1997).

For information on the local kurakas and their lives, see Horacio Villanueva Urteaga, *Cajamarca: Apuntes para su historia* (Cuzco: Editorial Garcilaso, 1975, especially 1–22); and *Los caciques de Cajamarca: Estudio histórico y documentos* (Trujillo: Universidad Nacional de Trujillo, n.d.). For background on the social organization of Cajamarca and the practice of polygyny, see the articles by Espinoza Soriano, "La poliginia señorial en el Reino de Caxamarca, siglos XV y XVI," *Revista del Museo Nacional (Lima)* 42 (1977): 399–466; and my book, *The World Upside Down: Cross-Cultural Contact and Conflict in Sixteenth-Century Peru* (Stanford: Stanford University Press, 1996), Chapter 4.

Finally, to compare don Melchior's will with others see Ella Dunbar Temple's article on three wills written by heirs of the Incas, "Los testamentos inéditos de Paullu Inca, Don Carlos y Don Melchor Carlos Inca," *Documenta: Revista de la Sociedad Peruana de Historia (Lima)* 2 (1949–50): 630–51; and my article, "Rich Man, Poor Man, Beggar Man, or Chief: Material Wealth as a Basis of Power in Sixteenth-Century Peru," in *Dead Giveaways: Indigenous Testaments of Colonial Mesoamerica and the Andes*, edited by Susan Kellogg and Matthew Restall (Salt Lake City: University of Utah Press, 1998), 215–48.

CHAPTER 3

Doña Isabel Sisa

A Sixteenth-Century Indian Woman
Resisting Gender Inequalities

Ana María Presta

The expansion of Tawantinsuyu set in motion a series of subtle religious and cultural changes affecting gender relationships. According to many Andean traditions, the panoply of indigenous gods and goddesses was arranged in a hierarchy characterized by gender complementarity. Human men descended from the male-oriented gods, who oversaw traditionally male activities—hunting game, caring for flocks, or waging war. Likewise, females descended from roughly an equivalent number of goddesses, who cared for the traditional female activities on Earth such as agricultural duties, rearing children, and weaving cloth, which held important ritual significance. Under the state religion of the Inca, however, the Sun god (Inti) and his descendant, the emperor or Sapa Inca (meaning unique or supreme ruler), were clearly superior to their female counterparts. Moreover, men's work seems to have become more highly valued. The Inca state religion also began controlling gender relationships directly, demanding that Andean communities supply set numbers of young women, called aclla, *to serve the Sapa Inca—spinning and weaving, serving in local temples, and preparing food and maize beer for festivals. In this way the Inca turned the aclla into symbols of state power by removing the labor, sexual behavior, and reproductive functions of these women from the control of their* ayllu *and families.*

The Spanish invasion and conquest of Tawantinsuyu moved Andean society much further toward the patriarchal values that permeated the Castilian legal code, particularly those laws governing inheritance. Nonetheless, Andeans soon began struggling to interpret and then to manipulate these new laws for their own advantage in the first century after the Conquest. One fascinating legal imbroglio over inheritance laws emerged between a wealthy and powerful Andean cacique principal in Santiago de Curi (near the provincial capital of La Plata, the seat of the Audiencia of Charcas, today's Sucre, Bolivia), don Domingo Itquilla, and his strong-willed indigenous wife, doña Isabel Sisa. According to Castilian law, a couple owned jointly any assets acquired during marriage, although the husband retained the right to manage all the couple's property during their lifetimes. When don Domingo wrote a last will and testament, he

35

declared that certain lands had been left to him by his ancestors, and so he felt free to bequeath them without regard to his wife's wishes. As a woman, doña Isabel could not openly dispute her husband's claims, so she filed her own will, claiming that these assets were joint property that she wanted to leave to her son and heir, Juan de Acuña.

During the legal proceedings over the inheritance, a series of scandalous revelations about the couple and their strategic maneuverings, illicit sexual relationships, and shady political and economic deals emerged. While he lived, don Domingo had the better of the legal battles, but soon after his death, the wily and resourceful doña Isabel prevailed through skillful litigation and her knowledge of Castilian law. The turning point came when she presented evidence that her husband had gained his post as cacique principal not through inheritance, but because his ability to read and write in Castilian had made him indispensable both to the community and to the Spanish authorities. He was one of a new generation of caciques who had usurped power from traditional ethnic leaders such as don Melchior Caruarayco of Cajamarca (see Chapter 2).

Ana María Presta is professor of history at the University of Buenos Aires and also holds a research appointment from CONICET, at the Instituto Emilio Ravignani in Buenos Aires, Argentina. She published numerous articles on a wide range of issues dealing with colonial Latin America before coming to the United States to earn her doctorate at The Ohio State University. Most recently, Professor Presta's research and writing have focused on the first Spanish settlers and encomenderos of Charcas (now Bolivia), which have led to her new book, Encomienda, familia, y negocios en Charcas Colonial: Los encomenderos de La Plata, 1550–1600 *(2000).*

During one of her customary trips through the rugged terrain between the small indigenous town of Santiago de Curi and the city of La Plata (now Sucre, the historical capital of Bolivia), doña Isabel Sisa fell from her horse. What provoked the accident remains unknown. Perhaps her horse was startled by thunder or lightning, which commonly occur during the Andean rainy season. Nevertheless, the fall happened on December 31, 1602. Upon her return home, doña Isabel, a true Catholic, suffering great pain and believing herself near death, summoned a notary to her bedside to take down her last will and testament.

Doña Isabel did not die from her accident, but this incident marked her first attempt to obtain her rightful share of the property accumulated during her marriage to a wealthy but domineering husband, don Domingo Itquilla. The ensuing battle between the couple over this estate subsequently revealed secrets, coverups, and scandals perpetuated by the desire of doña Isabel and her spouse to control wealth, power, and prestige. Because she married a member of the indigenous elite, doña Isabel enjoyed status, wealth, and power, but she was subordinate to her husband in a male-dominated society. Nevertheless, she proved to be a formidable foe in her battle to control her own destiny by skillfully using Castilian inheritance laws to resist the prevailing gender inequalities of society.

A last will and testament usually was a written text signed by the testator, if literate, and witnesses such as the attending priest and the notary. Although testaments varied in length, they usually began by identifying family members, kin, and the testator's social status. The will followed with provisions to pay for the burial, posthumous ceremonies and Masses, and donations to charity, and then with lists of the material belongings, debts, heirs, and debtors of the testator. In this way, testaments were ordinary, mundane documents, but they also reflected the cultural universe of the times and shed light on collective and personal representations of the supernatural.

The custom of producing a last will spread to the Spanish colonies and was practiced extensively among all kinds of people regardless of class, race, ethnicity, and gender. In many cases, for those who belonged to either the Spanish or the Indian elite, wills were inventories of their lives where private and public activities had their distinct place and meaning. Decoding those activities and the hidden practices that remain embedded in these texts is a fruitful challenge, allowing indigenous life stories and patterns of sociocultural changes to emerge. In some cases, testaments are the itineraries of life written before the passage into death.

It is through a number of testaments that the private story, the public life, and the hidden past of doña Isabel Sisa slowly come into view. Her initial testament, and the two that followed, tell a private story of desire, love, distrust, and resentment. Moreover, through her wills—along with those of her husband—it is possible to know more about how Spanish notions of wealth, status, and gender hierarchies influenced the lives of indigenous peoples in early colonial times. The Spaniards introduced new conceptions of property ownership and land tenure, enforced by a legal system designed to reproduce Castilian patterns of inheritance and the ideology of a society of estates, which established differential rights and privileges under the law and imposed rigid patriarchal structures, subordinating women to men. The story of doña Isabel also provides evidence about gender constraints, strategic liaisons, illicit relationships, and bitter claims sheltered from public view in order to protect the couple's wealth and status. Nevertheless, the story of secrets and lies evolved from the documents, demonstrating how property and inheritance formed the center of this woman's concerns when death seemed imminent. Doña Isabel's testaments portray in writing a determined woman who battled to secure her legacy for her son and designated heir, Juan de Acuña.

The first of the documents comprising the testament of doña Isabel followed the standard legal form by identifying her as the legitimate wife of don Domingo Itquilla, *gobernador* (governor) and *cacique principal* (ethnic lord) of Santiago de Curi. These titles demonstrated that don Domingo was recognized both by Spanish authorities and members of his own community as paramount lord of the town.[1] She also asserted her belief in the Holy Trinity, naming the Queen of the Angels as her mediator and the Angels as her lawyers; both were needed to guide her soul to the gates of Heaven. After placing her soul in God's hands, doña Isabel requested that her earthly remains be buried in the local church, in the chapel that she and her husband were building. If the chapel remained unfinished when she died, then doña Isabel wanted to be buried beside the main altar, after several Masses were said on behalf of her soul. She declared herself to be a member of the *cofradía* (religious brotherhood) of Our Lady of Guadalupe, and she wanted this sodality to sponsor Masses for her soul, paid for from her assets. Next, she asked her executors to invest 100 *pesos corrientes* (pesos of 8 reales) to support the celebration of seven Masses annually for her soul. Doña Isabel specified that she had no debts, although she claimed that the Indian community of Santiago de Curi owed her (and her husband) more than 600 pesos corrientes from the money payable to the *corregidor* (Spanish rural magistrate) for their taxes. One Hernando Chuquichambi also owed the couple an additional 60 pesos corrientes. Moreover, doña Isabel made it clear that she had the right to receive half of the money owed to the couple.

Regarding her personal belongings, she left her granddaughter, Juana de Acuña, 80 pesos corrientes and bequeathed some dresses to her granddaughters. After these items, she emphatically declared everything else community property. Among these goods, she listed a house and a lot located within the city of La Plata; houses, lots, and orchards in Santiago de Curi; one hundred cows, eight pairs of oxen, twenty-five mares, two mules, and a horse. Household goods included a Chinese satin tapestry (purchased for 120 pesos corrientes), a cloth with the image of the Mother of God and a crucifix, some furniture, and "siete libros de leer viejos" (seven old reading books). Also listed were 750 pesos in cash, 40 *cargas* (100 pounds) of wheat, 5 cargas of potatoes and 2 of maize sown in their fields, an unspecified quantity of stored wheat, corn, and potatoes, 80 cargas of dry wheat to be given to their Indians, 28 pesos corrientes owed to doña Isabel and don Domingo (by Juan de Tudela and his wife for 10 cargas of wheat), and agricultural tools. She included personal belongings—an *axu* (woman's outfit), a *lliqlla* (wide shawl), a pair of Castilian velvet sleeves embroidered with gold, and four new cotton shirts from Rouen. Finally, since she had benefited from the labor of the Indians of Santiago de Curi, she left the elderly and poor of that community a pair of oxen. Moreover, she named her husband, don Domingo, and her son, Juan de Acuña, as executors. She addressed Juan de Acuña as her "legitimate" son and sole heir. The husband and the son (as executors), the notary, and two witnesses signed the testament. One did so in her name, since doña Isabel was illiterate.[2]

One day later, while alone, doña Isabel asked the notary to add a codicil to her original testament. According to doña Isabel, her husband had forced her to dictate her testament in his presence, and she had accepted "because he is her husband and to avoid afflictions and because she is afraid of him."[3] Behind this admission were colonial notions of patriarchy, male domination, the weak social position of women, and even the threat of domestic violence. Determined to overcome her fears, however, doña Isabel asserted that there were some items she needed to add.[4] She stated that her husband had refused to give her half of the last harvest of wheat and maize, worth 1,000 pesos corrientes. Moreover, she declared that he had taken another 3,000 pesos corrientes that she had earned by selling *coca* (coca leaves) and *chicha* (maize beer). Although his wife had demonstrated her ability to earn money and transact business, don Domingo assumed the legal inferiority of women and their incapacity to administer assets, given the innate mental deficiency of the female sex (*imbecilitus sexus*). Castilian law allowed husbands and fathers to manage the assets of their wives and children. Thus, legalized gender prejudice denied doña Isabel the right to enjoy, administer, or invest her earnings.

Despite this legal support for patriarchy, Spanish law also provided that upon the death of one spouse, the other was entitled to half of the assets accumulated during the marriage. After the death of her husband, a wife had the right to get back her dowry, any other property that she had owned before the marriage, and one-half of the *gananciales* (community property) gained in common with her husband during their marriage. Since doña Isabel brought no dowry, she claimed that her earnings came from marketing goods and the property acquired during the marriage. She also claimed that don Domingo had not allowed her to include among their community property their *chacra* (small farm), called Chilcane, and their cattle ranch. Consequently, she named her "son," Juan de Acuña, the heir to her community property, including Chilcane and the ranch. Was doña Isabel really so near death when she dictated her will, or did she use her injury as an excuse to demand her share of valuable community property? Her first will and codicil may well have been a strategy to overcome gender constraints and contest her husband's will, which was dated two years before hers. It also served to remind her husband about her legal rights to their community property.

Don Domingo Itquilla had hired a notary to write his first will and testament on June 23, 1601, in La Plata.[5] Following convention, the cacique stated that he was the son of don Martín Chinori Guarachi and doña Ana Anama, former lords of Santiago de Curi. He declared his belief in the Holy Trinity and asked to be buried in the church of his hometown in the presence of the local priest and the members of the Brotherhood of Our Lady of Copacabana. He also requested Masses on his behalf to be celebrated in Santiago de Curi as well as at the four monasteries and cathedral in La Plata. Don Domingo designated for the statue of the Virgin of Copacabana in the church of Santiago de Curi a new cloak made of Chinese satin and embroidered with gold thread. He also left money to be applied to the canonization of Saint Isidore. After recognizing his debts to his Indians and others, don Domingo declared among his personal assets the chacra of Chilcane, which he "had inherited from his parents" before marrying doña Isabel. He also mentioned other properties and belongings that his wife had declared as communal property. Furthermore, he stated that thirty years ago he had married doña Isabel Sisa, who had neither brought a dowry nor given him heirs. Consequently, he named her as the sole heir to their remaining community property. Moreover, he left his "nephew," don Domingo Hamamani, the estate of Chilcane and the *cacicazgo* (chieftaincy) of Santiago de Curi. Additionally, don Domingo demanded that his nephew look after, support, and marry the child named doña María Chocoboto, daughter of the deceased don Domingo Andaca, as a condition of inheritance. Surprisingly, after this clause don Domingo asserted that he had no children, either with his legitimate wife or with another woman.[6] Finally, he named don Juan Prica, *segunda persona* (second in command) of affairs in Santiago de Curi, and his "nephew," don Domingo Hamamani, as his executors.

It seems clear that instead of going to court to resolve their disputes over communal property, the partners had chosen to use their wills to litigate the property rights. Doña Isabel prepared her wills and codicils as a strategy of defense under Spanish law, acting as the plaintiff. Accordingly, her husband, the defendant, promptly understood the game and responded in the same way. Thus, a confrontation of "wills" began between doña Isabel and don Domingo. These legal actions avoided any long, tedious, and costly lawsuits over the disputed communal property and kept the battle in the domestic sphere, once the pact of silence between husband and wife had been broken. While both spouses added more information in each new will, don Domingo introduced contradictions in his version of events that would eventually lead to his defeat in court.

All of these changes in the testaments involved efforts by both spouses to name their legitimate heirs, but, in so doing, they began to leave a number of questions unanswered about their kin relationship. Thus, new names and questions about kinship appeared in the wills. A "legitimate son" was soon thereafter addressed as a "son" in doña Isabel's statement, and in the last will of don Domingo the heirs to the alleged personal property were a "nephew" and a "child." At first glance, these puzzling contradictions seem difficult to resolve. For example, was don Domingo the father of doña Isabel's "legitimate" son? If so, why did he assert that he had no children? If not, was she married before? Why did don Domingo award his office to a nephew whose kinship was not clearly established in his will? Why did he show concern over looking after a child who had no ties of kinship to him? And how could caring for this child be a condition for having his nephew and heir inherit the most important office within an Indian community? The answers slowly emerge from a careful reading of the testaments themselves.

For six years doña Isabel kept silent, leaving aside her quest for community property and inheritance rights. Perhaps the spouses had reached some understanding or just decided to put off a family feud. Nevertheless, don Domingo produced two more wills between 1606 and 1608, and the clauses dealing with his personal information, burial plans, charity works, and donations remained the same as the one written in 1606. As before, he persisted in declaring that he had inherited the estate of Chilcane in addition to two previously unmentioned properties, Vilcaparo and Otavi, from his parents and grandparents. In keeping with Castilian law, don Domingo, like many other indigenous property owners, based his rights both on inheritance and genealogy. Since his genealogical proof of ownership did not extend beyond his grandparents, however, don Domingo stated that he also had formal written, legal titles to the chacras.

After mentioning other assets and people who owed him money, the cacique stated that he had married doña Isabel Sisa, a "palla" (noble woman) from Cuzco, thirty-four years earlier. According to don Domingo, when the couple had married they had no assets, with the exception of the estates of Chilcane, Vilcaparo, and Otavi, the properties bequeathed by his parents and grandparents. Accordingly, doña Isabel had the right to inherit half of everything acquired during their marriage: household belongings, houses, orchards, livestock, and harvests. Although don Domingo declared that he had no legitimate children, at this time he recognized "dos hijos bastardos" (two bastard sons) born after his marriage to doña Isabel: don Alonso and don Diego Itquilla, who both lived in his town. Don Domingo appointed Martín de Olmedo, a Spanish *vecino* (citizen) of La Plata and his "nephews" don Domingo Hamamani and Domingo Itquilla as his executors. Finally, he named his illegitimate children as heirs to his remaining assets.

According to Castilian law, parental assets passed to legitimate heirs, regardless of sex. One-fifth of this property could be given freely to any favored heir. From the remaining four-fifths, the testator could dispose of one-third, the *mejora* or supplementary bequest, to endow an heir. Demonstrating some knowledge of the law, don Domingo donated to his elder son, don Alonso, the supplementary bequest of one-third and the one-fifth of free disposition. Nothing was stated about the succession to the cacicazgo of Santiago de Curi, but don Domingo declared his previous testament invalid.[7]

When don Domingo ordered his last will and testament in 1608, he was ill in his house at Santiago de Curi. After repeating the clauses found in the earlier versions of his will about details of his burial, Masses to be said on his soul's behalf, and charitable works to be done in his name, don Domingo again declared that the properties of Chilcane, Vilcaparo, and Otavi were his personal belongings, inherited from his parents. He enumerated the debts that his executors should collect from several patrons, including his Indians and Domingo Hamamani, a native from Toropalca. Don Domingo took this opportunity to refer to Domingo Hamamani as an Indian, who allegedly claimed to be his relative and owed him 100 *fanegas* (1.5 bushels) of maize, twenty cows, two pairs of oxen, fifty sheep, and 50 cargas of wheat. Did don Domingo Itquilla's illness make him unable to remember that he had named Hamamani as "don," his "nephew," and his successor to the government of Santiago de Curi?[8] In truth, Hamamani was apparently a client of the cacique, serving merely as a tool in his dispute with doña Isabel. For some unknown reason, he was no longer useful to accomplish this initial role assigned to him by don Domingo. Finally, don Domingo requested his executors to pay 200 pesos to a "moza montañesa" (a young mestizo woman) who worked for a rich Spaniard in La Plata. Could she have been one of the elderly cacique's mistresses or perhaps even the mother of one of his illegitimate children? After those odd clauses, don Domingo described a series of debts owed to several individuals from La Plata and Santiago de Curi. It is possible that the cacique was a moneylender because his will mentioned that he had custody of money for several people, and these funds should be returned by his executors after his death.

Don Domingo insisted again that doña Isabel had brought no assets to the union, reiterating that he alone owned the estates of Chilcane, Vilcaparo, and Otavi, which he had inherited from his ancestors. By declaring these assets as property owned before the marriage, don Domingo tried to show that his wife had no claim over them, leaving him free to donate them to any heir of his choice. Subsequently, don Domingo stated that he had two illegitimate sons, don Alonso, a five-year-old born to Luisa, an Indian from Santiago de Curi who was no longer in town, and don Diego, a three-year-old who lived with his mother, the Indian Barbola, in the neighboring town of Guata. Don Alonso, the elder, was raised at don Domingo's home by his legitimate wife, doña Isabel. Consequently, don Domingo bequeathed legacies to these two illegitimate sons, naming don Alonso his successor to the cacicazgo of Santiago de Curi and the heir to the one-fifth and one-third of his remaining assets.[9] Until don Alonso came of age, don Domingo's nephew—an Indian of his same name—would remain in charge of the government and his assets. In an attempt to maintain control even after his death, don Domingo declared that if his elder child died, his office and belongings should pass to the younger son. However, his lands remained his greatest obsession. He demanded that his heirs never sell them, because they had to remain in the family "until the end of the world" ("que las dichas mis chacras no se vendan hasta el fin del mundo"). The executors of this last will were doña Isabel Sisa, her son Juan de Acuña, one don Diego Aricoma, and the nephew of don Domingo of the same name, whom he had also designated as governor until his elder son reached the age of majority.[10]

This last will finally made public the seamy personal affairs of don Domingo, including the names of his mistresses and illegitimate children. The offspring of his illicit liaisons were children of status who, like their father, enjoyed the title "don." In the absence of one child's mother, doña Isabel, his legitimate wife, was even raising the very youngster who was supposed to succeed her husband as cacique and as the owner of lands that she claimed as her own.

The office of cacique allowed don Domingo to take advantage of business opportunities while enjoying respect, status, and prosperity. Moneylending gave him the chance to add cash to his enterprises. The absence of a banking system during colonial times generated a market for people who made significant profits from lending money at interest. As the local lord, don Domingo received the tribute of his Indians (in specie and in kind), which gave him access to cash. Moroever, because of his prestige within the region, he enjoyed the confidence of a wide range of locals who were willing to allow him to invest their savings. As a result, the last statement of don Domingo left legacies to his heirs, satisfied the demands of creditors and business associates, and named executors to carry out his plans to control the patrimony that he had amassed so skillfully over his lifetime.

Despite this carefully designed scheme, the persistence of doña Isabel to realize her own goals checked and then undermined his efforts, both by unmasking his lies and deceptions and by using Spanish law to her advantage. According to Castilian law, as a married woman, doña Isabel could own property that her husband could only administer but never own. Nevertheless, the system of communal property, guaranteed by the same legal provisions, stated that assets acquired during a couple's married life—interest, salaries, real estate, rents, or any kind of investment—were jointly owned. Upon the death of one of the spouses, the profits from their joint enterprises were communal property, which could be divided among the surviving spouse and the remaining legitimate heirs without regard to how much money each partner brought to the union or invested during the marriage. Don Domingo and doña Isabel were aware of the law and both tried to turn it to their own advantage. If the estates of Chilcane, Vilcaparo, and Otavi, for example, were, as don Domingo asserted, his own possessions, inherited from his parents, and if his wife brought no dowry to the marriage, then there was no substantial community property to bequeath. On the contrary, if (as doña Isabel had declared) the chacras were common assets accrued during their long marriage, then she had a right to them regardless of whether or not she had brought any dowry to the marriage. Both spouses were fighting for their assets, but only one could win the bitter, gendered battle of "wills."

Don Domingo Itquilla, cacique of Santiago de Curi, apparently died soon after dictating his final testament in 1608. Months later, in 1609, doña Isabel, now a widow, asked a notary to write another will. Widowhood was a status that gave women a certain autonomy and freedom from male subordination. Now, no censorship, tutelage, or mistreatment could stop doña Isabel from undermining many provisions of her late husband's wills.

Doña Isabel pressed her case vigorously by presenting herself as a woman of noble blood and as a dedicated wife. She professed to be a palla from Cusco and the legitimate daughter of don Hernando Tupa and Juana Carua. As a respectful and loving wife, she asked to be buried in the church of Santiago de Curi in the grave of don Domingo and beside him. She requested that a Mass be celebrated during her funeral and that fellows of the Brotherhood of Our Lady of Copacabana should accompany the body. Doña Isabel left money to pay for more Masses and to buy candles and white wax for the altar of the church as well as for her grave. Her executors were to provide Juan de Acuña, her "natural" son, his wife Magdalena Gutiérrez, and their daughters Juana, Angelina, and Mariana de Acuña with mourning clothes for her funeral. According to a provision from her husband's last will, doña Isabel redirected the investment of 180 pesos corrientes to her granddaughters, Juana and Angelina. By playing the dutiful wife, instead of offending the memory of her deceased husband or calling him a liar, doña Isabel did much to advance her claims for their disputed property.

The widow then undermined her husband's last will by casting doubt on his testimony on the "venta y composición de tierras" (sale and verifications of land ownership) that had taken place in the district during the 1590s. According to both documents, she asserted that don Domingo had stressed before the notaries who signed his wills and the judge who confirmed his land ownership that "the lands *we* possessed" had been inherited from his parents and grandparents, all natives of Santiago de Curi. Nevertheless, doña Isabel boldly countered that don Domingo and his relatives were not natives of Santiago de Curi but came from Toropalca, a town near Potosí. She wisely set her claim in the center of a debate that was taking place in the Southern Andes at the end of the sixteenth century over the large-scale migration of indigenous people from their natal communities. What did doña Isabel expect to gain by disclosing that her husband was not a native of the town where he had held the office of cacique? If his family had migrated to Santiago de Curi, was he merely a migrant or "foreigner" (*forastero*), not a respected ethnic leader with long-standing kinship ties in the town? Moreover, if don Domingo were a lowly forastero, could he enjoy hereditary rights to the prestigious office of cacique principal?

Migration was a deeply rooted practice in the Southern Andes, an extremely harsh environment that offered remarkable climatic variations, even at short distances up or down the mountainsides. Permanent, cyclical migration from different ecosystems characterized the life of diverse Andean ethnic groups. Kinship, reciprocity, and redistribution were the principles that bound together the inhabitants of the highlands and lowlands and regulated their permanent exchange of labor and produce in the absence of a market economy. Depending on their needs and the geographical constraints, Andean peoples lived in dispersed settlements scattered across different altitudes and climates. This way of living, however, was totally alien to the Spaniards, who usually spent their lives in the same town or village where they were born. In the Andes, however, peoples from the high plateau dispatched kinsmen to found settlements in the valleys and lowlands to gain access to resources such as maize, chili, wood, cotton, and coca leaves, which complemented those in their highland natal settlements. Many natives of Toropalca, for example, had lived in the valley of Curi before the Spaniards' arrival. Curi was a peripheral settlement where peoples from different ethnic groups in the highlands became *mitmakuna* (permanent colonists from other regions) to contribute to their own group's self-sufficiency. After the Conquest, however, new European ideas about private property, land ownership, and citizenship linked to territorial origin were introduced into the Andean world, causing considerable confusion and numerous disputes over land ownership and what constituted legitimate kinship ties.

Before the 1570s, some ethnic groups from the highlands took advantage of the confusion generated by pre- and post-Conquest customs of property ownership to seize lands worked by their own colonists in the lowlands. This confusion was compounded during the last thirty years of the sixteenth century, when Spanish authorities tried to resolve such disputes between highland and lowland groups. Between 1572 and 1575, for example, the fifth viceroy of Peru, don Francisco de Toledo, conducted a *visita general* (general inspection) and a *reducción general* (resettlement program). He wanted to take a census of the indigenous population, organize the *mita* (cyclical forced labor draft) to provide a steady stream of workers for the mining center of Potosí, and concentrate the dispersed Andean settlements in *reducciones* (Spanish-style villages) to collect the head tax or tribute more effectively.

Toledo's survey allowed highlanders the opportunity to develop new strategies for maintaining access to their landholdings in the lowlands. Artificial divisions introduced by the Spaniards differentiated between the "natives" of a town and those who were merely colonists or recent migrants, who had originated in another community at a different ecological level. The colonists would be registered in highland or valley settlements as "natives" or in both towns by virtue of their dual residence. Thus, the disclosure that don Domingo was a native of Toropalca living in Santiago de Curi makes sense in an Andean world where kinship, descent, and ethnicity did not require only one residence. Pre-Conquest Andean ideas about "citizenship" were rooted in ethnicity rather than place of birth. Relying on traditional Andean beliefs, don Domingo stressed kinship, status, and residence to advance his claims as both cacique principal and the owner of lands in Santiago de Curi. Doña Isabel (or her attorney) relied on Spanish law, however, to emphasize her husband's natal community (Toropalca) to undermine his case, leaving aside the ethnic and kinship ties of don Domingo.

The second major move from the colonial administration to concentrate the scattered Amerindian population and gain land to be sold or granted to the Spaniards was to compel those who occupied lands to show their legal titles. Only those persons who could claim ancestral occupation and were able to pay a set fee to confirm their holdings could remain in possession of their lands. Don Domingo had obtained property titles to the lands allegedly belonging to his ancestors, with the land ownership confirmed during the general land survey of 1593–1595. Although doña Isabel was close to winning her battle for community property, her arguments were not strong enough to invalidate don Domingo's will. Nevertheless, she persisted.

Just as don Domingo had declared in his last statement, doña Isabel agreed that they had married in La Plata. However, she revealed that he was then a "particular"—an ordinary Indian, a commoner, a taxpayer, a status he had enjoyed before moving to Santiago de Curi, where "he became skillful at knowing how to write without being a cacique principal from this town . . . to which we came and being and residing there and letting the people be aware both notables and commoners that *he knew how to read and write* and since there was no one in town who knew how, they [the Indians from Santiago de Curi] said he was from their *ayllu* [kin group] and a relative and requested him to be their cacique."[11]

As this testimony indicates, don Domingo was not a cacique by birth but a commoner who had gained status by virtue of his literacy. Thus, apparently neither descent nor residence made a difference in this case, but both partners skillfully manipulated the concepts to support their arguments. What matters here is that don Domingo, the alleged cacique and landowner, had gained his office by being literate rather than by virtue of his kinship and hereditary status. As an ordinary Indian, penniless like his wife when they married, don Domingo acquired his estates during his marriage. For this reason, doña Isabel argued, Chilcane, Vilcaparo, and Otavi truly were the property of both spouses. According to the resourceful doña Isabel, don Domingo was persuaded by "someone" who knew how much he loved his sons to pass on to them assets that did not rightfully belong to him.

Only after don Domingo had died could doña Isabel raise the veil that had obscured the true story of the couple and their joint assets. While her husband was alive, doña Isabel could not reveal the true story of how he had gained community leadership despite his humble origins. As an ordinary Indian, don Domingo could not claim hereditary rights to ethnic leadership or hope to gain large amounts of property. His attempt to gain legitimacy by claiming lands supposedly inherited from his ancestors eventually undermined his pretensions. After his death, nothing prevented doña Isabel from calling on Castilian laws of inheritance, which worked to her advantage because they gave wives equal rights to inherit their husbands' estates. She did not have to rely on rank or status to gain her inheritance. By admitting her husband's humble origins, doña Isabel gained her community property. Like her husband, she was also moved by the power of blood ties and love. She persisted in gaining her share of the joint property for her son's sake. After finally winning her long inheritance battle, doña Isabel thus named as her heir Juan de Acuña. As her testimony revealed, however, Acuña was a mestizo, fathered by Diego Vásquez, a Spaniard from Jerez de la Frontera, who had returned to the Iberian Peninsula long ago. By addressing her son as a mestizo, she guaranteed that he would not be subject to the indigenous head tax, after losing the tax exemption that he enjoyed as a member of the household of a local lord. This may explain why she addressed her son as "legitimate" in her initial testament.[12]

In the final version of her last will and testament, doña Isabel detailed once again her community property and personal belongings. Among her own assets, she listed a house and two peach orchards in Santiago de Curi, 388 cargas of maize harvested from Chilcane (sown after don Domingo had died), animals, tools, and 600 pesos corrientes. She also included two outfits made of *cumbi* (finely woven cloth) with their axu, another axu embroidered in silver, 2 *varas* (1 vara equals 66 inches) of blue *paño* (woolen cloth) and silver thread to sew an axu, three *ñañacas* (cloth used as a turban) made of *abasca* (ordinary domestic wool), and five pairs of *topos* (pins for clothing) with their silver pendants. Among her household goods, doña Isabel owned two pairs of *cocos* (ceremonial drinking vessels) and several silver vases.

The story of doña Isabel Sisa—an indefatigable, indigenous woman—and her husband, the cacique of Santiago de Curi, fits the model of a new Andean elite that enjoyed political power through writing. As Joanne Rappaport puts it, "only those who knew how to write, or who were able to communicate with scribes, either through Spanish or through an interpreter, could lay any claim to the reins of power."[13] Writing gave a commoner his chance to become a lord, and written communication through an interpreter gave doña Isabel the opportunity to defend her rights and enjoy the assets that belonged to her by virtue of her marriage.

The newly made lineage of Itquilla was short-lived. Status and office were curtailed by doña Isabel's claims to her property, providing a clear example of how wealth prevailed over other traditional values. Finally, testaments had an additional meaning in colonial Latin American history. They were instruments of self-promotion, manipulation, and lies that showed the rapid sociocultural changes in the lives of those who wanted to climb the social ladder.

NOTES

1. *Cacique* is an imported Caribbean word for lord or chief, a title the Spaniards extended to address the Andean lords. *Cacique principal* means principal lord in Spanish. Although the name of an Andean ethnic leader is *kuraka* in Quechua or *mallku* in Aymara, I used the word cacique to address don Domingo Itquilla or his office since that was the word written on the documents.

2. Archivo Nacional de Bolivia, Escrituras Públicas (hereafter ANB, EP) 52 Francisco de Tovar notary–Santiago de Curi, December 31, 1602, 523–25.

3. "por ser su marido y por evitar pesadumbres y por miedo del."

4. ANB, EP Vol. 52 Francisco de Tovar notary–Santiago de Curi, January 1, 1603, 526.

5. ANB, EP Vol. 32a Diego Sánchez notary–La Plata, June 23, 1601, 448–52.

6. Ibid., 451.

7. ANB, EP Vol. 63 Juan Fernández de Castro notary–La Plata, July 19, 1606, 414–17.

8. ANB, EP Vol. 68 Andrés Gonzalez de Cavia notary–Santiago de Curi, May 31, 1608, 367–72.

9. Ibid., 370–71.

10. Ibid., 371.

11. ANB, EP Vol. 144 Diego de Adrada notary–Santiago de Curi, October 6, 1609, 715–19.

12. According to Castilian law, legitimate children were those born from a legitimate marriage. Legitimate birth gave heirs, regardless of sex, full rights to inherit equal shares from their parents' assets; however, the same law offered parents the chance to endow a preferred heir with additional assets. Naming an heir as legitimate meant to secure rights of inheritance to all the property and, in some cases, to offices and privileges held by one or both parents.

13. Joanne Rappaport, "Object and Alphabet: Andean Indians and Documents in the Colonial Period," in *Writing without Words: Alternative Literacies in Mesoamerica and the Andes*, ed. Elizabeth Hill Boone and Walter Mignolo (Durham, NC, 1994), 276.

SUGGESTED READINGS

The testamentary practices of Andean women can be seen in Elinor C. Burkett, "Indian Women and White Society: The Case of Sixteenth-Century Peru," in *Latin American Women: Historical Perspectives*, edited by Asunción Lavrín (Westport, CT, 1978); Frank Salomon, "Indian Women of Early Colonial Quito as Seen through Their Testaments," *The Americas* 44:3 (January 1988); and Susan Kellogg and Matthew Restall, eds., *Dead Giveaways: Indigenous Testaments of Colonial Mesoamerica and the Andes* (Salt Lake City, 1998). Gender ideologies and hierarchies are developed by Irene Silverblatt in *Moon, Sun, and Witches: Gender Ideologies and Class in Inca and Colonial Peru* (Princeton, NJ, 1987). Female urban commercial practices are depicted by Ann Zulawski in "Social Differentiation, Gender, and Ethnicity: Urban Indian Women in Colonial Bolivia, 1640–1725," *Latin American Research Review* 25:2 (1990).

Migration, labor, taxation, and patterns of indigenous control of resources can be seen in the outstanding works of Thierry Saignes, "The Ethnic Groups in the Valleys of Larecaja: From Descent to Residence," in John V. Murra, Nathan Wachtel, and Jacques Revel, eds., *Anthropological History of Andean Polities* (Cambridge, 1986).

For the Andean ambivalence toward the Spanish market economy, see Steve J. Stern in "The Variety and Ambiguity of Native Andean Intervention in European Colonial Markets," in Brooke Larson and Olivia Harris, eds., with Enrique Tandeter, *Ethnicity, Markets, and Migration in the Andes: At the Crossroads of History and Anthropology* (Durham, NC, 1995). The cultural impact of writing (including testaments) has been examined in Joanne Rappaport, "Object and Alphabet: Andean Indians and Documents in the Colonial Period," in Elizabeth Hill Boone and Walter Mignolo, eds., *Writing without Words: Alternative Literacies in Mesoamerica and the Andes* (Durham, NC, 1994); and idem, *The Politics of Memory: Native Historical Interpretation in the Colombian Andes* (Durham, NC, 1998).

CHAPTER 4

Domingos Fernandes Nobre

"Tomacauna," a Go-Between in Sixteenth-Century Brazil

ALIDA C. METCALF

The Portuguese settlement of Brazil followed a markedly different course than the Spanish pattern in Mexico and the Andes. The fleet of Pedro Alvares Cabral, en route to India, made the first recorded European land-fall on the coast of Brazil in 1500, but the Portuguese crown chose to focus its attention on India instead. No immediate settlement followed Cabral's discovery. Rather, a small but profitable trade in brazilwood developed along the coast. Portuguese merchants as well as interloping French rivals fostered contacts with the indigenous Tupi-Guarani peoples who lived along the long coastline of Brazil. With these tribes, merchants exchanged European trading goods for brazilwood. Over time, this mutually beneficial bartering relationship broke down and the enslavement of Indians began. The first Portuguese settlers arrived at São Vicente, in southern Brazil, in 1532. Other important early settlements were Salvador da Bahia, located in the northeast, which became the capital in 1549; and, farther north, Olinda, the major settlement of Pernambuco. In central Brazil the French established a small Protestant colony at Rio de Janeiro in 1555, which was taken by the Portuguese in 1560.

The success of sugar cultivation in the northeast, around Olinda and Salvador da Bahia, led to a growing demand for Amerindian slaves to work in the cane fields, producing escalating levels of conflict later in the sixteenth century. Gangs of Portuguese began penetrating the rugged wilderness interior (sertão) in search of Amerindian captives to sell as slaves for the coastal sugar plantations. The warlike indigenous peoples resisted these incursions, but ancient rivalries between tribes made any type of unified response to repel the invaders difficult. Moreover, Portuguese slavers began learning indigenous languages, marrying Amerindian women, and taking part in tribal affairs. Mixed-blood offspring of these relationships (mamelucos) often served as cultural mediators, living part-time in the interior among their Tupi-Guarani kinsmen and part-time in coastal Portuguese settlements. Over the years Portuguese and mameluco slave hunters cultivated their Amerindian allies to help them capture enemy groups, turning indigenous rivalries to their advantage and taking larger numbers of slaves for sale in the coastal settlements.

One of the more famous of these mameluco go-betweens, who made his living by slave trading in the sertão, was Domingos Fernandes Nobre, known among his indigenous kinsmen and followers as Tomacauna. Like his fellow mameluco traders and slave hunters, Fernandes Nobre lived a dual life, moving freely between the Portuguese in the capital and the frontier world of the Tupi-Guarani. When in the interior, Fernandes Nobre became Tomacauna, tattooing his body in the indigenous style and taking part in local religious rituals of the syncretic Santidade cult. Although his ability to function in both the Portuguese and indigenous worlds made him both feared and successful as a slave trader, he eventually ran afoul of authorities along the coast.

In June 1591 a visiting inquisitor from Portugal's Holy Office of the Inquisition arrived in Bahia, and several of the city's citizens denounced Fernandes Nobre for his heretical participation in the Santidade cult. Although he defended himself and escaped the most severe discipline, this case demonstrates the tensions between the hierarchical Europeanized society developing on the coast and the individualistic and pluralistic society evolving in the wilderness. To the inquisitor, the tattooed Tomacauna with his questionable ethics and heretical religious beliefs was a barbarian, a threat to the "civilized" Portuguese colonists in Bahia. Although the sugar planters of the coast relied on mameluco go-betweens to provide slave labor, these individuals also represented European fears that overseas colonies stood on the verge of lapsing into "barbarism" and social disorder. Men such as Tomacauna were necessary to the economic prosperity of sixteenth-century Brazil, but their rugged individualism threatened to undermine the Catholic, family-oriented, and civilized world of Salvador da Bahia.

Alida Metcalf is professor of history at Trinity University in San Antonio, Texas, and a leading scholar of colonial Brazil. She received her B.A. from Smith College in 1976 and her Ph.D. in 1983 from the University of Texas at Austin, where she studied with Richard Graham. A specialist in Brazilian history, she is the author of Family and Frontier in Colonial Brazil: Santana de Parnaíba, 1580–1822 *(1992), which was awarded the Harvey Johnson Book Award in 1993 and Honorable Mention for the Bolton Prize in 1994. In 1999 she published "AHR Forum: Millenarian Slaves? The Santidade de Jaguaripe and Slave Resistance in the Americas" in the* American Historical Review. *Her current research focuses on Jesuit and Mameluco go-betweens in sixteenth-century Brazil.*

When an inquisitor from Portugal's Holy Office of the Inquisition arrived in Brazil's capital of Salvador da Bahia in June 1591, Domingos Fernandes Nobre was not in the city. Neither was he in the Recôncavo, the rich forestlands around the Bay of All Saints into which Portuguese settlers had carved their sugar plantations. Instead, Fernandes Nobre was deep in the *sertão*, the wilderness, living in a camp with nearly one hundred other men who had left the coastal settlements of Bahia and Pernambuco a year earlier to trade for Indian slaves. Such expeditions, known as *entradas*, had become essential to supply the incipient sugar plantations of the Portuguese colonies of Bahia and Pernambuco with laborers. Many *mamelucos*, men of mixed Indian and Portuguese parentage like Domingos Fernandes Nobre, had become slave traders who used their ability to move between the worlds of the Indian wilderness and the Portuguese coast in order to make their living. Therefore, while Fernandes Nobre and the other leaders of this expedition negotiated with the Indian chief, Arataca, the inquisitor made his entrance into the capital. Thus, the men in the sertão missed the pomp and ceremony that marked the inquisitor's arrival and subsequent transformation of the rhythms of daily life in Salvador.[1]

These mamelucos were go-betweens—men who lived both in the wilderness and in the coastal settlements. Because of their facility with Indian languages and customs and their willingness to use that knowledge for the benefit of the Portuguese colonists, they were essential in the development of the sugar economy in Bahia and Pernambuco. Go-betweens supplied the Indian slaves who labored on the first sugar plantations in Brazil. Yet, as the inquisitor's sojourn in Bahia and Pernambuco would make clear, the Portuguese were not entirely comfortable with their reliance on these men.

The first go-betweens in Brazil were Europeans who had been shipwrecked along the coast and who had survived by joining Indian tribes. One such man in the south was João Ramalho, who, when the Portuguese began their first permanent colony at São Vicente, was living as an Indian. Ramalho forged an alliance between the Portuguese and his tribe that allowed the new colony to survive. As the colony grew, Ramalho became increasingly powerful and began to supply the colonists with Indian slaves from enemy tribes. In Bahia, another go-between was Diogo Alvares Caramurú, who had also been shipwrecked in the early years of the sixteenth century. Like Ramalho, he had married into a local Indian tribe and had considerable influence among them. Caramurú also became an ally of the Portuguese when they attempted to establish colonies in Bahia. The mameluco descendants of Ramalho and Caramurú continued to live as go-betweens, often becoming involved in the Indian slave trade.[2]

The early settlers of Pernambuco and Bahia intended to profit from the new colony, and to do so they needed an economic focus. They chose sugar. Sugarcane had been grown successfully in other Portuguese colonies off the coast of Africa, such as the islands of São Tomé and Madeira, but its planting, cultivation, harvest, and milling required many laborers. Who would work in the fields and in the mills? The Portuguese had become slave traders along the coast of Africa in the sixteenth century, and planters in Brazil might have thought of obtaining African slaves. But the settlers in Brazil had little capital to finance slave trading across the Atlantic. They turned, therefore, to a more immediate source: the Indians. Later, after the disastrous decline in the Indian population, planters would indeed look to Africa for slaves. But in the sixteenth century, planters had little sense that the combination of disease and slavery would drastically reduce the Indian population. Instead, they viewed Indians as an unlimited resource of cheap labor whom they could enslave for their own profit.[3]

The Portuguese crown saw as its moral obligation the conversion and baptism of the Brazilian Indians into the Christian faith. To this end the crown designated the Society of Jesus (or Jesuits) to evangelize in Brazil, yet the economic interests of the settlers clashed with the moral obligations of the distant crown. Moreover, the Indians of Brazil were not the peaceful "noble savages" that early reports described. Rather, they lived in many different tribes, some of which practiced violent warfare. Cannibalism was sometimes the result of such wars. Even some of the Portuguese who became parties to intertribal warfare were put to death in cannibalistic ceremonies. Thus, while the crown did not want to see widespread Indian slavery in Brazil, by royal legislation it provided the loopholes that colonists used to enslave Indians freely. According to law, Indians who made war against the Portuguese, or who practiced cannibalism, could be taken legally as slaves.[4]

Indian slavery became commonplace in Bahia and Pernambuco after the 1560s. And so, when the inquisitor arrived in Bahia in 1591, the men with Domingos Fernandes Nobre were trading for slaves. In the sertão, the leaders of the entrada sent gifts and promises each morning to Arataca. The chief was an avowed enemy of the Portuguese, but because of the size of this particular entrada, the gifts promised each day, and the skill of the expedition's leaders, he kept the peace. In return for swords, pistols, gunpowder, and the repair of arms that the Indians already possessed, Arataca exchanged Indians. The leaders of the expedition carefully controlled these negotiations and insisted that the men trade with the Indians only through them. But the men soon learned that if they patterned themselves after Fernandes Nobre, they too could deal on their own with the Indians.[5]

His fame as a man of the wilderness was legendary in Bahia. Fernandes Nobre was a mameluco—his mother was Indian and his father Portuguese—and he drew on this dual identity to exploit the wilderness. He was as accustomed to living in the sertão among Indians as he was to living in the city among the Portuguese settlers. In the wilderness he was known by his Indian nickname, "Tomacauna." He spoke Indian languages, and parts of his body were tattooed in the Indian style to signify that he was a brave warrior. Seeing and perhaps admiring his example, some of the men on this expedition also spoke in the Indian dialect and tattooed their bodies to more convincingly offer arms to be traded for slaves.

While Fernandes Nobre negotiated in the wilderness, his wife saw or most certainly heard about the procession, Mass, sworn declarations of faith, and decrees of of July 28, 1591, in honor of the inquisitor. To her it must have brought back memories, however sketchy, of her childhood in Portugal where the presence of the Holy Office and its procedures for ferreting out heretics were etched into the memories of local townspeople. On that Sunday in Salvador, the bishop of Bahia led a procession from the Church of Our Lady of Ajuda to the cathedral. The governor, judges, members of the city council, priests, and clerics solemnly accompanied the inquisitor, who was escorted under a canopy of golden cloth. Inside the cathedral, he sat on a red velvet chair beneath a crimson damask canopy in the main chapel. Mass was said in Latin, followed by a sermon preached in Portuguese by the provincial of the Jesuit mission. Then the archdeacon of the cathedral mounted the pulpit and read the edicts brought by the inquisitor from the king of Portugal. The notary of the inquisitor next stepped up to read, in Portuguese, a document of the late Pope Pius V in favor of the Holy Office and in opposition to those who dared to criticize it.

The inquisitor then moved to an altar in the middle of the chapel, which was richly adorned with a silver cross, four silver candlesticks, two missals resting on damask cushions whose pages were held open by two silver crosses. One by one, the governor, judges, councilmen, and other officials approached the altar, knelt, placed both hands on the crosses on the missals, and swore to uphold the faith. In a loud voice the notary asked the congregation to promise to do so as well. At the end of the ceremony, the notary affixed these documents to the door of the cathedral along with one that stated that under pain of excommunication, all residents of the city and one league around it must denounce within thirty days anything they knew, or had seen, or had heard, against the holy Catholic faith. He affixed another document to the church door stating that the inquisitor would grant thirty days of grace during which time those residents who confessed their faults would not lose their properties.[6]

The arrival of the inquisitor in Salvador brought to Brazil, for the first time, an institution well known in Portugal. The Portuguese Inquisition shared many similarities with the Spanish Inquisition, which had been brought to Spain by Ferdinand and Isabella in the fifteenth century. The Inquisition had as its mission the elimination of heresy from Catholicism. The Spanish inquisitors fixed their attention on the *conversos*, Jews who had converted to Christianity and who then had married into old and established Catholic families. Actively pursuing them, the inquisitors accused, tried, and punished thousands of conversos for crimes of heresy. When Ferdinand and Isabella expelled the Jews from Spain in 1492, many crossed the border into the kingdom of Portugal, where there was no Inquisition. But there too, the Jews faced pressures. A decree of 1496 forced all Jews in Portugal to convert to Christianity and to be known thenceforth as New Christians. In 1546 the Portuguese Inquisition began and the New Christians quickly became the major target. Many of them took refuge in Brazil. In 1580, when King Philip II of Spain took the crown of Portugal, the Portuguese Inquisition became even more influenced by the Spanish Inquisition. Because so many New Christians had settled in Brazil, the Inquisition authorized its first visit there in 1591. Brazil would never have a resident Holy Office, as did Mexico and Peru, but through occasional visits and the work of *familiares*, a privileged group of literate individuals who served the Inquisition, its presence was felt in the colony.[7]

With the arrival of the inquisitor in 1591, a new era in the history of the city of Salvador had thus begun. But the men of the wilderness were not there to see it. In Salvador and in the Recôncavo, many pondered the instructions brought by the inquisitor. Their thoughts may have turned first to the obvious heresies: secret Judaism, the reading of banned books, and covert Protestantism. Other crimes sought out by the inquisitor might have crowded into their thoughts: blasphemy, bigamy, bestiality, sodomy, and witchcraft. Only later, perhaps, did the go-betweens come to mind: the odd way that they moved back and forth between two worlds, stepping into and then casting off opposite identities at will.

When the men returned to the city of Salvador in December 1591, the period of thirty days of grace had ended. Unbeknown to Domingos Fernandes Nobre, four people had already denounced him. On August 7 a twenty-three-year-old mameluco accused him of worshipping an Indian idol in the wilderness seven years earlier. On August 21 a student in the Jesuit school denounced him for worshipping the same idol and participating in a heretical cult in the sertão of which the idol was a part. That same day, Paula d'Almeida gave an even fuller account of how Fernandes Nobre had knelt three times before the idol, rebaptized himself in the ritual of the cult, and offered fishhooks and knives to the cult's Indian leader. Then, on August 26, Diogo Dias, a mameluco farmer, gave a complete account of this sect, known as Santidade, or holiness. Dias appeared before the inquisitor, who sat with his assistants and the leading clergy of Salvador da Bahia at an inquisitorial bench, or court, that questioned each person who presented him or herself. Dias related that a number of Christian Indian slaves had fled from the Jesuit missions and from the estates of their masters into the wilderness. There, the members of the sect had built their own church with a baptismal font, an altar, a confessional, and an idol shaped like an Indian, which they called their god. Domingos Fernandes Nobre, Diogo Dias continued, was part of this movement for eight or nine months. Then, because the cult encouraged all the slaves to flee from their masters and because the masters feared that they would attack the city, the governor commissioned a company of men (of which Diogo Dias was a part) to apprehend the sect members and imprison its followers. But, according to Diogo Dias, Fernandes Nobre fled deep into the sertão and took the followers of the sect with him. From there, Fernandes Nobre took the Indians of the sect to the parish of Jaguaripe in the Recôncavo, to the estate of his own patron, a Portuguese sugar planter.[8]

The Santidade sect appealed to the Indians as well as to the small but growing number of African slaves in Bahia. It was a millenarian sect, and, as is common in such movements, it predicted imminent divine intervention to save the faithful who suffered under the yoke of oppression. Influenced by indigenous traditions of renewal and revival together with the Christian teachings of the Jesuits, the believers retreated into the wilderness where they built their own religious community. Mamelucos and free Indians were attracted to the rituals of the sect and to its baptisms, dancing, smoking of tobacco, and speaking in tongues. The sect appeared to validate those considered outcasts (such as slaves) or marginal (such as mamelucos) by the dominant Portuguese culture of Salvador. According to the standards of the Inquisition, it was clearly a heretical sect and one that required the punishment of any Christian who believed in it.[9]

On January 12, 1592, after the men from the expedition had returned to Bahia, the inquisitor granted another thirty days of grace, this time to the residents of the parishes of the Recôncavo, the agricultural hinterland of forests, sugar plantations, and small farms around the Bay of All Saints. Mamelucos tended to live in the Recôncavo as opposed to the city of Salvador, because in the Recôncavo they worked for sugar planters or claimed small farms cut from the forest. Men whom Fernandes Nobre had known for most of his life, including some who had been with him on the most recent expedition to Chief Arataca, began to denounce him. A Portuguese carpenter who had been with Fernandes Nobre on the recent entrada claimed that the men had eaten meat on Catholic holy days when meat was forbidden. Men such as Fernandes Nobre, he stated, had servants and slaves with them who easily could have obtained fish, beans, or fruit. A soldier who also had just returned from the same expedition stated that in the wilderness Fernandes Nobre told him that he had joined in the Santidade sect seven years ago out of fear that the Indians would kill him. Men who confessed their sins to the inquisitor also implicated Fernandes Nobre. One confessed to truly believing in the sect, while four others maintained that they "pretended" to believe in its teachings to fool its adherents. All of them implicated Domingos Fernandes Nobre as one who had bowed deferentially before the idol and told them to do the same.

On January 21, Isabel Beliaga, Domingos Fernandes Nobre's wife, went to the inquisitor to testify to what she knew. Isabel, forty years old and a native of northern Portugal, first denounced the habits of women she had known in Pernambuco. These women were New Christians, accused by Isabel of secretly practicing Judaism. Then she denounced her husband. Perhaps Isabel denounced him to protect herself, or perhaps she hoped to minimize his sins. She referred to her husband as Domingos Fernandes Tomacauna, thereby, perhaps inadvertently, reinforcing his dual identity. But she accused him only for the tattoos that his body bore. Isabel stated that she "had heard" that he tattooed himself to show Indians that he was brave and to escape certain death at their hands. She concluded by describing another man who she knew also tattooed himself. Isabel may have intended to show how modest her husband's sins were compared to those of the New Christians, or how explicable they were, given the dangers that he faced in the wilderness.

Domingos Fernandes Nobre "Tomacauna" arrived home after most of the rest of the expedition. He returned to Bahia via the northern cities of Pernambuco, apparently during the middle of the grace period. He may not have heard his local priest read to the assembled parishioners the document sent by the inquisitor to every parish of the Recôncavo, but he certainly would have known of its being tacked onto the church door. For reasons that we shall never know, he decided to confess his faults to the inquisitor on February 11, the last day of grace granted to the residents of the Recôncavo. By that time, fourteen people had denounced him and his name and his faults had come up in the confessions of eight more. Although every person who passed before the inquisitorial bench was required to swear to uphold the secrecy of the Holy Office, it is unrealistic to think that the inquisitor operated in total secrecy. Perhaps Fernandes Nobre feared for the fate of his soul as well as for the confiscation of his property if the inquisitor found him guilty of heresy.

This confession provides a fascinating glimpse into the life of a go-between. His dual identity was reflected in his Portuguese and Indian names. Born in Pernambuco, and presumably baptized Domingos Fernandes Nobre, his father was a Portuguese stonemason, while his mother was a free Indian woman. From the time he was eighteen years old, he confessed that although he remained a Christian at heart, he lived more as an Indian than as a white man. He went into the wilderness on many expeditions, lasting for many months, either in search of gold or Indians. It was during such expeditions that he became Tomacauna: he tattooed his legs, arms, and buttocks with red *urucu* and black *genipapo* inks, tied feathers in his hair, and walked naked among the Indians. He explained to the inquisitor that he tattooed himself for the same reason that Indian men did—to show that they were brave warriors. He danced, sang, and shook the rattles in Indian ceremonies; he smoked tobacco and drank fermented palm wines. He accepted women given to him—sometimes as many as seven—and lived with them as wives, according to Indian custom. This he did, he told the inquisitor, so that the Indians would accept him as one of theirs, call him nephew, and treat him well. On his last expedition as well as on others, he had knowingly violated the law by trading arms to Indian nations known to be at war with the Portuguese. During all of the time he spent in the wilderness, he never abstained from eating meat on holy days, nor did he pray or commend himself to God.

Tomacauna described in detail his association with the Santidade religious sect. In his version of events, he had led a company of soldiers into the wilderness with the goal of imprisoning the followers of the sect. When he met up with its members, he doffed his hat and bowed to their idol in order, in his words, "to make them understand that he believed in their heresy." Then he and his men took part in a procession with the idol. Having won their confidence, Tomacauna sent this branch of the sect back to the Recôncavo, where, on the estate of his patron, they built a village and church. Tomacauna continued on deeper into the wilderness in search of the rest of the sect. In a place known simply as Tall Palms, Tomacauna met the leader, "the one they call Pope." Tomacauna greeted him on bent knee, then "wailed and lamented" in the Indian style. He danced, celebrated, sang, played their musical instruments, "drank the smoke," and allowed himself to be revered and adored as a saint. All of this, Fernandes Nobre maintained to the inquisitor, he did to deceive them and to bring them to the Recôncavo.

Following his confession, as was customary, Fernandes Nobre reappeared before the inquisitorial bench. When asked why he had joined in the ceremonies of the Santidade sect, he responded that while he knew perfectly well that they were wrong, he took part only because of his material interest in bringing the believers to the Recôncavo, where, his patron hoped to make use of their labor. When told that he must confess if he had ever left the true faith—because he could be absolved only by the Inquisition—he replied that he had never left the holy Catholic faith.

And when asked how many times he had not refrained from eating meat on holy days, he replied that there were many times, but, being such a large man, he was obliged to do so.

Tomacauna's confession reveals that he lived in a complex and ambiguous world with few moral absolutes. Although he claimed to have kept the holy Catholic faith in his heart, his behavior suggests that he adopted whichever religious practices best suited the occasion. Apparently, he learned from a young age to use his imposing physical presence and cunning mind to survive in dangerous situations. How much did he really reveal to the inquisitor? How trustworthy is his confession? Given what is known about him, it seems likely that Fernandes Nobre, with a convincing display of outward humility, told the inquisitor what he wanted to hear.

In fact, while the inquisitorial bench did not believe Fernandes Nobre's insistence that because of his great size he could not exist without meat, the inquisitor did show mercy. He reprimanded the go-between for his many errors but recommended lenience, because he had confessed during the grace period. Various penitences were required. Among them, Fernandes Nobre was to make an even fuller confession of his entire life and to continue confessing regularly for six months. During those six months, he was to receive special religious instruction from a priest and was to fast on five Wednesdays following Easter. The inquisitor also imposed one onerous punishment: Tomacauna was never to return to the wilderness. From now on, Tomacauna would again be simply Domingos Fernandes Nobre.

This sentence paralleled those received by other mamelucos found guilty of similar faults. Together they reflect the inquisitor's willingness to forgive their past behavior, yet he was not willing to let them return to the sertão, the place where they had made their living. In the eyes of the inquisitor, the mamelucos had to maintain their Portuguese heritage; they could not continue to slide back and forth between Indian and Portuguese identities.

Seen through the eyes of such a bastion of Portuguese culture as the inquisitor, the mameluco go-betweens were rude, uncivilized, and backsliding Christians. They set poor examples for others because they encouraged relativism and an extreme individualism. In their world, moral decisions were made based not on principles but on the immediate need. Go-betweens remained true only to themselves; loyalty to an Indian tribe or to the Portuguese colony depended on the situation. Such attitudes served the go-betweens well in the fluid and ambiguous world in which they lived, but they were diametrically opposed to the values of Portuguese colonization. For the crown and the Church, colonization had moral imperatives such as the evangelization of Indians, the propagation of a

Portuguese culture in a new land, or the obedience of colonists to the officials of the crown and Church. As it turned out, the inquisitor could not prevent the go-betweens of the late sixteenth century from returning to the sertão. But, increasingly, they would be pressured to assimilate more fully into the Portuguese culture or else to retreat from the core of the colony and move with the frontier toward the wilderness.

The early Portuguese colony in Brazil depended on go-betweens, those men who could move easily between the very different Indian and Portuguese worlds. In the earliest days, the survival of colonists depended on good relations with neighboring Indians. Shipwrecked Portuguese go-betweens became essential first intermediaries. As the colonies became established, however, and as sugar emerged as the economic motor of Bahia and Pernambuco, the Portuguese depended on go-betweens not for good relations with neighboring tribes but for supplying the sugar plantations with Indian slaves. Mameluco slave traders such as Domingos Fernandes Nobre led expeditions into the wilderness to capture Indians, usually illegally, for the sugar planters. To take an expedition into the wilderness and return with hundreds of slaves required a special kind of leadership, cunning and treachery in dealings with Indian tribes, and a hardened attitude toward the future of the men, women, and children who would be reduced to slavery. Because of their own experiences, the mameluco go-betweens understood Indian life better than anyone else in the colony, but to make their own livings they chose to work on behalf of the sugar planters and to encourage the violence of slavery. The planters clearly recognized the contribution of the go-betweens to their success; indeed, many employed them on their own estates. But as the colony developed and became more Portuguese in its culture and outlook, the go-betweens, with their dual identities, embodied less and less of the ideals of the Christian Portuguese colonists.

First in Pernambuco, then later in Bahia, a disastrous decline in the Indian population forced sugar planters to search for other laborers. African slaves already outnumbered Indians on the sugar plantations in Pernambuco when the inquisitor finished his work in Bahia and began it anew in Pernambuco. By the seventeenth century, Bahian planters began to rely increasingly on African slaves. As the labor demands of the sugar plantations changed, the mameluco go-betweens had less to offer the planters. Indeed, the wilderness itself was rapidly disappearing beyond the cane fields. Only on the frontiers could go-betweens still cross from the Indian to the Portuguese world and live in the complex and contradictory ways suggested by the life of Domingos Fernandes Nobre "Tomacauna." In succeeding centuries, go-betweens paved the way for Portuguese, and later Brazilian, colonization of the wilderness to the north, south, and west. But they would not inherit the world they helped to create, nor would their distinctive lifestyle survive past the initial stages of colonization. Like the Indians they had exploited, the go-betweens found themselves cast aside by the advancing colonial culture.

NOTES

1. This dignitary came as a "visiting" inquisitor, meaning that his presence in Brazil was limited to a specific time. Brazil did not have its own formally established Holy Office of the Inquisition with a permanent, resident inquisitor, as did Mexico and Peru.

2. There are brief accounts of João Ramalho, Diogo Alvares Caramurú, and Domingos Fernandes Nobre "Tomacauna" in John Hemming, *Red Gold: The Conquest of the Brazilian Indians* (Cambridge, MA: Harvard University Press, 1978).

3. Stuart Schwartz, *Sugar Plantations in the Formation of Brazilian Society: Bahia, 1550–1835* (New York: Cambridge University Press, 1985), 28–72; Alexander Marchant, *From Barter to Slavery: The Economic Relations of Portuguese and Indians in the Settlement of Brazil, 1500–1580* (Baltimore: Johns Hopkins University Press, 1942). On the sixteenth-century Portuguese slave trade in Africa see A. C. de C. M. Saunders, *A Social History of Black Slaves and Freedmen in Portugal, 1441–1555* (New York: Cambridge University Press, 1982).

4. Dauril Alden, *The Making of an Enterprise: The Society of Jesus in Portugal, Its Empire, and Beyond, 1540–1750* (Stanford: Stanford University Press, 1996), 474–501; Thomas Cohen, *The Fire of Tongues: António Vieira and the Missionary Church in Brazil and Portugal* (Stanford: Stanford University Press, 1998), 13–49. Famous accounts of cannibalism in sixteenth-century Brazil include: Hans Staden, *Hans Staden: The True History of His Captivity*, trans. Malcolm Letts (New York: R. M. McBride & Company, 1929); and Jean de Léry, *History of a Voyage to the Land of Brazil, otherwise called America*, trans. Janet Whatley (Berkeley: University of California Press, 1990).

5. Trials of mamelucos, Inquisition Archive, Arquivo Nacional da Torre do Tombo, (hereafter ANTT), Lisbon, Portugal. For Portuguese readers, many of the confessions and denunciations have been published; see *Primeira Visitação do Santo Ofício às partes do Brasil pelo Licenciado Heitor Furtado de Mendonça: Confissões da Bahia 1591–1592* (Rio de Janeiro: F. Briguiet, 1935); and *Primeira Visitação do Santo Ofício às partes do Brasil pelo Licenciado Heitor Furtado de Mendonça: Denunciações da Bahia 1591–1593* (São Paulo: Paulo Prado, 1925).

6. This description of the ceremony marking the arrival of the visiting inquisitor is drawn directly from the documents written by the notary of the Inquisition. Portuguese readers may find it in *Confissões da Bahia*, pp. 39–45.

7. On the Portuguese Inquisition, see Francisco Bethencourt, "Portugal: A Scrupulous Inquisition," in *Early Modern European Witchcraft: Centres and Peripheries*, ed. Bengt Ankarloo and Gustav Henningsen (Oxford: Clarendon Press, 1990), 403–22. An excellent starting point for the Spanish Inquisition is Norman Roth, *Conversos, Inquisition, and the Expulsion of the Jews from Spain* (Madison: University of Wisconsin Press, 1995).

8. Trial of Domingos Fernandes Nobre, ANTT. Portuguese readers may find his confession and the denunciations of him in *Confissões da Bahia* and *Denunciações da Bahia*.

9. On the Santidade sect of Bahia, see Alida C. Metcalf, "AHR Forum: Millenarian Slaves? The Santidade de Jaguaripe and Slave Resistance in the Americas," *American Historical Review* 104 (1999): 1531–59.

SUGGESTED READINGS

Provocative insights on the roles of go-betweens in the conquest of the Americas are offered by Steven Greenblatt in *Marvelous Possessions: The Wonder of the New World* (Chicago, 1991) and by Tzvetan Todorov in *The Conquest of America: The Question of the Other* (New York, 1983).

Understanding Brazil in the sixteenth century begins with study of the indigenous peoples; John Hemming provides a highly readable overview in *Red Gold: The Conquest of the Brazilian Indians* (Cambridge, MA, 1978). A modern translation of a French Protestant's observations of sixteenth-century Indian life is Janet Whatlcy's *History of a Voyage to the Land of Brazil, otherwise called America* (Berkeley, 1990); another vivid firsthand account is *Hans Staden: The True History of his Captivity* (London, 1928). The early relations between Indians and Portuguese are explored by Alexander Marchant in *From Barter to Slavery: The Economic Relations of Portuguese and Indians in the Settlement of Brazil, 1500–1580* (Gloucester, MA, 1966), while the best discussion of the development of the sugar plantation is to be found in *Sugar Plantations in the Formation of Brazilian Society: Bahia, 1550–1835* (New York, 1985), by Stuart Schwartz. The early Jesuit mission is of paramount importance for understanding sixteenth-century Brazil; see relevant sections of Dauril Alden's *The Making of an Enterprise: The Society of Jesus in Portugal, Its Empire, and Beyond, 1540–1750* (Stanford, 1996), and Thomas Cohen's *The Fire of Tongues: António Vieira and the Missionary Church in Brazil and Portugal* (Stanford, 1998). Unfortunately, little has been written in English on the Portuguese Inquisition and Brazil, but an excellent overview is Francisco Bethencourt's "Portugal: A Scrupulous Inquisition," in *Early Modern European Witchcraft: Centres and Peripheries* (Oxford, 1990), edited by Bengt Ankarloo and Gustav Henningsen.

CHAPTER 5

The Mysterious Catalina

Indian or Spaniard?

NOBLE DAVID COOK

The Spanish Caribbean in the early seventeenth century was far removed from the centers of Amerindian population, mineral wealth, and political power in the Spanish Indies, yet it was a strategic area, protecting the sea lanes to Mexico and the north coast of South America. The first Spanish settlements, originally established by Christopher Columbus and his successors, appeared in this region from the late fifteenth century. After the exploitation of some gold deposits, pearls, and other wasting assets, however, the centers of wealth and power shifted to the more populous provinces of Mexico and the Andes. The Amerindian population of the scattered Caribbean islands declined catastrophically within two generations, the victims of European epidemics coupled with the depredations caused by warfare and overwork. Spanish efforts to resettle the dispersed Amerindians into European-style towns both changed indigenous lifeways and helped to spread the deadly European diseases.

Spanish entrepreneurs had begun to import African slave labor and to experiment with a variety of export crops, notably sugar, tobacco, and cacao (particularly on the mainland of northern South America), but the region still receded into an economic backwater of the empire. Nevertheless, the fleets from Spain still sailed with European wares to exchange for Peruvian and Mexican silver. The riches conveyed in these fleets attracted Spain's enemies, particularly pirates and privateers who sought to prey on Spanish commerce and its more isolated Caribbean outposts. Strongholds such as Havana or Cartagena were usually able to resist the incursions of these pirates and became the lynchpin of Spain's defenses in the region. More isolated outposts—Puerto Rico, Portobelo (in Panama), or Florida— remained dangerously exposed to attack. It was a violent and often unstable world.

The controversies surrounding the enigmatic young servant girl, Catalina, took place in the city of Havana where ships from Mexico and Peru, laden with silver, gold, and other American resources, rendezvoused for the return trip to Spain. While this fleet was taking on water and provisions, bureaucrats in Havana detained a prominent notary, Francisco de Ludeña, and his family for attempting to have an Amerindian (Catalina) accompany them to Spain, a practice expressly forbidden by crown law. Bureaucrats frequently tried to extract bribes or confiscate the goods of travelers returning to Spain to supplement their meager government salaries, but the case of this young servant girl proved particularly complicated and revealing about colonial ideas of caste and gender. Ludeña claimed that Catalina was a Spanish woman entrusted to his care, while his detractors used her lowly status as a servant, her appearance (dark skinned and short), and her lack of any education or refinement as proof that she was an Amerindian.

The controversy surrounding the case demonstrates the difficulty of maintaining clear, unambiguous categories of race, caste, and ethnicity in the volatile world of the Spanish Indies. Once away from orderly European social hierarchies, records could be easily falsified and a person could "pass" for someone of a higher or, in the case of Catalina, a lower social position. Indeed, the difficulty in determining the caste of people such as Catalina probably explains why settlers in the Indies became obsessed with questions of race, caste, and status throughout the colonial era. The case also demonstrates how biases, self-interest, and outright lies enter into the historical record, thus making it difficult for historians to extract the "truth" when attempting to reconstruct the past.

Noble David Cook is professor of history at Florida International University. His early work concerned demographic history, culminating in his seminal book, Demographic Collapse: Indian Peru, 1520–1620 *(1981). Since that time, he has explored a wide range of topics in colonial Spanish American social history, including his widely read study (coauthored with Alexandra Parma Cook),* Good Faith and Truthful Ignorance: A Case of Transatlantic Bigamy *(1991), and his edited and translated edition (with Alexandra Parma Cook) of Pedro de Cieza de León,* The Discovery and Conquest of Peru *(1998). His most recent synthesis is* Born to Die: Disease and New World Conquest, 1492–1650 *(1998).*

Colonial social labels such as Indian, *mestizo*, Spaniard, and black were markers of caste, an identity assigned at birth that largely remained fixed throughout a person's lifetime. Most Europeans thought that social position should remain unchanging, and in the Spanish Indies, for example, elites believed that an Amerindian tributary should remain one until death. Even ethnic lords who traced their ancestry to the Inca, Maya, or Aztec nobility or had accumulated great wealth could not become "European," regardless of whether they had adopted the dress, speech, or mannerisms of their colonial overlords. Likewise, someone of African ancestry would be given a label of color, whether slave or free. Sixteenth- and seventeenth-century colonial elites seemed obsessed by caste, much as their counterparts in Spain were preoccupied with demonstrating "purity of blood" (*limpieza de sangre*), proving that their ancestry was not "tainted" by the blood of *conversos* or *moriscos* (Jews or Muslims who had converted to Christianity). In Spanish America, the process of race mixture (*mestizaje*) was widespread, which always clouded issues of individual and collective identity.[1]

Despite Spanish efforts to establish fixed racial and ethnic categories, complications abounded in individual cases. Even a definition of what constituted "Indianness" in late sixteenth-century Spanish America could prove contentious and ambiguous. What characteristics set one person apart from others and placed him in a clearly defined category, "Indian"? What were the markers of caste, and how did contemporaries interpret them? These issues come into focus in a particularly contentious case in Havana in late 1605, when various witnesses volunteered testimony on "Catalina, a young Indian woman" who had allegedly arrived in the city from the port of Cartagena de Indias (in current-day Colombia). Their statements, extracted during legal hearings of the Casa de la Contratación (Board of Trade) and kept on file in the Archivo General de Indias, offer fascinating insights into the nature of societal stereotypes as well as the vexing problem of finding "truth" in documentary evidence.

Catalina, a seventeen-year-old servant girl, appeared in the record because her master, Francisco de Ludeña, a royal notary (*escribano del rey*) who had lived and worked in Cartagena de Indias for several years, was attempting to bring her along with his family to Spain. He understood that royal ordinances explicitly prohibited the transport of Amerindians to Europe. As a result, shortly after the fleet reached Havana, *alguacil* (constable) Francisco Báez of the port city, denounced the royal notary and filed charges before the Lieutenant-General (*teniente general*) of the Island of Cuba, Licentiate Bernardo de Argüello. Báez complained that Ludeña transported with him "an *india* (Indian woman), native of Cartagena, such being prohibited."[2] The accusation was so serious that local authorities jailed Ludeña immediately and sequestered his property en route to Spain. His case is just one of dozens; officials in Havana frequently scrutinized to the last detail the papers of travelers to Spain. It was profitable for authorities in the port city to denounce and prosecute unsuspecting travelers, and it was certainly one way to supplement their meager salaries.

Báez quickly found witnesses willing to implicate Ludeña. The first was Juan Fernández Jaramillo, Havana's public executioner, who by occupation might be considered a reliable observer. He swore that he had known the notary and his family for about a decade in Cartagena de Indias. His testimony (December 6, 1605) was explicit: "She [Catalina] was very young, and [I] know that she is an Indian, native of the city of Cartagena . . . , because [I] saw her growing up from a young child, and she was always viewed and taken for an Indian." Fernández Jaramillo added that he "had seen them whip her as a black woman" in the house where she served. Others provided similar testimony. A week later, Báez presented Juan Delgado, a supervisor of the butcher shops in Cartagena, who also knew Ludeña and his family there. One time, Delgado had heard Ludeña exclaim: "Here comes my india, give her something." He said that Ludeña always sent the girl to buy items for the family's table. Furthermore, during the five years he lived in Cartagena, he always heard the girl called an Indian. This last testimony, however, was undermined because Delgado himself was incarcerated at the time of his deposition.

The critical testimony against Ludeña had already been taken on December 7. On that day the Lieutenant-General of the island ordered that a girl who "seems Indian" be examined to determine her status. Captain Gómez de Roxas, the "Protector General of the Indians (*protector general de indios*) of the Island" was present for the questioning.[3] The court took Catalina's sworn testimony in Spanish, however, because she spoke the language, making an interpreter unnecessary. She promised to tell the truth. When asked, "What is your name and status?" she replied that she was "an Indian, a native of Cartagena, and was named Catalina." She then testified that her parents were Anton de Mairena and Catalina Rodríguez, both natives of Cartagena, and that she was eighteen years old.

Catalina was then pressed about why she gave this testimony, when not long before she had sworn to the Lieutenant-General that she was from the kingdom of Castile. The judges then demanded: "Who counseled you to say this?" Catalina replied that her master, Francisco de Ludeña, had ordered her to say that she was from Guadaira and to deny that she was an Indian. She now swore that she was indeed an Indian. "That is the truth," she insisted. Queried about who brought her and in what ship, Catalina said that she came with Ludeña in the vessel of Captain Pedro Sánchez, part of the fleet presently anchored in the harbor and under the command of General don Francisco del Corral. Catalina was then asked how long she had served Ludeña and how much he paid her. When her parents died, she replied, she was still very young, and her sister María proposed that she serve Ludeña. "In all this time he has not given [me] anything more than clothing and footwear." When questioned when and how Ludeña decided to take her from Cartagena to Spain, she said that "while serving he persuaded her, saying that if she would come with him to the kingdom of Castile he would give her clothing and whatever else was necessary."

To verify her story, the officials asked Catalina to provide the names of people who might know her and be able to support her new testimony. She said that the shipmaster, Cristóbal Gómez, and a sailor named

Jacomes as well as others on the boat knew of her identity. The girl seemed honest to the Havana officials, and, given the possibility of corroboration from other witnesses, they began civil proceedings against Francisco de Ludeña. Acting in Catalina's best interest, "Indian Protector" Gómez de Roxas secured an order from the Lieutenant-General to place "Catalina india in the house of Licentiate Suárez de Poago,[4] and be put under the care of his wife, Ana María, until the matter can be investigated further."

The alguacil, Francisco Báez, pressed the case against Ludeña. On January 30, 1606, he presented as a witness forty-seven-year-old Juan de Sequera, then residing in Havana. Sequera reported that he had seen the young Catalina in Cartagena in the service of Francisco de Ludeña and his wife. At times she "would go with a jug for water, coming from the garden of Governor don Pedro de Acuña, who had found her and brought her from the Xagueyes province."[5] Sequera further reported that he thought Catalina "had a carnal relationship with one Lucas Garcilán, a barber, who often absented himself from the service of the governor to spend time in the house of Catalina." Sequera also testified that Catalina was Indian because "it seems the said Catalina has the shape (*talle*) of an Indian, because her body demonstrates it." But he admitted not knowing her mother or father.

The following day, Báez secured the testimony of twenty-two-year-old Nicolás de Silva, who had seen Catalina three or four times in Cartagena de Indias. On board the ship to Havana he had observed Catalina serving Ludeña, "cooking and providing other services." But Silva was less certain of her Indianness: "I don't know if she is Indian or mestiza." In fact, he admitted that while in Cartagena, he "had always taken her for a mestiza."

A few days later, on February 9, Báez interrogated two forceful witnesses who claimed to be more certain of the girl's identity. Sixty-year-old Gerónimo de Valdes had worked for General Francisco del Corral and had also served in the house of the governor of Cartagena, don Pedro de Acuña, along with a companion, the barber Lucas Garcilán, Catalina's alleged lover. Valdes reported that whenever Lucas was missing from the household, it was said "he was with the Indian woman that the said Francisco de Ludeña had." The witness stated that he had seen the girl named Catalina serving Ludeña on the way from Cartagena to Havana, and when Valdes asked her if "she knew Lucas the barber, she had responded 'yes.' " He therefore thought that they were one and the same, and further he believed "it is very certain that she is by caste Indian (*de casta de india*), because by her looks one can easily see it."

The same day, Báez brought forth forty-year-old Havana resident Simón de Padilla, who had worked for Ludeña while in Cartagena. He had observed the young woman Catalina serving regularly in the household. Simón reported that many times he had heard Ludeña call to her, "Come here, india!" Since Ludeña and his wife always referred to Catalina in this way, Padilla also took her for an Indian. Furthermore, he stated, "by her looks she shows it and thus he knows [she is]."

Despite Catalina's confession that she was an Indian, the court sought additional proof of her caste. Another Indian woman, María Díaz of Santa Marta, testified before the alguacil on February 10 and corroborated Catalina's story. The witness was herself twenty years old and a servant of María Díaz, the wife of Luis González, a permanent resident (*vecino*) of Havana. María testified that she had known Catalina in Cartagena and saw her serving a married man who lived near the Indian settlement of Xagueyes del Rey. According to María, she had often observed Catalina going to fetch water from a well in the house of Anton Nesado, a vecino of Cartagena. The woman whom Catalina served many times called her an "Indian . . . , and she frequently whipped her." María Díaz added, "I saw her dishonoring her, calling her 'Indian bitch' (*perra india*)." She concluded, "This is the same Catalina who at present is in this city and who has been shown to me."

Three days later Francisco de Castilla, a thirty-two-year-old vecino living in the La Punta neighborhood of Havana, testified that about six years ago he had been in Cartagena and had seen Catalina treated by local people as an Indian, "a daughter of Indian parents." He saw her several times in Ludeña's residence and twice since she had arrived in Havana, so he was certain that it was the same person. As part of her service, she was ordered to bring water from the fountain "and other even lower things." Castilla said that he "had never heard anyone refer to her as a Spaniard or *mulatta*, rather always as Indian." He elaborated further that by her "looks and bearing Catalina seems to be an Indian." Moreover, "she has the color of such, and wide short feet, as the other Indian women do." The markers of identity for Francisco de Castilla and the other Spanish witnesses were clear—phenotype, body structure, and outward appearance as well as the menial occupation of servant girl. No Spanish woman in the Indies could look or act as Catalina did; therefore, she must be Indian!

While Francisco Báez collected testimony against him, Francisco de Ludeña attacked the integrity of the public executioner, Fernández Jaramillo, forcing the alguacil to recall him to testify. Fernández Jaramillo swore again that his earlier testimony was the whole truth. He now recalled that on the day that Ludeña was jailed, he demanded to know: "Why have you denounced me for this Indian woman?" Fernández Jaramillo confided to the interrogator that he replied: "I have not denounced you. . . . The Indian girl had spoken to him (Ludeña) earlier, and he knew it." Ludeña then said to Fernández Jaramillo, "If you join me, then you will know her." The executioner next claimed that Ludeña offered a bribe: "Why not ask me for four or five pesos? . . . Don't be someone who would denounce me, we have established a close friendship after all." Without question, Ludeña was attempting to pay off the executioner and abort the legal proceedings. If Fernández Jaramillo's testimony was truthful, Ludeña's guilt was clearly implied by the offer of a bribe.

Ludeña and Fernández Jaramillo apparently conspired to manipulate the sexuality of the defenseless Catalina. The testimony of Juan de Sequera and Gerónimo de Valdes, establishing a physical relationship between the barber and the young girl, already attested to her carnal relationship with a European male. The sexual affair occurred with or without the knowledge and control of her master. If Fernández Jaramillo were telling the truth, however, Ludeña was offering not only four or five pesos but also Catalina's sexual services.[6]

The testimony taken by Báez apparently established Catalina's status as an Indian. There was only some hesitation on the part of a few witnesses who indicated that she might be a mestiza. Nevertheless, over the weeks the alguacil had assembled numerous witnesses attesting to the Indian identity of eighteen-year-old Catalina. Although her parentage could not be established, several said that she probably belonged to an ethnic group settled near Cartagena de Indias, the Xagueyes del Rey. She served her masters as an Indian woman would, doing menial tasks that would not be done by any respectable Spanish woman in the Indies. She carried water, brought food from the market, cooked it, and did a thousand other things expected of a female Indian servant. Furthermore, her masters called her an Indian in the presence of many witnesses. Their treatment of her was clearly exploitative; there were frequent whippings and cutting verbal abuse. Even an Indian woman testified that Catalina was Indian. Most important, Catalina herself provided the proof by her sworn statement. By all accounts she fit the stereotype, and the colonial elite who glanced at her in the street recognized her as Indian. Her stature, her demeanor, her dress, her short stubby feet, and her skin color, as Francisco de Castilla indicated, demonstrated her essentially "Indian" nature.

Despite all of this evidence indicating Catalina's Indian identity, much of the documentation in such legal cases is filled with truth, half-truths, and even outright lies.[7] Francisco de Ludeña had been in the Indies for several years and was returning to Spain with his family and significant assets. During a decade of service overseas, most Spaniards made both friends and enemies. There were always astute officials in a port like Havana, where virtually all travelers spent a few days or weeks while the ships of the fleet returning to Spain were outfitted for the Atlantic passage. Cuban officials in Havana looked out for their own interests as well as the crown's, and any bureaucrat who denounced a civil crime could reap a handsome reward. It was into this type of environment that Ludeña sailed in the last days of December 1605. He had capital and plenty of enemies. His apparent attempt to transport an Indian servant girl back to Spain was the perfect pretext for ambitious officials in Havana to move against him.

Ludeña's initial defense was straightforward: he was innocent of the charges. He insisted that Catalina was a Spaniard. Her identity was clear, and he could prove it. Many years ago he had gone from Seville to nearby Alcalá de la Guadaira, serving with a judge under a commission from the Holy Office of Seville. There, he resided in the house of Rodrigo Caro, the notary of the local arm of the Inquisition. Caro and his wife doña Ysabel begged him, "for the love of God, please take on and raise the orphan girl Catalina," who was poverty stricken. The couple was keeping her temporarily out of charity. Convinced by their pleas and that of the girl's older sister, Ludeña took Catalina into his household to be a companion for his son Gerónimo. In the ensuing years, Ludeña and his family took Catalina with them to the Canary Islands, Margarita in the Caribbean, Caracas in Venezuela, and finally Cartagena de Indias.[8]

As Ludeña prepared a comprehensive questionnaire for use in his defense, many loathsome character traits emerged, particularly his insensitivity and overall bigotry. In addition to background questions on the case, he asked the witnesses to discuss why Catalina now said that she was an Indian because she "has been pressured and threatened by some people for her to say it." He also stated that "she is so simple and ignorant that with any bit of fear that you put into her, she will say whatever you put in her mouth." Some of his questions reveal Ludeña's low opinion of Amerindians, whom he considered so worthless as servants that he never used them. Instead, he had several black men and women serving him, and a black slave as a page. His son, Mateo de Ludeña Valdes, apparently shared his father's opinions. After marrying and settling in Cartagena, he kept more than "thirty head of slaves."

Ludeña did his best to collect witnesses who knew him in Havana; there was insufficient time to gather information from distant Cartagena, on the mainland coast. On January 4 he presented Ana Duarte, who had known his family seven years ago in the city of Santiago de León, Caracas; she later sailed on the same frigate with the Ludeña household to Cartagena. Duarte thought that Catalina was an "ignorant" Spaniard. The following day, another witness, Diego Enríquez, testified that he had stayed in the Ludeña house in Cartagena. During this visit, he asked Catalina about her background, and she told him that she was an orphan from Alcalá de la Guadaira, where she still had a sister and other relatives. He took her for "simple, ignorant, and of little knowledge." He further recalled that Ludeña had many slaves in Cartagena, and "ordinarily he took a young black page who followed along behind him through the city." Indians were not employed in the household. On January 7, Ysabel Gutiérrez, the wife of Diego Enríquez, testified that when the Ludeñas had moved to Cartagena, she often visited their household. She also had spoken to Catalina in Havana. Another household servant told Ysabel that "she (Catalina) was not thinking of anything other than returning with this witness to Spain, because all she wanted was to return to her homeland." Ysabel concurred that Catalina was "a simple girl of little understanding."

The same day, Ludeña summoned a fifty-eight-year-old soldier, Damián de Levia, stationed at the Morro fortress in Havana harbor, who claimed to remember Ludeña from the time of his service in the Canaries. Levia was in the Port Guard when Ludeña with his family and Catalina had first disembarked. He stated that he knew the whole household well because he frequently visited their house on business of Governor and Captain General don Luis de la Cueva. Two years later, Governor Cueva discharged his soldiers and returned to Spain, leading Levia to serve in Las Palmas, where he again met Ludeña. Levia later watched the notary and his family depart for America, taking Catalina with them. Before their departure, however, two of his fellow soldiers had told Levia that they had known Catalina's parents in Alcalá. Most important, while Catalina was being examined before the Lieutenant-General of Cuba, Levia asked her, "Why is it that you, a Spaniard, have said you are an Indian?" She replied that she did so "out of fear and consternation." He characterized her mental state in the same terms as Diego Enríquez: "simple, ignorant, and of little knowledge," reiterating the same labels used by Ludeña in the original testimony.

Ludeña also called several other witnesses, including a fifty-year-old Seville resident, Bartolomé Rodríguez, who provided on January 16 important facts corroborating Ludeña's case. According to Rodríguez, he had visited the house where Catalina was being held at Ludeña's behest. He asked her where she was born, and she replied Alcalá, but she could not remember her parish. She knew that it was the house of Rodrigo Caro and his wife Ysabel, on a wide street whose name she did not know. The witness knew Caro and the street in Alcalá de Guadaira where he lived, the Calle de la Mina, which was indeed very wide. The next day, Rodríguez continued his probing, and Catalina revealed that her father was a laborer from Gandil named Anton de Mairena. Her mother was Catalina Rodríguez. Bartolomé Rodríguez confided: "I knew the said

Anton de Mairena; he was a short man with a dark complexion (*moreno*)."
Moreover, the witness said that Catalina looked a lot like her father—
stature (short), occupation (servant), demeanor (weak-minded), phenotype (dark), and likely with straight black hair. Was Catalina a *morena*, an
Andalusian of lower-class background, or an *india*? Indeed, Catalina now
admitted to Bartolomé Rodríguez that she had falsely testified to being
an Indian "because they had terrorized me." Catalina's true identity now
became the central problem facing the local representatives of Spanish
justice in Havana. Their final decision had implications for the welfare
of both Francisco de Ludeña and Catalina. Long incarceration in early
seventeenth-century prisons damaged both a person's health and finances.

After several weeks of inactivity in the case, Ludeña demanded action from the court, but this request only encouraged his opponents to
take the offensive. On February 25, Francisco Báez appeared before the
Lieutenant-General of Cuba, claiming that he had proven his case well
enough "to secure victory." Catalina had confessed to being an Indian,
and her admission was corroborated by many witnesses. He wanted the
case settled. Whatever her true status, argued the alguacil on February 31, Francisco de Ludeña should be prosecuted for having transported
her without a license. It seemed to Báez that Ludeña was conspiring to
make it appear as though Catalina was a Spaniard in order to take her to
Europe. He said that he had clearly and definitively demonstrated that
Ludeña was breaking the law and thus should suffer the full penalties.

For his part, Ludeña responded on February 28, charging that the
entire proceedings were tainted and that the witnesses supporting the
accusers were untrustworthy and even dishonest. He did not mince words:
"They are infamous men of evil conscience, and without fear of God."
These allegations and the inquiry that followed delayed the decision on
the original case until mid-March. Ludeña continued to press the attack,
trying to discredit his accusers. He asked: "What of the witness Juan de
Sequera? Had he not been forced to serve ten years as an oarsman in the
galleys?" "What were his crimes," and why was witness Gerónimo de
Valdes forced into galley service in Cartagena? And Juan Delgado, were
not he and his father of the same name both infamous morisco rebels,
exiled from Spain? And Padilla, the butcher in Cartagena, was he not
publicly shamed in the city and finally exiled from the Indies? What was
the background of witness Francisco de Castilla? Most important, however, what about the public executioner, Fernández Jaramillo? Was he
not forced into galley service for deserting to the Moors in North Africa? Did he not commit murder in Cartagena? Were not his ears cut
off as a sign of his criminality? Did he not wreak havoc in Havana before
he was selected as public executioner, and even afterward? And who

authorized such a criminal to serve the crown when he had repeatedly stolen, killed, and lied? How and why had such a den of criminals been assembled to give testimony against Francisco de Ludeña, a royal notary?

As much as his enemies in Havana in early 1606 may have wanted to ignore Ludeña, his charges could not easily be silenced. The notary was an educated man with substantial connections in both Spain and the Indies, even if he were not the most caring and benign of masters. Ludeña wanted the testimony of those witnesses against him to be stricken from the record, arguing that the word of such people could not be trusted. Indeed, in the next weeks he did provide even more convincing evidence that many of his accusers were petty criminals at best, and traitors to the king or even murderers at worst—a veritable rogues' gallery.

Simón de Padilla, the butcher in Cartagena, had been found guilty of using false weights and had been put in the stocks. Juan Delgado was a branded morisco, son of another morisco, a butcher of Seville. Public executioner Fernández Jaramillo had a long criminal record. Most recently, María Rodríguez, the wife of a chief pilot of the galleys, reported that about a month earlier while at home in bed, she had been awakened about midnight by a loud noise in the yard. She got up to investigate and discovered Fernández Jaramillo with another soldier who was shouting: "Well, you scoundrel and thief, in the house of an honorable lady! You have come and jumped over the walls to rob her." Fernández Jaramillo, in front of the soldier and the surprised María, "fell to his knees saying for the love of God, do not let anyone know, because I have entered as a person who has lost all reason, and I am drunk." According to the witness, this event occurred even after Fernández Jaramillo had been whipped and paraded through the streets of Havana because of his theft of some cheeses from Captain Alonso Ferrera.

Given these serious accusations, the judge decided to examine Juan Fernández Jaramillo a third time, on March 13, in the Morro fortress. He simply denied several of the accusations; others he ignored. Fernández Jaramillo did admit, however, that while stationed as a soldier in the North African frontier fortress of Melilla for a "piddling thing," he had been sentenced to the galleys as an oarsman for ten years without pay. Much of the service was in Cartagena de Indias. He further admitted that he had escaped, and Governor Acuña had then sentenced him to an additional five years in the galleys. At about that time his ears were cut off. His escape was just one of those spur-of-the-moment things, he lamented, and he did not deserve such a harsh disfigurement. For his alleged murder of a soldier in the plaza of Cartagena, Fernández Jaramillo admitted to a sentence of another two years in the galleys, again without pay. More recently, he conceded that for a certain case involving cheeses, the Lieutenant-General of Cuba had condemned him to two hundred lashes and an additional ten years of galley service. Nevertheless, Lieutenant Gendias and Antonio Fernández Farias persuaded him to take the office of public executioner in Havana, and for this they forgave him the ten additional years in the galleys. Fernández Jaramillo, of course, accepted the offer and "began to use and exercise the said occupation."

To press his case, Francisco de Ludeña continued to challenge the integrity of his accusers. On March 14 he related even more complete and damning information about his enemies. He called back for cross-examination Juan de Sequera, who was part of the company of Governor Acuña. Sequera testified that Fernández Jaramillo had served ten years in the galleys because "being a soldier on the Barbary Coast he had gone over the walls of the fortress and had wanted to join the enemy Moors." Furthermore, Sequera had seen him whipped publicly in the streets of Cartagena de Indias for having "absconded with some cheeses and bottles of oil from the storeroom of Captain Alonso Ferrera," leading to a sentence of ten additional years of galley service. Sequera too had been an important witness against Ludeña, but the notary's questions revealed that his reliability was suspect. Sequera admitted that he had been condemned in the city of Córdoba in Spain for taking part in an uprising. He received a term of eight years' galley service, which he completed in Cartagena under Governor Acuña.

Three days later, Ludeña presented his summation before Judge Suárez de Poago, concluding his defense by attacking those who had brought charges against him and pointing out the weaknesses and inconsistencies in their testimony. Ludeña charged that these hostile witnesses were "a band of lost and infamous people, and bad Christians"; they were "all of them exiled, and they had fled from Cartagena for crimes." Then, using what he believed to be flawless logic, he critiqued point by point the weaknesses in the testimony of his accusers. They did not provide the names of the girl's parents, her *encomendero*, or the parish in her indigenous village. If she really were an Indian, she should have been placed in the house of the General Protector of the Indians, but she was not. It was clear to Ludeña that Catalina's testimony had been coerced and that her words should have been more closely scrutinized from the very beginning of the judicial process. He lamented that the investigating official did not take such precautions, particularly when it was public knowledge that she had complained of the "force that had been applied to make her say that she was an Indian." Furthermore, the proper protections legally available for minors had been denied Catalina in this case. In conclusion, Ludeña asked that all the charges against him be dropped. Instead, he argued that his accusers should themselves face punishment for "having wanted to make of a Spanish girl, a daughter of

Spaniards, an Indian, subject to servitude." He demanded justice and a conclusion to the case.

The following day, March 18, Judge Suárez de Poago gave his decision: "I find that regarding the . . . merits of the [case] . . . Francisco de Ludeña defended himself well enough. . . . I must absolve and do absolve in this instance the said Francisco de Ludeña." Despite this verdict, the tribulations of Ludeña did not end. His enemies persevered and took judicial action that left him in legal limbo. On April 8, Francisco Báez filed an appeal, directed to the president and judges of the Royal Audiencia of Santo Domingo. Such an action provided Ludeña's enemies in Havana and Cartagena de Indias with the excuse to keep him jailed and his properties sequestered. If Ludeña left for Spain, charges against him still would remain open. Furthermore, many important papers would still be under the control of his enemies.

When Ludeña, his wife, family, and servants did return to Spain several months later, it was only after a lengthy delay. The annual fleet remained in Havana harbor while the ships were checked for seaworthiness and provisioned. Ludeña and his party finally departed in late September or early October, at the height of the hurricane season. The return route took the ships off the Florida coast and west of the Bahamas, where they took advantage of the strong currents of the Gulf Stream. The fleet would pass not far from Bermuda, in the mid-Atlantic, and then sail toward Cape San Vicente in Portugal. From there it was only a day or two to the Andalusian ports of Spain. They finally landed at Sanlúcar de Barrameda, at the mouth of the Guadalquivir River, and on October 20, 1606, the Ludeña household was taken into custody. Alcalde Licentiate Martín Hernández Portocarrero, of His Majesty's Council, along with don Melchor Maldonado, treasurer of the Casa de la Contratación, reviewed the documents of the passengers on board the ships that entered the harbor. On the vessel of shipmaster Antonio de Obregón the officials found "Francisco de Ludeña with his wife, one son, and a female servant, and some slaves." Because the party could not "show a license for their voyage" and the royal inspectors discovered the problem in Havana with an "Indian woman," the officials took immediate action. Ludeña and his companions were "taken into custody to be turned over to the jail of the Casa de Contratación in Seville."

Here, in the records of the Casa de Contratación, the modern historian finally encounters documents that unravel part of the mystery surrounding the true identity of Catalina. Like all Spaniards leaving for the Indies, Ludeña and his party needed permits to depart, which officials filed in the registers of the Casa de Contratación. In most cases, the process proceeded quickly, but sometimes complications arose that led to costly delays. A royal letter authorizing the trip, however, could speed up the process. On September 30, 1591, in the palace at San Lorenzo, Philip II signed a letter authorizing Francisco de Ludeña, vecino of Seville, to travel to Tierra Firme with his wife, children, a male servant, and two women for their service. The document specified that the children and servants were not to be married. On the outbound voyage in the early 1590s, shipmaster Juan Camacho recorded the presence aboard of one Francisco de Ludeña, his wife doña Leonor de Valdes, and Mateo, Gerónimo, and María, their children, along with Juan López de Aguila, Juana de Mendoza, and Catalina de Villacis, all servants and natives of Seville. They carried a copy of the license to depart for Tierra Firme. It was standard procedure to briefly describe each traveler in order to prevent others from falsely taking their places. The descriptions are not as accurate as paintings, but they are the only evidence available to the historian. At the time, Francisco de Ludeña was forty-two years old, "of good body, a black greying beard and black eyes." Doña Leonor was forty, with a "clear rosy complexion and a mole on the middle of her nose." Mateo, aged nineteen, "had signs of a beard and a small wound on the right cheek," while thirteen-year-old Gerónimo had a "sign of a wound on the left eyelid." María was twenty, "white, and with a clear rosy complexion, and two small scars on the side of the face and another on the right arm." Juan López de Aguila was thirty, of a good body, with a straw-colored beard and two wounds on both eyebrows. Juana de Mendoza was "white, with a small mole in the temple on the right side."

Most important for unraveling the case and determining the veracity of Ludeña and his accusers, however, is the description of the servant, Catalina de Villacis. But here someone has tampered with the document. There is a small tear in the page where the critical text about Catalina was entered, and paper glued to cover the hole. All that can be discerned are the words, "de edad - - - p - - - - na [pequeña?] de cu - - [cuna?]" (aged - - - small in a crib), a scar above the right eyebrow and another on the right cheek. Why was the correct age of Catalina alone removed from the original page, unless someone wished to falsify the record? The fragmentary, altered text suggests that Catalina was still in a crib, therefore an infant. But this contradicts the testimony given by Ludeña while in Havana. Furthermore, officials in Seville seldom recorded full descriptions of infants, mentioning details such as scars in the licenses. They tended simply to mention small children as just that—small children—with no further identifying information, unlike young and older adults, where they provided a fuller physical description. A full description of an infant "servant" is even more suspicious. There is also the curious addendum dated December 23, 1595, signed by one Juan Caxal, for the ship *San Pedro* that confirms boarding by "Francisco de Ludeña and his wife and children, because his servants did not appear." This document too is torn at the most critical points, with paper glued on to cover the gaps. Who tampered with the records—Ludeña, or perhaps his enemies in Havana, who had access to his papers when his properties were sequestered? And who is *this* Catalina? Is she an Indian, or the orphan whom Ludeña claims to have taken into his household, or even someone else?

From jail in the port of Sanlúcar de Barrameda, Francisco de Ludeña wrote on October 21, 1606, complaining of his rapidly worsening plight; moreover, his wife was now seriously ill. He reminded authorities that he had returned to Spain on the *Santa María la Rosa* and that he remained unjustly incarcerated. He lamented the embargo of his property, especially of a black slave named Ysabel, pleading, "I have need of [the slave] for my personal service and for my wife, who has already received extreme unction and is at the point of death, and the said slave is ready to give birth." Ludeña requested that the slave and her clothing be released so she could serve her master and mistress, regardless of her advanced pregnancy. The treasurer and judge, don Melchor Maldonado, complied immediately and ordered the transfer of the party to a jail in Seville. Although the relevant documents are missing, the party apparently posted bond and was freed for fifteen days, with the stipulation that they appear at an agreed-upon time before the jailor of the Casa de la Contratación in Seville. Sometime between October 21 and November 16, doña Leonor died.

Nevertheless, the royal prosecutor (*fiscal*), Diego Lorenzo Navarro, pressed charges against Francisco de Ludeña on November 16 in Seville. That same day Ludeña appeared and, in his name and that of his son Gerónimo, requested that the justices hear testimony in the case. He also asked that Catalina, who was under twenty-five and therefore legally a minor, be assigned a guardian, Francisco de Mesa, a *procurador* (solicitor) of the Royal Audiencia. Two days later, the court of the Casa de la Contratación complied with both petitions.

The officials took Ludeña's sworn "confession." He was now listed as fifty-seven years old, and he testified that he had been the king's notary in Seville several years before departing for the Indies. Court attorneys then asked if he had returned to Spain with his wife, children, and servants this year in the fleet commanded by General don Francisco del Corral, "without orders or license . . . carrying as he did much merchandise, gold and silver, without registering it." Ludeña admitted that he did sail with his wife and one son as well as with one slave and a servant woman, proceeding from Cartagena de Indias where they had resided for some time. The group first traveled on the ship of Juan Martínez de Murgia to Havana, but when this vessel began to take on water, they transferred to the ship of Antonio de Obregón. Ludeña "carried the license of the Governor and royal officials and the Inquisition of the said city of Cartagena." In Havana, however, the Lieutenant-Governor of Cuba had "taken all the baggage that I had, among which they took the said license." The justices then asked him if he had brought one "Catalina india who at present is in your service," despite knowing the laws prohibiting the transport of Indians to Spain from the Indies. He replied no, that he had dealt with these charges in Havana, where he had been imprisoned, "and I was freed because she is a Spanish woman, a native of these kingdoms, raised in Alcalá de la Guadaira." The same day the officials also took the sworn testimony of Gerónimo, whose evidence corroborated that of his father. Gerónimo too provided critical testimony that the license authorizing their return to Spain remained among the properties seized in Havana.

Officials of the Casa de la Contratación took the testimony "of a woman imprisoned in the jail of the Royal Audiencia" on November 18, 1606. The young woman "says that she is Catalina de Mairena and is seventeen years old, and is a servant of Francisco de Ludeña." She reported that she had returned from Tierra Firme and was a native of Alcalá de la Guadaira. When asked why she had confessed in Havana that she was an Indian from Cartagena, she replied: "I said it because the Lieutenant of Cartagena advised me to say it." Catalina told the court officials that he had actually forced her to say that she was Indian. Asked if she had come without an official travel license, she replied that she had served Francisco de Ludeña from the time that he left Spain in the company of Judge Milla until their return. Moreover, she had traveled in the service of her master, with his license.

Two days later solicitor Francisco de Mesa appeared before the president and justices of the Casa to speak on behalf of his clients, Francisco, Gerónimo, and Catalina. He argued that there was no legal cause not to free them, and they certainly did not constitute a public danger. Furthermore, he declared that Diego Rodríguez Sierra, a wealthy Seville silk merchant, had agreed to post bond for the imprisoned Ludeña and his household. His efforts prevailed, and on that day three officials of the court signed the release order.

For Ludeña, the whole affair had been a close call, fraught with risks. Shipping an Amerindian and illegal merchandise back to Spain was a serious crime, and his position had been made especially precarious by the confiscation of his papers in Havana. Did those papers include damaging reports on colonial officials in Cartagena and Havana, which motivated the American officials who brought charges against him? Certainly, his personal situation, and the family's, became even more unfortunate by the death of his wife. Nevertheless, he did secure his freedom, and documentation about his case in the court of the Casa de la Contratación ended.

Fortunately for anyone interested in unraveling the case, the paper trail in the Archivo General de Indias is extensive and fills many gaps in the story. Although someone (Ludeña or his enemies) tampered with his original license to travel to the Indies, other papers exist because both the originals and copies of supplementary documents regarding Ludeña's voyage to the New World were filed elsewhere in the Casa de la Contratación.[9] The critical piece for reaching the "truth" is the license authorizing Catalina de Villacis to travel to the Indies as a servant of Francisco de Ludeña. In these papers the original Catalina is described in detail, and she could not be the same seventeen-year-old who testified in Seville in 1606. According to the documentation, on December 19, 1591, Ludeña had appeared before the Casa to request an authorization, which he signed in his own hand, for Catalina de Villacis to accompany the family as one of two female house servants. Two days earlier, Catalina had presented witnesses attesting to her background and "purity of blood," a requirement that was not easy to circumvent because the crown was exceptionally diligent in attempting to keep "undesirables" from the Indies. Pedro Suárez, a tailor, testified that he had known Catalina from as long as he could remember. She was a native of Seville, from the parish of San Pedro, unmarried (*soltera*), and her parents and grandparents were Old Christians, untainted by the blood of Muslims, Jews, or anyone recently converted to the Catholic faith.[10] The family had never been called before the Inquisition. Two other witnesses confirmed his statement, and the description of Catalina provided by all three witnesses was consistent—she was about thirty years old, small of body, with a scar above the right eyebrow and another on the right cheek. In the documentation used in Ludeña's defense in 1606, Catalina's age was removed along with the term "small of body" (*pequeña de cuerpo*). Someone had left just enough text so that it appeared to read, or could be read, as "pequeña de cuna," an infant girl in a crib.

Who, then, was the Catalina who accompanied Ludeña in 1605? Was she Catalina india, Catalina de Mairena, or Catalina de Villacis? Where was the real Catalina de Villacis, now about forty-five years old? Did she really go to the Indies, and was this Catalina india perhaps her daughter? Or were the charges against Ludeña in Havana really true? And what of the story of the servant girl, the orphan Catalina from Alcalá de la Guadaira, who had been taken in by Ludeña's family fifteen years or so ago? Was she brought by them to the Indies without an official license? She was, it seems, the person responsible for the events narrated in the record. Her charges, true or false, brought into action the legal representatives of the royal government in the Indies. What were her motives? How could she be so easily forced to testify under oath that she was an Indian when she was not? Had she been so mistreated by Francisco de Ludeña and his wife that she acted in revenge? Were there personal reasons why she might have hoped to remain in Cartagena de Indias rather than return to Spain? Was she sexually linked to Gavilán the barber, or to someone else? We do know that Ludeña was lying in his testimony. But how far did the lie extend?

The real identity of Catalina india remains a mystery. Certainly, her case demonstrates the caution that historians must use in their search for the "truth." Evidence is always suspect and must be examined from all angles. Court cases, with multiple testimonies from competing parties, often permit scholars to probe for answers, but multiple points of view are rare in colonial documentation. Too often, historians hear only one voice—that of a colonial bureaucrat, a clergyman, or a person in the strongest position of power and authority. But which of the witnesses was telling the "truth"? We know that witnesses lied, even under oath. If the evidence today is ambiguous about Catalina's identity, then what of her contemporaries who tried to label her "Indian"?

The varied descriptions provided by witnesses in the case permit a slightly better understanding of the nuances of colonial descriptors of caste and class. And in the early seventeenth-century Spanish Caribbean, it was the "perception" that counted most often. What made Catalina an Indian or mestiza in the minds of the witnesses was color and physical attributes together with her menial occupation. Yet other witnesses testified that she looked like her father—small, dark, or moreno. If she were a Spaniard and simply resembled her father, her occupation as a servant would not have been uncommon for the daughter of a day laborer in Alcalá de la Guadaira. Unfortunately, authorities in the Indies obscured Catalina's true background and used her for their own ends. Officials in Cartagena de Indias and Havana, for whatever reasons, were clearly manipulating her identity to exert pressure on Francisco de Ludeña. He, in turn, manipulated her identity to protect himself and his family. Catalina's own shifting statements, back and forth from Indian to Spaniard, probably reflect not so much her confusion as her attempt at survival in a male-dominated world where she was merely a pawn in the hands of those in power. Her identity would change in keeping with the relative strength of those who controlled her life and her voice.

NOTES

1. Claudio Esteva-Fabregat, *Mestizaje in Ibero-America* (Tucson: University of Arizona Press, 1995), sharply contrasts the different attitudes in Anglo versus His-

panic America. Catalina's story was uncovered during research for another project in Spain in 1998–99 under support of a Fellowship from the American Council of Learned Societies and Florida International University. The author thanks the students and faculty of Tulane University for their comments at a presentation in March 1999, and especially Alexandra Parma Cook for constructive criticism.

2. Unless otherwise noted, the quotes are taken directly from the case in Seville's Archivo General de Indias, Contratación 151B, ramo 6.

3. The Protector General of the Indians was a position bestowed on someone, usually with legal experience, who was charged to assist in the defense of Amerindians. Bartolomé de las Casas was the first to be given the office in 1516, by Cardinal Jiménez de Cisneros. By the early seventeenth century there were many salaried Indian defense attorneys scattered throughout the Indies. See Lewis Hanke, *The Spanish Struggle for Justice in the Conquest of America* (Boston: Little, Brown, and Company, 1965).

4. Licentiate Melchior Suárez de Poago served as royal fiscal in the Audiencia of Panama from January 30, 1613, to February 19, 1619, when he was appointed fiscal of the Audiencia of Quito, where he served until retirement in 1647. Ernesto Schäfer, *El Consejo Supremo y Real de las Indias* (Seville: Escuela de Estudios Hispanoamericanos, 1947), 2:472, 516.

5. The governor of Cartagena de Indias, don Pedro de Acuña, was named to office on October 26, 1592. On December 24, 1599, he was appointed governor of the Philippines, where he later died. His successor in Cartagena, don Jerónimo de Zuazo Casasola, was named to office on March 9, 1600. Schäfer, *Consejo de las Indias*, 2:526, 534.

6. Sexual exploitation on the conquered, male and female, is stressed by Richard C. Trexler, *Sex and Conquest: Gendered Violence, Political Order, and the European Conquest of the Americas* (Ithaca: Cornell University Press, 1995).

7. Lies under oath are frequent, as described in a case of one Spaniard charged with bigamy and illegal shipment of bullion to Spain; see Alexandra Parma Cook and Noble David Cook, *"Good Faith and Truthful Ignorance": A Case of Transatlantic Bigamy* (Durham: Duke University Press, 1991). The historian must even take care in analyzing ecclesiastical records. As W. George Lovell succinctly points out, Dominicans and Franciscans could view and portray a series of events in an entirely different light, acting out of interests for their own order. See W. George Lovell, "Mayans, Missionaries, Evidence, and Truths: The Polemics of Native Resettlement in Sixteenth-Century Guatemala," *Journal of Historical Geography* 16:3 (1990): 277–94.

8. For the city see María del Carmen Borrego Plá, *Cartagena de Indias en el siglo XVI* (Seville: Escuela de Estudios Hispanoamericanos, 1983).

9. Archivo General de Indias, Contratación 5234B, #1, ramo 19.

10. In Archivo General de Indias, Contratación 5234B, # 1, ramo 18 we learn her parish in her testimony about Juan López del Aguila.

SUGGESTED READINGS

The unsavory side of port cities in the circum-Caribbean during the sixteenth century is portrayed in John Esquemeling, *The Buccaneers of America*

(New York: Dorset Press, 1987). For the seamy side of life in Seville, see Ruth Pike's *Artisans and Traders: Sevillian Society in the Sixteenth Century* (Ithaca: Cornell University Press, 1972), and Mary Elizabeth Perry's two books, *Crime and Society in Early Modern Seville* (Hanover, NH: University Press of New England, 1980), and *Gender and Disorder in Early Modern Seville* (Princeton: Princeton University Press, 1990). For the case of Catalina de Erauso, "the nun-ensign" who shocked Seville society in this period, see Stephanie Merrim, "Catalina de Erauso: From Anomaly to Icon," in *Coded Encounters: Writing, Gender, and Ethnicity in Colonial Latin America*, edited by Francisco Javier Cevallos-Candau, Jeffrey A. Cole, Nina M. Scott, and Nicomedes Suárez-Araúz (Amherst: University of Massachusetts Press, 1994), 177–205.

For motives for emigration, see Ida Altman, *Emigrants and Society: Extremadura and Spanish America in the Sixteenth Century* (Berkeley: University of California Press, 1989). The trials of crossing the Atlantic are beautifully detailed by Carla Rahn Phillips, *Six Galleons for the King of Spain: Imperial Defense in the Early Seventeenth Century* (Baltimore: Johns Hopkins University Press, 1986). To examine socially defined sex roles, see Asunción Lavrin, ed., *Sexuality and Marriage in Colonial Latin America* (Lincoln: University of Nebraska Press, 1989); Steve J. Stern, *The Secret History of Gender: Women, Men, and Power in Late Colonial Mexico* (Chapel Hill: University of North Carolina Press, 1995); and Ann Twinam, *Public Lives, Private Secrets: Gender, Honor, Sexuality, and Illegitimacy in Colonial Spanish America* (Stanford: Stanford University Press, 1999).

PART II

THE MATURE COLONIAL ORDER, 1610–1740

During the seventeenth century a more stable colonial social, political, and economic order developed in the Spanish Indies. By 1600 the Spaniards had subjugated the major Amerindian peoples, ended the squabbles among the initial conquistadors, and imposed an imperial bureaucracy to ensure their political dominance. Over time, however, the fiscally strapped Spanish crown began systematically selling appointments to most key colonial bureaucratic posts, which allowed *creoles* (people of European descent born in the Indies) to gain unprecedented political clout, which they often used to advance local rather than imperial interests. During these years the settlers also laid the foundations of a prosperous market economy tied to Europe. Silver mining remained a cornerstone of the colonial economy, but as production stabilized in Mexico and declined in South America, investment capital increasingly flowed to other prosperous economic sectors such as agriculture, grazing, manufacturing, and artisan production. With the economic diversification of the Indies, commercial exchanges expanded beyond the convoy system of transatlantic shipping, as trade links in legal and contraband merchandise evolved in the Caribbean and the Pacific, extending even to Spain's Asian possessions in the Philippine Islands.

For its part, the Roman Catholic Church had converted thousands of Amerindians, but persistent signs of enduring indigenous religious practices disturbed many in the Church hierarchy. In fact, some churchmen in the Andes initiated systematic efforts to "extirpate" indigenous religious practices. Nonetheless, widespread acceptance of Church rituals and popular devotions demonstrated the inroads made by Roman Catholicism throughout the Indies. In short, a hegemonic colonial political, social, and economic order slowly became entrenched during the long period from 1610 to 1740.

In Brazil the seventeenth century saw not only the consolidation of royal institutions but also the instability and conflict occasioned by the Dutch invasion and occupation of Salvador da Bahia (1624–25) and much of the captaincy of Pernambuco (1630–1654). The Portuguese crown dispatched royal governors to each of the major provinces, with a governor-general in Salvador (called viceroy after 1720) who theoretically supervised the other provincial leaders. In reality, his powers outside of Bahia were strictly limited, as each governor controlled his own province and communicated directly with Lisbon. It was not until 1609, however, that Portugal established a high court in Salvador da Bahia, which heard criminal and civil cases and appeals from lower courts. A municipal council in the major cities also administered local affairs in their immediate jurisdictions. The entire bureaucracy, however, was much smaller than in Spanish America.

The economy of Brazil remained mainly focused on sugar, produced on large plantations (*engenhos*), and, from the 1690s, on gold mining. The capital-intensive engenho consisted of large cane fields and a mill to process the cane into sugar and, for a fee, the crop of neighboring small-scale producers. The demand for labor at the mills eventually exceeded the supply of Amerindian slaves, so plantation owners began importing Africans. It was the very success of the sugar economy in Brazil that attracted the Dutch invaders, who sought to control this profitable colonial industry. After expelling the Dutch, the crown provided a fleet of warships in 1649 to guard the annual convoys of merchant vessels involved in the sugar trade. The discovery of gold and diamonds in the 1690s in the interior provinces of Minas Gerais, Mato Grosso, and Goiás added a new dimension to the export economy, and the ensuing mining boom prompted a major movement of people from the coast. By the eighteenth century, Brazil too had begun to establish a more stable colonial social, political, and economic order.

The chapters in Part II deal with the struggles of a diverse group of individuals, who were attempting to cope with a hegemonic colonial order. Ursula de Jesús was an African slave living as a servant in the Convent of Santa Clara in Lima who later became a mystic, famous for having divinely inspired visions and conversations with souls in Purgatory. Despite gaining her freedom and leading an exemplary life in the convent, Ursula could not escape the racism of her day. Indeed, she had even internalized some of these prejudicial attitudes, admonishing slaves who disobeyed their masters or had pretensions above their social station. While Ursula de Jesús accepted the values of the hegemonic colonial order, the Afro-Brazilian slave leader, Zumbi, resisted them by ruling Palmares, a coalition of communities of escaped slaves in the interior of Bahia that survived from the 1590s until its downfall in 1694. During the turbulent years of the Dutch occupation of Pernambuco, Palmares grew to between 20,000 and 30,000 inhabitants, an independent state based on a mixture of African and European customs. Zumbi, its most formidable military and political leader, defeated several Portuguese military expeditions until the final successful assault in 1694 and his capture and death the next year.

The journey of the Jeronymite friar, Diego de Ocaña, highlights the rise of the diverse forms of popular piety in the seventeenth century. In contrast to Ursula de Jesús, who lived in one of the proliferating urban religious houses in Lima during the period, Ocaña traveled through the countryside and to provincial capitals, such as Saña on the north coast of Peru, to spread the popular devotion of Our Lady of Guadalupe. To this end, he made small paintings of the Virgin of Guadalupe (which he claimed were divinely inspired), and when one of these images gained fame for its curative powers, it attracted the attention of a disreputable local parish priest who only wanted it for his private collection. The encounter between Ocaña and the priest gives us a glimpse into notions of divine intervention in human affairs, popular piety, and clerical fears about heterodoxy.

The resistance and agency of the indigenous peoples also formed a common theme during the seventeenth century. Felipe Guaman Poma de Ayala's failed attempt to gain control over lands claimed both by his family and a rival group of Andeans, the Chachapoyas, demonstrates how well indigenous elites understood and manipulated the Spanish legal system. The Maya lord, AhChan, like Guaman Poma, tried to collaborate with Spanish colonial authorities seeking to subdue the Itza, one of the last independent Maya kingdoms in the tropical forests of Petén, Guatemala. AhChan also became disillusioned with the Spaniards and later fled to the remote interior of Belize, where he led a multi-ethnic enclave of fugitive Maya. Accommodation held few benefits for the Andean nobleman, Guaman Poma, and the Maya lord, AhChan, and, like many ordinary people, they felt compelled to resist injustices perpetrated by the hegemonic colonial order.

CHAPTER 6

Ursula de Jesús

A Seventeenth-Century Afro-Peruvian Mystic

NANCY E. VAN DEUSEN

Seventeenth-century Lima was a rapidly growing cosmopolitan viceregal capital whose population rose from nearly 25,000 in 1619 to perhaps as high as 80,000 by 1680. This demographic growth ended abruptly, however, in 1687 when a devastating series of earthquakes struck, forcing people to flee the destruction, famine, and diseases that ensued. Lima was also the seat of the viceregal court, the most important royal audiencia in the realm, and the center of a prosperous colonial economy, at least until the tragedy of 1687. The crown made Lima the commercial entrepôt for the Andean region, and each year highland silver mines (particularly the famous "red mountain" at Potosí, in Bolivia) shipped bullion to the capital. Here it was exchanged for European wares (gathered from the trade fairs at Portobelo), illicit contraband merchandise, or colonial products from overland and seaborne trade routes. In addition, the city's urban population had become highly stratified: émigrés from Spain and Creoles occupied the highest social positions, followed by those of mixed racial ancestry (castas); then came the Amerindian residents of the city's indigenous sector (called the cercado), and the African freedman and slave populations. In short, for most of the century the viceregal capital was a vibrant, sophisticated urban center with a diverse citizenry.

A reflection of Lima's prosperity was the plethora of stately churches, monasteries, convents, and other religious buildings constructed during the seventeenth century. As the religious capital of the viceroyalty, Lima was the seat of an archbishopric as well as the Holy Office of the Inquisition and most of the principal monasteries or convents of the religious orders operating in South America. Each of these ecclesiastical organizations had its own edifice, ranging in splendor from the imposing cathedral in the central plaza to more modest parish churches in the cercado. These buildings formed the center of a vital religious life that included veneration of the cross, cults of the saints, and ritual use of music, dances, and prayer. Such expressions of piety reflected the grandeur of the capital, but they also mirrored colonial ideals about social stratification. A person's role in a religious festival, seat in the cathedral at important services, and admission to certain religious orders or sodalities (cofradías) depended on social status. Even convent life was rigidly hierarchical, with nuns of the black veil occupying the highest rank, followed by nuns of the white veil, novices preparing to take their vows, donadas *(servants recognized for spiritual gifts or contributions to the community), and regular servants, who tended to worldly needs—washing, cooking, cleaning, and other household chores.*

One of the servants in the large and prestigious Convent of Santa Clara was a black slave, Ursula de Jesús. According to her later writings, Ursula began serving a wealthy nun of the black veil, but she chafed at her humble post, displaying signs of vanity and a rebellious spirit. After narrowly escaping death by falling into a deep well, however, Ursula changed her ways and led an exemplary and holy life. In fact, she became a well-known mystic who had divinely inspired visions and the ability to communicate with souls in Purgatory. Over time her reputation led one of the convent's nuns to purchase her freedom, and Ursula became a respected donada valued for her piety and visions. Despite her reputation, Ursula could not escape racial prejudices against Afro-Peruvians, even in the Convent of Santa Clara. She could never hope to attain the status of a nun or even gain a small measure of the recognition accorded to the creole mystic, Saint Rose of Lima. Nevertheless, her piety and links to the divine served as models to other women of color in Lima. Even today, in Lima's poor neighborhood of Barrios Altos, where the Convent of Santa Clara still stands, people continue to recount tales of her miraculous visions and her holiness.

Nancy E. van Deusen is associate professor of history at Western Washington University. A well-known specialist on female religious in seventeenth-century Peru, she has published numerous articles and a book, Between the Sacred and the Worldly: Recogimiento in Colonial Lima *(2001). She is also completing a critical edition of writings about the mystical experiences of Ursula de Jesús (forthcoming).*

One day, just as Ursula de Jesús, an Afro-Peruvian religious servant (*donada*), finished taking communion in the Convent of Santa Clara in Lima, the ghost of the deceased Licenciate Colonia appeared to her, asking her to plead with Jesus Christ to have mercy on his soul. Although he claimed that the intervention of the Virgin and Saint Rose of Lima had aided him, he continued to suffer terrible and interminable anguish in Purgatory. He then explained that his flagrant mistreatment of his slave, Francisca, had determined in part his lengthy sentence. Shocked by this request, Ursula went into a meditative trance to communicate with Jesus Christ, who confided to her that this soul faced perpetual torture and damnation and that her supplications would be of no use.[1]

Such otherwordly requests for intercession directed to the holy women of convents by those in Purgatory were not considered remarkable in colonial Latin America. What is indeed remarkable about this petition is that the spirit of a high-ranking colonial official contacted a former slave of African descent and that many of the elite nuns in her religious community had faith in the mystical abilities of the unassuming but powerful Afro-Peruvian servant in their midst. The question to be addressed here is how Ursula de Jesús, an enslaved woman of humble origins, gained both the experience and authority to claim such transcendent abilities as well as a reputation for sanctity that only a few achieved during that period.

Born in 1604 in Lima, Ursula inherited her status as a slave from her mother, and the two resided with their owner, Gerónima de los Ríos. Ursula spent her formative years in a large household filled with African, Spanish, and Peruvian people who shared and exchanged elements of their distinct cultural traditions. Both familial and occupational positions placed her owner in contact with a number of highly placed peninsular members of *limeño* (resident of Lima) and Andalusian societies. Like other elite Spanish women, Gerónima actively engaged in business negotiations (usually giving power to a male figure to represent her), especially the buying and selling of slaves. She had no children, but the household consisted of other family members, including her niece, Inés de Pulgar, and a few orphans as well as an abundance of Spanish, mestiza, and black girls working in her service as cooks, laundresses, maids, and gardeners.

Ursula's early childhood years replicate the circumstances facing many slaves who spent their lives working for others and whose family relations and destinies remained intricately linked to their patrons. Like many young girls living in a society where Catholic tenets often dictated cultural norms, Ursula developed a particular devotion to the Virgin of Carmen and prayed the rosary and fasted once per week. But she was unique in other respects. In 1612, Ursula went to live with a wealthy *beata* (pious laywoman) and mystic named Luisa de Melgarejo Sotomayor (1578–1651). During her years in doña Luisa's household, she met a number of men and women deeply committed to mystical practices. Although in 1617 she then entered the Convent of Santa Clara to serve Gerónima de los Ríos's niece, sixteen-year-old Inés, her unconventional spiritual education expedited her change in status from a slave serving her mistress into a freedwoman working in the service of God.

We have access, fortunately, to the inner musings and experiences of someone who easily could have slipped into oblivion because, at the request of her spiritual confessor, Ursula recorded her visions and mystical experiences. Her diary, kept between 1647 and her death in 1666 and later copied and altered by her confessor, accesses three important issues current during a period of spiritual efflorescence in seventeenth-century

Lima. First, as a woman of color and a mystic, Ursula faced particular choices and contingencies that elite women living in convents did not. Second, although female visionaries claimed a degree of objectivity as conduits of divine knowledge, Ursula's recorded visions revealed the social tensions resulting from her experience of racism and the maintenance of social hierarchies characteristic of the convent and society at large. Undoubtedly, her singular experiences affected the choices she made.[2] Third, her visions enhance our knowledge of popular spirituality and notions of the beyond because Ursula specialized in communicating with departed souls caught in the fires of Purgatory and desiring redemption.

According to the Jesuit chronicler Bernabé Cobo, by 1630 the "mystical body" of the "Christian Republic" of Lima had reached a level of piety comparable with that of the best European cities. Six "sumptuous" convents for females and fourteen male monasteries formed an integral part of the urban landscape, and Cobo estimated that in 1630, 3,600 individuals lived in monastic institutions, including more than 1,000 nuns, 1,000 servants, slaves, and laywomen in convents, compared with 1,126 priests and 500 donados, servants, and slaves in male monasteries.[3] In addition, mystical practices already condemned by Inquisition authorities in Spain reached their zenith. A number of Jesuit friars, many of whom served as the confessors of famous beatas, including Luisa de Melgarejo, explored the tenets of mysticism and influenced a generation of young male and female charges. Ursula's short stint in Melgarejo's home brought her in direct contact with a number of "living saints": individuals recognized by the community as worthy of sanctification, including doña Luisa herself. As mystics they claimed to receive divine knowledge through visions and "mental prayer"—direct, unmediated union with God—and served the Lima community as prophets and healers. The general populace, including influential authorities such as the wife of the viceroy, frequently solicited their spiritual advice on marriage, health, lost objects, and auspicious travel dates. Doña Luisa's celestial revelations circulated throughout Lima, and Saint Rose (1586–1617) was said to consult her confidante's writings.[4] Ursula also met a number of beatas who openly discussed theological matters. Unfortunately, many of these women were tried and, with the exception of Luisa de Melgarejo, convicted by the Holy Inquisition in 1625.

Although the Inquisition attempted to curtail what it considered to be heterodox forms of Catholic expression, young black women such as Ursula were fortunate to participate actively in the spiritual renaissance occurring in Lima, either through direct, intimate relations with creole mystics or through their own efforts. For instance, many wanted to be Saint Rose's spiritual protégées, including Mariana, a native Andean servant who introduced the servant of God to a famous pious *cacica* (female ethnic leader), Catalina Huanca. Mariana diligently obeyed her mistress by placing lime on Rose's hands when she was told that they were pale and lovely, and later she confessed under duress that the saint wore a tunic of rough pigskin under her Dominican habit.[5] Unobtrusive, submissive devotional practices could also be found among exemplary *casta* men and women who generally served as donada/os in convents or as members of a Third Order of the Regular clergy. Frequently mentioned in the convent chronicles composed at the time, they were also recognized for their spiritual gifts and contributions among both the religious community and Lima's inhabitants. The Franciscan chronicler, Diego de Córdova y Salinas, for instance, extolled the virtues of Estephanía de San Joseph (d. 1645), a *mulata* freedwoman and beata who charmed the elite with her vibrant personality; she preached daily sermons, tended to the sick and the poor, and collected alms for the nuns of Santa Clara. Her mestiza companion, Isabel de Cano, sewed mattresses for the sick and also spoke in public about spiritual matters. Word traveled throughout Lima that Francisco de la Concepción, a humble African donado, could appear in two places simultaneously and had the gift of prophecy. Hundreds of rich and poor limeños knew of the sensational curative abilities and charitable efforts of the Dominican mulato Martín de Porras (1579–1639) long before his elaborate funeral procession took place. Not only did casta men and women situate themselves within the pantheon of Lima's popular "saints," but the cult of the Señor de los Milagros (an image of Christ) grew steadily during Ursula's lifetime and reached a fevered pitch among people of African descent following the 1655 earthquake.

While aware of the various forms of popular religious expression in the "world," Ursula's main contacts after 1617 remained with holy women cloistered in the Convent of Santa Clara. Founded in 1605, it attracted scores of elite women who aspired to become nuns of the black veil. Those who could only afford to pay a modest dowry or were not members of the aristocracy often became nuns of the white veil. Race and economic status were certainly key in perpetuating an assemblage of "durable inequality," and yet humility, strict observance of the rules, and spiritual gifts also served to elevate status within the convent.[6] A few of Ursula's contemporaries deserve specific mention. Catalina de Cristo worked as a baker in the convent; swore before the Abbess that Saint Clare awakened her each morning by saying, "let's go and knead the dough, Catalina"; and also reported seeing souls in Purgatory during Requiem Masses.[7] In another example, Agustina de San Francisco had the reputation of supervising the slaves (including Ursula) and servants working in the convent with a firm but kind hand. Juana de Cristo gave spiritual counsel to the convent's servants and at night slept on a wooden plank in tribute to Christ's suffering on the cross. Another nun, Gerónima, signed her name "Slave of the Blessed Souls of Purgatory" and collected alms to pay for Masses that might release them from their temporary prison. She kissed the feet of the dead (including blacks), and during Requiem Masses she imitated the corpse by covering herself with a shroud while the choir sang.

The original constitution of the Order, written by its founder, Clare of Assisi (d. 1253), encouraged all able sisters to do manual labor and share in communal tasks.[8] She hoped that the nuns of the Order would devote themselves to a life of poverty and independence in a self-sufficient environment. However, medieval convents supported a much smaller population. In the seventeenth century, Santa Clara in Lima required huge capital investments to support a population that grew by nearly 20 percent between 1630 and 1650 and consumed vast quantities of supplies. Each month the residents ate at least 140 chickens and large amounts of wheat flour and sugar; hundreds of pesos were spent on corn to feed the chickens raised in coops inside the cloister, on cords of wood for the ovens in the kitchen, and on the organ.[9] Male carpenters transported goods and repaired and built additions to the convent, but it depended chiefly upon female workers housed there.

In spite of Saint Clare's wishes, the convent maintained a large female servant population, in part because the majority of the nuns of the black and white veils disdained manual labor. During Ursula's lifetime, nearly 20 percent of the total convent population consisted of servants and slaves who served individual nuns and carried out communal tasks. For twenty-eight years, Ursula was one of hundreds of women whose exhausting daily work regime afforded no spare time to contemplate religious matters. Each day she attended to the needs of her *ama* (owner) in her cell: she prepared her food and washed her clothing and linen. Once those tasks were completed, Ursula worked with the other servants in the kitchen and infirmary until late each evening.

Although extremely hardworking, Ursula described herself during her years in bondage in the convent (1617–1645) as self-centered, temperamental, and vain. Like many slaves in Lima, she was known for her frippery and desire to wear stylish clothing. However, an event occurred in 1642 that transformed Ursula's life and permanently altered her reputation for vanity. Angry that she had lent a skirt to someone who returned it soiled, she washed it and then spread it out to dry on a plank covering the mouth of a deep well in the center of the convent. While she was arranging the skirt, the platform she stood upon collapsed, leaving Ursula suspended above the pit and trying to hold on, literally, for her life. Unable to help her, the nuns and other witnesses fervently prayed that she would not suffer a painful death. Ursula claimed that her own supplications to the Virgin of Carmen rescued her, and miraculously she recovered her balance and gained enough leverage to reach safety.

This fortuitous event led the now deeply humbled Ursula to sell her finery and dedicate her spare moments to prayer. From her brush with death she gained a sense of a greater purpose in life and beseeched God to instruct her in spiritual matters. The nuns began referring to her as a "servant of God," as Ursula now took pride in the exacting labor required of her and subjected herself to even more demeaning and burdensome tasks. In the infirmary she cared for the most contagious and repulsive patients and volunteered to wash infected clothing and rags wet with loathsome pus. Whenever she felt repugnance, she would place the rags in her mouth. Such mortification resonated with the sufferings and Passion of Christ and, above all, with his humanity.

Indeed, Ursula's sense of self-sacrifice, humility, and charity toward others conformed to notions of sanctity among holy women and men of the period. Her spiritual "résumé" replicated a common hagiographic model: a life of vanity and worldliness followed by a miracle and subsequent spiritual conversion. Like other holy women in Latin America and Catholic Europe, Ursula began to have visions and reported in her diary that she communicated frequently with Jesus Christ. Her "education" may seem odd to someone in the twenty-first century, but many female visionaries admitted to having intimate, emotional communication with God and other celestial beings. Still, in order to conform to contemporary notions of humility, they expressed astonishment that such a "worm," "ant," or lowly being as themselves would merit divine attention. Ursula echoed this sentiment. One day, while meditating, Ursula felt a tremendous desire to kiss the hand of Christ. She reported "experiencing" his presence and watched as he freed his nailed hand from the cross and placed it on her mouth. Deeply grateful for this divine favor, she asked, "My Lord, am I Saint Catherine [of Siena] or Saint Gertrude?" To which the Lord responded, "I am the one who benefited them and I am able to benefit you." Stunned by this reply, the humble Ursula wondered how she could possibly be compared to two famous saints who were noblewomen and who received "gifts" and personal visits from Christ.

In many ways, Ursula's path followed that of many other female visionaries, with one important exception: she was still a slave. After 1642, misunderstandings between Ursula and her owner developed because she neglected her daily work in order to attend to spiritual matters. By 1645, she felt despondent and desperate and requested permission to leave the convent to search for a new owner.[10] Concerned that the convent might lose a gifted holy woman and that Ursula's spiritual "career" would be cut short, doña Rafaela de Esquivel, a nun of the black veil, purchased Ursula's freedom—a considerable expense for that period. Ursula appreciated doña Rafaela's generosity but declined a subsequent invitation to become a donada for several reasons. Although the circumspect Ursula no longer wanted to leave the convent, neither did she want to continue a life of servitude, which the status of donada might prolong. Clauses in "letters of freedom" often specified that freed slaves should continue to "assist" their owner for a determined number of years. Like many freedwomen, she was proud to be her own mistress after forty-one years in bondage, and wished to be "free" from draining communal tasks to devote herself entirely to God's service.

Ursula also resented the convent's donadas whom she considered to be pompous. The religious servants would have considered her, as a slave, to be of a lower status and may have mistreated her. In retrospect, however, Ursula regretted her vanity and tenaciousness. After receiving a "sign" from Heaven when several religious objects in the main chapel caught fire, and encouragement from a black novice about to take her vows as a donada, Ursula decided to follow the same course in 1646.

In fact, becoming a donada clearly presented Ursula with the best option to pursue her spiritual interests in a more dedicated and untethered fashion. Many donadas of Santa Clara held more prestigious posts than the servants and slaves of the convent. Some were *sacristanas*: they cleaned religious objects and washed the linen for the altar. Each morning they prepared the chapel for Mass by lighting candles and ensuring that the flowers, incense, and religious objects were readied for the priest. Others rang the bell to announce the liturgical hours; those with great strength carried the heavy cross during the religious processions held within the convent. The nuns welcomed donadas who showed a flair for fashioning candles for processions, festivals, and special Masses. Finally, many convents boasted several donadas renowned for their remarkable expressions of piety, including a reputation for mortification and other acts of humility or mental prayer.[11]

Religious servants were a significant presence in Santa Clara; a 1633 report enumerated forty-seven professed donadas and sixteen novices, representing 26 percent of the total population of female religious.[12] Nearly all were native Andeans or castas; like Ursula, a few girls of African descent had received their freedom. Many were illegitimate or orphaned and had few family ties outside the convent. Most applicants were under the age of twenty and had spent years working in the service of a nun as a *criada* (servant). Cloistered since childhood, a donada was guaranteed economic and social security that the dangers and cruelties of the world could not provide. Moreover, a life in the service of the Holy Virgin seemed a natural recourse to many applicants. Still, most candidates were judged on their ability to carry out communal tasks and serve individual nuns. If they were fortunate, a nun would sponsor their vocation by promoting their candidacy to the religious community and by paying the required dowry of 500 pesos.

Once she decided to become a donada, Ursula spent the year 1647 preparing for her formal profession. She earned the reputation of being exceptionally pious because she lived with "singular advancement of her spirit, continuous mortification of her senses, and [served as a] rare model of penitence, and repeated fasts." Her evenings were spent lying prostrate before an image of Christ in the choir; she also wore a hair shirt and a crown of thorns hidden beneath her hair together with iron-studded straps around her waist and arms. On her back she carried a cross with barbs tightened with a bodice made of pigskin, with the bristles turned inward to intensify the effect. Each day she whipped herself before retiring, and once again at four in the morning. Ursula professed on June 13, 1647, the day of the Holy Trinity, "with great devotion and humility." At that decisive moment, she expressed a fervent desire to comply strictly with her vows of poverty and chastity and obedience to the rules of the Order of Saint Clare.

From 1647 until her death in 1666, Ursula's spirituality—and particularly her ability to intercede on behalf of souls trapped in Purgatory—continued to grow. The nuns of Santa Clara, her numerous confessors, and the Lima community considered her to be unusually gifted and blessed. For two decades, Ursula became intimately familiar with the world of dead souls, who began communicating with her in the belief that her prayers might alleviate their suffering in Purgatory. In her diary, she recorded these phenomenal otherworldly "visits" from a variety of individuals: priests revealing their peccadilloes, nuns regretting their impudent conduct, or servants and children recounting the grave illnesses and excessive work that they had endured. Often she heard the voice of Jesus Christ and felt his presence or saw images of him, her guardian angel, or the Virgin Mary. Each offered assistance in alleviating the suffering of the pleading souls in Purgatory who appeared frequently before her.

Most Catholics in early modern society believed in free will, which corresponded with the conviction that each person, after death, was judged before a holy tribunal and then sentenced to a specific length of time in Purgatory in order to purge his or her sins. All souls knew that their stay in Purgatory was temporary, and salvation and access to Heaven guaranteed. Depending upon the gravity and number of transgressions, "time" spent in this intermediary space between Heaven and Hell varied from several hours to several centuries. Only the most unsullied souls went directly to Heaven; most resigned themselves to the fact that they would have to spend some time in Purgatory. As one spirit explained to Ursula,

"In order to go to Heaven, souls had to be purified with fire: to become like the purest crystal—without a single imperfection—before entering into Glory."

Once there, many awakened, as though their life had been a dream and they then witnessed their wasted hours and acts of folly. This realization formed an initial stage of their purgation along with the knowledge that their sins might have been expiated by prayer, contrition, and good works. Many reported being subjected to horrible torments, including extreme temperatures: from flames licking at their ethereal bodies to being plunged into icy waters. While in a deep trance, Ursula once had this vision of souls close to Hell: "She saw an enormous and ferocious mouth of a formidable dragon, and inside, multitudes of souls covered in voracious flames. It was like when a pot boils and bubbles appear: some rising to the surface, others disappearing below. The descending souls plunged beneath with a terrible force and [she could see] them all completely water-logged and lodged in between horrible flames of burning tar and brimstone. But, once again, they would return to the surface, in strife and in constant motion."

The obsession with Purgatory, and sordid details of tales of horror and woe found in Ursula's diary, reached a fever pitch in seventeenth-century Lima—to some degree because the dead formed an integral part of the lives of the living. Family members expressed concern for those in the beyond through prayers and requests for Masses, or by fasting, and buying indulgences. They believed that these efforts could accomplish two goals: they might alleviate the suffering and diminish the length of time of their loved ones' stay in Purgatory, and their charity might eventually assist their own case. In Lima, Masses said for souls in Purgatory were popular; in the cathedral alone, priests said 3,000 Masses each year for departed souls. Even the nuns of Santa Clara founded chaplaincies on behalf of the souls of Purgatory, and Ursula herself established a confraternity in the name of the Virgin of Carmen, known for saving lost souls.[13]

Saving souls in Purgatory was seen as a selfless and beneficial enterprise, both for the living and the dead. Intercession on behalf of troubled souls eased the concern of the living for their loved ones; served as a source of moral authority and as a disciplinary measure for those involved in similar wrongdoing; provided a direct, celestial education for the holy women working as intercessors; and offered visionaries such as Ursula the opportunity to gain a sense of power and authority which, under other circumstances, might evade them.

Communication with those from the beyond was believed to be real, but why would the souls of the dead wish to "speak" with Ursula? Many holy women throughout early modern Catholic Europe and Latin

America experienced visions of departed souls, particularly of family members or people with whom they had been close. Several of the singular beatas circulating in Lima during Ursula's adolescence, including Luisa de Melgarejo, reported seeing the souls of Church dignitaries in Purgatory; described the torments of souls; traveled to Heaven, Hell, and Purgatory; or predicted whether the living would be condemned or saved. Most of these women, however, lived quiet, unremarkable cloistered lives. And of these, only a few accepted the difficult, lifelong task of releasing souls in Purgatory. Those who did, like Ursula, believed that God had chosen them for that purpose.

Ursula's diary is unique because she communicated with souls from all walks of life. Among the deceased nuns who approached her, a number lamented that they had not paid enough attention during Mass: they whispered in the choir or spread malicious gossip. The spirit of one nun who had spent years in Purgatory said, "Don't admire us, Ursula, twice I held the position of Prelate and now I am paying [dearly] for my faults." She expressed a commonly held belief that male and female religious had a greater moral responsibility than lay people. If they sinned and disobeyed the convent's rules or the Ten Commandments, they suffered harsher punishment in the hereafter. Ursula asked the nun's spirit if many souls from Santa Clara were in Purgatory, to which it replied, "yes." It explained to Ursula that those Brides of Christ who spent their time in business negotiations instead of spiritual endeavors would pay a high price for their cupidity in the beyond. Ursula also inquired after the soul of her beloved doña Rafaela, the nun who had purchased her freedom, and a voice assured her that Rafaela had ascended into Heaven.

Despite her status as a donada and freedwoman, Ursula's spiritual authority prevailed on certain occasions. Once, Christ explained to her His disappointment in the lax morals of his Brides. He ordered that celestial "decrees" be posted in the choir enjoining the nuns to center their thoughts upon spiritual matters before, during, and after Communion. The nuns were required to deliberate on the ways they had been remiss. This was a tall order, because it forced Ursula to criticize indirectly nuns who had been her superiors for decades. Fortunately, both her confessor and the Abbess took the directive seriously, and no one in the community doubted its veracity. The Abbess called a general meeting and read out the reforms dictated to Ursula from Christ. Clearly, the threat of Purgatory served as a reminder that nuns and servants would be judged accordingly before the eyes of God. As Christ once explained to Ursula, even the ashes of the most powerful viceroy could easily dissipate in water. Perhaps Ursula's "reform" visions were also far more effective than any ecclesiastical visitation from the Archbishop, because they originated within a humble woman who understood the hierarchical structure of the convent and her place within it.

Concerns with racism and race relations were a constant in Ursula's life. Acutely aware of the centrality of patron-client relations as well as the necessary attributes of obsequiousness and humility for those in bondage, she never forgot her former position as a slave. This is evidenced by the fact that deceased younger and older slaves and servants frequently asked her to intercede on their behalf and to advise the living that they should behave honorably. One female slave appeared in her earthly form in the hope that Ursula would recognize her. She feared becoming one of the many lost, forgotten, and "orphaned" souls (*ánimas solas*) in Purgatory without anyone to care about their well-being. Another slave explained that she had committed a mortal sin for having had a licentious love affair with a nun (causing a tremendous scandal), but that her prayers to Saint Clare and to Saint Francis had saved her from the flames of Hell. She thought that her thirty years in Purgatory were well deserved, but Ursula pleaded to God on her behalf—arguing that she had served the community well—in an effort to reduce her punishment. On another occasion, Ursula awakened with a horrible fright at 3 A.M. because she felt the presence of the soul of a dead slave who had worked as a cook and baker in the convent. She had erred by paying more attention to her own needs than to those of the "common good," and she advised Ursula to bring this matter to the attention of the Abbess, so that others would become aware of the consequences of their pernicious conduct.

Ursula's diary entries often recorded complaints about the demands of pampered nuns, the onerous kitchen work, and the trial of being spat upon and ridiculed. Frequently, when she asked Christ why she had to work excessively long hours, He reminded her of the excruciating suffering that He had endured during the Passion. On one occasion she wrote: "Saturday, I was exhausted from so much cooking and other things, desiring only to be in the mountains where there are no people. I turned to God and said, were it not for Him I would not persevere in this. He responded that although the Son of God was quite well off in His kingdom of glory He came to suffer travail for our sake." And about one difficult companion she wrote: "I am such a bad black woman. Sometimes I feel—I don't know what—toward my companion, with all her scolding I don't know how to get along with her. If I ask her, bad, if I don't ask her, worse. I can't find a way. Other times she will say, why don't you take your provisions, and I go and ask for alms for the infirm. Or, why don't I cure them? And other things of this nature that make me laugh. God only knows how I survive, and they tell me to suffer all that is offered me."

At times, Ursula found herself caught between her position as a visionary and freed black woman. She was not the only one to face this dilemma. The mulatto friar, Martín de Porras, dealt valiantly with the stark realities of racism and yet was known to admonish slaves who disobeyed their masters.[14] Ursula understood that slaves and servants often suffered the cruelties of abuse, physical exhaustion, and unjust recrimination but also comprehended the fact that they were property. On one occasion, the convent set off fireworks in honor of the June celebrations of Corpus Christi. In the tumult, a large ember landed on the head of a slave, causing a deep, mortal gash. Still, Ursula's concern rested not with the slave but with his master, a priest well known among the nuns. She felt troubled by the inconvenience that the loss of his slave would cause him. But when she begged Christ to have mercy on the poor sick priest, a voice immediately chastised her:

> Ursula, it is not for the convenience of the owner that the servant should die. This [act] begins to open [the slave's] eyes to the world, and if he lives any longer he will lose [this knowledge] and it is better that he should die. When you are here sleeping in Heaven, the scales fall from the eyes, and each individual can see clearly that which is best for the salvation of the soul. This costs God a lot, and he is his Wise Majesty, the Universal Lord of the Heavens and the Earth, by whose hand pass so many things. The servants [in the world] all have a particular Providence.

Not all of Ursula's visions were laden with tales of anguish and suffering; she often witnessed the positive results of her efforts. After employing various means to ensure their safe passage from Purgatory, many transfigured souls—now radiant and dressed in flowing white garments—appeared to thank her before ascending to Heaven. One servant whom she had "saved" described to Ursula how Heaven differed depending on one's "station" in life: "[In Heaven] great harmony prevailed; everyone had their place according to their position; nuns belonged in one part, male religious in another, and lay persons and priests all occupied their places in order and harmony. Indians, blacks, and other people were punished in accordance with their standing and the obligations of their class."

In the realms of the beyond, everyone had a designated place that replicated the social hierarchies in the world, but those spaces also eradicated socially constructed differences. According to Ursula's visions, all souls were capable of ascending to Heaven. For instance, the deceased María Bran, a slave of Santa Clara, appeared to Ursula dressed in an ecclesiastical garment tied with an ornately embroidered cord and wearing a crown of flowers similar to that of Saint Rose. María assured Ursula that blacks and donadas went to Heaven, a concern that a white mystic would not have. The fact that a slave, dressed as a saint, would occupy a space in the lofty heights of Purgatory and then enter "Glory" reveals

Ursula's conception of Purgatory as a place where social justice prevailed. From the point of view of a mystic who fought against racism and brutality her entire life, Purgatory equalized differences, but it also functioned as a prism of the complex hopes and fears of a broad cross-section of Lima's colonial inhabitants.

Near the end of her life, Ursula became aware that she too would be granted a direct and safe passage to Heaven because of her selfless efforts to help others. After suffering a mortal illness for over three weeks, Ursula died on February 23, 1666, and doña Leonor Basques, a well-respected nun of the convent, declared that the servant of God entered Heaven in a state of ecstasy with her eyes raised toward the skies and her soul "nailed to the crucified Christ." She died a "good death" because she prepared her will, disposed of her worldly possessions, confessed her sins, and received extreme unction. The nuns of Santa Clara deeply mourned her passing, and a number of high ecclesiastical and secular authorities, including the wife of the viceroy, attended her funeral. Because of her lifelong devotion to Our Lady of Carmen, Ursula was buried beneath her chapel in the convent.

Ursula never gained the recognition that Saint Rose achieved in the seventeenth century. Nevertheless, she served as a model for women of color in Lima in small but significant ways. Five months after her death, the Abbess petitioned for twenty-year-old Francisca de la Cruz to become a donada "following the example of the Mother, Ursula de Cristo." The nuns commissioned a casta artist to paint her portrait, and in 1686, one of her Franciscan confessors recopied and edited her diary. Today, religious histories mention her name only in passing. Until recently, people in the humble neighborhood where the Convent of Santa Clara is located were permitted to enter the vestibule to kneel before her image and pray for her intercession on their behalf.

NOTES

1. Most information on Ursula and the quotations cited in this chaper are derived from two manuscripts: the original diary, "Vida de la Hermana Ursula," Archivo del Monasterio de Santa Clara, Lima, Libro 5, 1928; and a version copied by her Franciscan confessor, "Vida de la Venerable Madre Ursula de Jesucristo," located in the Franciscan Archive of Lima, Registro 17, no. 45, n.d., 585r-603r.

2. Elizabeth Alvilda Petroff, "A Medieval Woman's Utopian Vision: The Rule of Saint Clare of Assisi," in idem, *Body and Soul: Essays on Medieval Women and Mysticism* (New York: Oxford University Press, 1994), 3–4.

3. Bernabé Cobo, "Historia de la fundación de la ciudad de Lima," in *Monografías históricas sobre la ciudad de Lima* (Lima: Imprenta Gil, 1935), 1:137, 233–34.

4. Juan Meléndez, *Tesoros verdaderos de las Yndias* (Rome: Nicolás Tinassio, 1681), 2:311.

5. Ramón Mujica Pinilla, "El ancla de Santa Rosa de Lima: mística y política en torno a la Patrona de América," in *Santa Rosa de Lima y su tiempo*, ed. José Flores Araoz et al. (Lima: Banco de Crédito del Perú, 1995), 195.

6. Charles Tilly, *Durable Inequality* (Berkeley: University of California Press, 1998).

7. Diego de Córdoba y Salinas, *Crónica franciscana de las Provincias del Perú*, ed. Lino G. Canedo (Washington, DC: American Academy of Franciscans, 1962), 900.

8. Petroff, "A Medieval Woman's Utopian Vision," 66–79.

9. Archivo Arzobispal de Lima (henceforth AAL), Monasterio de Santa Clara, Leg. III, exp. 23, "Cuentas del monasterio . . . 1626 hasta 1629," 1r-2r.

10. Church authorities were responsible for the physical and spiritual well-being of slaves, and ecclesiastical law stated that a slave who suffered excessive brutality from his owner could petition a judge to be resold.

11. Francisco Echave y Assu, *La estrella de Lima convertida en sol sobre sus tres coronas* (Antwerp: Juan Baptista Verdussen, 1688), 228–33.

12. AAL, Monasterio de Santa Clara, Leg. IV, exp. 42, "Relación de religiosas y donadas del Monasterio de Santa Clara," 1633.

13. Archivo General de la Nación (Perú), Protocolos, Sebastián Muñoz, 1643–45 (February–March 1645), no. 1192, "Fundación de capellanía, doña Francisca de Aguilar, monja en Santa Clara." On Masses in the cathedral, see Echave y Assu, *La estrella de Lima*, 72–75.

14. J. P. Tardieu, "Genio y semblanza del santo varón limeño de origen africano (Fray Martín de Porras)," *Hispania Sacra* 45 (1993): 572.

SUGGESTED READINGS

Amaya Fernández Fernández et al., *La mujer en la conquista y la evangelización en el Perú* (Lima, 1997), includes a brief biography of Ursula de Jesús. Luis Martín's *Daughters of the Conquistadores* (Albuquerque, NM, 1993) provides an insightful overview of convent life in the Viceroyalty of Peru. Kathryn Burns treats the economic and social realities of Cuzco's nuns in idem, *Colonial Habits: Convents and the Spiritual Economy of Cuzco, Peru* (Durham, NC, 1999). Nancy E. van Deusen's *Between the Sacred and the Worldly: Recogimiento in Colonial Lima* (Stanford, CA, 2001), and Fernando Iwasaki, "Mujeres al borde de la perfección," *Hispanic American Historical Review* 73:4 (1993): 581–613, both examine forms of spiritual expression among women in seventeenth-century Lima. The best monograph on slavery in colonial Lima is Frederick Bowser, *The African Slave in Colonial Peru, 1524–1650* (Stanford, CA, 1974).

Both English- and Spanish-language excerpts of female spiritual writings in Peru, Mexico, and Spain are provided in Electa Arenal and Stacey Schlau, eds., *Untold Sisters: Hispanic Nuns in Their Own Works* (Albuquerque,

NM, 1989); and Asunción Lavrin gives a general overview of Latin American female spirituality in "Women and Religion in Spanish America," in Rosemary Radford Ruether and Rosemary Skinner Keller, eds., *Women and Religion in America*, vol. 2, *The Colonial and Revolutionary Periods* (New York, 1983), 42–78, which includes a translation of the life of the mulatta terciary, Estefanía de San Joseph. Finally, Jacques Le Goff's *The Birth of Purgatory* (Chicago,1986) and Gil Fernández Martínez's *Muerte y sociedad* (Madrid, 1993) enable the reader to understand the medieval and early modern European attitudes toward death and the afterlife that influenced Ursula and other visionaries.

CHAPTER 7

Zumbi of Palmares

Challenging the Portuguese Colonial Order

MARY KARASCH

Sugar exports fueled the economy of Portuguese Brazil in the seventeenth century, and as profits from European sales increased, sugar planters imported more slave labor, especially from Angola. These enslaved Africans proved to be a more efficient, productive labor force than the Amerindians. Large sugar plantations dotted the landscape in the Northeast, sometimes employing hundreds of slaves who planted the crop, cut the cane, and processed it into sugar loaves and aguardiente *(white rum) for sale in coastal urban centers, such as Salvador in Bahia and Recife in Pernambuco. Few of these complex operations were entirely self-sufficient in basic supplies (manioc, corn, beans, livestock, etc.), which they bought from farms and ranches in the interior. Finished goods and many artisan products came from the nearest urban marketplace. In short, the economic life of much of coastal Brazil revolved around sugar production, supported first by indigenous and later by a mixture of Amerindian and African slave labor.*

Slaves in Brazil resisted bondage in numerous ways: work slowdowns, sabotaging of machinery or tools, violence, and flight. By the seventeenth century, settlements of fugitive slaves called quilombos *or* mocambos *emerged in the frontier zones. Most of these mocambos in the Northeast were small encampments, but one settlement, called Palmares, developed into an independent confederation of eleven towns that spanned the rugged frontier zones in the states of Alagoas and Pernambuco. At its peak, Palmares was an autonomous state, based on African political and religious customs, with between 20,000 and 30,000 inhabitants. Probably founded in the 1590s after a slave revolt, the eleven mocambos of Palmares survived for one hundred years supported by agriculture, fishing, hunting and gathering, trade, and raiding nearby Luso-Brazilian settlements and plantations. The Portuguese and the Dutch mounted many expeditions to conquer Palmares, but each suffered defeat by its determined defenders. The final, successful assault on Palmares took place in 1694, when a Luso-Brazilian force of over 1,000 men encircled the main mocambo of Macaco, battered down its walls with artillery, and then captured and looted the town. The smaller, weaker mocambos also fell to the attackers, who took the few surviving captives to sell as slaves in Rio de Janeiro. For the Portuguese, Palmares represented not only a military danger but also a bea-*

con to all slaves intent on resisting colonial authority. Such a threat to the social and political order was unacceptable and had to be destroyed, regardless of the cost.

The most famous "Great Chief" or king of the Palmares confederation was Zumbi, who forcibly overthrew his predecessor, Ganga Zumba, for failing to mount an effective resistance against the Portuguese. Although Zumbi was born in Palmares, he was captured by a military expedition and raised in Porto Calvo by a Catholic priest, Antônio Melo, who baptized the boy and taught him both Latin and Portuguese. At fifteen, however, he ran away and returned to Palmares, where he ultimately usurped the position of Great Chief from Ganga Zumba in 1677. Given the scarcity of women in Palmares, many females had multiple husbands, but leaders such as Zumbi could have one or more wives of their own. Indeed, popular traditions record that Zumbi's wife was dona Maria, a white woman captured from her father's sugar plantation by a raiding party from the federation. Nevertheless, upon becoming the king of Palmares, Zumbi became a formidable political and military leader convinced that peace with the Portuguese promised only betrayal and enslavement. As a result, he fought off each Portuguese and Brazilian military expedition sent against Palmares until the final, successful conquest of Macaco in 1694. Zumbi escaped the carnage following the capture of Macaco only to fall into an ambush in November 1695; his body was mutilated and his severed head was displayed in Recife. Although Palmares and its most famous leader had perished and the Portuguese colonial notion of order had prevailed, Zumbi's memory continued to inspire all those who sought freedom in Brazil.

Mary Karasch is professor of history at Oakland University in Rochester, Michigan. She is a noted authority on slavery in Brazil and received her doctorate at the University of Wisconsin. Professor Karasch has written numerous articles in her field and is the author of a seminal book on Brazilian slavery, Slave Life in Rio de Janeiro (1987).

Mythic hero, or traitorous enemy? Zumbi of Palmares is a man of legend celebrated in the movie *Quilombo* and honored by Afro-Brazilians every year in November. He was born in 1655 and died resisting capture in 1695. His life and the drama of Palmares, which have been told and retold in Brazil for centuries, have inspired generations of slaves and their descendants. It is one of the defining moments in colonial Brazilian history that reveals both the order—that is, the colonial system and its profound inequities—and the disorder (in the view of the Portuguese) of the slaves who escaped their world of *engenhos* (sugar plantations) and *senzalas* (slave barracks). In contrast, however, I would argue that the order was in Palmares and the disorder was on the coast, as fugitive slaves re-created in the forested hillsides of Palmares their own autonomous society, free of slavery and of Portuguese colonialism. This essay will first, define *quilombos*; second, describe Palmares before the revolt that brought Zumbi to power; and third, assess the role of Zumbi in the final years of Palmares before its destruction by the great army of the 1690s. It will conclude with the elevation of Zumbi to a national hero who inspires those who struggle against or endure the legacies of slavery in modern Brazil. In myth and popular belief, Zumbi has not died but lives on to continue the struggle of his people.

Wherever slavery existed in colonial Brazil, settlements of fugitive slaves were sure to be nearby. They came to be called *quilombos* from the Jaga term (*ki-lombo*) for a fortified camp in Angola, and their inhabitants *quilombolas*. An alternate term, *mocambo*, derives from *mukambu* in Quimbundo, another Angolan language. In the case of Palmares, as in much of the Northeast, the more common usage was *mocambo*. They were often no more than small encampments where a group of slaves could hide out from their masters and overseers. Others grew to considerable size under the leadership of kings or queens. Those that existed on the fringes of plantations or mining camps sometimes served as temporary respites where slaves could escape from work for a brief period before being returned to the rigors of life as a slave.

Palmares, however, was different. It evolved into an autonomous community in the interior of the states of Alagoas and Pernambuco and posed a military threat, especially under Zumbi, to Portuguese colonial society on the coast. Its very success challenged the colonial order on the coast in a way that no other mocambo had ever done, and its destruction, so the Portuguese hoped, would deter all other such attempts in the interior of Brazil. But they were wrong. Slaves did not give up the struggle for freedom and formed quilombos as long as slavery lasted, or they learned from the brutal destruction of Palmares to remain hidden and preserve their autonomy in secret until discovered by the outside world a century after the abolition of slavery in 1888. They could escape destruction because they either settled in remote regions of Brazil, such as Kalunga in Central Brazil or the quilombos of the Amazon region and Mato Grosso, or they remained small and did not pose a military threat.

In contrast, Palmares was both remote from the coast yet close enough for expeditions to reach it. The mocambo took its name from a region where palm trees were plentiful—that is, *palmeiras* (palm groves) in Portuguese. A seventeenth-century description suggests why fugitives took refuge there. It was "a naturally rugged site, mountainous and forested," where the light could not penetrate and lush vegetation impeded one's steps and obscured the trunks of trees.[1] The tangled forests were penetrated by numerous rivers, which provided secure sources of water, even in the dry season. In addition to the hostile vegetation, Palmares included a series of tall mountains with sharp escarpments. One of them was shaped like a stomach (*barriga*); hence it was named the Serra da Barriga, from which the inhabitants were able to view the region all around for a great distance and flee to the interior upon the approach of a hostile expedition. In the Serra da Barriga of what is now the modern state of Alagoas, formerly a part of the captaincy of Pernambuco in the colonial period, was constructed the principal mocambo of Palmares known as Macaco.

The chroniclers do not document when the first fugitive slaves fled to the Serra da Barriga. Décio Freitas, one of the historians of Palmares, argues that the first to establish themselves in a mocambo were a group of fugitives from a sugar plantation in the south of the captaincy of Pernambuco at the end of the sixteenth century. They had risen in revolt and killed their masters and overseers. If Freitas is correct, then Palmares began in a slave revolt of the late sixteenth century. When they chose to flee to the interior, these runaways were invading unknown lands, reputedly controlled by hostile Indian nations. What they found, however, in the Serra da Barriga was a terrain so difficult that even the Indians avoided it. According to tradition, about forty fugitives made it to the mountains and there built the first thatched-roof huts.[2] Their daring brought them freedom, and this generation died as free men who never again had to work on a sugar plantation.

The ancestors who began Palmares forged a new society in the mountain fortress. Reconstructing its "golden age" before the 1670s, when internal dissension combined with destructive expeditions led to disaster, is somewhat difficult because historians are dependent on outsider accounts and/or popular traditions. At the beginning of the seventeenth century, aggrieved planters began to complain about the blacks of the Serra da Barriga who were raiding their plantations for women. Not only did they capture black women but also white women and their daughters, *mulatas* (women of mixed African and European ancestry), and Indian women. Some women, however, may have fled voluntarily to escape abusive spouses and masters or, in the case of at least one prostitute, life on the streets of Recife. Since their numbers were small in the early seventeenth century, the men of Palmares also recruited other men to join them, including Portuguese soldiers who were fleeing forced recruitment. Whether plantation slaves were stolen, as in the Luso-Brazilian traditions, or voluntarily opted for freedom is unclear from the sources. There is no doubt, however, that recruiting through either capture or persuasion was a marked feature of the early period in the history of Palmares. In 1597 a Jesuit priest complained that the "first enemies are the blacks of Guiné [Africa] in revolt, who are in some mountains, from where they come to make assaults and give some work."[3]

As they recruited their new members, the black, mulatto, Indian, and white inhabitants of Palmares created an economy based on subsistence agriculture, trade, and raiding. The first Palmarinos may have lived by hunting, fishing, and gathering palm products and cultivating the small plots of land they planted with corn and manioc, but as the settlement evolved, so too did the diversity of economic activities needed to sustain thousands of people. The basic communal principle that challenged Portuguese mercantile and capitalist ideals on the coast was that all property belonged to the mocambo, with the exception of one's own personal property. As a spy reported, "Everything was [belonged to] of all and nothing was of no one." In other words, as Freitas concludes, "the palmarino blacks had created a communitarian economy of self-subsistence."[4]

Families received the land on the condition that they give any surplus to the community. To obtain access to land, one had to belong to the community of the mocambo; later they had to be a part of a particular polyandrous family. A new recruit had to submit to a long period of trial, including raiding and capturing a replacement for himself, after which he would be incorporated into a family and given access to land. Men were the labor force; women were the ones who organized and supervised the work as "chiefs of the family." Each woman might have as many as four or five husbands who labored for her and their household, which was obviously an inversion of patriarchal Luso-Brazilian society on the coast.

The basis of the economy was agriculture. Two weeks before planting began, the families cleared the fields using the techniques of slash-and-burn agriculture, although the burnings must have announced their presence to neighbors and expedition leaders. Working together, they tilled the fields, planted the seeds, and harvested the crops. Because the soil was so fertile, they could plant two crops of corn each year. Their workday comprised six hours from dawn to noon as opposed to the twelve- to eighteen-hour days on coastal plantations. At the end of the harvest, they feasted and danced for a week. Their labor was not devoted to Europe's consumers of sugar but to their families. They harvested food crops—that is, corn, beans, manioc, sugarcane, and sweet potatoes. Any surplus was deposited in a warehouse located in the center of the town for the benefit of the mocambo—its chiefs and warriors, its children, the old, and the sick. They also set aside a surplus for emergencies, especially drought and external attacks. Additional foodstuffs were traded to nearby planters for manufactured items that they could not make themselves.

They also exploited tree crops, especially bananas. They planted orchards of fruit-bearing trees such as mangoes, which must have provided them with vitamin-rich fruits and fruit drinks. They also harvested the rich resources of the palm trees. They ate the palm fruit with manioc flour or made it into an oil to be used in lamps or as butter. They even ate the large worms that lived on the trees. With palm leaves they covered their houses and wove mats and baskets. For their clothing they wove cloth from tree bark and used the husk of the palm fruit to make pipes. They undoubtedly enjoyed palm wine as they smoked their pipes.

For animal protein, they hunted and fished and raised chickens and pigs but did not raise cattle, which suggests that pastures were unavailable or that they easily acquired beef by raiding or trading for cattle with nearby ranchers. The chroniclers certainly complained about the blacks of Palmares killing cattle. The quality of their diet was reflected in their fine physical shape. When the captives from Palmares were paraded through the towns, the malnourished poor marveled at their health and strength.

Sometime after settling in the mountains, Palmarinos solved one of the most difficult challenges that faced quilombolas—that is, obtaining iron and weapons. Initially, they raided nearby plantations for iron weapons and tools, but they soon found a source of iron ore, which they mined. Since many Africans had worked iron before their enslavement in Brazil, they undoubtedly applied their knowledge to iron mining and smithing. In the Serra da Barriga, they placed the forge next to their religious "temple" and council house, which suggests an African religious attitude toward the significance of iron. Although they were unable to make firearms, they could meet most of their needs for tools and weapon points. They also acquired firearms and gunpowder in tribute from the whites whom they permitted to live on their lands. Their ceramics included Amerindian pots and jars and Delftware imported from Holland.[5] They also used hammocks and carved objects of wood.

What they could not make, they then had to acquire by trade or raid. The Palmarinos not only traded their surplus foodstuffs for guns and salt but also for manufactured goods. Since sugar planters tended to focus on monoculture and did not plant enough food for their slaves, the Palmarinos ran a thriving trade in corn and manioc with nearby planters who protected them, since they were dependent on Palmares for food for their slaves. Portuguese complaints about the white protectors and tributaries of Palmares help to document the ways in which it was linked to the local economy. Its residents did not live in isolation or avoid contact and relations with whites.

In this way, the people of Palmares lived by agriculture, fishing, hunting and gathering, trade, and raiding for an entire century. They were able to exploit the same environment without exhausting their food sources while at the same time increasing their population size. Furthermore, they were able to produce a sufficient surplus to maintain a political and military elite and militia forces that defended their towns from attack. They even had settlers who lived on their lands and paid them tribute. Zumbi was supported from this surplus, and he and his people may have suffered from hunger only in time of war, drought, or crop failures.

The culture and society of Palmares are more difficult to describe. According to Governor Francisco de Brito Freire, they spoke their own new language, which at times appeared to be from Guiné or Angola, or Portuguese, or Tupi, a coastal Indian language. Whites could not understand their language and had to speak to them through interpreters.[6] How those interpreters had learned the Palmarino language is uncertain, but Zumbi could also speak Portuguese and knew Latin. He would not have needed an interpreter to communicate directly with the Portuguese.

Just as their language was a mixture—apparently a creole language— cultural traits appear to have been drawn from both the Africans and Amerindians. The majority were black men who were increasingly removed from their African traditions as the generations passed, although new runaway Africans tended to reinforce some cultural traditions. Amerindian captive women brought their languages and cultures and undoubtedly transmitted them to their children and grandchildren. The central position of women in Palmares must have tended to reinforce the Amerindian influence. The fabrication of ceramics in Amerindian forms and designs is suggestive of the strength of their culture.

Since women were rare, especially at first, and highly valued, the Palmarinos evolved codes of conduct around polyandrous marriages to avoid constant fighting over women. The polyandrous family was the basic social unit of Palmares, and family relationships were established through the maternal line. The best surviving description of the polyandrous households of Palmares derives from a document of 1677, which gives a summary of a spy's report. He had lived among the Palmarinos for six months.

> Each black who arrives at the mocambo [who has] fled from his masters is soon heard by the council of justice, which has to know his intentions because they are greatly distrusting, nor are they trusting solely due to the fact of being [a] black who presents himself; that as soon as they certify the good intentions of the black who comes, they give him [a] wife which he possesses along with other blacks, two, three, four, and five blacks, since [there] being few women they adopt this style to avoid conflicts; that all the husbands of the same wife live with her [in] the same mocambo, all in peace

and harmony, in imitation of a family, . . . that all these husbands are obedient to [the] woman who orders all in life as in work; that to each of these families the chiefs [*maiorais*], in council, give a piece of land to cultivate, and that the woman and her husbands do; . . . that in war they impress all in the moments of greatest need, without exception of the women who on those occasions appear more like *feras* [wild animals] than persons of their [own] sex.[7]

On the coast of Brazil, this lifestyle stood in marked contrast to the patriarchal planter-dominated society in which powerful white men lorded it over large households of women, including a wife, mistresses, and numerous slave concubines. Zumbi's mother may have ordered her household of men and children before losing her newborn to raiders from the coast, or she may have been one of the wives in a chiefly household, since the chiefs were permitted to have more than one woman. Ganga Zumba, Zumbi's predecessor, had three: a mulata and two black women. The children born in the quilombo of polyandrous or polygynous marriages never knew slavery. Zumbi, however, was the exception because he had been born free in Palmares but was then raised in the household of a Catholic priest after he had been stolen away.

The religion practiced in Palmares is uncertain, but it is unlikely to have been that of the *orixás* found in Candomblé, a contemporary Afro-Brazilian religion. Due to the slave trade from Congo-Angola to Brazil after 1580, the majority of Palmarinos were probably Central Africans. According to tradition, the first fugitives to settle Palmares were Angolans.[8] There was also a minority of slaves imported in that period from what are now the modern countries of Ghana and Benin. Ganga Zumba was an Ardra from the slave coast, and he may have followed practices more similar to Dahomeian Vodun. Zumbi had been raised Catholic by a priest, as had other Palmarinos who kept statues of Jesus Christ, Our Lady of the [Immaculate] Conception, and St. Brás in the "church" in the largest mocambo of Palmares in 1645. There are references to priests and to non-Christian religious specialists at Palmares, and even the name Ganga Zumba suggests *nganga*, a common term for a religious specialist in Central Africa. Did Zumbi continue to practice some, if not all, of his Catholic beliefs, or did he abandon them for the new religion he found in Palmares, which may have been a mixture of Central African, Christian, and Amerindian religious traditions? There is one glimpse in the documents of a young Zumbi continuing to maintain a relationship with the priest who had raised him in his household, risking capture on three separate occasions to bring him gifts. Were Zumbi's furtive visits those of an adopted son to a beloved father, or as a Christian to a respected priest? Or was there a forbidden sexual relationship between the priest and the young Zumbi? Because of his capture at an early age and his intensive education in Portuguese, Latin, and Church teachings, apparently Zumbi's religious formation was Luso-Brazilian in contrast to the more African and Amerindian quilombolas. On the other hand, he clearly chose a Central African name with religious and chiefly connotations after he was free to do so.[9]

Those who followed the more African religious traditions in Palmares were undoubtedly concerned with protection and security. Shrines with statues, amulets, and charms may have been common. Religious specialists would have been needed to protect the Palmarinos from spiritual harm, but they did not rely solely on spiritual safeguards. They fortified their towns with walls of wood or stone, and in time of war with tall palisades and hidden traps with sharp pointed poles that impaled men and horses. Before the Dutch invasion, the Palmarinos had a great council that met in the council house and elected a chief or a maioral, who had many powers but not the absolute ones of a hereditary king or dictator. The most crucial decisions were resolved in a popular assembly. Thus, the early image of the leader of Palmares is of a nonhereditary and elected chief who had to consult an assembly. His subjects were few—perhaps no more than 1,000 in the Serra da Barriga in the 1630s. All this changed, however, with the Dutch invasion, which transformed the colonial Northeast and enabled thousands of slaves to flee to Palmares. Zumbi was born a year after the expulsion of the Dutch in 1654, and he entered a more complex society—that is, a confederation of town-sized mocambos led by the Great Chief, Ganga Zumba, in the 1670s. Under his leadership, Palmares had grown to enormous size. Macaco had 8,000 inhabitants, while Amaro may have had 5,000. Some 20,000 to 30,000 men, women, and children may have lived in the eleven mocambos of Palmares.[10]

The personal history of Zumbi of Palmares begins shortly after the expulsion of the Dutch from Pernambuco in 1654. A year later the governor of Pernambuco sent an expedition against Palmares. Confident in having defeated a powerful European enemy, the Portuguese governor commissioned Brás da Rocha Cardoso to lead an expedition of 600 men to eliminate their "internal enemy" who had grown in strength and numbers during the Dutch wars. Although the expedition of 1655 failed to destroy Palmares, the troops took prisoners, including a newborn who was only a few days old. The little boy was given as a present to a Portuguese parish priest, Antônio Melo, who served in the district of Porto Calvo until he returned to Portugal in 1682. The priest baptized the child Francisco and later taught him to read. By the age of ten, the boy knew both Latin and Portuguese. Until age fifteen, Francisco lived in a clerical household as the priest's servant and assisted him in his religious duties, such as saying Mass. Many priests in the colonial period maintained large households that included slave women, and some may have cared for Francisco and imparted their values and religious beliefs. At the same time, the priest undoubtedly taught him Catholicism. The young Francisco may have absorbed both Afro-Brazilian and Portuguese beliefs and expressed them as an altar boy. The traditions do not make it clear whether the priest treated him kindly as an adopted son or badly as a captive.

Suddenly and inexplicably the teenager fled the life that he had known and took refuge in Palmares in 1670 at the age of fifteen. The reasons are uncertain. Had he continued to maintain contact with the people of Palmares and with his mother's family during the long years of exile as a priest's servant? Or had a particular act of cruelty or racial discrimination led him to flee the slave society of the coast? A more sinister motive is hinted at in a denunciation registered with the Inquisition. The charge against Padre Melo was sodomy. Did the young Francisco flee to escape unwanted homosexual abuse?[11] The latter theory seems unlikely because Zumbi later returned at the risk of his own life to give presents to Padre Melo, which suggests that he was fond of his adopted father. Because Padre Melo maintained a relationship with Zumbi until his return to Portugal, his enemies may have falsely denounced him to the Inquisition to ruin his reputation. Nevertheless, by 1685, Zumbi had a wife and children. According to popular traditions from Alagoas, his wife was dona Maria, a white woman who was the daughter of a sugar planter of Porto Calvo and who had been captured by the Palmarinos. When the theatrical dance of Quilombo is performed in Alagoas, she appears as Zumbi's queen, who at the end of the performance is handed over to an influential white man after the destruction of Palmares. Oral traditions suggest that within Palmares she had become a person of stature, who was no longer held against her will. When whites raided quilombos elsewhere in Brazil and discovered captive white women, they returned them to their families. Instead, Zumbi's wife (and his children?) were treated like fugitive slaves. Otherwise the usual sources do not refer to her except in one letter in which the Portuguese offered freedom to Zumbi, his wife, and children if he would make peace.[12]

Except for the brief visits to the priest who raised him, Francisco's future lay with Palmares. Perhaps because of his knowledge of the outside world as well as his literacy skills, he rose rapidly within the mocambo of Osenga, located near Porto Calvo. Two years after his return to Palmares, he was elected maioral. Reflecting his reintegration into Palmarino society, he changed his name to Zumbi and his mocambo was renamed Zumbi. At eighteen years of age in 1673, he led a force that defeated an expedition led by Antônio Jácome Bezerra and achieved the rank of *cabo de guerra*. Two to three years later in 1676, he courageously resisted the attack of the expedition of 280 men led by Major Manuel

Lopes, who invaded and burned one of the mocambos that then had 2,000 houses. The Palmarinos suffered heavy losses, and Zumbi was wounded in the leg. After this battle, one chronicler described him as "crippled."[13] In spite of that setback, it took him only four years more to become the general commander of the Palmarino militia forces as general of arms (*mestre de campo*). Zumbi thus led the militia forces when they confronted the expedition of Fernão Carrilho, which killed so many Palmarinos in 1677.

The former altar boy had quickly earned the trust and respect of the Palmarinos for his leadership abilities, but where had they come from? Padre Melo testified to his intelligence in a letter he wrote about Zumbi, but who had trained him to lead men into battle? The sources are silent. His political skills, however, were honed when he challenged Ganga Zumba, the chief of the mocambo of Macaco and Great Chief of the confederation of mocambos. Although the Portuguese called him *rei* (king), Ganga Zumba had to consult a council composed of the chiefs and cabos de guerra of each mocambo. Zumbi, in the role of chief of his mocambo, must have participated in the deliberations of the council. As a cabo de guerra, he was also subject to the commander-general of the militia. Since Ganga Zumba's powers were not absolute nor based on hereditary rights, he ruled at the wishes of the Council of Chiefs. In order to survive, the Palmarinos required a strong political and military leader able to mobilize the people in defense of Palmares. If he failed or showed weakness, the very existence of Palmares would be threatened.

The threat came in the powerful expedition of Fernão Carrilho, who attacked Palmares in 1677, killing many, wounding Ganga Zumba, capturing Field Commander Ganga Muiça, and taking numerous captives back to slavery on the coast. His people blamed Ganga Zumba for this disaster, accusing him of being drunk when he commanded one of the military forces. In all of the mocambos, except for Macaco, popular assemblies called for Ganga Zumba's removal. When the great council in Macaco took up the question, Zumbi assumed a leadership role and spoke for the opposition. He denounced Ganga Zumba for "military ineptitude" and corruption and used his oratorical skills to wage a "legal" battle to remove him. In spite of his efforts, however, he lost. Ganga Zumba remained as Great Chief of Palmares to the distress of those who feared the consequences of his inept leadership.

The opposition (possibly led by Zumbi) soon began to conspire to remove him by force. Learning of the plot against him, Ganga Zumba struck first by deciding to make peace with the governor of Pernambuco. He sent to Recife a delegation that included two of his sons to ask for "peace and friendship." In the words of an anonymous chronicler,

The appearance of those barbarians caused amazement, because they came naked, and with their natural parts alone covered. Some wore their beards in braids, others wore false beards and mustaches, and others were shaved, and nothing more. All were husky and powerful, armed with bows and arrows, and carrying only one firearm. One of the king's sons rode a horse because he still bore an open bullet wound that he had received during the fighting.[14]

The peace accords negotiated in 1678 included the provisions that those who made peace would receive lands at Cucaú and be able to trade openly with their neighbors, and that all blacks born in Palmares were free vassals of the king of Portugal. But the price for peace and the right to occupy Cucaú was Ganga Zumba's agreement "to return all the runaways who had come from our populated places."[15] Since native-born Palmarinos had ties of friendship and family with the former slaves who had joined them, they feared that their family members and friends would be forced back into slavery on the coast. The peace accords thus cost Ganga Zumba majority support. Only 300 to 400 persons agreed to follow him to Cucaú, where he established a separate community under Portuguese "protection."

With Ganga Zumba no longer resident in Macaco, Zumbi seized the initiative. Using the militia forces of his mocambo, he moved against the mocambos that had remained loyal to Ganga Zumba. Some he took by force of arms, others by the power of persuasion. After consolidating his power over the other mocambos, he unified all adult men into a great army that then conquered Macaco, an easy victory because Ganga Zumba and his followers had retreated to Cucaú. With Ganga Zumba isolated and defeated, the Great Council then elected Zumbi as the head of the confederation of mocambos. What Zumbi had achieved was a palace coup in which he had seized upon popular discontent to organize militia forces that had unseated an unpopular ruler. His daring victory was then legitimized by the Great Council.

As Zumbi consolidated his power in Macaco and prepared for future wars, Ganga Zumba's people faced incursions on their land by white planters seeking their fugitive slaves. Supporters of Zumbi in Cucaú also plotted to seize weapons and foodstuffs to take to the defense of Palmares; but when they were discovered, they struck first, poisoning Ganga Zumba and killing his principal advisers. The Portuguese then took advantage of the conflict to repress Zumbi's supporters in Cucaú and executed four of the principal conspirators and enslaved 200 others. Ganga Zumba's attempt to live at peace in Cucaú in the midst of a slave society had divided the people of Palmares and ended tragically with his death in 1680.

Perhaps Zumbi and the Palmarinos concluded that to make peace was to be betrayed and enslaved. Why they henceforth fought the Portuguese and the planters so tenaciously may have been due to the terrible lessons learned at Cucaú: the Portuguese were not to be trusted, and to live in peace with them would only lead to enslavement. To preserve their freedom, they had to resist and fight for their people and their own way of life. What is clear from the documentation is that a newly unified and revived Palmares under the leadership of Zumbi took the offensive. Troops of forty to fifty men attacked plantations and towns, carrying off slaves, foodstuffs, and weapons. One wonders if they particularly raided plantations where their former comrades had been reenslaved. Not even the great sugar mill owners were safe from attack as they traveled from the coast to their plantations. For a period of thirteen years (1680–1693), Luso-Brazilian expeditions were ineffectual in stopping Palmarino attacks. Troops raised by forced recruitment in Bahia and Pernambuco were unable (or unwilling?) to defeat the Palmarinos. Thus, Zumbi and his people lived in freedom because they were able to defeat militarily all the small expeditions sent against them.[16] In 1685 the king of Portugal tried to make peace with Zumbi and offered to pardon him if he would move to an *estancia* (ranch) with his wife, children, and captains, where they would receive royal protection from enslavement. Was Zumbi tempted to abandon his people? We can only judge from his behavior, because he continued to fight and did not make peace.[17]

That same year of 1685, Zumbi was helped by a great epidemic of yellow fever that struck coastal Brazil for the first time. The severity of its impact on Europeans meant that the colonial forces were unable to organize large expeditions. The year 1690, however, marked a shift in government policy from the support of small, poorly trained, and badly organized forces to the recruitment and provisioning of an enormous expedition designed to conquer Palmares and enslave its people. To attract men, the government promised the lands of Palmares to the victors.

First, the government ordered convoys of foodstuffs sent to Porto Calvo, the town where Zumbi had been raised. From there, they constructed a road to move oxcarts of supplies to the Serra da Barriga. A month later 3,000 unruly recruits arrived, including prisoners from the jails of Recife, whites, Indians, *mamelucos* (mestizos), and even blacks organized in Henriques regiments. By the time that they had gathered all of the men together, they had raised an army of 9,000, the largest ever put together in the colonial period. Included in this great army were the men from São Paulo (Paulistas), who were led by Domingos Jorge Velho. Thus, Zumbi and the Palmarinos were to face an army larger than the

Dutch had sent to capture Pernambuco.[18] Unfortunately, the documents do not reveal the size of Zumbi's army.

The final assault on Palmares began with an attack of 1,000 men led by Domingos Jorge Velho, but Zumbi and his men easily repulsed them. The governor of Pernambuco then sent Bernardo Vieira de Melo to re-inforce them. Once again, Zumbi and his troops defeated them. Palmares was then protected by hidden shafts that killed men who fell into them as well as by a great palisade that encircled the defenders of Macaco. On January 5, 1694, as Zumbi went to inspect the fortifications of Macaco, he saw the approaching artillery of the huge expedition. According to tradition, he questioned the sentry who had failed to warn the people of the army's approach: "And you let the whites encircle us? Tomorrow we will be invaded, and dead, and our wives, and children [will be] captives." He then ordered the negligent sentry executed and convened his war council.[19]

Meanwhile, the great army was attempting to surround Macaco, and cut off all routes of escape. While the army closed in, the people of Macaco slipped out in the early morning at about 2:00 A.M. All but the rear guard led by Zumbi had left the town when a sentry spied the fleeing Palmarinos and opened fire. Zumbi and about 500 men then fought desperately at the edge a steep precipice in the black of night. In the confusion, many tumbled over the side while the fortunate ones escaped to the forest, but so many had been wounded that their flowing blood "served as [a] guide to our troops." The survivors were then hunted down by the troops of Vieira de Melo, who reported killing 200 men, only saving the lives of the women.[20]

At dawn the artillery batteries broke the walls of Macaco and the troops sacked the town, killing any of the defenders who remained. According to Frei Loreto de Couto, the troops advanced on Macaco "cutting and killing all they met" until there was no place to put all the bodies. Only 510 captives survived to be taken and divided as slaves among the victors in Porto Calvo. Macaco itself was looted and burned. After Macaco's destruction, the victorious army fell on the weaker mocambos and continued to kill the men and capture the women and children. Few of them lived, however, because the mothers killed their children so they would not be enslaved and afterwards starved themselves to death. Eighty of the survivors were sold as slaves to Rio de Janeiro.[21]

The victorious troops returned to the coast with their captives and left the Paulista Domingos Jorge Velho to "clean up." Rather than pursue the fugitives from Palmares, he seems to have furthered his own interests by "acquiring" cattle from nearby ranches and contrabanding captive blacks for sale in Bahia. Meanwhile, Zumbi could not be found. Somehow he had escaped the slaughter at Macaco with perhaps 200 of his people. At this time, he remained hidden in an effort to regroup his small band of men.

Once the governor learned that Zumbi had escaped, he put a price on his head. However, Zumbi continued to raid for arms and ammunition. He was seen at the town of Penedo and recognized by the scars from his wounds. Nonetheless, he and his men remained in the area of Penedo. One of his principal lieutenants was a mulatto named Antônio Soares of Recife, who was captured on one of the raids. A Paulista and his men tortured him to reveal Zumbi's hiding place. Although Soares initially refused to inform on Zumbi, he yielded after receiving the promise of his life and his freedom and led the Paulistas to the forests, possibly in the Serra Dois Irmãos. At dawn, Soares left the forest and called out, "Zumbi! Zumbi! Zumbi!" When Zumbi appeared, Soares walked up to him like Judas going up to Christ. Rather than kiss him, however, he plunged a dagger into his stomach.[22]

Although severely wounded, Zumbi fought valiantly, as did his companions who came to his aid. Only one of them survived. Zumbi died in the fighting on November 20, 1695. The Paulista and his men delivered his "small and thin body" to the officials of the City Council of Porto Calvo. An examination revealed fifteen gunshot wounds and innumerable blows from other weapons; after his death he had been castrated and mutilated. The last degredation by his enemies occurred in a public ceremony in Porto Calvo, where his head was cut off and taken to Recife, where the governor had it displayed on a pole in a public place. His objective was to destroy the belief that Zumbi was immortal. The mulatto Soares received his reward of a pardon, ratified by the Overseas Council in 1696, and lived to an advanced age in Recife.[23]

Zumbi's betrayal and death, however, did not eliminate his influence or appeal to the slaves of Brazil and their descendants. Some of his followers who escaped the destruction of Palmares continued to live freely in quilombos, and the memory of Zumbi and Palmares led slaves to flee to quilombos as long as the institution existed in Brazil. Unlike Palmares, however, many remained hidden and unconquered, and their descendants lived in freedom until discovered in the twentieth century. They now claim rights to lands given to them by the Constitution of 1988.

In the cities of contemporary Brazil, Afro-Brazilians celebrate Zumbi's life and honor his memory each year on November 20. He has become the epic hero of Afro-Brazilians who celebrate his courage, leadership qualities, and heroic resistance. On the other hand, many in Brazil ignore him. One senses a reluctance to make him a national hero because he and the Palmarinos offered a direct challenge to Luso-Brazilian life and culture as well as to the colonial order. A society in which women organized the households, the people worked on a communal basis, and elected black leaders governed a multiracial society that included tributary whites was the opposite of the colonial society on the coast. Zumbi was a powerful black leader who had defeated numerous Luso-Brazilian expeditions, and Luso-Brazilian authorities who had imposed a patriarchal, racially stratified, and inequitable colonial order on the coast could not tolerate such a man. Perhaps the former altar boy fought so valiantly for his people because he knew both worlds—the world of slavery and racial discrimination in which he had been raised, and the world of freedom and autonomy to which he escaped at the age of fifteen.

NOTES

1. Décio Freitas, *Zumbi dos Palmares* (Luanda: Ministério da Cultura, 1996), 7. My thanks to Flávio dos Santos Gomes for this reference.

2. Ibid., 7–8.

3. Ivan Alves Filho, *Memorial dos Palmares* (Rio de Janeiro: Xenon Editora, 1988), 5.

4. Freitas, *Zumbi*, 10.

5. The evidence for Amerindian and European pottery in Palmares is from the archaeological investigations reported by Pedro Paulo de Abreu Funari, "A arqueologia de Palmares," in *Liberdade por um fio: História dos quilombos no Brasil*, ed. João José Reis and Flávio dos Santos Gomes (São Paulo: Companhia das Letras, 1996), 26–51. This chapter also includes maps and the only known picture of Palmares from 1647 (p. 33).

6. Freitas, *Zumbi*, 12.

7. Ibid., 11–12.

8. For Angolans as fugitives, see Ernesto Ennes, *As Guerras nos Palmares* (São Paulo: Companhia Editora Nacional, 1938), 24.

9. Freitas, *Zumbi*, 21.

10. Ibid., 15–16. Freitas believes that the total population of the mocambos did not exceed 20,000.

11. My thanks to Matthias Röhrig Assunção in a letter of October 13, 1999, for calling my attention to the *Veja* article of May 24, 1995, on the theory that Zumbi was a homosexual. The historian Luiz Mott located the denunciation of Padre Melo to the Inquisition; but Freitas, while considering the hypothesis "plausible," has not found any allusion to a sexual relationship in the correspondence of Padre Melo.

12. On Zumbi's wife, see "Quilombo" [of Alagoas] in *Dicionário do Folclore Brasileiro*, ed. Luis da Camara Cascudo, 5th ed. (Belo Horizonte: Editora Itatiaia, 1984). A brief and incomplete version in English is " 'White Man Won't Come Here': A Twentieth-Century Folk Memory of Palmares," in *Children of God's Fire: A Documentary History of Black Slavery in Brazil*, ed. Robert E. Conrad (University Park: Pennsylvania State University Press, 1994), 377–79. The document that refers to the peace offer to Zumbi, his wife, and children is reprinted in Décio Freitas, *Palmares: A Guerra dos Escravos*, 3d ed. (Rio de Janeiro: Edições Graal, 1981), 144.

13. Edison Carneiro, *O Quilombo dos Palmares*, 4th ed. (São Paulo: Editora Nacional, 1988; Brasiliana, vol. 302), 40.

14. "The Great Seventeenth-Century *Quilombo* of Palmares: A Chronicle of War and Peace," in Conrad, *Children of God's Fire*, 375.

15. An English summary of the peace treaty and its provisions is in ibid.

16. Carneiro, *Quilombo dos Palmares*, 43–44. He lists at least thirteen expeditions between 1672 and 1694 that Zumbi would have fought against.

17. For the peace offer of the king of Portugal in 1685, see Freitas, *Palmares*, 143–44.

18. Freitas, *Zumbi*, 24.

19. Zumbi's words are recorded in document 54, "Requerimento . . . de todos os officiaes e Soldados do terço de Infataria São Paulista de que hê M.e de Campo Domingos George [*sic*] Velho," in Ennes, *Guerras nos Palmares*, 323.

20. Freitas, *Zumbi*, 25.

21. Ibid.; Carneiro, *Quilombo dos Palmeres*, 163.

22. Freitas, *Zumbi*, 26–27.

23. Ibid., 27.

SUGGESTED READINGS

Four brief biographies of Zumbi are by: Décio Freitas, *Zumbi dos Palmares* (Luanda: Ministério da Cultura, 1996), which is the best; Severino Vicente da Silva, *Zumbi dos Palmares* (São Paulo: Edições Paulinas, 1990); Joel Rufino dos Santos, *Zumbi* (São Paulo: Ed. Moderna, 1985); and Leda Maria de Albuquerque, *Zumbi dos Palmares*, 2d ed. (São Paulo: IBRASA; Brasília: Instituto Nacional do Livro, 1978).

General histories of Palmares, some with published documents, include Jayme de Altavilla, *O Quilombo dos Palmares* (São Paulo: Comp. Melhoramentos, 1931); Ivan Alves Filho, *Memorial dos Palmares* (Rio de Janeiro: Xenon Editora, 1988); Edison Carneiro, *O Quilombo dos Palmares*, 4th ed. (São Paulo: Editora Nacional, 1988; Brasiliana, v. 302); Ernesto Ennes, *As Guerras nos Palmares* (São Paulo: Companhia Editora Nacional, 1938); Décio Freitas, *Palmares: A Guerra dos Escravos*, 3d ed. (Rio de Janeiro: Edições Graal, 1981); and Mário Martins de Freitas, *Reino Negro de Palmares*, 2d ed. (Rio de Janeiro: Biblioteca do Exército, 1988). Additional printed documents on Palmares are in Robert Edgar Conrad, ed., *Children of God's Fire: A Documentary History of Black Slavery in Brazil* (University Park: Pennsylvania State University Press, 1994); and Leonardo Dantas Silva, ed., *Alguns Documentos para a História da Escravidão* (Recife: Editora Massangana, 1988).

On *quilombos* in Brazil see João José Reis and Flávio dos Santos Gomes, eds., *Liberdade por um fio: História dos quilombos no Brasil* (São Paulo: Companhia das Letras, 1996); Richard Price, ed., *Maroon Societies* (Garden City, NY: Anchor Books, 1973); and Stuart B. Schwartz, "Mocambos, Quilombos e Palmares: A Resistência Escrava no Brasil Colonial," *Estudos Eonômicos* 17 (1987): 61–88.

CHAPTER 8

Diego de Ocaña

Holy Wanderer

KENNETH MILLS

Spreading Christianity was central to the Spanish colonial enterprise in the New World, and Roman Catholic clergy founded convents and churches as they sought both to convert the Amerindian population and to police the faith among all Christians. Evangelizing took place not only in major cities such as Lima or Mexico City but also in smaller provincial centers such as Saña, on the north coast of Peru. In the sixteenth century, the rural economy of northern Peru had revolved around the city of Trujillo, yielding bountiful harvests of wheat, corn, beans, rye, grapes, olives, and fruits. Trujillo remained the home of the region's most prominent European families, and it was also the seat of local government, a bishopric, and several important religious houses. By contrast, Saña (founded in 1563) remained a smaller place, nestled among the forbidding sand dunes of the coastal desert, with only a parish church and three convents. Nevertheless, in the seventeenth century Saña experienced greater economic prosperity with the introduction of sugarcane cultivation, which later would become the foundation of the local economy and make it the preeminent city in the region. When the Jeronymite friar Diego de Ocaña visited the area in 1599, however, Saña was still a small provincial city with an ethnically diverse population in need of spiritual guidance and supervision.

The familiar festivals, saints' days, and devotional objects associated with Catholic devotion provided stability and structure to Spanish society in Iberia and the New World, but the crown and clerical authorities believed that they could also pose serious dangers if the laity did not adhere to orthodoxy. The Inquisition policed the actions of all but the native Andean population, but by 1610 the Archbishopric of Lima clerical and lay officials would initiate visitations to the Amerindian parishes to root out or "extirpate" not only lingering pre-Christian religious practices but also what were viewed as errant forms of Christianity. Apart from such direct efforts to maintain the faith, Churchmen also monitored the veneration of holy images such as Our Lady of Guadalupe from Spain or New World devotions such as the Virgin of Copacabana, the original image of which was enshrined in 1583 on the eastern shores of Lake Titicaca in what is today Bolivia. These powerful expressions of faith could win new peoples to Catholicism in the New World, but officials of the Church hierarchy also

121

wanted to ensure that the laity adhered to pure Catholic principles. In the seventeenth-century Spanish empire the lines dividing Church and state remained blurred. For the crown, preserving Roman Catholic orthodoxy formed a bulwark against social disorder and political chaos, particularly in the remote provinces of the Indies.

The mission of the Jeronymite friar, Diego de Ocaña, was designed to advance the spread of an important popular devotion, the "miraculous" sculpted image of the Virgin of Guadalupe from the kingdom of Extremadura in what is today western Spain. Ocaña and his companion, Father Martín de Posada, were sent from Extremadura to the Viceroyalty of Peru as agents (demandadores) *to inspect the cult of the Virgin and to gather alms for the home sanctuary and monastery. Before arriving in Saña on the arid northern coast of Peru, however, the elderly Posada died, leaving Ocaña to carry on their mission alone. Once in Saña, the now hungry and bedraggled friar found a thriving cult of the Guadalupan Virgin in a nearby valley under the supervision of the Augustinian Order, leaving him little hope of controlling devotions to the Virgin at this shrine or seeking alms. Feeling himself divinely inspired, however, Ocaña painted images of the Virgin of Guadalupe, which he hoped would serve as the basis for an authoritative new series of Marian shrines in Peru all providing alms and answering to the Jeronymites at the home shrine in Extremadura. One of his portraits gained fame for its curative powers in Saña and attracted the attention of a covetous and unsavory parish priest who invited the impoverished and near-starving Ocaña to his house. An elaborate negotiation ensued, with the friar torn between his mission of religious control and propriety and his need for food and the means to continue his journey. In the end, Ocaña accepted the wily priest's offer of silver for the portrait, not as payment but as a donation that would allow him to continue his mission throughout the Spanish Indies. Like many devoted religious, Ocaña saw himself as an instrument of divine power, and his retelling of this curious affair displays both his faith and the "playful" influence of the picaresque literature of the day. Further, the author of this chapter contends that Ocaña reveals a special concern that he shared with not a few of his clerical contemporaries—a fear of being ineffectual and forgotten or, even worse, of becoming an inadvertent spark of Christian heterodoxy and error.*

Kenneth Mills is associate professor of history and the director of the Program in Latin American Studies at Princeton University. He took his doctorate at the University of Oxford. He has published numerous articles and has co-edited a popular sourcebook of primary texts and images (with William B. Taylor), Colonial Spanish America: A Documentary History *(1998), a revised edition of which, integrating Portuguese and Brazilian sources with the help of Sandra Lauderdale*

Graham, will be published by Scholarly Resources in 2002. Professor Mills is also the author of An Evil Lost to View? An Investigation of Post-Evangelization Andean Religion in Mid-Colonial Peru *(1994), and the work for which he is best known,* Idolatry and Its Enemies: Colonial Andean Religion and Extirpation, 1640–1750 *(1997).*

𝒟iego de Ocaña was a Castilian and a friar of the Order of Saint Jerome. As an agent of his home-monastery at the sanctuary of a miraculous image of the Virgin Mary, Our Lady of Guadalupe, in the Villuercas mountains of Extremadura in western Spain, he traveled to and through much of Spanish South America between 1599 and 1605, gathering alms, propagating devotion, and recording what he found. Most of what can be learned about Ocaña begins with what he himself wrote, drew, and rendered in watercolor and ink sketches in a cross-genre account of this journey created en route.[1]

Ocaña wrote and sketched principally for his Jeronymite superiors and brethren in Guadalupe, but he also heeded a succession of royal commands for all kinds of information about the Indies "from any person, lay or religious," who traveled there.[2] Thus, significant sections of his manuscript amount to highly purposeful reporting with these religious and imperial interests in mind; Ocaña attempts to bring narrative order both to the series of devotional centers he founded and to his various experiences. That said, his manuscript also has a powerful personal dimension. He was not composing an "autobiography" in the modern sense or even engaged in "life-writing" in the manner of the explorations of self pursued by his saintly contemporaries and their disciples. His kinds of self-revelation emerged more indirectly.

After introducing Diego de Ocaña and his role as a representative of the holy image of Our Lady of Guadalupe, my principal way of capturing something of his life and significance in a short chapter is to explore this indirectness as well as to illuminate a small event at the edge of larger things, centering on one of Ocaña's many apparent departures not only from the focus of his journey but also from the main trunk of his narrative. On the surface, the incident seems to document a simple change of fortune along the way—the kind that Ocaña and his readers expected from their traveling heroes, fictive and otherwise. Yet the entertaining respite from apparently more serious matters that this friar's excursion into the world might seem to offer is not really a respite at all. The story that is light in tone and told with an amusing flair is also a desperate tale, heavy with unease. It represents one in a succession of narrative episodes in which Diego de Ocaña seems to steal away—and consequently to steal his readers away—from his central mission and into his creative mind; and yet, I contend that the story's uncertainty is undoubtedly registered for a reason, which requires close consideration alongside Ocaña's most deliberate narrative forays. While his telling of a single incident cannot encapsulate him, it throws light on a few of his thoughts and actions. Further, it reveals "more" than he, and others of his ilk, could express in any other way. Students of evangelization, missionary activity, and religious change in various social and ethnic communities in colonial Latin America run the risk of depending too fully on an established assembly of examples and texts to fire their understanding. Diego de Ocaña offers a fresh angle onto the uneven transplantation and multiform communication of Catholic Christianity in colonial settings, suggesting much about early modern religious enterprise and about the aftermaths it generated.

DIEGO DE OCAÑA AND THE MISSION TO PERU

Diego de Ocaña was born around the year 1570 in Ocaña, near Toledo. All that is known of his early youth is that he made his way to the shrine of Our Lady of Guadalupe in Extremadura. This home of the carved image of the Virgin Mary had attracted pilgrims and prayers since at least the early fourteenth century. There, the boy entered the monastery of the Jeronymites, the Virgin's guardians since 1389. He made his full profession of vows in the Order of Saint Jerome on June 8, 1588, on that day appearing to choose the promise of a spiritually full but sequestered life of prayer, obedience, and manuscript illumination in the convent's bustling scriptorium.[3] His physically adventureless days in Guadalupe were, in fact, numbered, lasting a little more than a decade. On January 3, 1599, as a late replacement for another friar, Diego de Ocaña and an older Jeronymite companion, Martín de Posada, were bound for the New World.[4]

Among the royal privileges and entitlements conferred by a series of medieval and early modern Castilian monarchs on the Jeronymite guardians of Guadalupe was the right to send out representatives to inspect and spread devotion and to gather alms that would maintain a cult befitting the Mother of God and assist in the care of the thousands of pilgrims who flocked to the sanctuary each year. Ocaña and Posada were two such agents, called *demandadores*, or questors, from the house at Guadalupe who, in the age of King Philip II, extended their field of operation beyond the Spanish and Portuguese heartlands and into what the Jeronymite chronicler and future prior of the monastery of Guadalupe, Gabriel de Talavera, in 1597 called—in apparent reference to any number of newly contacted peoples—"the most remote regions of the Indians."[5] Ocaña and Posada crossed the Atlantic and passed through the Caribbean and over the isthmus of Darién before sailing down the northern coast of South America as far as the port of Paita, where the older man, already gravely ill, died in a rented room. Ocaña carried on alone, traveling through much of Spanish South America until 1605, at which point he went to New Spain, where he died in Mexico City in 1608.[6]

Gabriel de Talavera viewed matters, including demandadores, from a great distance. He placed his monastery's holy wanderers within a universal network of alms collection and divine favors that linked not only diverse and expanding terrestrial settings of Catholic Christendom but also Heaven and Earth. Yet the extra-European paths of these representatives from Guadalupe were not nearly so well trodden as Talavera dreamed. If the Virgin of Guadalupe had become known and venerated in certain American parts, the Jeronymites—who had been, at best, sporadically involved in New World expansion and who remained without their own monastery there—most often were not. False alms-gatherers in all manner of habits abounded, and even legitimate ones such as our two demandadores from Guadalupe could expect cautious, if not cool, receptions as they arrived in cities and towns. They had to be carefully introduced and authorized by official papers carried both from their Jeronymite superiors and from the crown.

From such papers as well as from the reporting of their activities such as the detailed account made by Ocaña within the larger surviving relation of his journey, it is clear that urban centers were these representatives' principal targets and that their brief was extensive.[7] Guadalupan demandadores expected a contribution from the coffers of any municipality that could afford it. Ocaña also mentions begging alms door-to-door, often assisted by the legitimating and cajoling presence of some respected local notable. Yet a demandador promoted devotion and collected alms principally through the founding of religious associations (*cofradías*) among the laity. The recruited groups of pious men and women were themselves to be governed by hand-picked local stewards (*mayordomos*) among whose chief tasks were the maintenance of the flow of alms and bequests and the choice of secure successors to their office. People and piety were organized around sacred images of Our Lady, which the Guadalupan agents either inspected and approved or, as in Ocaña's case, might even make and then put directly into a cofradía's care. Ocaña wrote of how the Virgin Mary herself guided his hand as he created seven painted renderings of the original sculpted image of Our Lady of Guadalupe, at least five of which Ocaña saw enshrined in South American churches (in Lima, Potosí, Chuquisaca [La Plata, today Sucre], Cuzco, and Ica).

Ocaña also orchestrated an array of devotional activities, a kind of audiovisual assault on a city or town's different social communities that included programs of preaching, special Masses, elaborate local festivals and processions, and even theatrical performances to promote the Virgin of Guadalupe, attract people to join a lay religious association, and inspire local residents to give alms and veneration. Ocaña himself delivered sermons, but in diverse and populous places such as the great mining center of Potosí (in what is today Bolivia) he also recruited others, including gifted local preachers in native Andean languages as well as in Spanish.[8] The sermons as well as the hymns and a play composed by Ocaña himself were peppered with miracle stories exemplifying the history and power of Our Lady of Guadalupe.

The ultimate goal in each setting was a new sacred foundation, a fresh beginning for a local cult of the Virgin. Yet some of these beginnings were only achieved at the expense of existing Guadalupan images whose cults had grown untethered from obedience to the shrine of the original image in Extremadura. Demandadores in the late sixteenth century were scrutinizing and correcting local devotion even as they were exciting it. In this sense, these agent-inspectors reflected their centers, in Ocaña's case, the increasingly jealous attitude of the home-monastery of Guadalupe, and also the caution of the larger Catholic Church in matters surrounding the veneration of images and relics (and also the related authorization of miracles and human sanctity) in the years following the promotion of the decrees of the Council of Trent (1545–1563). It was Ocaña's task to bring and maintain order in a particular Marian corner within the Christianizing Indies. He was to visit and inspect existing Guadalupan cults in the New World, with an eye to reforming or otherwise counteracting any wayward devotion and replacing any unauthorized images that he might find. And he was also to ensure—beyond the amounts needed by local devotees for basic maintenance and the purchase of wax and other necessities—that an appropriate bulk of any alms gathered in the name of Our Lady of Guadalupe was flowing back to the home shrine in Extremadura.

Ocaña's efforts to spread and maintain correct devotion to the original image and cult of Our Lady of Guadalupe in promising places in the Indies were capped off by his own narratives describing what he had done and experienced as a demandador. These narratives were a crowning part of his orchestrations. In them, he both fantasized about, and attempted to fasten down, the cultic beginnings he wanted to achieve. He thought, too, of his readers. As the first champion and participant-teller of these new sacred foundations of Our Lady of Guadalupe, Ocaña sought to influence the consequences of his actions and how they might be remembered.

It is easy to be carried along by Ocaña's purposefulness and systematized narrative effort toward new and secure devotional foundations, to concentrate on his dream of control and permanence. Indeed, being carried along in this way is an important part of the central task of trying to understand Ocaña's priorities and ways of seeing. But it is only a first part. The reader's engagement with what Ocaña trumpeted should not obscure what he could not help but whisper. Indeed, as I shall attempt to show, the Jeronymite also tells of traveling, and faring, much less certainly. He finds himself, more often than expected, at a considerable distance from his determined choreographies of alms collection and propagation. Significantly, he writes of these misadventures—these moments when things grew difficult or awkward or went completely awry. Put more accurately, Ocaña attempts to write *through* them. It is to one of these moments that I now turn.

THE INCIDENT IN SAÑA

Diego de Ocaña arrived in Saña (just south and east of what is today the city of Chiclayo) in the northern coastal region of Peru in late September 1599, having buried his companion and fellow Jeronymite Martín de Posada in the port of Paita only a few days earlier. Saña was at this time an abundant provincial town in a well-watered valley of this arid region. Pueblos of Indians remained, even after the devastation wrought upon native numbers by waves of disease in the coastal zone. The pueblos surrounded a substantial and growing Spanish settlement that included a parish church and the convents of three religious orders.

In another valley only about 4 leagues (c. 12 miles) away was a shrine dedicated to an image of Our Lady of Guadalupe, an already famous sculpted likeness that had been in the care of Augustinian friars near Pacasmayo since 1563. Ocaña marveled at the Augustinians' fine house, their school, and extensive properties, and especially at the wealthy and thriving cult of Our Lady, which commanded alms and veneration up and down the coast of Peru. The image had its stirring foundational legend and was now famous for miracles, with pilgrims arriving even from the viceregal capital of Lima to the south.[9] It may have been sought by a Spanish devotee and carved by an approved sculptor as a faithful likeness of the original, but from Ocaña's perspective, devotion to Our Lady of Guadalupe on the north coast had gone badly wrong. From promising beginnings, the cult had strayed and transformed into an example of disobedience. Neither in the north coastal region nor (as Ocaña would discover) in populous Lima was any thought given to the original image of Our Lady of Guadalupe, and not a peso of alms raised in her name was being sent to the Spanish home-sanctuary. The image's

Augustinian guardians had declared a kind of religious independence and had no intention of operating their satellite shrine differently. Alms, rents, and other incomes gathered in the name of the Virgin of Guadalupe would stay in this American place.

Ocaña later presented his short sojourn in Saña as the point at which he began to formulate not only a clear-headed response to the rival image of Our Lady of Guadalupe but also his larger strategy, his dream-narrative of replenished control. He had seen the established prosperity and devotion at the Augustinians' shrine, and he judged it locally insurmountable. "I could do nothing in this town," Ocaña later wrote, referring to Saña, "beyond empowering two people [to oversee collection and dispatch] in case someone sought to make a donation to Our Lady of Guadalupe of the kingdoms of Spain through their will or by some other means." Appreciating the Augustinians' foundation and shrine (and thinking it unassailable) "was one of the things . . . which moved me to build chapels in Lima and in other places," he explained.[10] And these plans for a rival image in populous Lima (in 1600, a city of some 20,000) were only the beginning. For it was then that this demandador would truly get to work. Within such chapels, Ocaña planned to position portrait-copies, images of Our Lady of Guadalupe which, with the Virgin's help, he himself would paint and see approved by ecclesiastical authorities. Around these new images he would recruit lay religious associations and organize festivals and liturgical devotion, intensive programs of preaching and, of course, systems of alms collection that he meant to be protected in perpetuity. These would be the sacred beginnings that he could then champion as a first chronicler.

Oscana's understanding of himself as a messenger, a conveyor of authority, is a recurring theme in his story. He was God's instrument, one who enjoyed a spiritual conduit to Heaven. More particularly, he perceived himself as one whose lack of formal artistic training beyond some manuscript illumination in the scriptorium at Guadalupe would be overcome, like any other obstacle—from a tempest at sea to a wornout mule. He wrote of how the Virgin herself guided his brush strokes. Ocaña described himself further as the carrier of a simple and legitimate spiritual authority—"a friar from her [Mary of Guadalupe's] own house" who could paint faithful copies, "so very like the one in Spain." The fresh and direct connection to the original image and shrine is what is important. He counted on devotees in the New World to appreciate the authenticity of his channel to the heavens, and also on their capacity to share at least some of his understanding of how the celestial court functioned.

Two principal messages on this score were exemplified in his own sermons, just as they would have echoed through those delivered by preachers whom he recruited to his cause. The first concerned the proven power of the Virgin Mary in her advocation of Our Lady of Guadalupe as a prime intercessor before God. And the second asserted Ocaña's capacity to deliver the goods, in contrast to what he had only to imply were the lesser and even dubious claims to such authority ventured by the conveyors, guardians, and devotees of certain other images. Ocaña's understanding of Mary of Guadalupe as a permanent and singular advocate for all kinds of people partook of a highly developed Marian theology in shrines such as the one in Extremadura. Moreover, his attachments to orthodox power and devotional propriety reflected not only his home-monastery's increasing sensitivity toward the proliferation of image-copies but also his Counter-Reformation moment, one of simultaneous caution and vigorous defense when it came to matters such as the veneration of images, relics, and the investigation of purported miracles.

As justified as Ocaña may have felt as a creator and dispenser of holy images in New World settings, however, there were concerns and dangers which he did not mask. Like many other missionaries who found themselves in evangelization settings far from the comfort of confirming centers, he was taking important matters into his own hands. Later in his manuscript, as he was taking stock of the various images he had gone on to paint and enshrine in Peru, his recognition of this fact prompted a revealing defensiveness. "I know full well," Ocaña explained to his readers, both Jeronymite and otherwise,

> that there are and will be those in Spain who argue that it is not wise to make these images [as I have done]. But, for these reasons, they will begin to see their importance. For now, and each year hence, from wherever there is a house and image of Our Lady of Guadalupe, many alms will leave the Indies which [otherwise] would have stayed. And now the *majordomos* [of the lay religious associations he founds]—who are like *demandadores*, and whom I leave [in office]—are masters of all, and [themselves] remain subordinate to the Justices and the royal and ecclesiastical courts which will annually take account of the alms they have collected.[11]

What Ocaña does not include in this passage—especially a discussion of the arguments of the nameless critics who he suspects will question the wisdom of his actions—seems more significant than his overt defense of the devotional centers he has founded and the reassertion of his dream of permanence and perpetual alms. His insecurity is registered. Rather than gliding over his sense of the dangers that the painted image-copies might bring to the mission of replenished control, he works through it. And within his self-defense and line of reasoning is a glimpse of self-awareness, which invites us toward a closer examination of Ocaña's adventures in Saña.

THE TEMPTATION OF DIEGO DE OCAÑA?

In the days before his arrival in Saña, the reality of severe want, of life alone on the road, and of the possibility of his own insignificance began to press in on Ocaña. Traveling overland through the coastal desert, even with a native Andean guide who knew the area, there was the danger of becoming disoriented, of losing the trail, and of draining the last drop of water from their gourds. Somewhere in the sands stretching between the city of Piura and the "Indian town" of Olmos, Ocaña recalled musing further. Like the path he and his guide were traveling, he seemed dangerously close to disappearing. "As soon as the horses pass," he observed, "the wind fills their footprints [with sand], and there is no trace." In Ocaña's case, the prospect of himself and the Virgin of Guadalupe being forgotten almost as soon as they passed arose from more than a contemplated erasure of his way through the sand. Impermanence had a name. Fray Diego del Losar ("de Losal" in Ocaña's rendering), also from the shrine in Extremadura, had been a Jeronymite predecessor who traveled throughout Peru for some twelve years promoting the advocation of Our Lady of Guadalupe. Del Losar was little remembered by people whom Ocaña met, and he became for Ocaña a powerful reminder of all that might not come of his own efforts. There was barely more memory of Diego del Losar than if he had not been there at all, Ocaña stated, and what had happened with del Losar could happen with him: "as soon as his back was turned, all would come to an end, be abandoned and forgotten."[12]

When Ocaña reached Saña, only a few days later, the place turned out to be the site of more than the adjustment and rise of his resolve. Indeed, his lofty plans for countering the Augustinians' shrine and avoiding the apparent failures of del Losar by painting and enshrining a small empire of images of Our Lady, which might endure in Lima and other carefully chosen places beyond, would have to wait. Ocaña had spent his last *real* on the rented horses and the Indian guide who had accompanied him into town. He was starving, without the means to continue, casting about for options and forced to act. In his manuscript, Ocaña worked to make sense of some further adventures in Saña. "Finding myself in need," he explained, "I began to sell some of the things I carried, my appealing images in particular. I had a very striking image I made in Panama, and I brought it out for some people to see. They took it to a person who was ill and, before everyone's eyes, he [soon] appeared well; and I said that if they paid me, I would leave it there."

News of the apparently miraculous recovery of this person—and doubtless of the visiting friar's offer, too—spread, and Ocaña was soon fielding requests. But humans (neither Ocaña nor the individual townspeople) were not acting alone. According to the Jeronymite, the people "begged and pleaded" with him to leave the image behind. He claimed to have been surprised neither by the miraculous cure nor by the local burst of requests for the image. Interest in the image was, for him, evidence of a devotion awakened by God, a celestial reward after the Virgin of Guadalupe had heard her friar's call and interceded on his behalf. "I had earlier prayed to Our Lady," Ocaña explained, "[asking] that they [the townspeople] would take a liking to her portrait."

For the praying friar, God's miraculous cure had drawn fervent interest in his image at just the right moment, yet the precise direction of the image's appeal begs further attention. One of the people who came forward to see the Jeronymite's image was "a rich and inquisitive priest." Ocaña presents this cleric as a crude and single-minded collector of curious sacred objects, not the stable and influential sort of person whom Ocaña characteristically sought out to assist his local missions, let alone to take an image of the Virgin into his care for the future. The priest, for his part, seems to have regarded Ocaña as a fellow down on his luck from whom something remarkable and powerful might be gotten. He also appears to have assumed that Ocaña was a little like him, one who might both appreciate and serve his collecting passion. The priest invited the Jeronymite back to his home to show off the many *curiosidades* that he had collected in his oratory. Ocaña claims to have accepted the invitation not out of politeness or any particular desire to see the fruits of this man's obsession, but because he was famished. As it turned out, he saw in this rich priest someone likely to be able to produce even more than a decent meal. As the Jeronymite's stomach rumbled, the story continued--a story that contains more meaning than might first meet the eye. A seemingly amusing comedy is also an elaborate dance between religious propriety and caution, on the one hand, and worldly temptation and even the prospect of heterodox danger, on the other. What Ocaña leaves out in his reporting of the various steps in this dance seems as illuminating as what he chooses to relate.

His reservations about the rich priest notwithstanding, Ocaña arrived with his locally renowned image of Our Lady of Guadalupe hidden, literally, up his sleeve. After showing Ocaña around his oratory crowded with oddities and sacred marvels, the priest came straight to the point: he was hoping to make his next acquisition. And what he proposed was simple enough: if Ocaña would only leave his painted image of the Virgin of Guadalupe with him, the priest would be all too happy to help the needy friar on his way.

Here, Ocaña's self-consciousness takes over. He first stresses the care he has taken to follow his order's restrictions about personal property and the receipt of money by any friar who finds himself on the road. It was imperative that he not break the rule, or even seem to do so, for either kind of departure offended God and set a scandalous example to lay people.[13] He writes of his polite and public response to the priest's unseemly directness as having been an expression of how pleased he would be to leave his image amid so fine a collection for no recompense at all. And yet, behind the spoken effort not to oblige the priest to pay him, he confessed a more private thought. "Relieving my need," he admitted, "mattered more to me than all his indiscretion." Ocaña had been praying again, and he owned up to how eager he had been for matters to proceed precisely as the priest was suggesting: "I was at my wit's end and at such a point that, like another Esau, I would have sold my birthright for a bowl of lentils."[14]

As Ocaña's relation of the episode continued, it grew simultaneously more tense and entertaining. It was as if the famished yet painstaking friar and the crude and worldly priest had been preparing for the roles all their lives. The cleric ventured some details, saying that if Ocaña would just part with the miraculous image, he would give him a bar of silver to support his mission and travels. Yet even in Ocaña's desperation, this assurance was not enough. The Jeronymite's asides confirm that he felt obliged by his vows to play a more innocent figure than he could possibly have been at this stage. "But, sir," he claims to have inquired, "what is the value of a bar of silver?" The priest's quick answer was a further inducement and just the right touch to allow Ocaña to advance a step further. While most *barras* of silver were worth about 250 pesos, the priest explained, he would give Ocaña one that would easily fetch 300. With this offer, according to the Jeronymite, the priest began pleading that he accept the arrangement. Ocaña wrote that the comforting prospect of 300 pesos worth of silver coming as a kind of gift from a pleading man made him swallow hard at his good fortune: he was refusing to take payment, and the offer in exchange was more than he had dreamed of! After going quiet for some time, the Jeronymite wrote that he burst out laughing at this further evidence of God and Mary answering his prayers and causing the priest to implore him to accept the silver in this way.

Ocaña snapped back to attention when he realized that the priest was taking his reaction the wrong way. Fearing that the traveling friar was a clever campaigner laughing off the 300 pesos as a paltry sum, or perhaps imagining that some monkish reluctance to receive payment still lingered, the priest began begging the Jeronymite to reconsider. According to our author, the priest cried that he would give Ocaña anything he desired, just as long as he left the portrait copy in his oratory. This heightened level of beseeching was even better. It provided further reassurance, if any were required, both for Ocaña and for his Jeronymite readers in Guadalupe that vows were kept and propriety observed. The friar was acting as any wandering religious would act in such circumstances, thinking only of how to proceed with his mission. Ocaña writes that he calmed the priest by assuring him that the painting of the Virgin of Guadalupe would be his, and by saying once more to the man that if he had not been in need, he would have parted with it for nothing.

Even with his prospects so suddenly improved, the world still seemed a treacherous place. The sight of the large bar of silver made Ocaña uncomfortable. He could not relax with the temptation, like a misdeed, right there in front of him and everyone else. ... if the priest now able to pay him in worth in cattle or ...ear. When the priest, having gotten what he wanted, finally went to claim the supper for which the friar had been long... ...lt so nervous in the presence of his prize that he declined ... wrote that he considered it better to leave quickly, before ...m to gaze tenderly upon the silver and think better of the ...

Ocaña's story raced to its conclusion: it was time for a somewhat inglorious getaway. The Jeronymite instructed his servant to hide the silver in his cloak and carry it directly to the inn, where he would meet up with another servant who was waiting, bored and disconsolate at their impoverished predicament, and watching their belongings. Ocaña describes the scene that the travelers later must have reflected upon together. When the man who had been waiting saw the first servant enter, sweating under a load, and then throw a silver bar to the ground, he began to cheer up. "All three of us," Ocaña wrote, "delighted to find ourselves, at last, with money, called for the innkeeper to bring us something to eat." Yet the Jeronymite still could not quite relax. He remembered that "I asked them [the innkeeper and his family or helpers] to close the door, and I instructed that if anyone came looking for me or asking after me they should say that I was nowhere to be found (*que no estava en el mundo*)."

Ocaña tried to capture how he felt, explaining that he meant precisely what he wrote; rendered more literally, he was wishing not to be found in the world, and also feeling not of or in it: "It is true that, just then, I was not there," he added.[15] Behind a tavern door with his two servants, still feeling a little deprived of his senses and strength but aware of having solved the puzzle of how he would obtain horses and continue down the coast to Lima, Ocaña tried to shut himself off from the mundane uncertainties of Saña. He was finally about to eat his fill. Yet just seeing and touching the bar of silver was somehow not enough to persuade him that either it, or his adventure, was real. "It seemed to me that it was a dream, and that I did not have it [the silver] for certain." It was not the last time that Diego de Ocaña would describe what he saw before him, and what was happening to him in America, as a dream.

CONCLUSION

For a demandador charged with the foundation and inspection of holy images in secure settings—places in which devotion would be regular and monitored, and from which a steady supply of alms would flow—he was paying a surprising amount of attention not to the fate of an image he had created but to a newly acquired hunk of silver. What about the portrait-copy of Our Lady that he left behind in the oratory of a priest of questionable piety? Where precisely would the image be placed, and were there arrangements for its care and protection as well as for the alms that might be gathered in the name of Our Lady of Guadalupe? Was the painting now a curiosity within a larger private collection and around which a local bore could spin marvelous stories? Or would reports of the miracle spread, leading others to visit and venerate the image in a shrine that would grow? These are the possible futures about which Ocaña was nothing short of obsessed in other urban centers in Peru, but he was not in a position to face them in Saña.[16]

It can be tempting to view the episode in Saña as atypical and largely unimportant. Arguably, events there unfolded so differently from how they developed in one of Ocaña's orchestrated acts of foundation or correction in Lima, Potosí, Chuquisaca, Cuzco, or Ica, that the two kinds of action are unrelated. In Saña, once Ocaña had abandoned any idea of founding a devotional center to rival the Augustinians, perhaps he was simply using anything at his disposal to relieve a bitter want and to proceed to the larger centers in which he would truly go to work, carefully performing his demandador's functions of spreading correct devotion and of gathering and guiding alms. But, then, why did Ocaña write of his experience in Saña in the way that he did, justifying and entertaining in equal measure, and not concealing difficult matters that he might well have reported differently or not at all? What happens if we do not look away or take Ocaña entirely at his word—if we do not cleave his adventure in Saña from our company as light entertainment, as the desperate measure of a traveler in need, or of a friar with an eye on bigger prizes?[17] What happens if we take the episode seriously as a revealing invitation toward Ocaña's manner of seeing what he was doing?

Two matters seem most pertinent. First, Ocaña was a friar who had joined a religious order and pledged his life to obedience and service to God and a miraculous image of His mother; he prayed often and, as I have emphasized above, he expected divine involvement in worldly affairs. The Jeronymite had carefully recorded reasons for believing himself one of God's favored servants. Aboard a ship, descending the face of a cliff, crossing a swift river, considering his own survival within a building collapsed by an earth tremor, menaced by people he does not know or understand, and, in seemingly countless other predicaments in the Indies, Ocaña reminds the reader of his manuscript of how he understood his own fate to be in celestial hands. His expectation of heavenly help and comfort meant that for Ocaña there was a special opportunity, not something to fear or avoid, in elaborating a narrative about experiences such as he had had in Saña. Our Lady of Guadalupe and God were looking out for him, placing certain people in his path, moving human hearts. Ocaña, literally, could not have seen himself, or explained things, in any other way.

Second, narrating such an episode was an opportunity for playfulness—albeit an early modern Castilian friar's kind of playfulness—that was not appropriate at points in the manuscript in which he was reporting his official foundational and reformative efforts. It was a reader's and a writer's playfulness. To fuel these more personal portions of his account, Ocaña could draw on his familiarity with contemporary genres of literature that featured the adventures and changes of fortune of a various band of God's human instruments with whom the friar, as a traveler in a strange land, could easily identify. The incident that became a "detour" or "trial" or "challenge" in the life of an exemplar or protagonist was a crucial and comfortably repetitive feature in most tales of apostolic suffering, in hagiographic narratives, and in all manners of edifying stories. And such elements were just as integral to the plots of the popular romances of chivalry (one of which Ocaña explicitly cites at another point in his manuscript), to their more pious offshoots, the so-called *libros de cabellerías a lo divino*, and to the picaresque literature. There is not space to exemplify these influences sufficiently here. But suffice it to say that, together, these merging literary forms provided highly developed, elastic, and entertaining patterns into which a writer such as Ocaña could tip the details of his own experiences. Such events and close scrapes as happened to Ocaña in Saña positively invited such a tipping. Rather than simply distorting his record of an actual happening, these patterns enabled Ocaña's telling and his extraction of meaning from it while, in the process, coating real events in a contemporary and receivable humor and thus considerably enhancing his narrative's appeal for contemporary readers.

The future remained a region of hope. Dreams of permanence were not fully punctured—in part, because, for Ocaña, uncomfortable reality seemed to intrude as expected, almost on cue. Diego de Ocaña, the divinely inspired creator of painted images of the Virgin of Guadalupe and the orchestrator of new sacred foundations meant to overcome all barriers in the Andes, does not so much go absent as step aside. Diego de Ocaña, the wanderer and writer, arrives to reflect on the various tests of his devotion and effect of his prayers. Saña and other places in America became proving grounds for his trust in the Marian protector and in her influence before God. But, as he composed his account, he also sought to console himself, to find a little protection. The act of writing allowed him to cast his mind back to Saña, to try and sort out what had occurred there; attempting to write through such events brought the prospect of achieving some understanding. Ocaña could take a few crucial steps away from haunting impermanence, away from his memory of that place surrounded by sand, away from a full realization of the imperfection and transitory nature of what he, like other Christian missionaries, might achieve, much less control, in the Indies. He could decide he did not wish to be found there. When not with his paintbrushes, then with his pen and ink, Ocaña could creep back from the world toward the more certain walls of his cloister in Guadalupe. Yet his simultaneous determination to come and go from those walls, to tramp around in the world rather than only transcend it, and his enthusiasm for attempting to record a range of what he did and experienced there, meant that Diego de Ocaña never quite disappeared.

NOTES

1. Biblioteca de la Universidad de Oviedo, Spain, M-204, is untitled, but it has been called the "Relación del viaje de Fray Diego de Ocaña por el Nuevo Mundo (1599–1605)."

2. *Real cédula* of Philip II to the chancellería of the Nuevo Reino de Granada and other officials in the Indies, San Lorenzo, August 16, 1572; *Relaciones geográficas de Indias*, ed. Marcos Jiménez de la Espada, Biblioteca de Autores Españoles, vol. 183 (Madrid: Ediciones Atlas, 1965), *Perú*, vol. 1, 50.

3. Archivo del Real Monasterio de Guadalupe, Leg. 39. Ocaña must have been at least eighteen years old by this date in 1588, the minimum age for entrants according to the Jeronymites' constitutions, "because at a younger age they cannot understand the rule they take." Biblioteca Nacional de España, Madrid, Ms. 1099, "Compilación de las constituciones extravagantes de la Orden de S. Gerónimo desde su principio hasta el año de 1513," Título 7, fol. 7v.

4. On his late inclusion as one of two monks permitted and commissioned by an ailing King Philip II, see Archivo General de Indias, Indiferente General, Leg. 2869, Tomo 5, fols. 165v, 168r-169v, 207r; and Carlos G. Villacampa, *La Virgen de la Hispanidad o Santa María de Guadalupe en América* (Seville: Editorial de San Antonio, 1942), Appendices, docs. 4–10: 325–31. Martín de Posada and Diego de Ocaña set sail from Sanlúcar on February 2, 1599.

5. *Historia de Nuestra Señora de Guadalupe* (Toledo: Thomas de Guzman, 1597), Observaciones, Treatise 4, fol. 454r.

6. Archivo del Real Monasterio de Guadalupe, Códice 61 (Necrología de monjes, 1600–1747), fol. 7r.

7. Accounts were composed by other Jeronymites who traveled across the seas on behalf of the monastery of the Virgin of Guadalupe, but the pressures of space do not allow their treatment here. Suffice it to say that none of the surviving records is as extensive or articulate as Ocaña's "Relación."

8. Ocaña's reporting of his sojourn of some fourteen months in the great mining center of Potosí, while not entirely typical, was the culmination of these first tellings. See Kenneth Mills, "Diego de Ocaña's Hagiography of New and Renewed Devotion in Colonial Peru," in *Colonial Saints: Hagiography and the Cult of the Saints in the Americas, 1500–1800*, eds. Allan Greer and Jodi Bilinkoff (forthcoming from Routledge); and idem, "Diego de Ocaña e la organizzazione del miracoloso a Potosí," in *Il santo patrono e la città. San Benedetto il Moro: culti, devozioni, strategie di età moderna*, ed. Giovanna Fiume (Venice: Marsilio Editori, 2000), 372–90.

9. Rubén Vargas Ugarte, *Historia del culto de María en Hispanoamérica y de sus imágenes y santuarios más celebrados* (Lima: Imprenta "la Providencia," 1931), 454–56. Ocaña writes of the shrine on the northern coast (in 1599) at "Relación," fol. 213v. On the Guadalupe of the north coast from a later and supremely Augustinian point of view, see Antonio de la Calancha, *Corónica moralizada*, ed. Ignacio Prado Pastor (Lima: Imprenta de la Universidad Nacional Mayor de San Marcos, [1638] 1974–1781), esp. vol. 4, 1225–1385. See also the celebratory Francisco de San Joseph, *Historia universal de la primitiva y milagrosa imagen de Nuestra Señora de Guadalupe* (Madrid: Antonio Marín, 1743), Chs. 24 and 25, 168–84.

10. Ocaña, "Relación," fol. 30r. Unless otherwise noted, from this point forward all quotations of Diego de Ocaña are from "Relación," fols. 29r–32v.

11. Ocaña, "Relación," fols. 214v–215r.

12. Diego del Losar was a native of Puente del Arzobispo, near Toledo, who professed his vows in the Monastery at Guadalupe in 1563. Sebastián García, *Guadalupe de Extremadura en América* (Guadalupe and Madrid: Comunidad Franciscana de Guadalupe and Gráficas Don Bosco, 1990), 109.

13. Biblioteca Nacional de España, Madrid, Ms. 1099, "Compilacion de las constituciones," Título 8: de lo concerniente lla honestidad de nra. religión, fol. 8v.

14. In the Bible, Esau, son of Isaac, notoriously sold his own birthright to his brother Jacob; he also lived for the moment and held nothing sacred. See Genesis 25: 29–34.

15. Sebastián de Covarrubias's third sense of *mundo* (world) in 1611 catches an essential portion of what Ocaña meant here. Covarrubias (translated by the author) writes: "Sometimes 'world' means the instability [or fragility] of things, their changeability." *Tesoro de la lengua castellana o española*, ed. Felipe C. R. Maldonado, rev. Manuel Camarero (Madrid: Editorial Castalia, 1995), 768.

16. See Mills, "Diego de Ocaña's Hagiography."

17. In his edition of Ocaña's "Relación," Arturo Alvarez goes so far as to offer an apology for the incident, reassuring the Jeronymite's new generations of readers that "the hardships he [Ocaña] suffered in the course of his odyssey excuse the freedom [the lack of preoccupation, *desenfado*] with which he relates to us such human

anecdotes as this one from Saña." Arturo Alvarez, *Diego de Ocaña, Un viaje fascinante por la América Hispana del siglo XVI* (Madrid: Studium, 1969), 48, n. 31.

SUGGESTED READINGS

Diego de Ocaña's untitled manuscript resides in the library of the University of Oviedo, Spain, catalogued as M-204, and called the "Relación del viaje de Fray Diego de Ocaña por el Nuevo Mundo (1599–1605)." Evidence within the manuscript suggests that Ocaña drafted and illustrated the work between 1599 and 1607. The "Relación" has seen a serviceable, if problematic, modern edition by Arturo Alvarez, *Diego de Ocaña, Un viaje fascinante por la América Hispana del siglo XVI* (Madrid: Studium, 1969), reprinted in paperback, with additional editorial changes in the interests of brevity, as *A través de la América del Sur* (Madrid: Historia 16, 1987).

Sustained discussions of Ocaña have been few, but readers should consult especially Francisco de San Joseph, *Historia universal de la primitiva y milagrosa imagen de Nuestra Señora de Guadalupe* (Madrid: Antonio Marín, 1743); Germán Rubio, *Historia de nstra. Sra. de Guadalupe; o sea: Apuntes históricos sobre el origen, desarollo y vicisitudes del santuario y santa casa de Guadalupe* (Barcelona: Industrias Gráficas Thomás, 1926–27); and Carlos G. Villacampa, *La Virgen de la Hispanidad o Santa María de Guadalupe en América* (Seville: Editorial de San Antonio, 1942). Notable is also Rubén Vargas Ugarte's pioneering work that discusses Extremadura's Our Lady of Guadalupe and Ocaña within a helpfully larger Marian theater in Spanish America: *Historia del culto de María en Hispanoamérica y de sus imágenes y santuarios más celebrados* (Lima: Imprenta "La Providencia," 1931). More recent, still surveying, but usefully juxtaposing Ocaña's work with an account produced by a Jeronymite successor in the Andes is Javier Campos y Fernández de Sevilla, "Dos crónicas guadalupenses de indias," in *Guadalupe y Extremadura, toda en la evangelización de América*, ed. Sebastián García (Madrid: Talleres Gráficas Don Bosco, 1993), 47–54. Exploring Ocaña as a special kind of early modern travel writer is Elena Altuna, " 'En esta tierra sin memoria': El viaje de Fray Diego de Ocaña (1599–1605)," *Revista de Crítica Literaria Latinoamericana* 22, no. 43–44 (1996): 123–37. For more on Ocaña as a Jeronymite *demandador* and for a more fulsome bibliography in general, see Kenneth Mills, "Diego de Ocaña e la organizzazione del miracoloso a Potosí," in *Il santo patrono e la città. San Benedetto il Moro: culti, devozioni, strategie di età moderna*, ed. Giovanna Fiume (Venice: Marsilio Editori, 2000), 372–90; idem, "La 'memoria viva' de Diego de Ocaña en Potosí," *Anuario del Archivo y Biblioteca Nacionales de Bolivia* (1999): 197–241; and idem, "Diego de Ocaña's Hagiography of New and Renewed Devotion in Colonial Peru," in *Colonial Saints: Hagiography and the Cult of the Saints in the Americas, 1500–1800*, eds. Allan Greer and Jodi Bilinkoff (forthcoming from Routledge).

The flavor of Ocaña's time in the Monastery of Guadalupe in Extremadura is best gained from the contemporary Gabriel de Talavera, *Historia de Nuestra Señora de Guadalupe* (Toledo: Thomas de Guzman, 1597). But readers seeking sound context and information in English on the Extremaduran image and sanctuary of Guadalupe as well as on the development of Spanish Jeronymites at Guadalupe and elsewhere are directed to Gretchen Starr-LeBeau, *In the Shadow of the Virgin: Religious Identity, Inquisition, and Political Authority in Guadalupe, Spain* (forthcoming from Princeton University Press); Albert A. Sicroff, "The Jeronymite Monastery of Guadalupe in 14th and 15th Century Spain," in *Collected Studies in Honour of Américo Castro's Eightieth Year*, ed. M. P. Hornik (Oxford, UK: Lincombe Lodge Research Library, Richard Kronstein Foundation for the Promotion of Jewish and Cognate Studies), 397–422; and J. R. L. Highfield, "The Jeronimites in Spain, their Patrons and Success, 1373–1516," *Journal of Ecclesiastical History* 34, no. 4 (1983): 513–33. On the monastery and shrine as a miraculous pilgrimage site, see especially Françoise Crémoux, *Pèlerinages et miracles à Guadalupe au XVIe siècle* (Madrid: Casa de Velázquez, 2001); and also the ranging compilation by Sebastián García and Felipe Trenado, eds., *Guadalupe: historia, devoción, arte* (Seville: Editorial Católica Española, 1978).

CHAPTER 9

Felipe Guaman Poma de Ayala

Native Writer and Litigant in Early Colonial Peru

Rolena Adorno

Before the European invasion in 1532, the Andean peoples had no formal system of alphabetic writing. In Tawintinsuyu the quipu, *a system of knotted cords, communicated meaning through the color, texture, size, form, and arrangement of the cords. Quipus did not attempt to reproduce phonetic sounds as in European script. Instead, they imparted numerical information and some basic narrative ideas much as today's road signs do (such as the red, octagonal "stop") without using alphabetic symbols. Trained specialists, known as* quipucamayocs, *interpreted the quipus by examining and manipulating the knotted cords. They could then pass on this information to interested parties, much like literate European scribes.*

Although Andeans continued using quipus early in the colonial period, by the late sixteenth century Spanish officials became suspicious and even hostile to evidence drawn from them. Since any such information was only decipherable by an Andean, it could not be verified independently by a European. Spaniards feared investing the power of recordkeeping solely to native quipucamayocs and judged the knotted cords much inferior to European alphabetic writing. Clerical authorities also feared that the mysterious quipus might represent a link to Andean religious beliefs and hence idolatry. This attitude led Spanish friars, entrusted with converting the Andeans to Roman Catholicism, to learn the principal indigenous languages and translate them into alphabetic script. As a result, by the early seventeenth century, quipus gave way to alphabetic writing in Castilian and, to a lesser extent, in the principal indigenous languages, Quechua and Aymara.

The efforts of European missionaries to translate Andean languages into alphabetic script and to teach Andeans Castilian Spanish (the most common language in Spain) ultimately encouraged an impressive but brief Andean literary awakening. The production of literary texts written in Castilian and in indigenous tongues culminated in 1615 with the completion of Felipe Guaman Poma de Ayala's masterpiece, El primer nueva corónica y buen gobierno. *This massive manuscript (nearly 1,200 pages, of which 398 are full-page illustrations) was written mostly in Castilian with occasional passages in the author's native Quechua, and it provided a history of the Andes before and after the founding of Tawantinsuyu, the*

Quechua name of the Inca empire. It also focused on the abuses perpetrated by the Spaniards on the conquered population since 1532 and made sweeping proposals for colonial reform. Guaman Poma's intended audience for his work was King Philip III of Spain.

By the time that Guaman Poma finished his opus, the Andean author Joan de Santa Cruz Pachacuti Yamqui Salcamaygua already had written his Relación de antigüedades de este reyno del Pirú *(1613), and the mestizo author, Garcilaso la Vega, also had produced the first part of his famous history, the* Comentarios reales de los Incas *(1609), the second part of which would appear posthumously under the title* Historia general del Perú *(1617). Meanwhile, the Spanish priest, Francisco de Avila, had compiled a series of religious traditions, written entirely in Quechua and known today as* Ritos y tradiciones de Huarochirí *(circa 1610). Despite the rapid outpouring of texts produced about the Andean past by indigenous and mestizo authors in the early seventeenth century, this literary renaissance ended abruptly, and future Andean authors would write only in Castilian. Moreover, none of the later works attained the majesty, scope, and originality of these earlier ones, particularly the* Nueva corónica y buen gobierno *of Guaman Poma.*

During his lifetime, Felipe Guaman Poma de Ayala went from collaborating closely with the colonial regime to denouncing its abuses in his long manuscript to the king of Spain. One important clue to this change in attitude may be found in documents relating to a dispute over land in the valley of Chupas (in Huamanga) between the kinsmen of Guaman Poma and an ethnic group, the Chachapoyas, originally from northern Peru, who also had settled in the region. The viceroy granted lands presumed to be vacant to the Chachapoyas in the Chupas area in 1586, but the following year a member of the Tingo/Guaman clan claimed and received the same lands. In the series of litigations between the parties that followed, the Chachapoyas and the Guaman/Tingo family accused each other of being recent interlopers. The legal dispute dragged on until 1600, when the Chachapoyas gained the upper hand by claiming that Felipe Guaman Poma (the leading figure in the litigation for the Guaman/Tingo clan) was neither a nobleman nor a cacique principal but a humble Andean named Lázaro. By discrediting Guaman Poma, the Chachapoyas won their case and secured the lands. For his part, Guaman Poma was sentenced to 200 lashes and a two-year exile from the city of Huamanga and its six-league radius. It was a bitter blow that no doubt led Guaman Poma to rethink his position regarding the colonial regime that he had so loyally served in the past. The vehicle for his protest was Nueva corónica y buen gobierno.

Rolena Adorno is Reuben Post Halleck Professor of Spanish at Yale University and has published on a wide range of subjects in colonial textual studies, including Guaman Poma and His Illustrated Chronicle from Colonial Peru/Guaman Poma y su crónica ilustrada del Perú colonial *(2001); (ed.)* Nueva corónica y buen gobierno, *digital edition of the Royal Library of Denmark (2001)* (www.kb.dk/elib/mss/poma/); Guaman Poma: Writing and Resistance in Colonial Peru *(1986, rev. ed., 2000); (with Patrick Charles Pautz)* Alvar Núñez Cabeza de Vaca: His Account, His Life, and the Expedition of Pánfilo de Narváez, *3 vols. (1999); and (coedited with Kenneth J. Andrien)* Transatlantic Encounters: Europeans and Andeans in the Sixteenth Century *(1991).*

𝒯he life story of Felipe Guaman Poma de Ayala illustrates the challenges that arose in the early colonial period for members of the first generation of ethnic Andeans born in Peru after the Spanish conquest. The record of that personal experience is contained in the 1,200-page "letter" that Felipe Guaman Poma wrote to the king of Spain as well as in other types of documents that bear his name and explain his activities. Pulling together the elements of his story as it is contained in the writings that span a twenty-year period (1594–1615) demonstrates the transformations of outlook that defined his personal experience. Guaman Poma's example shows how social roles and identities could evolve in the course of a single individual's lifetime when it coincided with the establishment and consolidation of the Spanish colonial regime.

Guaman Poma was descended from *mitmaqkuna* (members of an ethnic community sent with special privileges by the Inca to settle a newly conquered area), who originated in Huánuco and eventually settled in Huamanga; the timing of this migration has been estimated to have occurred in the fifteenth century. Guaman Poma's *mitmaq* heritage was central to the events that defined his position and fate in colonial society; it affected the way he defended his lands, and it also shaped his literary work. For these reasons, it is important to clarify the Inca concept of mitmaq and its evolution into colonial times.

In the Inca state, the mitmaqkuna often settled newly conquered areas (as in the case of Guaman Poma's Huánuco forebears), providing military garrisons along the vulnerable eastern borders of the kingdom or populating potentially productive but uncultivated and vacant lands. While mitmaqkuna obeyed administrative rule in their new place of residence, they maintained the dress and symbols of their own ethnic homeland. Their duties were to teach the superior ways of Inca culture, primarily the solar religion and the imperial language (Quechua), to facilitate the local community's assimilation into the Inca empire. After the arrival of the Europeans in 1532, the status and prestige of mitmaqkuna suffered a decline as the concept took on new meanings. To put it succinctly, the ambassadorial settlers who in earlier times represented the Inca's power and prestige and carried out his imperial mission were viewed

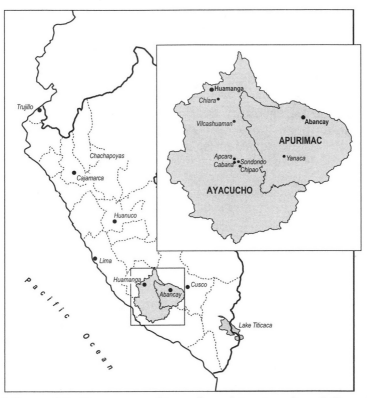

Map 3. Peru and the Departments of Ayacucho and Apurimac (insert). Reproduced from Adorno, *Guaman Poma and His Illustrated Chronicle*, 10–11. Courtesy of Museum Tuscalanum Press, Copenhagen.

at present as mere newcomers or outsiders (*forasteros*) to the communities they inhabited.

To give an idea of the precarious situation in which Andeans such as Guaman Poma found themselves, it is useful to consider the series of distinctions among migrant groups set up by the Spanish colonial regime. In the 1570s, Viceroy Francisco de Toledo (1569–1581) fixed permanent residences for the mitmaqkuna, or *mitimaes*, as they were called in Spanish. They were assigned to the places where they were residing at the time, thus separating them and their descendants from the local *ayllu*, the basic kin unit of native Andean society, which held title to land, organized cooperative labor teams, and carried out other collective functions.

The viceroy's administration thus divided the indigenous community into two clearly defined categories: *originarios*, that is, native-born members of traditional, organized Andean settlements, and *yanaconas*, Andeans detached from their ayllu affiliations and living in the service of Europeans. "Forastero" and "yanacona" were terms used to refer to "outsiders" or "migrants to the community from elsewhere," and former migrants retained the name "forastero" regardless of the length of their residence in new communities and the degree of their assimilation. Removed from indigenous society, yanaconas constituted a heterogeneous and transitional social group. Despite Toledo's provisions seeking to order and fix the populations of forasteros, the very act of doing so brought to the fore the question of migrant status and resulted in considerable social chaos. A little later, in the seventeenth century, colonial officials attempted to distinguish between "*forasteros revisitados*, those 'who live in their respective *ayllus* because their ancestors were born here and were integrated into these communities,'" and "*forasteros advenedizos* and other recent arrivals who at present are found within the *ayllus* but leave at will."

Guaman Poma's experience allows a glimpse from within as to what the mitmaq heritage meant in colonial times. When he set out to defend his interests in lands he claimed as his rightful inheritance in the area of Huamanga, he identified himself as both a member of the local native elite (*cacique principal*) and as an appointee of the Spanish colonial government (*gobernador de los indios y administrador de la provincia de los Lucanas*). The documentation for this litigation is contained in two sets of documents: one from the Departmental Archives in Ayacucho, edited by Juan A. Zorrilla; and the other from a private Peruvian collection, commonly called the "Expediente Prado Tello" in reference to the present owner (and editor).

Later, in the *Nueva corónica y buen gobierno*, Guaman Poma used a similar title, "administrator, Indians' advocate, deputy of the administrator of the colonial district" (*administrador, protetor, tiniente general de corregidor*), and, through his corrections to the manuscript, elevated the hereditary title of cacique principal (principal lord) to that of *capac ques prencipe* (*qhapaq*, which means prince). His actions reveal the need that he felt to assert and enhance his traditional inherited status, changing it from local lord to dynastic prince as well as to claim a new status within the colonial hierarchy. The inflated titles that he used in passing from the Expediente to the chronicle correspond to the development of his literary pursuit in the face of his judicial defeat. Taken together, the Expediente Prado Tello and the *Nueva corónica y buen gobierno* reveal Guaman Poma's transformation from local claimant and petitioner to someone who considerably enlarged his perspective without ever losing sight of his interests.

By his own claim, Guaman Poma was born "after the time of the Incas," and he declared himself to be eighty years of age when he finished writing his work.[1] Although his calculations are unlikely to be precise, the period of his birth was between the mid-1530s and the mid-1550s and his death, after the year 1615. Determining his place of origin is more complicated. The itinerant life and forced resettlements that defined the lives of so many Andean members of his generation characterized Guaman Poma's own familial and personal experiences as well. The first issue is geographical. Placing Guaman Poma's life experiences on a map gives the clearest idea of what living under colonial rule meant to the natives of the Andes more generally (see Map 3).

While Guaman Poma claimed Huánuco as his ancestral home, Huamanga (today's Ayacucho), the new colonial city in the Andes of south central Peru, was the site of his recollections of events from the period of his youth as well as the focal point of his decade-long litigation to support claims to hereditary properties. It is likely that Guaman Poma considered Huamanga his home; it was possibly even the place of his birth. Nevertheless, the province of Lucanas, located in the southern Andean region of present-day Peru, was another major site of his activities. He traveled through Lucanas as a church inspector's assistant in the late 1560s, worked there as a low-ranked colonial Indian administrator in the late 1590s, and settled there after his expulsion from Huamanga in 1600. Lucanas is located about one hundred miles to the south-southeast of Huamanga.

As a native Andean "assimilated" to Spanish language and religion, Guaman Poma would have been known as an *indio ladino*, that is, as someone who was presumably proficient in Castilian, Christian in belief, and Hispanicized in custom. Besides denoting ostensible assimilation to Hispanic language and religion, the term *ladino* connoted negative values of craftiness, cunning, and untrustworthiness. It was a colonial term applied by Europeans, never one of self-identification by Andeans. Because of the effective erasure of elite status that its use commonly connoted, the term "indio ladino" was never used by Guaman Poma to refer to himself (although he used it to refer to others of his race). He surely felt the sting of its negative connotations when he mentioned that he and others were scorned as *ladinejos* or *santicos ladinejos*, that is, as great and impertinent talkers, overzealous converts, and busybodies.

Regarding his assimilation of European ways, Guaman Poma presented himself as a devout Christian, and his insistence on this point is a measure of the suspicion with which ethnic Andeans' conversion to Christianity was held. With respect to his literacy, Guaman Poma wrote that he learned reading and writing from a mestizo priest, Martín de Ayala, whom he identified as his half-brother and whose piety he celebrated. Despite the presence of a mestizo in his own family and his admiration for his half-brother, Guaman Poma condemned *mestizaje* (racial mixture) and the growing numbers of *mestizos* (persons of mixed race) in Spanish colonial society that threatened, in his view, the survival of the Andean race.

Guaman Poma's artistic apprenticeship was likely carried out under the supervision of another priest, the Mercedarian friar Martín de Murúa, whose two manuscript chronicles of Inca history include drawings made by Guaman Poma. Murúa was working as a parish priest in the province of Aymaraes located in the present-day Department of Apurimac. Aymaraes is located nearly due east from the clustered pueblos of San Cristóbal de Suntunto, Concepción de Huayllapampa de Apcara, and Santiago (San Pedro) de Chipao that Guaman Poma frequented in the province of Lucanas. His detailed account of Murúa's conflicts with the local native community suggests his sustained contact with the friar. Guaman Poma's discussion of local Andean governance in Yanaca, the native settlement where Murúa lived, and his mention of a score of traditional customs that were practiced there but prohibited by the Church, also point to his considerable acquaintance with that community.

There are two central facts in Guaman Poma's life that allow us to take the measure of his experience. The first is that he wrote and drew his enormous book, which, contrary to his aspirations, was not published until three centuries after his death. The second (the first in order of occurrence) is that he was expelled from Huamanga in the year 1600. The expulsion may have been one of the principal factors that inspired him to write his work because the immense manuscript finished in 1615 represents a complex change in Guaman Poma's outlook. He went from a position of collaboration with the Spanish colonial regime as a Church assistant and minor functionary in local civil administration to an attitude of exposing its injustices and excesses. Putting no faith in the civil administration of justice after his 1600 debacle, he turned to the king as his ultimate recourse. Whether between the time he began writing his letter/chronicle and the moment he finished it, Guaman Poma maintained the conviction that the monarch could or would take remedial action on behalf of the Indians of Peru is a question that remains unresolved. We turn now to the events and circumstances that led up to Guaman Poma's writing of his 1,200-page "letter to the king."

FROM HUAMANGA TO LUCANAS, LIMA, AND CUZCO: SERVING CHURCH AND STATE

Guaman Poma's pursuits were typical of many Andeans who were in command of the Spanish language and who could therefore negotiate between Andeans and non-Andeans, including Europeans, Creoles (individuals born in America of European parentage), and enslaved black Africans. Guaman Poma's activities first come into view for the period of the 1560s through the early 1580s, and we can best appreciate them through the pictures in his chronicle. His earliest reference to colonial affairs is vividly portrayed in a drawing depicting a colonial census (Figure 1). Identified as a "general inspection tour" carried out by Damián de la Bandera in 1557, the survey was a census undertaken to measure the size and constituency of the Andean population to assess tribute and cyclical state corvée labor service (*mita*). Guaman Poma calls the depicted event "the first general inspection of the Indians of this kingdom," but its scope was actually limited to the province of Huamanga. He illustrates a typical census interview in which the inspector, Bandera, asks the mother of a young boy to identify her son. She responds in Quechua that the child, who is her own, is the son of a powerful lord. The specificity of this Huamanga encounter suggests that Guaman Poma, as a native Andean, was well acquainted with colonial census-taking and that similar questions had been put to him and his family, who likely were living in Huamanga at the time.

Another drawing orients us to Guaman Poma's experience in the service of the colonial Church (Figure 2). He writes of having served the ecclesiastical inspector (*visitador*) Cristóbal de Albornoz in the identification and punishment of practitioners of traditional Andean religion in the first campaigns to "extirpate idolatry" in early colonial Peru. Although he does not picture himself here, Guaman Poma shows Albornoz supervising the punishment of a weeping Andean male as carried out by another Andean member of the priest's inspection team. It is likely that Guaman Poma was recruited in Huamanga for Albornoz's 1568–1570 campaign to the provinces of Soras, Lucanas Laramati, and Lucanas Andamarca. Guaman Poma mentions the names of inspection team personnel who appear in Albornoz's reports on this specific tour as well as the names of local Andeans punished. His youthful participation in the campaigns to root out native Andean religions by playing the crucial, intermediary role of interpreter and informant was a hallmark of his life experience.

Albornoz's extirpation-of-idolatry campaigns probably provided Guaman Poma with his earliest significant exposure to the policies and

Fig. 1. A Spanish colonial census taker inquires about the identity of the male child. Guaman Poma, *Nueva corónica*, 410. Courtesy of the Royal Library of Denmark, Copenhagen. Reproduced in facsimile by the University of Paris and republished by Siglo XXI Editores, Mexico City.

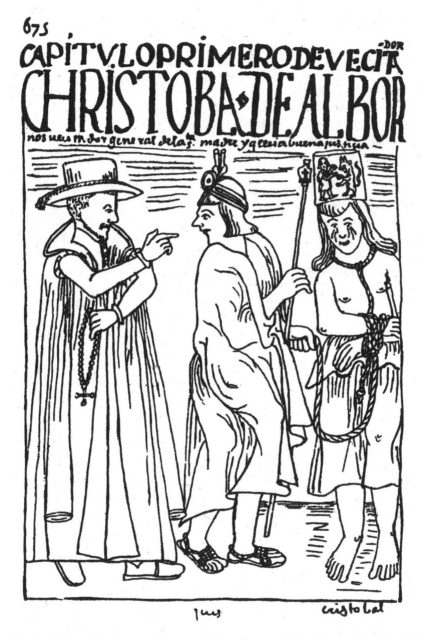

Fig. 2. A Spanish priest punishes an Andean for practicing his traditional religion. Guaman Poma, *Nueva corónica*, 689. Courtesy of the Royal Library of Denmark, Copenhagen. Reproduced in facsimile by the University of Paris and republished by Siglo XXI Editores, Mexico City.

practices of the missionary church in native Andean communities. He expressed approval of the work carried out by Albornoz and pointed out that the priest punished the practitioners of Taki Unquy, a radical nativist movement that preached the triumph of Andean gods over the Christian god, advocated rejection of all that was European, and coincided with the threat of armed rebellion against the Spaniards from the neo-Inca stronghold at Vilcabamba. (Albornoz has been broadly credited for the suppression of the Taki Unquy movement.) Guaman Poma's reference to the practitioners of Taki Unquy as "false shamans" (*hechiceros falsos*) suggests that he viewed its leaders as exploiting for their own personal or political gain the traditional rituals that in Inca times had been mounted for the expulsion of illness.

In another area of the activities of the missionary Church, Guaman Poma reveals his familiarity with the provincial Church councils held in Lima to establish and refine policies for evangelizing the Andean peoples. His enthusiastic support of its decrees on a broad range of issues suggests that he viewed rigorous and thorough evangelization as a pressing need in Andean society. Together with his militant defense of the need for surveillance of the Andean communities and his detailed exposition of all the prohibited practices that survived in his day in the provinces of Lucanas Andamarca and Soras, Guaman Poma's religious perspective is orthodox and inflexible. Its expression is in no way syncretic or ambiguous, and it reflects the outlook that he must have developed in his youth or early adulthood when he was accompanying Cristóbal de Albornoz on his inspection tours. Guaman Poma was at the same time strongly critical of the Churchmen who failed in their pastoral duty or subverted it by their actions. This criticism takes the form of an internal critique of the Church, that is, of one who presents himself as being integrated into its fold.

In addition to his knowledge of Church council edicts, Guaman Poma's mention of some of the men who participated in the important Third Church Council, convened in Lima in 1582–83, leads us to wonder if his skills as an interpreter had been employed there. Yet his references to one of the Council's principal theologians, the Jesuit José de Acosta, as well as to Luis Jerónimo de Oré, a Franciscan priest from Huamanga, and the secular priest and author Miguel Cabello Balboa, evoke them not as persons whom he had met or worked for but rather as authors of the books that they had written. The question remains as to whether his contact with these Churchmen was as a reader of their works or as an observer and informant at the Council. His praise of the Jesuits, for example, may reflect his indirect acquaintance with the prominent role they played there. However, Guaman Poma mentioned only two Jesuits by name in the course of his entire work, which indicates that he

probably knew few of them personally. In general, the priests who populate Guaman Poma's chronicle are overwhelmingly those who served in
local Andean parishes in the provinces of Lucanas Andamarca, Soras,
and Aymaraes in the southern Peruvian Andes.

Guaman Poma recounts seemingly firsthand recollections of Cuzco
and the administration of Viceroy Toledo, pictured here in death after
the Spanish monarch refused to grant him an interview upon his return
from Peru (Figure 3). The first years of Toledo's regime in particular
seem to have constituted for Guaman Poma one of the most significant
periods of colonial affairs with which he was familiar. He registered as
the most permanent economic and social effects of the Toledo years the
systematic census-taking and one of its consequences, the *reducciones*,
whereby native communities were removed from their traditional dispersed homelands and relocated to larger Spanish-style towns, in order
to levy taxes and assess mita labor more efficiently. Guaman Poma gave
an extensive account of the legislation promulgated by Toledo in Cuzco
and examined Toledo's inspection tour of the viceroyalty.

The tour was carried out after the resettlement program had been
undertaken, according to Guaman Poma. He named two of the inspectors appointed for Huamanga, again revealing that the province was the
locus of his close acquaintance and, no doubt, the sphere of his activity.
He described Toledo's late 1570 journey from Lima to Cuzco, starting
his account with Toledo's visit to Huamanga and reporting events of the
subsequent journey to Cuzco as if he had been an observer and participant. Recounting Toledo's reception in the city of Huamanga, he described the highly theatrical and symbolic act that the viceroy carried
out at the Inca site of Vilcashuaman on the stone step pyramid from
which the Inca presided over his court. Toledo ascended the steps to the
Inca's seat (*usnu*) and was "received like the Inca himself by all the principal lords." He then commanded the oldest and most highly ranked
lord present to ascend to the top of the pyramid and be honored with
him.[2]

The crucial episode that Guaman Poma recalls from Toledo's regime is the execution of the Inca prince, Túpac Amaru (Figure 4). He
portrays with considerable drama Túpac Amaru's 1572 entrance into the
ancient Inca capital of Cuzco as a prisoner and his subsequent execution
and burial. Again, as if he had been an eyewitness, Guaman Poma created this picture of the powerful scene in which the Inca prince was be-
headed (he was actually garrotted) while noble Andean men and women
wailed in protest and grief.

In general, Guaman Poma's assertions reflect the attitudes and actions of the Andean provincial elite from the midsixteenth century on-
ward. On the whole, the native elite responded eagerly to the chance to

Fig. 3. Don Francisco de Toledo, the viceroy of Peru who executed the last Inca prince, dies of grief. Guaman Poma, *Nueva corónica*, 460. Courtesy of the Royal Library of Denmark, Copenhagen. Reproduced in facsimile by the University of Paris and republished by Siglo XXI Editores, Mexico City.

Fig. 4. The last Inca prince, Túpac Amaru, is executed by Viceroy Toledo as noble Andeans lament the tragedy. Guaman Poma, *Nueva corónica*, 453. Courtesy of the Royal Library of Denmark, Copenhagen. Reproduced in facsimile by the University of Paris and republished by Siglo XXI Editores, Mexico City.

seek offices and privileges in the colonial system. From the 1550s on-ward, native lords had served as subordinates to Spanish administrators (Guaman Poma's documented experience is an example), and they con-tinued to compete for positions in the colonial bureaucracy even after the reorganization of native society under Toledo. In the 1570s the vice-roy revamped the ethnic power structure, institutionalizing state control over the succession of *kurakas* (Andean lords) and converting them into agents of the state for overseeing the directed activities of the local com-munity. Toledo had dismissed Inca rule as illegitimate and tyrannical, and he fused the local hereditary leadership with colonial governmental functions.

Toledo's legacy is crucial to interpreting Guaman Poma's position and claims. Like many others, he participated in the transactions of offi-cial society, yet his colonial affiliations were no match for those of the ethnic group against which he and his kin competed for the disputed lands. Guaman Poma's case illuminates the situation of Indians desig-nated as forasteros, and illustrates the principle that "land-tenure cases were among the most hotly contested within the colonial judicial sys-tem. The rising value of land and the shrinking assets of indigenous com-munities provoked bitter disputes. Migration complicated the debates over land inheritance and titles in ways which were reflected in the courts throughout the seventeenth century."[3]

IN LIMA AND HUAMANGA: LITIGATION
AND LEGAL DEFEAT

During the six-year period from 1594 to 1600, Guaman Poma was serv-ing as an interpreter and witness in proceedings in Huamanga that con-firmed land titles and implemented the policies resulting from Viceroy Toledo's *reducciones*. At the same time, Guaman Poma was busy in legal pursuits, defending in the courts his and his kin's claims to lands in the valley of Chupas, just a few leagues from the colonial city of Huamanga. Losing these legal battles and later acknowledging them only by allusion in the *Nueva corónica y buen gobierno*, Guaman Poma nevertheless let slip the observation, in discussing the pretensions and criminal activities of "common Indians," that he first became aware of such social disintegra-tion—Andean society being turned "upside-down"—when he began his travels, that is, "in the year that we left, of 16[0]0 and afterward."[4]

Guaman Poma's adversaries in the legal disputes that culminated in the year 1600 were the Chachapoyas, an ethnic and possibly a linguistic group originating in the eastern highlands and western Amazonian slopes of today's northern Peru. They had been assigned by the Inca state to the Quito area, where they were living at the time of the Spanish invasion. The Chacha groups have been characterized as "small homogeneous enclaves forming a far-flung net of small mitmaq operations" that were found "at the outskirts of former aboriginal sites which had been converted into Inca centers," possibly with "responsibility for controlling the interaction of aborigines with the privileged population of the new citadels."[5] The Chachapoyas had not been conquered until the reign of the Inca Huayna Capac, but when the Spanish took over Peru the Chachapoyas quickly assimilated themselves into the royal forces as "modern soldiers," continuing the role they had played in late Inca times.

In mid-1538 the powerful Chachapoyas joined as allies the Spanish royal forces that eventually defeated the rebellion of Diego de Almagro the younger in one of the most important battles between the Spanish crown and rebellious conquistadores in the 1540s. (In the *Nueva corónica y buen gobierno*, Guaman Poma repeatedly asserts that his father don Martín de Ayala and clansman, the Cavinga Inca don Juan Tingo, had served the crown in the same signal effort.) After the royal victory, the Spanish governor settled the Chachapoyas nearby at Santa Lucía de Chiara in the valley of Chupas and exempted them in perpetuity from tribute payment in recognition of their loyalty and military prowess. They were identified as being in service to the "justice officials of this city [Huamanga] and the royal crown."[6]

The struggle over the lands of Chiara, located some two leagues from the city of Huamanga, began in 1586 when in Lima the viceroy Fernando de Torres y Portugal granted the presumably vacant lands to the Chachapoyas under the leadership of their lord, don Baltazar Solsol. Reasons given were their status as mitmaq as well as their ongoing service to the crown in law enforcement in Huamanga. Granting them land on which to settle was thus presumably based on need and merit. The lands are described in the decree as being vacant "for more than fifty years, since they had been the lands of the Inca."[7] On such a basis, lands were typically considered to be vacant—unencumbered by any legal claims to ownership.

Just two months after the lands of Chiara were surveyed in February 1587 and the Chachapoyas established there, a member of the Tingo-Guaman families claimed and received the same lands from the same corregidor's deputy. The next recorded legal action occurred seven years later in September 1594, when the rights of the Chachapoyas were confirmed. Again, just a few months later, the Guaman-Tingo families' claim to Chiara of April 1587 was also upheld. Notwithstanding the protests of the Chachapoyas, local colonial authorities honored the renewed Tingo-

Guaman claims. In subsequent years, both parties filed petitions and counterpetitions, each side accusing the other of being recent immigrants (*advenedizos*) to contradict their claims as longtime residents and landholders. For a while, it seemed that Guaman Poma and the Guaman-Tingo families would prevail. On September 5, 1597, a ruling was made in Lima in favor of the two families, and Guaman Poma carried the disposition with him from Lima back to Huamanga. However, the summons that had been directed to the Chachapoyas by Guaman Poma's family and the Tingo heirs on September 14, probably in 1597, suggests a weakness to those claims that the Chachapoya leader Domingo Jauli would later exploit against Guaman Poma after the dispositions in 1598 and 1599 were made in the latter's favor.

On that September 1597 occasion the Indians' legal advocate representing Guaman Poma made a reference to one of his relatives, Martín de Ayala, as a yanacona. This reference to one of Guaman Poma's family members (evidently another Martín de Ayala, not his father or his half-brother) as someone detached from the ethnic community casts a shadow over all of them as recent immigrants and potential outsiders to the Huamanga area. Although Guaman Poma earlier had accused the Chachapoyas of being recent immigrants and runaways, the tide of events on this issue now turned dramatically against him.

On March 23, 1600, in Huamanga and before the corregidor's deputy and justice official Pedro de Rivera, the Chachapoya leaders Domingo Jauli and Juan Sota accused Guaman Poma of falsely presenting himself as a cacique who called himself don Felipe; they claimed that he was instead a humble Indian named Lázaro. They charged that this "don Felipe/Lázaro" had secured a royal order to have the Chachapoyas' lands surveyed under false pretenses and that he had then failed to appear on the designated date at the Chiara site where the survey was to have been carried out. The municipal notary accompanying the survey team corroborated the Chachapoyas' claim.

On December 18, 1600, the Chachapoyas' rights to Chiara were confirmed. On that same date, a criminal sentence was imposed on Guaman Poma. As condemned in the verdict, he was accused of being a "common Indian who, through deceit and trickery, called himself a cacique and was neither a cacique nor a principal, yet he subordinated Indians so that they respected him as such. He always behaved and sought offices with malicious intentions and deceits and was an Indian of evil inclinations and all the rest, as should be evident."[8] Thus, Guaman Poma was sentenced to two hundred lashes to be administered publicly, and he was condemned to two years of exile from the city of Huamanga. If he violated the conditions of the sentence, his exile would be doubled to four years. The costs of the suit, furthermore, were to be borne by him. On December 19 in Huamanga the sentence was proclaimed publicly.

Were the punishments elected for Guaman Poma unusual? Were they carried out? Committing false actions and misrepresenting the truth of matters constituted some of "the greatest evils man can commit," and banishment or death was considered the appropriate punishment, according to the *Siete partidas*, the fundamental legal code in sixteenth-century Castile that was carried over to Indies legislation. Although it is not known whether the corporal punishment was administered to Guaman Poma, his banishment surely was effected.

Why had Domingo Jauli singled out Guaman Poma for criminal charges? He was clearly the most persistent of Jauli's adversaries as well as the most successful. Twice, Guaman Poma had traveled to Lima (on September 10, 1597, and again on March 6, 1599) to appear before the Royal Audiencia. In both instances, he came back to Huamanga armed with certified documents upholding his land titles. Under such circumstances, Jauli evidently was able to triumph over him only by successfully convincing the authorities that Guaman Poma was an interloper—a fraudulent representative of the clan whose legal claims had been upheld by the highest court in the land. Removing him was tantamount to nullifying those claims.

IN LUCANAS AFTER 1600: WRITING TO EXPOSE INJUSTICE

References to Guaman Poma's activities in the years after 1600 are found in his letter of February 14, 1615, to King Philip III as well as in the *Nueva corónica y buen gobierno*.[9] Most of Guaman Poma's experience during those years was probably limited to the Lucanas region; his trips to Lima would take him via Huancayo or Nazca and Ica. The twenty-odd settlements and the majority of local colonial officials whom he named in regard to this period—the chronicle is suffused with these myriad references—are from the province of Lucanas. Local events span the years from 1608 to 1615, and he made several references to noteworthy occurrences of the years 1611, 1612, and 1613. For example, he mentioned an inspection of the local priests and parishes in Lucanas as part of a general tour carried out in 1611, and he remarked that he had been imprisoned at the time for seeking to defend local Andean citizens whom he represented as an appointee of the colonial administration.

One other significant area of Guaman Poma's activity, documented in the *Nueva corónica y buen gobierno*, is illustrated in Figure 5. One of his

Fig. 5. An Andean commoner dictates his complaints to an Andean lord to seek justice through the Spanish colonial legal system. Guaman Poma, *Nueva corónica*, 784. Courtesy of the Royal Library of Denmark, Copenhagen. Reproduced in facsimile by the University of Paris and republished by Siglo XXI Editores, Mexico City.

best-known drawings depicts an Andean commoner enumerating his grievances on the fingers of one hand while an Andean lord, dressed in European garb and sitting at a desk, drafts in Spanish the complaint that later will be submitted to the colonial authorities. This is the idealized realization of Guaman Poma's efforts as social activist and mentor in teaching fellow Andeans the skills of reading and writing. He spoke of having "disciples" whom he taught how to advocate for their rights, filing petitions and making legal claims to the colonial government. In his chronicle/letter to the king, Guaman Poma recommended dozens of times that literacy in Spanish be extended to the upper echelons of the Andean population. He understood that in the world of colonial affairs the written word was the essential means by which to document abuses, record laws and legal actions, and demand and authorize the redress of grievances. This faith in the written word is fully realized in the writing of his remarkable book.

Guaman Poma probably turned to the writing of *Nueva corónica y buen gobierno* after the year 1600 and his expulsion from Huamanga, "in the year that we left, of 16[0]0 and afterward." When he finished it, he signed it from Lucanas. His illustrated chronicle and treatise of more than a thousand pages had two main purposes: to give Philip III an account of ancient Andean history from the beginning of time through the reign of the Incas and to inform the monarch about the crisis in Andean society that was a result of Spanish colonization. Calling his work "El primer nueva corónica y buen gobierno," that is, the first of the "new chronicles" and a treatise on "good government" or governmental reform, Guaman Poma set forth his account of Andean history as "new" because it gave a version of pre-Columbian and Conquest history unfamiliar to readers of the Spanish-authored histories of Peru then in print. He presented an elaborate and complex cosmology that wove the dynasties of the Andean past into a Christian model of universal history, and he made the Incas not the first and only great Andean dynasty but the last one, succeeding the earlier royal dynasty of the Yarovilcas of Allauca Huánuco from which he claimed descent.

With respect to the theme of good government, Guaman Poma wanted to convince the king to take action to combat the dire situation that he described in these terms: the traditional Andean social hierarchies were being dismantled. The native Andeans were being exploited in the mines and in the countryside and were fleeing to the cities, where they engaged in the dissipated lifestyles of rogues and prostitutes. The mestizo population was increasing due to miscegenation and intermarriage, and the ethnic Andean population was declining dangerously due to mestizaje, colonial violence and exploitation, and European diseases.

Guaman Poma thus fashioned himself in his work as a trustworthy adviser to the king, the importance of which is demonstrated by his fine portrait of the hypothetical royal interview, visualized here as a face-to-face meeting for which the presentation of his chronicle is the written surrogate (Figure 6). As his credentials he claimed that he was the heir to the Yarovilca dynasty that preceded the Incas and that his grandfather and father, their merits having been recognized by the Incas, had served the lords of Tawantinsuyu in important posts.

The long prose text in which Guaman Poma presented these views was written mostly in Spanish with occasional sections (unreadable to the king) in Quechua. He explained his creation and use of pictures by remarking that he understood the king to be fond of the visual arts. Yet his heavy reliance on the pictorial mode to state his positions and argue his points, particularly about the colonial abuse of the native population, suggests instead that he considered his drawings to be the most direct and effective way of communicating his ideas to the king and persuading him to take action. Guaman Poma wrote that he hoped the king would have his work published to encourage colonial officials to halt abuses and improve the situation of native Andeans.

Did Philip III ever receive and read Guaman Poma's book? Probably not, although it seems likely that the manuscript arrived at the Spanish court because its ultimate and present location is in the Royal Library of Copenhagen in Denmark. This fact suggests that there had been some form of diplomatic acquisition such as, for example, the possible receipt of Guaman Poma's extraordinary manuscript by a Danish ambassador and collector of books who came upon it while at the Madrid court. It seems certain that the pictures, because of their intrinsic interest, ensured the work's survival. It is likely that the Scandinavian destination can be attributed to the interest that the *Nueva corónica y buen gobierno* held for its contribution to the Black Legend of Spanish history in the ideological war between Catholic southern Europe and the Protestant countries of the north.

By the writing of his book, we might assume that Guaman Poma displayed his faith in the power of the written word and his certainty of the king's willingness to act on it. Yet after reading the words he wrote at its conclusion, "There is no god and there is no king. They are in Rome and Castile,"[10] we as his readers might wonder, finally, how strong that confidence really was. From Guaman Poma's early occupation as a Church inspector's assistant to his failed legal disputes in claiming ancestral lands to his years-long research and writing of a work that he sent to the king of Spain, the trajectory of his experience reveals the precariousness of native Andean life under colonial rule. Even more than the itinerancy of such a life, Guaman Poma's personal testimonial reveals the ambiguities

Fig. 6. King Philip III receives Guaman Poma, whose book is a surrogate for this face-to-face interview. Guaman Poma, *Nueva corónica*, 975. Courtesy of the Royal Library of Denmark, Copenhagen. Reproduced in facsimile by the University of Paris and republished by Siglo XXI Editores, Mexico City.

and internal contradictions of the colonial experience. His story reveals the complexities that raise many questions for which there are no simple, absolute answers.

NOTES

1. For documentation of all sources used in this essay, see Rolena Adorno, "Introduction to the Second Edition," *Guaman Poma: Writing and Resistance in Colonial Peru* (Austin, TX, 2000), xxiii–xxvi, xxviii–xxxviii, xlv–xlix, liv–lv.

2. Felipe Guaman Poma de Ayala, *El primer nueva corónica y buen gobierno*, ed. John V. Murra and Rolena Adorno, Quechua translations by Jorge L. Urioste (Mexico City, 1980), 447. Numbers refer to Guaman Poma's pagination as corrected in the 1980 print edition and the 2001 digital edition of the Royal Library, Copenhagen (*www.kb.dk/elib/mss/poma/*).

3. Ann Wightman, *Indigenous Migration and Social Change: The Forasteros of Cuzco, 1570–1720* (Durham, NC, 1990), 135.

4. Guaman Poma, *El primer nueva corónica*, 886, 918.

5. Frank Salomon, *Native Lords of Quito in the Age of the Incas: The Political Economy of North Andean Chiefdoms* (Cambridge, Eng., 1986), 160.

6. Juan A. Zorrilla, "La posesión de Chiara por los indios chachapoyas," *Wari* 1 (1977): 49–64, see 59.

7. Ibid., 51, 57.

8. Ibid., 63.

9. This letter is freshly transcribed and translated into English in Rolena Adorno, *Guaman Poma and His Illustrated Chronicle from Colonial Peru/Guaman Poma y su crónica ilustrada del Perú colonial* (Copenhagen, 2001), 79–86.

10. Guaman Poma, *El primer nueva corónica*, 1136.

SUGGESTED READINGS

For Guaman Poma's own writings, see the Royal Library of Denmark's online digital edition of the original *Nueva corónica y buen gobierno* manuscript (*www.kb.dk/elib/mss/poma/*), especially for the 398 drawings. For the prose text, transcribed, see Felipe Guaman Poma de Ayala, *El primer nueva corónica y buen gobierno*, edited by John V. Murra and Rolena Adorno, Quechua translations by Jorge L. Urioste (Mexico City, 1980; rpt. 1992). For Guaman Poma's letter to Philip III announcing the completion of his work, see its Spanish transcription and English translation in Rolena Adorno, *Guaman Poma and His Illustrated Chronicle from Colonial Peru/Guaman Poma y su crónica ilustrada del Perú colonial* (Copenhagen, 2001). In "Chronicles of the Impossible: Notes on Three Indigenous Peruvian Historians" (*From Oral to Written Expression: Native Andean Chronicles of the Early Colonial Period*, edited by Rolena Adorno, Syracuse, 1982) and "Testimonies: The Making and Reading of Native South American Historical Sources" (*Cambridge History of the Native Peoples of the Americas. Part 3: South America*, edited by Frank Salomon and Stuart B. Schwartz, 1999), Frank Salomon discusses the writings of Guaman Poma and his peers from the perspective of Andean categories of historical and cosmological thought interpreted under colonial circumstances. In *Guaman Poma: Writing and Resistance in Colonial Peru* (Austin, TX, 2000), Rolena Adorno examines the visual and verbal compositional features of the chronicle and the meanings given by Guaman Poma to his work.

The Americas Society's multi-authored *Guaman Poma de Ayala: The Colonial Art of an Andean Author* (New York, 1992) provides insights into Guaman Poma's art at the intersection of Andean and European traditions. The interdisciplinary volume *Transatlantic Encounters: Europeans and Andeans in the Sixteenth Century*, edited by Kenneth J. Andrien and Rolena Adorno (Los Angeles, 1991), discusses the political, economic, social, and symbolic forces shaping colonial Andean society and highlights Guaman Poma as a central source and subject. On the important topic of colonial migration and its impact on Andean society, see Ann Wightman, *Indigenous Migration and Social Change: The Forasteros of Cuzco, 1570–1720* (Durham, NC, 1990). For the complexities of religion and ritual in the post-Conquest Andean world, see Sabine MacCormack, *Religion in the Andes: Vision and Imagination in Early Colonial Peru* (Princeton, NJ, 1991); and Kenneth Mills, *Idolatry and Its Enemies: Colonial Andean Religion and Extirpation, 1640–1750* (Princeton, NJ, 1997). Steve J. Stern's *Peru's Indian Peoples and the Challenge of Spanish Conquest: Huamanga to 1640* (Madison, 1982) and Karen Spalding's *Huarochirí: An Andean Society under Colonial Rule* (Stanford, 1984) examine the process of change in Andean society from pre-Columbian to midcolonial times, the former focusing on Guaman Poma's home territory and the latter on the province about which he had much to say at the end of his work.

CHAPTER 10

AhChan

The Conquest of the Itza Maya Kingdom

Grant D. Jones

The politically divided Maya polities of the Yucatán peninsula resisted the Spanish invasion of Francisco de Montejo from 1527 to 1535, and it took an additional decade for the Europeans to secure a firm foothold in the region. Nevertheless, sporadic hit-and-run guerrilla tactics allowed some Maya groups to maintain their nominal independence until the end of the seventeenth century. One such group was the Itza kingdom, whose rulers traced their lineage to Chich'en Itza, a once-powerful city that had dominated large portions of Yucatán before AD 1000. By the time of the Spanish invasion, however, the Itzas had established an independent indigenous polity in the remote tropical forests of Petén, Guatemala, with its capital of Nohpeten on Lake Petén Itzá. The Maya had long used flight into such frontier regions to resist indigenous invaders and burdensome taxes or other unwelcome impositions, and they continued these practices to resist Spanish domination from Mérida, the colonial capital of the peninsula. While the Itza successfully maintained their independent kingdom, they faced periodic Spanish encroachments among other Maya groups along their frontiers, and they often responded with military force to annex these areas and protect their borders. Since the region contained no precious metals or other resources of interest to Europeans, it remained largely free from total Spanish colonial domination for many years.

By the end of the seventeenth century, because of the difficulty of overland travel between Yucatán and Guatemala, the Spanish crown in 1693 approved the opening of a new road across the unconquered territories separating these provinces. The governor designate of Yucatán, Martín de Ursúa, used this opportunity to clear the forests all the way to those occupied by the Itza, whose conquest he made a top priority. The Itza king, Ahaw Kan Ek', reportedly wanted to pursue a policy of peaceful submission, but other Itza leaders favored war in alliance with another rival Maya group, the Kowohs. To pursue his plan of conciliation with the Spaniards, Ahaw Kan Ek' dispatched his nephew, AhChan, to Mérida in the winter of 1695.

In a carefully orchestrated ceremony in Mérida, AhChan declared (in the name of Ahaw Kan Ek') that the Itza wished to be vassals of the king of Spain; later he and his companions converted to Christianity. Under

Spanish law, once the leaders of a nation converted to Roman Catholicism, local authorities did not have to pursue policies of "peaceful conversion." As a result, Ursúa was now legally free either to accept the Itza as vassals or to subject them by force. At the same time, the Itza war faction, ignoring the authority of Ahaw Kan Ek', attacked Spanish soldiers in the region, and Ursúa began preparations for war. AhChan and his companions, who had left Mérida after the ceremony was concluded, fled from his Spanish escort along the way south. He later arrived at the Spanish camp, however, in March 1697 just as the invaders prepared to storm Nohpeten. Although the Spaniards captured the Itza capital, it took several days before they found Ahaw Kan Ek' and his family. Nevertheless, when the Spaniards inflicted various punishments and indignities on Ahaw Kan Ek' and his family members, a disillusioned AhChan fled with his kinsmen to the interior, where they could be free of Spanish control. Spanish authorities captured the Itza in 1702 and eventually made him cacique of San Miguel, a mission town in the region. After an indigenous uprising in 1704, however, AhChan escaped the Spaniards once again, apparently becoming the leader of a multiethnic enclave of Maya groups in a remote region of southern Belize. Regardless of how much the colonial authorities attempted to conquer the Maya and force them to accept the "orderliness" of Christian society, some groups, such as the Itza Maya led by AhChan, preferred to live in the forestlands where they could live according to Maya, not Spanish, societal rules.

Grant D. Jones is professor of anthropology at Davidson College. He is a noted authority on the Mayas, having written numerous articles on the subject. He has edited Anthropology and History in Yucatán *(1976) and (with Robert R. Kautz)* Transition to Statehood in the New World *(1981). He is also the author of two major books:* Maya Resistance to Spanish Rule: Time and History on a Colonial Frontier *(1989), and, dealing with the conquest of the Itza,* The Conquest of the Last Maya Kingdom *(1998).*

𝒯he Itza Maya noble AhChan played a critical role in the events surrounding the 1697 Spanish conquest of the Itzas, the last surviving native kingdom in Spanish America. We are fortunate to know much about his adult life, his political strategies and actions, his relationships with both Spaniards and his fellow native leaders, and the poignant personal dilemmas that he faced as his society collapsed upon the destruction of its political leadership and the coming of harsh colonial rule. This chapter follows his career across the many borders—cultural, political, and spatial—that he traversed over his long and challenging life. Because there are few colonial-period cases of such important native individuals whose biographies are as well known as his, it is a privilege to know this man and to imagine the rapidly changing, even dislocated times and places in which he lived.[1]

HISTORICAL SETTING

At the time of the Conquest several million lowland Mayan-speaking peoples occupied a vast tropical region that today encompasses the three Mexican states of the Yucatán peninsula (Yucatán, Campeche, and Quintana Roo), eastern Tabasco, the lowland tropical forests of eastern Chiapas, the departments of Petén and Baja Verapaz of Guatemala, northwestern Honduras, and all of Belize. At the time of first Spanish contact the native peoples of this extensive territory, which extends more than 650 kilometers north-south and about 450 kilometers east-west at its widest point, spoke primarily mutually intelligible dialects of Yucatecan Maya. A smaller number of speakers of several related Cholan Maya languages occupied the southern and western portions of the lowlands.

The Mayas of the northern lowlands, the first to be conquered by Spaniards in the early sixteenth century, comprised a single ethnic group whose members spoke the Yucatec Mayan dialect. At the time of the Conquest these were divided into between fourteen and eighteen politically distinct territories or provinces of varying degrees of centralization. Some of these provinces had earlier formed a confederation with its capital at Mayapan, but by the midfifteenth century this alliance had collapsed.

To the southeast of this region, between the Bahía de la Ascención and the New River in northern Belize, were the predominantly coastal provinces of Waymil and Chetumal (or Chaktemal). The capital towns of these two provinces commanded positions near the mouths of the Hondo and New Rivers and played a central role in trade with the interior peoples to their south and southwest. South of Chetumal, in Belize, was the Tz'ul Winikob' province, whose capital town was Tipuh, located on the upper Belize River.[2]

Of the southern Yucatecan-speaking populations the most important was found along the lakes of central Petén. This region was ruled primarily by a kingdom known as the Itzas, who, according to their own histories, had migrated to Petén from Chich'en Itza in the north, probably during the fifteenth century AD. Their less populous immediate neighbors, the Kowohs, also claimed to have migrated from the north, around the time of the sixteenth-century Spanish conquest of northern Yucatán. Both groups, whose aggressive military prowess impressed Spaniards and other natives alike, remained fully independent from Spanish rule until their conquest in 1697, nearly a century and a half after the 1542 establishment of the colonial capital, Mérida, in the north. Most of the Mayas known as Mopans, who lived in Petén and Belize within and beyond the boundaries of Itza territory, also remained independent until this late date as did those known as Kehaches, who occupied regions to the north of the Itza lands.

The Itza capital was located on the island in Lake Petén Itzá that is today Ciudad Flores, the capital of the department of Petén. The Itzas called their capital Nohpeten, "Large Island," and modern writers often refer to it as Tayasal. Until 1697, when Spanish forces from Yucatán finally captured Nohpeten in a bloody battle, the Itzas had exerted independent political and military influence over much of Petén and, on occasion, even much of Belize. They, and to a lesser extent their neighbors, the Kowohs, are the principal subjects of this chapter, in particular one member of their nobility, AhChan, whose remarkable life and accomplishments unfold in the Spanish documents that chronicle the conquest of the Itzas and their political disintegration due to disease, warfare, and colonial rule.

Why the Itzas survived as an independent native political entity is a question of great historical complexity. The famous conquistador Hernán Cortés passed along the northern and western coasts of the Yucatán peninsula in 1519, stopping in Tabasco before moving on to Veracruz in pursuit of the conquest of the Mexica (Aztec) capital of Tenochtitlan in central Mexico, which he accomplished by 1521. While in Tabasco he apparently learned of the Itza kingdom deep in the forests to the southeast, and in 1525 he led a massive overland party of Spanish troops and native retainers across Itza territory on his way to Honduras. He met Ahaw Kan Ek', the Itza ruler, at Nohpeten, and he provided the first descriptions of the broad territorial and economic influence of the Itzas, who were not officially contacted again by Spaniards until Franciscan missionaries reestablished communication in 1618.

The Spanish conquest of northern Yucatán dragged on slowly and intermittently from 1527, when Francisco de Montejo initiated the project, until 1542, when his son and nephew founded the city of Mérida. The balkanized nature of the Maya polities in the north required that much of the battle for control over the region be fought by means of separate regional wars against a fiercely resistant population. Over the following decades the colonial government gradually established control over only the northern part of the peninsula, with a single southern outpost, Salamanca de Bacalar, just north of the present-day border between Belize and Mexico. While the Mayas of Belize were nominally conquered by the mid-1500s, Petén remained an independent native territory. Itza influence over the region grew, thus limiting efforts by Spaniards to establish full control over the vast region between the northern colony and Nohpeten.

The northern colonial province of Yucatán was impoverished, with few natural resources of interest to Europeans, and devasted by the impact of European epidemic diseases. The menace of foreign piracy around its long coastline required constant military outlays and prevented the costly pursuit of the conquest of the province's unconquered southern frontiers. By the early seventeenth century, however, adventurous soldiers and missionaries from Yucatán pursued several expeditions into these regions. Armed Itza attacks, however, repulsed virtually every such effort. By 1638 the Itzas had reconquered Belize and forced the Spaniards to withdraw completely. Tipuh, the former capital of Tz'ul Winikob', now became a provincial capital of the expanding Itza kingdom. Not until the last years of the century would an ambitious politician and soldier, Martín de Ursúa y Arizmendi, manage to devise a strategy to conquer the Itzas and their neighbors, the Kowohs.

AHCHAN: AN INTRODUCTION

AhChan, an Itza Maya noble, was born about 1667, probably in the eastern region of the present-day department of Petén, Guatemala. A member of the Itza royal family, AhChan played an important role as a mediator between Itza and Spanish political forces both before and after the 1697 conquest. In this role, however, he remained deeply troubled over his conflicting and shifting loyalties to colonial authorities and to his own people. He epitomizes the tragic personal anguish that colonialism brought to once-independent native leaders as well as the astuteness with which many such individuals managed the contradictions imposed upon them by situations over which they had only marginal control.

AhChan's mother, known to us only as IxKante, came from Chich'en Itza far to the north of Itza territory, a place that had been the most important urban center in northern Yucatán until it began to decline about AD 1000. The Itzas of Petén traced their roots to Chich'en Itza, stating that their forebears had migrated from there, probably beginning in the fifteenth century. By the time of IxKante's birth the Spaniards had been in full control of northern Yucatán for over a century, and although Chich'en Itza was then only a small village, it remained for the Itzas both a symbol of their proud history and a ritual pilgrimage site for their nobility. IxKante, who had died when AhChan was young, was the sister of Ahaw Kan Ek' (Lord Serpent Star), the last king of the independent Itzas. All of their kings bore the dynastic name Kan Ek', signifying that their mothers descended from a line of females named Kan and a line of males named Ek'. Her name, IxKante, indicates that her mother was a Kante and that she was therefore actually a step-sister of Ahaw

Kan Ek', reflecting the fact that their father, like most Itza nobles, had more than one wife. (Ah- and Ix- are, respectively, male and female prefixes for Maya surnames.)

AhChan's father, also AhChan, was from Tipuh, a town located in western Belize near the present-day town of San Ignacio. Following IxKante's death he married another sister of Ahaw Kan Ek'. Tipuh, located on the frontiers of Itza territory, had been under Spanish control until 1637, when the Itzas staged a revolt that reverberated throughout the colonial mission towns of Belize and resulted in the expulsion of Spanish priests, administrators, and merchants. When the elder AhChan was born, perhaps about 1640, the Itzas controlled Tipuh, which had long been the most important Maya town in the region. His own father was probably a military administrator sent from Nohpeten to govern the area. As an adult, AhChan's father followed in his own father's footsteps, leading the military occupation of a region between Tipuh and Nohpeten then controlled by enemies of the Itzas known as the Kowohs. AhChan himself was probably born in the principal town of this region, known as Yalain, following this occupation, which most likely occurred during the 1630s.

Following the Itza occupation of the Yalain region most of the Kowohs, whose ancestors had also migrated there from northern Yucatán, relocated along the northern shores of Lake Petén Itzá. Relations between the Itzas and Kowohs remained fragile and even hostile thereafter, and AhChan's marriage to a member of the principal Kowoh ruling family reflected some effort to secure an alliance. Although he was not in the dynastic line, AhChan's high-ranking status as a member of the royal family, combined with his political astuteness and charismatic personality, destined him to become the principal Itza diplomat during the confusing and stressful closing years of the seventeenth century. He apparently neither spoke nor wrote Spanish prior to the conquest of the Itzas, although it seems likely that he later developed these skills. Ultimately he was to lead his subjects in a bold creation of his own independent kingdom in southern Belize.

The Itza system of governance in which AhChan participated was a complex one, grounded in principles of dual rulership (the king and a high priest, his cousin), a quadripartite division of elite governance over territories, and a cross-cutting system of representation on the ruling council from outlying towns and regions. These principles reflect ancient cultural features long recognized to have characterized the civilizations of Mesoamerica, in particular the Mayas. Nohpeten, densely covered with homes, palaces, and temples, served as the headquarters of the ruling elite. Most of the Itza population lived as cultivators in towns and villages on the surrounding mainland.

There is much more about AhChan's life and personality that remains unknown. Spanish documentation about individual lives, especially those of native peoples, was controlled by the interests of the individuals writing, and sometimes censoring, them. In the case of a Conquest activity such as the one in which AhChan was an important native player, politicians, military men, and missionaries all had their own interests at stake and were anxious to portray both enemies and friends in particular lights and to construct reports that would please and satisfy their superiors. The ethnohistorian focuses on the experiences and perspectives of the native "other" more than on those European voices in the documents in an attempt to move beyond the colonial gaze that colors all such writings. In them, however, when the native voice on rare occasions does speak, the message emerges only through the filter of European translation, interpretation, and even misrepresentation. Overcoming this limitation of the historiography of European-native interaction, without engaging in undue speculation, is an immense challenge.

We may wish that we knew more about AhChan's personal and family life, his inner thoughts about Itza versus Christian values and beliefs, his appearance and personal demeanor, the content of the orations that he delivered to his own allies—the list could go on for many pages. Yet we do know some things about him that allow us to paint in broad strokes a coherent but incomplete biography of a man whose actions and personal decisions seem to make sense to us today.

THE CONQUEST OF THE ITZAS: AN OVERVIEW

In 1693 the Spanish crown authorized Martín de Ursúa y Arizmendi, a Basque bureaucrat and governor-designate of Yucatán, and the president of the Audiencia of Guatemala to open jointly a new road that would connect Yucatán and Guatemala. While the "pacification"of the Itzas was not specified in official orders, Ursúa quickly made it his principal goal, rerouting the original direction of the road to have it terminate at the western end of Lake Petén Itzá.

As troops began to advance toward Itza territory in 1695, rumors about prophecies associated with the 256-year cyclical Maya *k'atun* calendar began to circulate, predicting a new age when the Itzas would surrender peacefully. The arrival of AhChan as the king's ambassador in Mérida at the end of 1695 further reinforced these rumors. AhChan claimed that Ahaw Kan Ek' wished to submit peacefully to Spanish colonization, which led Ursúa to press the king to fulfill his promise. A Franciscan friar, Andrés de Avendaño y Loyola, spent several days with the king at Nohpeten in early 1696 and left a detailed account of his journey and visit that revealed that many Itzas by then regarded Ahaw Kan Ek' as a traitor to his own people.[3]

The Itza king's enemies forced Avendaño to leave Nohpeten, and Itzas soon captured and murdered Yucatecan and Guatemalan soldiers and missionaries arriving separately at the lake. Ursúa and his troops reached the western port of the lake in February 1697. There boat builders completed and launched a sizeable oar-driven, heavily armed attack boat or *galeota*. The Spanish attack on Nohpeten on March 13 was brief but caused significant loss of Maya life. The occupiers found a deserted island but soon captured the ruler and other high-ranking Itzas. Ursúa returned to Campeche, leaving a small garrison isolated on their fortified island *presidio* (named Nuestra Señora de los Remedios y San Pablo) to cope with declining food supplies and a sea of hostile Mayas on the mainland.

A military rescue mission arrived from Guatemala in 1699, joined by Ursúa. The Guatemalans stayed only three months while conditions deteriorated even further. They brought a devastating epidemic that killed many Spaniards and further ravaged the native population. When they left, they took with them, in shackles, Ahaw Kan Ek', his son, and two cousins, including the high priest. Of these only the king and his son survived the long journey to Santiago de Guatemala (now Antigua Guatemala), where they spent the rest of their lives under house arrest.

Priests from Yucatán established a dozen mission towns among the surviving Itzas and Kowohs during 1702–03. In 1704, Maya leaders executed a well-planned but brief rebellion that brought about the permanent abandonment of most of the mission towns. Additional missions were later established in the region as Spaniards captured and relocated other fugitive Mayas. From a native central Petén population in 1697 of at least 60,000 persons, only about 7,000 remained by 1708. The primary cause of this tragic decline was disease. Today, due to numerous historical factors, including generations of ethnic group intermarriages and official linguistic suppression, only several dozen individuals still speak the Itza language.

THE KING'S AMBASSADOR

In 1695 the Itzas, anticipating a military attack from Yucatán, were deeply divided over strategies of defense. Whereas Ahaw Kan Ek' appeared willing to surrender, thus hoping to avoid a battle with superior Spanish forces, he faced violent opposition within the royal family, some of whose members allied with their former enemies, the Kowohs. So effective was this alliance that sometime during 1695 the Kowohs attacked Nohpeten and burned some of its buildings, probably in an aborted effort to dethrone the king.

When Ahaw Kan Ek' appointed AhChan in 1695 as his ambassador to Mérida, the ruler drove the wedge between these warring factions even deeper. AhChan's diplomatic actions were clearly intended to maintain Ahaw Kan Ek' as the legitimate supreme ruler, even if that meant colonial submission of the Itzas to the Spaniards. The ruler's uncle and the Kowohs, on the other hand, opposed any diplomatic negotiation with the Spanish enemy, viewing both the ruler and his nephew as traitors. Colonial officials, unaware that AhChan's diplomatic actions had intensified what already amounted to a state of war in central Petén, understandably failed to grasp these indigenous conflicts.

Ursúa and his political allies publicized AhChan's visit to Mérida at Christmastime in 1695 as a turning point in Yucatecan history. AhChan, they claimed, delivered official promises from his uncle, the king, that at last the Itzas had submitted to the Spanish crown and accepted Christianity as the one true religion. AhChan, previously unknown in Spanish circles, was baptized and became an overnight hero and the subject of widespread admiration, gossip, and speculation. For a time the governor's principal preoccupation would be the political significance of AhChan's message of the Itzas' peaceful surrender. Ursúa was, at least for the moment, convinced that he was within sight of winning the great prize— tens of thousands of Itza souls and tribute payers who passively awaited the arrival of occupation forces.

AhChan's first encounter with Spanish politics is a complex tale filled with intrigue, misrepresentation, and subsequent charges by Ursúa's political enemies that AhChan was a "false ambassador" of the Itza "king." Because his legitimacy and goodwill were unquestioned by Ursúa, the governor touted his attainment of this Itza noble's sincere loyalty as one of his major political accomplishments. Ursúa and AhChan were to become uneasy friends and allies in an unlikely drama that ended in tragic events that neither could have predicted. This, then, is AhChan's story.

FIRST MISSION TO MÉRIDA

During 1695 several interested parties in Mérida and Guatemala began making concerted efforts, sometimes in competition with one another, to contact the Itza rulers. All sought to achieve a peaceful solution to the Itza "problem" by negotiating peace terms that would somehow result in the nonviolent incorporation of the Maya kingdom into colonial political, social, and religious institutions. Ahaw Kan Ek' and his co-rulers became aware of the seriousness of Spanish intentions during April of that year, when armed Guatemalan troops, native archers from Guatemala, and several Dominican missionaries who accompanied them journeyed from Verapaz northward toward Itza territory. Although they sought peaceful contact with the Itzas, the result was violence, with several elite Itzas taken prisoner and others killed and wounded. The Guatemalans, discouraged by these events, abandoned their project.

Simultaneously, Spanish troops from Campeche, under Ursúa's orders, attempted but failed to reach Itza territory, retreating in late April after a violent encounter with Kehaches northwest of the Itzas. Ursúa immediately authorized a second campaign with a much larger military force, a military engineer, and construction workers who would begin opening a road through the forest into Itza lands. Accompanying these were three Franciscan missionaries whose task was to convince any Mayas they encountered to relocate their settlements along the road and accept Christian instruction. The leader of these missionaries was Fray Andrés de Avendaño y Loyola, of Spanish birth and a scholar of Yucatecan language and culture. He believed that certain widely circulated reports of Maya prophecies, said to be shared by the Itzas, were part of a divine plan to lead the Itzas to Christianity. He hoped to facilitate this outcome, working arduously but unsuccessfully over the next year to do so. His efforts would soon bring him into direct contact with AhChan in Mérida, with AhChan's relatives in Yalain, and even with Ahaw Kan Ek'.

Beginning in June 1695, Avendaño and his missionary companions, accompanied by Christian Mayas from Yucatán, nearly reached Itza territory. Dismayed by the violent excesses of Spanish troops against the Mayas captured along the road, however, Avendaño abandoned his attempts and returned to Mérida in September. He thereupon began to plan a second journey, determined to reach the Itza capital, Nohpeten. This time, embarking on December 13, he would succeed.

While these events were taking place, others were occurring on the eastern frontiers of Itza territory that would result in a little-publicized advance visit by AhChan to Mérida in September. On July 7, Captain Francisco Hariza y Arruyo, the Spanish *alcalde* (mayor) of the outpost villa of Bacalar-at-Chunhuhub' in present-day Quintana Roo, wrote to Ursúa from the village of Saksuus on the upper Belize River. He was at last making progress in baptizing uncontacted Mopan Mayas in this remote area, but he also wrote, "I hope in God and the holiest Virgin of the Rosary that before long Your Lordship will have to sign the elections of the Indians of Tah Itza island [that is, Nohpeten], because I have sent an Indian ambassador with a letter and other explanations." Hariza had also appointed Tipuh's town council and planned to send its members to

Mérida at the beginning of the year for the traditional annual confirmation of their so-called elections.

Hariza's ambassador to Nohpeten, Mateo Wikab', was from Tipuh. The alcalde had sent him there in April with gifts and a letter. He had waited in vain several months for Wikab' to return but was so keen to present the first fruits of his success to Ursúa that he departed in August for Mérida. Hariza and his seven Maya companions stood before Ursúa in Mérida on September 7 with a gift of Itza clothing, and Ursúa confirmed their "elections."

The governor's confirmation of Tipuh's council members' appointments was a standard requirement for all Maya town councils throughout Yucatán, but the ceremony usually took place near the beginning of January. Clearly, he intended to accomplish something else by rushing these Tipuhans before Governor Ursúa. In fact, some of them were not from Tipuh at all but part of an advance party of Itzas sent by Ahaw Kan Ek' to explore peace terms with the Yucatecan Spaniards. The leader of this party was AhChan himself, who must have arrived at Tipuh during August with news from Ahaw Kan Ek' that the Itzas were prepared to begin negotiations of surrender with the governor of Yucatán.

Avendaño, who had just returned from his first journey along the new road leading to Itza territory, later reported having served food to this delegation at his quarters in the Franciscan convent known as La Mejorada, in Mérida. They were, he said, from Yalain, AhChan's hometown. When he visited Yalain in 1696, Avendaño learned that those who accompanied AhChan to Mérida were his younger brother, known as AhChant'an and Nikte Chan, and two other Itzas, AhTek and AhK'u. The remaining three Mayas in Hariza's party were the only ones from Tipuh and therefore the only ones who actually received their staffs of office.

At this meeting, AhChan and his Itza companions invited the friar to visit Nohpeten by traveling through Tipuh and Yalain, where new houses would welcome him and his Franciscan companions. Later events indicate that Ahaw Kan Ek' had authorized his nephew's journey to Mérida and that it was he, the king, who was the source of this invitation to visit Nohpeten. The alcalde Hariza and Ursúa were well aware of the delegation's ultimate diplomatic purpose. Shortly after this meeting, AhChan and his party left Mérida with Hariza and the Tipuhans. Hariza carried with him a letter from Ursúa to be delivered to Ahaw Kan Ek' himself. Learning nothing of the outcome of the trip made by Mateo Wikab' to Nohpeten, he sent another Bacalareño, Pablo Gil de Azamar, to escort AhChan and his six companions back to Tipuh, which they reached on October 28. There Gil found Wikab', who recounted to him the surprising news that when he had arrived at Nohpeten:

the said Indians were preparing three or four thousand Indians to make war against some Spaniards, who they say consist of more than one hundred. These entered on horses. . . . Then [the Spaniards] made war against them during which thirty Indians died and one was taken prisoner. The said Uicab [*sic*] says that he saw one who had been axed and struck in the middle of the head with the butt of a musket; he returned to his town [with his wound] full of worms. Because of this the reyezuelo [Ahaw Kan Ek'] was found to be very upset.

This encounter was the one, noted earlier, that had occurred in April with Guatemalan troops.

At Nohpeten, Ahaw Kan Ek' had not only accepted gifts from Hariza, delivered by Wikab', but had also made a stunning offer in poetic language that Ursúa was to quote many times as the first official Itza recognition of Spanish supremacy:

So tell that captain [Hariza] that I shall receive him with pleasure. And I promise to surrender myself at his feet with eighty thousand Indians that I have under my command, subdued and subjected, and that with a thousand affections I shall receive the water of baptism, I and all my vassals. And tell him also that he must not deceive me in order to kill me; that I promise his governor four thousand Indians for the city of Mérida, because I desire much to see his king. Tell him [Hariza] also that when he arrives at that town [an unidentified port town on the lake] he should send for me to call [on him], advising me by whomever, that at his dispatch I shall descend to see him, to know if it is he who grants me peace, because if he comes directly to my town, I shall make war.

Hariza's letter to Ahaw Kan Ek' included a request for an audience with the king, a proposal for his peaceful surrender and baptism by a priest who would accompany Hariza, and a statement concerning the significance of pending k'atun prophecies. Wikab' read the letter to Ahaw Kan Ek', and in response the king said "that everything was true and that the time of the prophecies had already arrived, and that he wished to see our governor, since he had offered him peace. 'Because the others (he says) wish not to conquer towns but only to kill us. And because of that we proceed to give them wars. But [he said] that to your governor I shall render vassalage, because my descent is from that province.' "

After meeting with Wikab' at Tipuh in October, Gil decided to send one of the new alcaldes of Tipuh, Andrés K'eb', as a second emissary to Ahaw Kan Ek'. Accompanied by AhChan and his three kinsmen from Yalain, K'eb' carried a machete and earrings as gifts for the Itza ruler and possibly Ursúa's letter to the king as well. This was a difficult time for further negotiations at Nohpeten because rumors were circulating among the people around Lake Petén Itzá that the Guatemalans would return to kill them all. Nonetheless, Ahaw Kan Ek' decided to send his representatives again to Mérida, where they would make a formal public offer of peaceful submission. Gil urged Hariza to communicate this message from Ahaw Kan Ek' to Ursúa quickly, before the Guatemalans made further moves against the Itzas. He also offered to leave Tipuh with a group of Nohpeten representatives to Mérida before the end of November, promising that they would confirm the Itza peace offering.

SECOND MISSION TO MÉRIDA

On December 13, 1695, Avendaño set off from Mérida on his second journey toward Nohpeten. He carried with him official letters, including one from Ursúa to Ahaw Kan Ek', and gifts for the Itza ruler. Even before Avendaño left Mérida, Pablo Gil was already escorting the Itza representatives once again to the Yucatecan capital. AhChan and his Itza companions arrived at the ancient site of Bacalar, just north of the present-day boundary between Belize and Mexico, on December 7. There Gil wrote to Hariza, who was awaiting their arrival on the road ahead at Bacalar-at-Chunhuhub', that "there are here four Indians from the island of Noh Peten. One of them is the nephew of the monarch, who brought his uncle's crown in order to turn it over to your mercy and to the lord governor [as well as] the other gifts that he brings." In addition to AhChan and three other Itzas, Gil had with him several Mopans ("Muzuls") from the Tipuh area and the two Tipuhan alcaldes, who were to serve as interpreters. In addition to the gifts brought by AhChan, Gil forwarded to Hariza the Itza clothing received by Mateo Wikab' on his earlier visit to Nohpeten.

On December 12, Ursúa received in Mérida the news of the impending arrival of the Itza party. He immediately wrote a brief, ecstatic letter to the viceroy of New Spain: "I have just received a letter from Captain Francisco de Hariza, *alcalde ordinario* of the villa of Bacalar, with a note from Pablo Gil concerning his arrival from Tipu with four Indians from the great island of the Itzas, and among them a nephew of the petty king of that opulent nation, who comes in the name of his uncle to give obeisance, in sign of which he carries his crown. Very singular news and of great pleasure for me as well as this entire city, reflecting that the hour has arrived that His Majesty Our Lord is served to bring so many souls to the pale of the Holy Church."

Over the next few weeks each party rushed to secure its plans and interests. Hariza hurried with AhChan and his delegation on their long journey to Mérida. The secular clergy hastened their preparation for AhChan's baptism. Avendaño rushed to meet Ahaw Kan Ek' at Nohpeten to confirm his surrender. By December 20, Ursúa was prepared for the official reception of the Itza delegation. It was to be a grand affair, involving as many of the Spanish elite of Mérida as possible. He hoped that these public rituals would symbolize for the Mayas of Yucatán the end of the free forest frontier and the beginning of full colonial control over the last independent kingdom. Ursúa appointed the chief governmental secretary to prepare an official record of the Itza delegation's arrival, the attendant festivities, and the emissary's statement. Meanwhile, the ecclesiastical council of the cathedral was preparing for the religious ceremonies that would follow the diplomatic reception. The council, too, had appointed a secretary to prepare a parallel record of events.

Christmas Day, 1695, fell on Sunday. While Hariza waited outside Mérida with AhChan and the rest of the Itza delegation, the clergy celebrated Mass in the city's magnificent cathedral and offered prayers for the following day's events. On Monday morning at about ten o'clock Governor Ursúa was notified of the approach of four Itzas, who were nearing the entrance to the city. He left his offices immediately with the principal government clerk, Captain Francisco de Avila, and other officials to meet the arriving group. By the time the greeting party stepped out of their carriages and dismounted from their horses at the convent of La Mejorada on the outskirts of town, the visitors were already waiting. There, in the convent church's patio, Captain Avila reported:

> Preceding the courtesies, His Lordship invited [the Itza ambassador] into the carriage with him, and with all the said retinue and multitude of people who had crowded around to see the arrival of the said ambassador he took him to the holy cathedral church of this said city, from where, His Lordship having made a speech, he came to the palace and royal dwellings, where I joined [them]. And in the presence of His Lordship, the venerable dean and Cabildo Vacant See, many clergy, priests of the Company of Jesus [Jesuits], the city council, and other personnel already mentioned, the said ambassador took in his hands a crown that he carried, made of feathers of different colors in the style of a tiara, and he handed it over to His Lordship, the said ambassador saying to him . . . these words:
>
> Lord: Representing the person of my uncle the great Ah Canek, king and absolute lord of the Itzas, in his name and on his behalf, I come to prostrate myself at your feet and offer before them his royal crown, so that in the name of your great king, whose person you represent, you would receive and admit us into his royal service and under his protection, favor, and patronage; and that you would grant us fathers-priests who would baptize us and administer and teach the law of the true God. This is for what I have come and what my king requests and desires with the common sentiment of all his vassals.

Following Ursúa's formal response, "there entered and prostrated themselves in the presence of the said lord governor and captain general two Indians who came in the company of the said ambassador, from another nation who are called Muzuls . . . to render obeisance to him or as he who represents the person of His Majesty."

This diplomatic ritual was carefully planned, precisely staged, and apparently well rehearsed. The visitors' entrance into the city was timed to the hour. AhChan's short speech was written for him; the choice of every word and phrase was that of a Spaniard knowledgeable in such matters. He said to Ursúa exactly what Ursúa wanted him to say, using the phrasing that was legally necessary for the representative of a nation submitting itself to Spanish sovereignty. After AhChan was taken to the cathedral, Mass was celebrated, following which Ursúa delivered a sermon. The principals returned to the governor's residence, where additional ceremonies were staged in honor of AhChan and his three Itza companions.

Then, on Wednesday, December 29, Ursúa ordered AhChan to make a formal declaration in his presence before the government secretary and through the interpreter general. Ursúa, as on other similar occasions, asked the questions himself. A satisfactory declaration would pave the way for AhChan's baptism, which would take place the following Friday. The questions were carefully worded. AhChan's answers indicate that he was being manipulated by the governor, who sought clear and unambiguous legal justification for his designs on the Itzas.

When asked, "Who sent him to this province and for what purpose?" AhChan repeated the major points of his speech delivered on Monday, stating:

> he came there under orders of the great Ah Canek, his uncle, king of the provinces of the Itzas, to make a covenant and establish peace between the Spaniards and [the Itzas], and likewise that they might be in communication with one another, ceasing all war, and also to solicit commerce and trade for the things that they needed; and that he should say to the lord governor that he [Ahaw Kan Ek'] sent him his crown and prostrated it at his feet, requesting of him that they drink of the same water and inhabit the same house, because the designated ending of the prophecies of his ancestors had been completed, as a result of which he and the four kings who obeyed him at once rendered the owed vassalage to the King Our Lord in order that with that they might secure his favor and patronage, and also that they might obtain fathers-priests to be sent to them who would baptize them and teach the law of the true God.

It is doubtful that AhChan spoke in precisely these words; more likely he replied affirmatively, with minor additional details, to several subsidiary questions. This conclusion is inescapable when the wording of the reply is compared with a crucial section of Ursúa's letter of December 8 to Ahaw Kan Ek', which at this moment was being carried by Avendaño to Nohpeten: "And now also in the name of our great king don Carlos II, I ordered that you be given notice of all these things that I have said. And you, Ah Canek, have replied that if it is for peace and not war, you will surrender with all the Itzas to the obedience and service of our true king don Carlos, because the time has arrived in which your plate and your calabash might be one with the Spaniards, and in which you might be Christians."

In addition to confirming the offer made by Ahaw Kan Ek', as communicated by Mateo Wikab', the answer as stated—as well as Ursúa's letter—carefully noted that the offer of obedience was made with the understanding that war might cease and peace might reign between Spaniards and Itzas. AhChan's answer contained the additional understanding that peace would lead to the opening of trade between Yucatán and the Itza kingdom. This condition—that of peaceful conversion and the fostering of trade—was a primary requirement of the Spanish king's initial 1693 *cédula* to Ursúa, and the governor was eager to confirm that the Itzas understood and agreed to these terms. No less determined to avoid conflict had been Avendaño himself, who repeatedly insisted that military action not be used against any of the forest Mayas.

BAPTISMAL RITUALS

Over the next several days, AhChan and his companions remained in the governor's residence, where they received religious instruction in preparation for their baptism and first communion. Joining them as pupils were two unconverted Kejach Mayas who had been sent separately to Mérida. These two men were chosen as the first recipients of baptism on Friday, December 30, in the cathedral. Their ceremony was the prelude to the climactic Saturday baptisms of the Itzas.

Following these baptisms the musicians played while the entire party moved to the altar of the Virgin next to the choir, where an additional ensemble of four of Ursúa's black slaves provided recorder music, joined by a group playing bugles and trumpets and beating native turtle shells and drums. From there they moved to the presbytery, where the archdeacon presided over a Mass in which the two newly baptized Kejach Mayas received their first communion. Following the ceremony they were returned to the governor's residence.

The next morning an identical ceremony, with the same personnel and musical accompaniment, was carried out for the baptisms of AhChan and his three Itza companions. The ecclesiastical notary now described AhChan in impressive terms as "the ambassador of the great Ah Canek, monarch of the empire of the island of the Itzas in the forests." He was baptized Martín Francisco in honor of his godfather, Martín de Ursúa. His brother, sponsored by Pedro de Garrástegui Oleada, the Count of Miraflores and treasurer of the Santa Cruzada, received the name Pedro

Miguel Chan. His sister's husband was baptized Manuel Joseph Chayax in honor of his godfather, Sergeant Major Manuel Bolio, Ursúa's brother-in-law. Finally, AhTek, sponsored by Captain Juan Bernardo de Madrid, received the name Juan Francisco Tek.

With the completion of the nominal Christian conversion of three Itza notables, no further impediments could delay the conquest of this "infidel" nation. A fundamental principle in Spanish policies of conversion and conquest was that crown demands for peaceful conversion could be overlooked once a people's leadership had come to recognize the true God. Ahaw Kan Ek', having now accepted Christianity through his sister's son, was no longer the ruler of an independent foreign nation. AhChan's baptism represented the moment at which the Itzas ceased to fall under the protection of crown policies barring them from military conquest.

RETURN TO ITZA TERRITORY
AND ESCAPE FROM TIPUH

While AhChan was in Mérida, Avendaño, well aware of the Itza ruler's decision to send his nephew as his emissary, was on his way to Nohpeten. Once there he succeeded in reinforcing the king's previous decision to surrender but soon discovered that most Itzas regarded Ahaw Kan Ek' as a traitor. Avendaño, a party to this treason and in mortal danger, hastily slipped out of Nohpeten with his companions and nearly died trying to find his way back to Spanish-held territory. It soon became clear that Spanish optimism for the peaceful surrender of the Itzas was premature and misinformed.

The perceived failure of peaceful initiatives led to a series of violent encounters between Itzas and Spaniards. Ursúa became convinced that the only option was military conquest. Following Avendaño's expulsion from Nohpeten, the Itzas attacked, captured, and reportedly murdered Yucatecan and Guatemalan soldiers and missionaries rushing to Lake Petén Itzá. Ursúa, infuriated, was now determined to strike a military blow at the Itzas, whom he considered to be renegade subjects of the Spanish empire. His aims, which he pursued against great opposition in Mérida, were not only to complete the royal road to Itza territory but also to move troops and heavy artillery to the lakeshore for a large-scale attack on Nohpeten, the island capital.

As these events unfolded, AhChan and his Itza companions set off once again for Tipuh in mid-January 1696. Their initial "escort" consisted of only twelve Spanish soldiers, commanded by Hariza, and ten secular priests. Hariza and the priests learned of Avendaño's forced departure from Nohpeten, but they stuck by their intention to accompany

AhChan to present Ahaw Kan Ek' with Ursúa's demand for peaceful submission. These plans ground to a halt when, a few days after their arrival, AhChan ran away from Tipuh. Hariza and the priests decided that it was now too dangerous to make the journey to Nohpeten on their own.

AhChan was not seen again until March 10, 1697, when he appeared at Ursúa's camp at Ch'ich' on the western end of Lake Petén Itzá, only three days before the Spaniards stormed Nohpeten. There Ursúa questioned him about the circumstances of his sudden departure from Tipuh. Ursúa's version of his testimony (which I quote showing Ursúa's voice in italics) reported that two weeks after AhChan arrived there, the *cacique* of Tipuh, named Sima, said to him, "What are you doing here? Why don't you go, [because] they will cut off your head?"

> *Asked what cause or motive the cacique Sima had to say that they would cut off his head and to tell him that he should run away or go, he said that*:
> The cacique Sima told him that on the Petén they had caused injury and death to the Spaniards, and that [he] answered him that he had not been there and that he was not guilty.
> *Asked how it was that, not being guilty, and having received such news, he fled, he said that*:
> The same cacique frightened him and was the cause of his running away.

Sima knew full well that as soon as Hariza learned of the Itzas' murders and kidnappings of Spaniards on the shores of Lake Petén Itzá on February 2, he would accuse AhChan of having falsified or misrepresented himself in Mérida. AhChan did the only thing he could do under the circumstances—escape from Tipuh as quickly as possible. He went on to report that he then went home to Yalain, where he learned that other leaders had joined in armed opposition to Ahaw Kan Ek'. At that point he went into temporary hiding, continuing to fear, with good reason, that enemies of Ahaw Kan Ek' would kill him. Leaving Yalain as Spanish troops neared the Itzas' lake, he sought the protection of one AhPana at the small island of Motskal (possibly Islote Grande, just east of Nohpeten), close enough to have soon been discovered by "the king's people."

Upon being called for by Ahaw Kan Ek', AhChan moved his encampment to the lakeshore but at an unspecified location, where he feared attack by his neighbors; he did not risk visiting Nohpeten itself. He had spent four days before his meeting with Ursúa patrolling the bay against squadrons coming to attack the Spaniards. Although his testimony reads as if AhChan had gone alone with AhPana to Motskal and then alone to his new location on the lakeshore, this was not the case. We can assume that he took a substantial group of followers from Yalain—in essence, a small army—to both places and set up defensive encampments in each one. The aim of his military actions, I believe, was to provide support for the beleaguered king whose enemies sought to depose him for his friendly overtures to the Spaniards. Had it not been for AhChan's military protection these enemies might have overthrown the dynasty before Ursúa could launch his attack on Nohpeten on March 13.

Although AhChan's desertion stirred up a flurry of speculation and accusations in Yucatecan circles that he was a false ambassador, all available evidence, including his testimony on March 10, suggests that this was not the case. AhChan was a man caught between historical events over which he had, temporarily at least, lost control. His extensive testimony before Ursúa contained undisguised indictments against various Itza subrulers whom he accused of murdering Spaniards, while he defended his uncle, Ahaw Kan Ek', who, he claimed, attempted unsuccessfully to stop them from committing these acts or to punish them afterward.

Ursúa took AhChan into custody following his testimony, regarding him as a potentially useful future ally in his pacification of the Itzas. AhChan and his brother-in-law Manuel Joseph Chayax were placed aboard the armed attack *galeota* that left the Spanish encampment with troops before dawn on March 13. As the boat neared the fortified island of Nohpeten, canoes filled with Itza archers surrounded it, letting their arrows fly. Ursúa ordered that no shots be fired, but what followed was mayhem. AhChan, it was said by the officers and priests, spied from the galeota a small canoe near the shore to their north and identified the young man in it as a neighbor of Ahaw Kan Ek'. He called to the person in the canoe, who paddled close to the galeota. Ursúa ordered AhChan to tell him to go to Ahaw Kan Ek' and "tell him on his behalf that he would give him three chances to make peace." At that moment the defenders released volleys of arrows from the shore and the canoes. One arrow struck Sergeant Juan González in the arm; another hit a soldier named Bartolomé Durán who, "perhaps as a result of the pain," fired his gun. At that point, according to Ursúa, González lost control of the infantry, as did the officer in charge of landing the galeota and deciding when to release the troops.

The Spanish troops apparently began firing their rifles indiscriminately, resulting in the rapid retreat of the Itza defenders. Those who were not killed abandoned their canoes and defensive posts on the island and swam desperately toward the mainland. While accusing them of sheer cowardice, the commanding officers later wrote that AhChan "disembarked with us with such courage and valor that with a musket or *trabuco* he killed one of the Indians who had started to swim away." AhChan, of course, may have had his own reasons for choosing to kill that particular individual.

ANOTHER ESCAPE

During the days immediately following the Spaniards' occupation of Nohpeten, according to Ursúa, AhChan behaved as a loyal colonial ally. Four days after the attack, seventeen persons from Yalain visited Ursúa at Nohpeten, "offering their obedience" to the king of Spain. Among these was AhChan's brother and his wife and her sister. AhChan, Ursúa reported, had "behaved with inexpressible loyalty, and he has served me with much guidance and assistance." These people from Yalain had been given responsibility for apprehending the royal family. Although Ursúa had ordered Manuel Chayax, AhChan's brother-in-law, to bring Ahaw Kan Ek' and his relatives to Nohpeten, other persons from Yalain received credit for the accomplishment. Chamach Xulu, a leader of Yalain, was cited by Ursúa and his officers as having been the principal party responsible for the capture of Ahaw Kan Ek'. Several of Ursúa's officers later testified, however, that it was actually AhChan who had brought Ahaw Kan Ek' and his family to the island.

The followers of Chamach Xulu and AhChan were apparently eager to see the rulers brought before the Spaniards. Later reports that Christian conversion took an early hold among the relatives and allies of AhChan and Chamach Xulu may indicate that at this early date the Yalain elites simply wanted to see the Kan Ek' family forced to accept Christianity—that they believed that a peaceful resolution with the Spaniards and with each other could be achieved only through conversion.

As Spanish reprisals against the captured Itza ruler, his cousin the high priest, and others increased during the months to follow, however, AhChan became disillusioned with his colonial allies. On September 24, 1697, a soldier at the presidio wrote that he had run away from the island with "all of the Indians," who would have included his brother, brother-in-law, and other relatives. Ever since they had departed, every Spaniard had been anxious and on the lookout for attacks. The surrounding Itzas went about menacing the troops, presumably from canoes in the lake, in the hope that they would abandon the presidio altogether. Apparently the native population on the island had grown considerably over the intervening months: AhChan was said to have slipped away in the night, silently and without alerting the guards, with more than five hundred people.

The loss of the Spaniards' friend Martín Francisco Chan, who had served Ursúa, in the general's words, "as a light and guide for the capture of the principal island and as an inducement for the rest who gave themselves up," was an ominous sign. AhChan was now in a position to mount a major resistance against the vulnerable presidio with the support of the eastern province and perhaps even with his new allies among the Kowohs. Nonetheless, he sent a message from Yalain, where he had sought refuge, that he had not run away but rather had gone there to wait until he learned more about a report that he and other native leaders were to be killed by the Spaniards. His wait lasted five years.

FROM CACIQUE TO KING IN EXILE TO CACIQUE

Not until 1702 did secular priests, working with the Spanish military, begin to resettle these runaways into mission settlements around the main lake. One of the twelve missions established during that and the following year, San Miguel, was placed under the authority of none other than AhChan, who was captured and brought to the presidio along with his wife and children on May 20. He said that he had run away from the Spaniards for the second time because he had heard rumors that Ursúa planned to execute him. Since his escape from the presidio he had become the leader of the sizable and virtually independent Yalain province.

Ursúa agreed with Aguilar's suggestion that AhChan be pardoned for his errors and that, given the long history of their relationship, this prodigal godson should be sent to Mérida to live with him, lest AhChan inadvertently set off new unrest in the Petén wilderness. By December, unaware that AhChan had attempted to escape yet again, Ursúa had reconsidered the matter, thinking it might be better to send AhChan to live either with Guatemalan general Melchor de Mencos, who had led reinforcements to Petén during 1699, or in another household in Guatemala.

AhChan and his family were immediately placed in San Miguel, where he was made cacique as a means of attracting others to join him. This was a rational choice, considering his identification with Yalain, the probable origin of the first families to arrive. All but six or seven of the forty-four original families, however, already had run away, and AhChan immediately disappeared with everyone else on May 23. A Spanish officer chased them all down again and brought them back.

AhChan remained head of San Miguel through 1704, when an anti-Spanish plot among the mission inhabitants resulted in a brief but bloody rebellion. Although he was absolved of complicity in the plot, AhChan soon thereafter disappeared from Spanish eyes one more time and reassumed his role as a leader of Mayas living beyond Spanish control. What subsequently happened to him can be only partially reconstructed, but even the bare outlines found in the documents tell an evocative story.

Between 1705 and 1710 a Guatemalan settler in Petén, Nicolás de Lizarraga, produced a multicolored map of the "forest of Peten Itza." The map itself has been lost, but his detailed legend, written on a foldout, has survived. In one section of this legend he describes a native "province" that he calls "El Chan," where don Martín Chan, alias AhChan, had been made "king" over Mopans and Chols. He undoubtedly had Itzas among his followers as well. Lizarraga's geographical description of El Chan clearly identifies it as the southern coastal plain of Belize, a region known to have been occupied by Chols and Mopans.

Apparently, AhChan had been accompanied to this region by his followers. On a 1770 map, across the region between Verapaz and the Belize River, is written the phrase "Tierras yncultas havitadas de Yndios Gentiles Ytzaes" (uncivilized lands inhabited by Gentile Indians, Itzas). AhChan would therefore have been the leader of a multiethnic population comprising Itzas, Mopans, and Chols. These were people who had apparently put aside any previous enmities, perhaps convinced by AhChan himself that their only hope for continued independence was to join forces in this relatively remote region.

In 1708, Lizarraga wrote that 40 leagues from Los Dolores there were two towns founded by five native youths from Petén. Melchor de Mencos had taken them with him to Santiago de Guatemala when he left Petén in 1699 and had kept them in his own home to teach them Christian doctrine. They had been baptized, and he arranged for them to be taught to read and write under the tutelage of a Jesuit, Antonio Valtierra. One of the pupils was named Juan Chab'in, indicating that he was an Itza; his companions must have been Itzas as well. Chab'in was so talented that Valtierra started to offer him instruction in grammar, and all five learned how to offer confession and communion in the absence of a priest.

These five young men, according to Lizarraga, sought and received government permission in 1707 to teach the Gospel among their "companions" in the forest. Mencos and Lizarraga gave them money to buy religious instructional materials, and the Jesuits presented them with images of Our Lady of Carmén and Saint Francis Xavier. Their mission, as it turned out, was twofold: named as captains, they succeeded in rounding up 700 families to settle in two communities, and as missionaries, they taught the reduced settlers something about the Gospel and saw to the construction of two churches. Their military mission, moreover, had another facet: they led battles against "the rest of the forest Indians, in particular with don Martín Chan, apostate and Prince among them."

These two towns were almost certainly in the Toledo district of southern Belize, a short distance west of San Luis, the colonial name of the old native settlement known as Mopan. The "battles" that led to their establishment were against AhChan, whose forest headquarters must also have been in southern Belize. In October 1757 a sixty-year-old Mopan named Francisco Sumkal, identified as the cacique of San Luis, testified at the Petén presidio that about ten years earlier, while hunting wild pigs, he had seen signs of "infidels" near his town. He said simply—and no more—that although the San Luis cacique of that time, one Martín Chan, "intended to follow the said signs, he never did it."

Spaniards had estimated AhChan's age in 1697 to be about thirty. He would therefore have been about eighty when the event described by Sumkal took place. This Martín Chan, who refused "to follow the said signs," may well have been the same AhChan who had spent much of his adult life tortured by personal conflicts over his loyalty to his own people versus their conquerors. At some point in his middle or old age, Spaniards and their native allies had, we might infer, captured him one last time—in southern Belize—and placed him once again in a position of authority in a native mission town, this time San Luis. As an old man in about 1767, one of his last acts as an Itza leader over his Mopan, Itza, and Chol subjects and allies was to ignore intentionally the signs indicating that others among his people still enjoyed their independence.

EPILOGUE: LIVING HISTORY

While a young graduate student of cultural anthropology at Brandeis University in the summer of 1965, I traveled with other students and my wife to British Honduras, now Belize, to gain experience and training in ethnographic field methods. I planned to work in the southernmost Toledo District, whose inland region is the home of several thousand Mopan and K'ekchi' Mayas. There, in the Mopan village of San Antonio, Mary and I received a warm welcome, and I instantly knew that I would devote my career as an anthropologist to learning more about the Maya people and their history. While I spent only that one summer in Toledo, I have returned to Belize many more times, primarily to work with Yucatec-speaking Mayas in the northern part of the country and to carry out historical research in the Archives of Belize. In subsequent years my interests turned to the Mayas of the Spanish colonial period in Belize and in neighboring regions in Guatemala and Mexico, and I found myself carrying out archival research in Seville, Spain, and in Guatemala City.

That early experience with my Mopan hosts in Belize and my colonial-period historical research came full circle in an unexpected way in 1997, when the staff of the Indian Law Resource Center, an organization devoted to representing the legal interests of indigenous peoples worldwide, approached me concerning a lawsuit with the government of Belize that they were pursuing on behalf of the Toledo Maya Cultural Council (TMCC), which since 1978 has worked to represent the interests of the Mopan and K'ekchi' peoples of that district. Would I be able and willing to write an affidavit that would support these Mayas' claim before the Supreme Court of Belize that they were the original inhabitants of the region and that they could therefore legally assert aboriginal property rights on logging concessions granted to foreign corporations by the government of Belize?

Along with two other anthropologists with historical knowledge of the area, I prepared the affidavit and responded with a second one to counterarguments presented by the attorney for the government of Belize. This is a complex legal case, with many other documents, including local land-use maps, presented by and on behalf of the TMCC. For me, as an ethnohistorian, this was a valuable opportunity to utilize the results of years of archival research on behalf of indigenous peoples who have for centuries lived under difficult (and worse) conditions imposed by colonial and postcolonial governments of foreign origin. The historical evidence that I cited in support of the TMCC's case spanned most of the known colonial history of the region, including evidence for AhChan's Itza-Mopan kingdom in exile as related above. While the Supreme Court of Belize has declined to hear the TMCC's case, it is now before the Inter-American Commission on Human Rights, which at the time of writing had not yet issued a ruling.

History matters deeply for people such as these Mayas. Dozens of similar human-rights claims by "first nations" throughout the world, supported by historical evidence framed in terms of international law and local customary law and practice, are currently being debated and developed. Some of these cases have already succeeded in gaining territorial and other special rights for indigenous peoples, and the power of historical evidence has been a central element in every one of them.

NOTES

1. Unless otherwise indicated, all information concerning AhChan and the events in which he participated is drawn from original documents in the Archivo General de Indias, Seville, Spain, and in the Archivo General de Centro América, Guatemala City. These unpublished primary sources are cited in Grant D. Jones, *The Conquest of the Last Maya Kingdom* (Stanford, CA, 1999), where much more information about these and related events may be found.

2. The spelling of Maya proper names in this chapter closely follows the orthography of the Academy of Mayan Languages of Guatemala, with the principal

exception, for the benefit of English-speaking readers, of the substitution of the letter "h" for the letter "j." Spoken Maya vowels approximate the sound of Spanish vowels. An apostrophe following a consonant or a vowel indicates that the sound is glottalized.

3. Jones, *The Conquest*, 187–220. Fray Andrés de Avendaño y Loyola, *Fray Andrés de Avendaño y Loyola: "Relación de las dos entradas que hice a la conversión de los gentiles ytzáex y cehaches,"* ed. Temis Vayhinger-Scheer (Möchmühl, 1997); idem, *Relation of Two Trips to Petén Made for the Conversion of the Heathen Ytzaex and Cehaches*, ed. Frank E. Comparato; trans. Charles P. Bowditch and Guillermo Rivera (Culver City, CA, 1987).

SUGGESTED READINGS

For a narrative analysis of the 1697 conquest of the Itzas, see Grant D. Jones, *The Conquest of the Last Maya Kingdom* (Stanford, CA, 1999). Jones's *Maya Resistance to Spanish Rule: Time and History on a Colonial Frontier* (Albuquerque, NM, 1989) provides earlier background on Maya-Spanish relations on the southern frontiers of Yucatán. His overview of a much larger region, "The Lowland Maya, from the Conquest to the Present," includes a comprehensive bibliographic essay (in Richard E. W. Adams and Murdo J. MacLeod, eds., *The Cambridge History of the Native Peoples of the Americas*, vol. 2, *Mesoamerica*, Part 1, 346–91 [New York, 2000]). See also Victoria Reifler Bricker's chapters on Spanish conquests in the Maya lowlands in her *Indian Christ, Indian King: The Historical Substrate of Maya Myth and Ritual* (Austin, TX, 1981). For two excellent examples of works that include the written Maya voice in the history of northern Yucatán, see Matthew Restall, *The Maya World: Yucatec Culture and Society, 1550–1850* (Stanford, CA, 1997) and the same author's *Maya Conquistador* (Boston, 1998).

The conquest of the Itzas was first described in a 1701 pro-colonial apology by the Spanish chronicler Juan de Villagutierre Soto-Mayor, available in English translation as *History of the Conquest of the Province of the Itzá* (Culver City, CA, 1983). The Franciscan missionary Andrés de Avendaño y Loyola described his 1696 encounters with the Itzas in a fascinating report, *Relation of Two Trips to Petén Made for the Conversion of the Heathen Ytzaex and Cehaches*, ed. Frank E. Comparato and trans. Charles P. Bowditch and Guillermo Rivera (Culver City, CA, 1987). Temis Vayhinger-Scheer has edited a Spanish transcription of the same work, *Fray Andrés de Avendaño y Loyola: "Relación de las dos entradas que hice a la conversion de los gentiles ytzáex y cehaches"* (Möchmühl, Germany, 1997). For the Guatemalan conquest of the Chol-speaking Lakandons during the mid-1690s, an event closely related to the conquest of the Itzas, see *Nicolás de Valenzuela: conquista del lacandón y conquista del Chol*, edited with commentary by Götz Freiherr von Houwald, 2 vols. (Berlin, 1979), which contains extensive primary source documentation.

PART III

REFORM, RESISTANCE, AND REBELLION, 1740–1825

*W*hen the last Habsburg king of Spain, Charles II, died childless in 1700, it took fifteen years of bloody conflict to ensure the succession of the French Bourbon claimant to the throne, Philip V. As the new king surveyed his devastated patrimony, the pressing need for commercial and fiscal reforms became obvious. The transatlantic trade with the Indies had reached its nadir, and contrabandists plied the Caribbean and Pacific with impunity. Policymakers in Madrid desperately searched for ways to reinvigorate commercial ties with the colonies and increase revenues for the empty royal coffers. At first, their effort to revive Spain and its empire largely involved reestablishing the old imperial system, but the loss of Havana in 1762 to the British during the Seven Years' War highlighted the need for more drastic measures.

During the reign of Charles III (1759–1788), the crown began dispatching royal inspectors (*visitadores*) to various parts of the Indies to gain information and begin the process of making administrative, fiscal, commercial, and military reforms. By 1750 it ended the sale of appointments to all high-ranking colonial offices and began replacing Creoles with younger, well-trained, peninsular-born bureaucrats. Officials in Madrid also created two new viceroyalties in regions of South America famous for being centers of contraband trade: New Granada in 1739, and the Río de la Plata in 1776 (see Map 4). In many areas of the empire the crown also sent out a series of intendants (responsible for administration, fiscal affairs, justice, and defense) who linked provincial magistrates with audiencias of the major cities. The government also shored up local defenses, enlarged the fleet, and built up the regular army and local militias. To pay for these costly reforms, colonial authorities raised taxes and created royal monopolies for the sale and distribution of key goods such as tobacco. Finally, the crown ended the transatlantic fleet convoys in 1740 and allowed individual licensed merchant vessels from Spain to trade with the Indies. Although this remedy increased colonial commerce, the Madrid government went further and allowed free trade with the empire between 1778 and 1789. It was a time of sweeping imperial changes.

Under the leadership of its chief minister, Sebastião José de Carvalho e Melo, the Marquis of Pombal, Portugal also initiated reforms designed to tap the resources of its chief colony in Brazil. Like his counterparts in Bourbon Spain, Pombol sought to increase tax yields, secure colonial

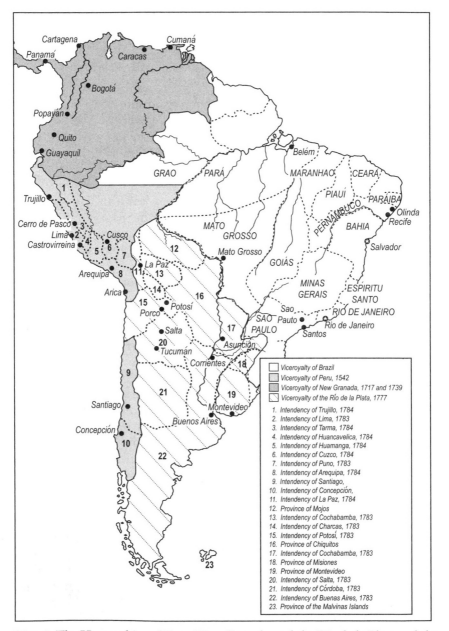

Map 4. The Viceroyalties of Peru, New Granada, and the Río de la Plata and the Viceroyalty of Brazil in the Late Eighteenth Century

defenses, and expand commercial ties between colony and metropolis. A particular concern was Portugal's reliance on Great Britain for manufactured goods needed in both the homeland and Brazil, and the large quantities of British contraband goods entering the colony. Pombol promoted Portuguese industries to curtail dependency on the British and to supply Brazilian markets. Moreover, to regain control over the colonial trade the chief minister abandoned the fleet system in 1765 and chartered three monopoly companies (which allowed only limited foreign participation) to trade with Brazil. He also revamped the colonial administration in Portugal and Brazil by establishing a new royal treasury in 1761 to centralize accounting, collect taxes more efficiently, and control expenditures. While these innovations had some impact on renovating the colonial ties with Brazil, Pombol's fall from power in 1777 limited their long-term effectiveness. Finally, lower gold production by 1750 and the slow decline of the sugar economy in Brazil also curtailed the success of the reform effort.

While the Bourbon reforms in Spanish America and Pombol's innovations in Brazil resulted in increased revenues and enhanced colonial commerce, they also produced a number of specific grievances in the Indies. In some areas, this unrest exploded into violent upheavals (such as the Rebellion of the Barrios in Quito in 1765, the Comunero Revolt in New Granada in 1781, the Túpac Amaru and Túpac Katari revolts in the Andes in 1781–1783, and the Inconfidencia Mineira in Minas Gerais in 1788). Nevertheless, Spain's and Portugal's rule continued unchallenged in most of the regions of their empires until Napoléon's army invaded the Iberian peninsula in 1807 to attack Portugal, a close ally of Great Britain, the French emperor's most bitter foe.

The Portuguese king, dom João VI, along with the entire court (nearly 12,000 people), fled in a British fleet to Brazil, where he ruled from 1808 to 1820. The king made profound changes in the colonial relationship, such as initiating free trade for Brazil, removing restrictions on manufactures, and granting British subjects extraterritorial rights. These changes culminated in his decision to raise Brazil to the status of a kingdom coequal with Portugal in 1810. When João VI reluctantly returned to Portugal in 1820, he left his son and heir, Pedro, in Brazil to rule as regent. After the Lisbon government reduced Brazil to colonial status and recalled Prince Pedro, he declared Brazil's independence, winning it with minimal bloodshed in 1822. The prince became the country's first emperor, Pedro I.

After his invasion of Spain, Napoléon forced its king, Charles IV, to abdicate on May 6, 1808, and his heir, Ferdinand, to renounce his rights to the succession. Napoleon then placed his elder brother, Joseph, on the throne, which led to a popular uprising against the French usurper. This tumult in Spain prompted a serious constitutional crisis in the Indies, where many Creoles believed that without a legitimate monarch, power reverted to the people. As a result, creole elites felt emboldened to establish provisional *juntas* in many major cities of the empire, usually to rule until a legitimate monarch was restored. Local Spanish authorities crushed many of these juntas, and others fell later to the Spanish armies sent by Ferdinand VII when he returned to the throne in 1814. Nevertheless, bloody wars for independence ensued that ultimately led to the independence of Mexico and Central America in 1822 and of South America by 1825.

As part of their reforms, the Spanish government allowed citizens born out of wedlock to purchase an edict of legitimation (*cédula de gracias al sacar*) that erased the "defect" of their birth. These edicts also allowed people to buy the honorific title of "don" and permitted those of mixed racial ancestry to purchase "whiteness." The wealthy mulatto merchant from Panama, Pedro de Ayarza, sought to purchase a cédula to raise his own social status and that of his three sons. Although the crown granted "whiteness" to one son, officials in Madrid denied it to Ayarza and the two younger ones, which demonstrates the difficulties involved in negotiating race and status in the uncertain world of the Spanish Indies. Problems of gender also plagued citizens in eighteenth-century Spanish America, such as the female merchant from Quito, Victorina Loza. Quito's economy had experienced a long decline as textile imports from Europe eroded the market for locally produced woolen textiles, leading to an outmigration of males seeking better economic prospects elsewhere. Resourceful women such as Loza took advantage of the opportunities provided by the relative shortage of men in the city to become merchants, a male-dominated job in most of the Indies. Nevertheless, Loza needed a husband to travel the difficult overland trade routes. After her first spouse died, she married a younger man, Francisco Xavier Sánchez de la Flor. Although this union proved to be an unhappy one, the tough and practical Victorina Loza remained a successful merchant, even in the uncertain and declining economy of Quito.

The great reforms of the eighteenth century had little impact on the life and loves of Captain José Antonio da Silva, who lived in the rural parish of Santana in the province of São Paulo, Brazil. Although da Silva married a woman who was his social equal, he also carried on sexual affairs with women beneath his station and fathered several illegitimate children. Despite contravening Church prohibitions against concubinage, da Silva's philandering did little to disrupt the prevailing social hierarchies of his day. Moreover, his slave mistresses actually reaped some tangible benefits from their relationship—wealth, higher status, and freedom for their children. In this way, Brazilian elites managed to perpetuate rigid hierarchies but also inadvertently allowed some social mobility.

The lives of many ordinary people were swept up in the larger events of their day. Eugenio Sinanyuca, the ethnic leader (*kuraka*) of Coporaque, was forced to chose whether to join the rebellion of his friend, José Gabriel Condorcanqui, who called himself Túpac Amaru II. Despite sharing many of the same complaints against the colonial regime as the rebel leader, local disputes between clerical authorities and government officials separated both men, and Sinanyuca decided to remain loyal to the crown. A rumored slave revolt in 1795 in Buenos Aires, allegedly led by the city's small French community, prompted local authorities to prosecute Juan Barbarín, a merchant apparently guilty only of believing in the principles of liberty and equality within the colonial social order. Barbarín was little more than an innocent pawn punished by colonial government officials who panicked at the prospect of revolution.

The life of Miguel García illustrates how black slaves, willing to fight in the independence struggles in exchange for their freedom, still gained few tangible benefits at the end of these wars. Despite his long years of brave service, García's wife was denied her freedom at the close of the independence struggles when a relative of her former master claimed ownership. Finally, a slave woman, Angela Batallas, used the prevailing political rhetoric of the independence era to demand her rights: she challenged the Great Liberator, Simón Bolívar, to grant her the freedom that was guaranteed in the public pronouncements of the creole governments of the time. The turbulent years of reform, resistance, and independence allowed some of these colonial subjects, such as Angela Batallas, some additional opportunities for negotiating a more favorable place for themselves within society.

CHAPTER 11

Pedro de Ayarza

The Purchase of Whiteness

ANN TWINAM

Although historians have written a great deal about the military, fiscal, administrative, and commercial reforms in the Spanish empire, they have paid scant attention to the Bourbon social agenda. The crown issued a series of landmark pieces of legislation dealing with questions of birth and race in the Indies, beginning in 1778 with the Royal Pragmatic on Marriages. This edict attempted to bolster the colonial social hierarchy by giving parents more direct control over their children's marriage choices. Whereas the Church had generally taken a strong stand in favor of spousal choice, even in cases of unequal marriages, the Pragmatic effectively allowed parents to appeal to royal officials, who could prevent the union if either the potential bride or groom had a "defect" of race or birth. In contradiction to the Pragmatic Sanction that impeded mobility, in 1795 the monarchy published a price list of favors called the gracias al sacar *that encouraged those with "defects" to move upward. Colonists who were illegitimate might purchase an official edict of legitimation (cédula de gracias al sacar) that erased the stain of their birth; people of mixed racial ancestry might purchase "whiteness" or even buy the honorific title of "don."*

These seemingly divergent policies concerning social and racial mobility stemmed from the piecemeal and occasionally haphazard nature of the Bourbon reform effort. They also embodied the long-standing Spanish tradition of allowing the king to alter rank, status, or heritage even when it involved an individual's birth or race. Such negotiations of race, class, and ethnicity were delicate matters that had to be scrutinized and adjudicated carefully by the Cámara, a subgroup of the Council of the Indies, on a case-by-case basis.

A crucial principle guiding members of the Cámara was the fundamental tension between status in the private world of individuals (family, kin, and intimate friends) and the public sphere (everyone else). Issues of race and illegitimacy were not necessarily immutably fixed at birth; a child might be known to be illegitimate or racially mixed by the private world of family, kin, and friends but in the wider society this fact might remain secret. As a result, individuals could "pass" as legitimate or even as white and maintain their "honor" (public reputation) and social status, despite any private "defects" in their birth or racial status. Passing also occurred when individuals who were illegitimate or racially mixed were able—given their family connections, wealth, education, and public service—to persuade outsiders to accord them the status of legitimates or whites in spite of their private reality. In this sense, questions of honor and status were negotiated and sometimes even contested, challenged, lost, or regained over time. Since honor was situated in the public sphere, a petitioner had to provide substantial evidence in a request for a cédula that he or she was seen by the community as a person of character. By granting an edict of legitimation or whiteness, the Cámara was validating honor already acknowledged by the wider colonial society. Through its legislation such as the Pragmatic on Marriages and the cédula that legitimated and whitened, the crown sought to mediate and promote social order.

The case history of Pedro de Ayarza gives a compelling example of the tensions that emerged over questions of race, honor, and status in the late eighteenth century. Ayarza was a well-respected Panamanian merchant with connections throughout the region, but he was also a dark-skinned man (pardo) of dubious ancestry. Nevertheless, prominent officials felt free to stay at his home; he was a captain in the local pardo militia regiment, and his wealth and commercial connections were unquestioned. In those ways he had informally "passed" in that he was often accepted and treated as if he were white.

Ayarza was also a solicitous father. When his eldest son, Josef Ponciano, was denied a degree at the university in Bogotá because of his race, the merchant began a legal process lasting from 1795 to 1807 to purchase official whiteness and the honorific title of "don" for himself and his three sons. Arguing that his many services to the crown, social standing in Panama, considerable wealth, and the virtues of his children (who were well educated) outweighed his racial defect, Ayarza spent a weighty sum on lawyers' fees to obtain whiteness through a cédula de gracias al sacar. Many officials in the Indies supported his request, while others feared the consequences of allowing the sons of a pardo merchant to obtain university degrees and, in the case of Josef Ponciano, to practice law. In the end, the members of the Cámara declared Josef Ponciano "white" and a "don," but they failed to approve a change in status for Pedro de Ayarza and his other two sons. This odd compromise left the family divided, with one member white and the others pardo, and demonstrates the difficult process of negotiating race, legitimacy, and honor in the closing decades of Spanish colonial rule.

Ann Twinam is professor of history at the University of Cincinnati and a noted authority on Colonial Spanish America. Her first book, Miners, Merchants, and Farmers in Colonial Colombia *(1982), provided a path-breaking socioeconomic history of the Bourbon reforms in Medellín Colombia. She has explored questions of gender, sexuality, and honor in a*

wide range of published articles and in her prize-winning recent book,
Public Lives, Private Secrets: Gender, Honor, Sexuality, and Illegitimacy in Colonial Spanish America *(1999). Professor Twinam has
just finished a pamphlet for the American Historical Association entitled
"Women and Gender in Colonial Latin America."*

$\mathcal{P}$anamanian Pedro de Ayarza was a solicitous father, willing to sacrifice
much for the welfare of his three beloved sons, Josef Ponciano, Pedro,
and Gaspar. As they grew up he "observed . . . [their] great inclination
toward a literary career" and so he decided to provide them with the best
education possible.[1] He sent them away from their Portobello home to
attend a boarding school in Cartagena. When his eldest, Josef Ponciano,
reached the age of twenty-one, he traveled with his twelve- and nine-
year-old brothers to Santa Fe de Bogotá. He attended the university while
they studied at the *colegio* of San Bartolomé. It was in only 1794, when
Josef Ponciano was ready to graduate, that the family's troubles as well as
this story begin. Even though he had attended classes for three years, the
university registrar and then the viceroy refused to let him graduate.
The reason: the Ayarzas were *pardos*, and the Laws of the Indies and a
royal *cédula* of 1765 specifically denied permission for racially mixed persons to receive university degrees.

And so father Pedro de Ayarza began a quest, from 1795–1807, to
purchase whiteness for himself and for his sons. What Pedro could not
know as he began this twelve-year campaign was that it would ultimately
end with his family divided. His eldest son would eventually be deemed
white and a don, while Pedro and Gaspar would remain pardos, as would
Pedro himself. To understand how this outcome occurred is to probe
critical years in the development of late eighteenth-century Bourbon
policies toward race, and particularly toward racial whitening. Tracing
the principal players in the Ayarza quest for whiteness—Pedro and his
sons, their friends and acquaintances in Panama and Bogotá, New
Granadan viceroys and officials and, the Council and Cámara of the Indies
as well as the Minister of Justice and King Charles IV—reveals intriguing variants on how race was conceptualized together with the limits and
extent to which it might be negotiated as the colonial era drew to a close.

The first question that naturally arises is: Why would a pardo from
Panama ever believe that he could successfully plead with a Spanish
monarch to make him white? Pedro had several excellent reasons to forward such a request. First, a historic Hispanic mentality had always validated the monarch's power to alter an individual's rank or heritage.
Second, at the same time that Pedro petitioned, the crown issued a 1795
arancel or price list of favors that might be purchased through a process
known as *gracias al sacar*. One provision made it possible for pardos to

buy whiteness while another set a price for the purchase of the honorific title of "don." Third, there were precedents of others who had been whitened. Understanding this background provides some framework for Pedro's initial optimism.

From the beginning of the Spanish state, monarchs had been able to alter rank and heritage, including race. As one Spanish historian succinctly characterized it, "The king counts more than blood" (*Mas pesa el rey que la sangre*).[2] Underlying the royal ability to transform status was a mentality that accepted a distinction between a person's private reality and any publicly constructed reputation. Since the monarch was superior to positive law, he could literally change an individual's public and legal persona. Throughout the centuries Spanish kings had declared persons who were *conversos* (of Jewish origin) to be Old Christians, transformed non-nobles into nobles, changed those born illegitimate into legitimates, and converted the nonwhite into white.[3] Echoes of the medieval origin of this bargain resounded when Pedro begged the king as "universal father" to demonstrate "clemency" toward "those vassals who demonstrate proper conduct in service to God and the monarchy."

By the end of the eighteenth century, the king was active only at the end of the process. Petitioners purchasing a gracias al sacar followed a well-defined routine.[4] They had to provide documentation concerning their birth, evidence of their service to the king, and letters of reference and recommendations from distinguished citizens. These were forwarded, sometimes with additional comments, by royal officials in the Americas—in the case of Pedro it was the viceroy of New Granada. The packet arrived at the Council of the Indies, which then sent it to the Cámara of the Indies, an elite subgroup composed of Council officials who handled issues of patronage, or *gracias*. Within the Cámara, attorneys (*fiscales*) first summarized the submitted documentation. They usually recommended approval or denial and then submitted a report to the Cámara, which met and discussed the application. If the Cámara's verdict was favorable, it was forwarded to the Minister of the Indies and the monarch who usually—but not always—gave final approval for the issuance of the official decree (cédula). In Pedro's case, he went a step further: he engaged an *apoderado*, a legal representative in Spain, to keep him informed of developments and to facilitate the movement of his case through bureaucratic channels.

Although the Cámara had issued gracias al sacar for centuries, it was only in 1795 that a royal decree publicized, detailed, and expanded those privileges as well as set prices to be charged in the Americas.[5] In the case of whitening the arancel fixed a price for *quinterones* (those of one-fifth mixed race) of 800 reales while, somewhat inexplicably, the presumably darker-skinned pardos paid a lesser 500 reales "for the dispensation of

[that] quality." Another new provision charged 1,000 reales for purchase of the title of "don," an honorific that carried with it the assumption that the bearer was white, legitimate, and a person of honor. In a backhanded way, "don" proved to be another avenue for those who were legitimate but racially mixed to advance socially, because those who received it were automatically considered white and persons of honor.

Certain provisions of the 1795 decree—for example, the granting of legitimations—were part of a Hispanic tradition of published and purchaseable gracias reaching back to the fifteenth-century beginnings of the Spanish state. These included the 244 eighteenth-century American legitimations explored in *Public Lives, Private Secrets*.[6] Others, such as whitening or the award of the title of "don," had only rarely been granted and had never been codified in a price list before 1795. This gap is notable, because Cámara officials appeared to have been surprised by some of the provisions in the 1795 legislation; they had apparently not been involved in either its compilation or composition.

On one level this may not be surprising, for in bureaucracies it is not uncommon for some officials to write legislation and others to enforce it. In this case, since the gracias al sacar was a money-making measure, bureaucrats in the treasury (Contaduría General) listed and priced the gracias to be sold. The result was that officials in the Cámara of the Indies had to deal with the social and racial consequences of a 1795 decree that either contradicted or altered their current policy. In the case of legitimations, the decree facilitated purchase by the offspring of adulterers or of priests even though the Cámara had an established policy of denying such requests.[7] In the case of whitening or purchase of the title of "don," Camaristas had to figure out how to award privileges that had rarely been granted and never before been institutionalized in a royal decree. Since Pedro's case started in 1795, when officials began to figure out their response, and extended to 1807, when some decisions were finally crystallized, it provides unique insight into those ways that imperial bureaucrats at a number of levels reacted to provisions concerning whitening and bestowal of the status of "don."[8]

It is notable that even though Cámara officials had seldom officially altered an individual's race prior to 1795, they had implicitly done so on a few occasions, one of which bore directly on the Ayarzas case. This was a ruling issued in 1765 after don Cristóbal Polo, a mulatto, had graduated from the university in Bogotá and had tried to practice law in Cartagena. When local lawyers protested, royal officials reviewed the case and decided that Polo's father's service in defense of that city and his own legal abilities were sufficient cause to admit him to the bar. Their decision additionally reveals how, with university graduation and admission as a lawyer, don Pablo informally leaped over racial and social barriers. Even though no official cédula of whitening or title of don was ever issued, Polo's education and profession meant that he was thereafter considered to be white and was commonly to be addressed as "don."

Even though royal officials had decided in favor of this Cartagena lawyer, they had also issued a 1765 decree that his case should "not serve as an example" for other petitions. Officials ordered that henceforth the university in Bogotá should prohibit those ineligible by statute—presumably illegitimates and the racially mixed—to enroll. That prohibition had later been violated when the eldest Ayarza son attended classes. Ironically, father Pedro de Ayarza tried to flip the 1765 decree because he cited it not as a prohibition for granting a university degree but as a precedent that such exceptions had already been made. Additionally, he admitted that the publication of the 1795 arancel for gracias al sacar had "inspired [him] to ask for this favor." And so it was within this context of Janus-faced precedents and ambiguous legislation that Pedro de Ayarza began to document his own accomplishments and those of his sons.

FIRST PETITION, 1795–1797

When asking for gracias, it was mandatory to demonstrate service to the king and the state. Pedro de Ayarza's first application, in 1795, provided a list of relevant activities. For twenty years he had served as a captain in the pardo militia, he had personally subsidized his militia company and had never collected any of the salary due him, and he had managed the finances of the local parish church as well as the Franciscan monastery. A man of means and one of Portobello's most prominent merchants, he was married and all three sons were legitimate. Yet a knowledgeable observer might have noted what he had not done—although his wealth more than qualified him, he had never held local public office, almost certainly due to his race.

Documentation of Pedro's service brought another group into the gracias al sacar process—friends and notables to testify in his favor. From Pedro's perspective, it was essential to round up the most prominent witnesses to support his argument. Some of these no doubt testified because his patronage was valuable, others likely were personal friends, and some were advocates for his sons. Such recommendations were largely formulaic: a notary would take a prepared witness list and go from one person to the next asking a series of questions crafted to elicit the sought-after answers. There are two aspects, however, inherent in this common type of colonial documentation that has often been underestimated. First, many witnesses did not follow the formula and give the pat or obvious answer—instead, their own authentic voices and comments sometimes emerged. Second, witnesses customarily used such testimony to send coded or implicit messages that went beyond the obvious affirmation of the facts. Cámara officials proved particularly alert to such transmissions. In Pedro's case, witnesses not only confirmed his service and wealth but also demonstrated the degree to which the Ayarzas were accepted by the white elite and thus the extent to which a gracias al sacar might disturb the social and racial status quo.

Some of the highest officials in Panama and Colombia rallied to support Pedro's petition. In Portobello, don Lorenzo Corbacho de Espinosa y Albares, the royal treasurer, noted that Pedro was a respected merchant—not an inconsiderable achievement for someone who was a pardo. Long-distance merchants had to lend and borrow money for extended periods, which meant that they had to be men of confidence and trust. These qualities were attributed to white merchants who were men of honor and thus denied to the racially mixed who lacked status. The treasurer confirmed, however, that Pedro was trusted by the commercial elites because "the merchants of Panama, Cartagena and other ports . . . consign to him with the greatest confidence." Cartagena merchant don Tomás Andrés Torres agreed. He observed the "lack of subjects . . . in Portobello" of "equal circumstance" and noted that Pedro handled "all the business of that province . . . his intervention not only is useful to commerce and its individuals but necessary."

On a more personal note, the Portobello treasurer, don Lorenzo, testified that Pedro received the "general applause . . . of all the persons of distinction of this city." His comments served to reassure royal officials that Pedro already informally enjoyed some of the privileges of whites so his upward mobility would not disturb local notables. The royal official who oversaw Portobello's mail service also validated Pedro's social acceptance. He noted that "the governors and all the other subjects of the first order without the least objection had visited and frequently visit [Pedro's] house." Another indication of this near-elite status was that when distinguished persons such as the archbishop of Nicaragua and the army brigadier passed through Portobello, they lodged with the merchant.

Pedro de Ayarza's fine reputation extended beyond his home in Panama to the viceregal capital in Bogotá. Particularly telling here was how he was able to enlist Bogotano elites to support the whitening of his son, Josef Ponciano. Early in the case the potential for whitening this eldest son became a particular focus of Cámara officials. They seem to have been most impressed by the enthusiastic support accorded this university student not only by his professors but also by some of the most important people in the viceregal capital. A lawyer of the audiencia of New Granada, for example, recalled that he had known Josef Ponciano since his school days in Cartagena, where he had earned the "highest esteem because of his manners" and where he had been treated with "respect by the highest subjects." The lawyer added that his cousin, who happened to be the governor of Panama, had given him "fervent recommendations" concerning Pedro's eldest son.

Witnesses sent coded messages not only concerning the Ayarzas' social acceptability but also concerning their race. One of the few negative voices was that of the director of studies at San Bartolomé, who had been the first to deny Josef's graduation. He made it clear that the Ayarzas did not have fair skin or straightish hair; they did not look white. When the official referred to Josef Ponciano's attempt to graduate, he mentioned the prohibitions of the 1765 cédula and added that it "seems to exclude . . . mulattos, which quality is notorious in this pretendent." This remark is notable because in other gracias al sacar cases when petitioners were whiter-looking, this factor worked to their advantage. Appearance did not apparently improve the chances of the Ayarzas.

Rather, when witnesses commented on the Ayarzas' race, it was to weigh it as an unfavorable "quality" that could be dismissed, given that it was counterbalanced by positive virtues that merited peer treatment. When audiencia justice don Francisco Xavier de Ezterripa praised Josef Ponciano's "good conduct," for example, he stated that "in spite of this quality he has made himself deserving of the general esteem, and he is distinguished in civil treatment with those who are considered persons of the superior class." Don Josef Rey, a Bogotá lawyer who had known the university student for three years, praised his "irreprehensible conduct" that clearly demonstrated those "zealous principles of education that since childhood have inspired him." He concluded that Josef Ponciano was "deserving (in spite of this characteristic) of the greatest attentions that could be given in this place." Such enthusiasm was seconded by don Pedro Groot, the royal treasurer in Bogotá, who observed that Josef Ponciano had "enjoyed in this city the esteem of the most prominent and notable subjects who, aware of his good talents, do not disdain from consulting with him and favoring him, washing away whatever fault . . . of his birth." He added that the manner of the eldest Ayarza son more than made up for any "defect that could be noted" and that he was treated with "distinction and appreciation." One of his former teachers even awarded him the title of "don" prematurely in referring to Josef Ponciano in his testimony.

While the elites of Portobello and Bogotá had considerable praise for Pedro and for his elder son, they were less specific about the virtues of the two younger boys, then thirteen and sixteen. Yet one of their professors at San Bartolomé had noted that all three brothers had won the "esteem of the most prominent persons" because of their "proper conduct," "modesty," "good education," and "courteous and Christian behavior." And so with these and a number of similar recommendations, Pedro's petition was forwarded through the viceroy in Bogotá to the peninsula for a decision by the Cámara of the Indies.

How did Spanish officials respond to this barrage of information? It is telling that when the document first arrived in July 1795, the Cámara fiscal wrote a note in the margin that the price list for gracias al sacar charged 1,000 reales for "don" and 500 for dispensation of pardo. He did this even though Pedro had not asked to be whitened but rather to purchase the title of "don." Officials seemed aware that this was one of the first post-1795 gracias al sacar cases and so it might set some precedent for whitening in the Americas. The reviewing attorney was not sympathetic to Pedro Ayarza's petition. He applauded what he considered to be the "just opposition" of university officials and the viceroy who had prohibited Josef Ponciano's university graduation. He recommended that the Cámara deny Ayarza's petition given that it ran against the "spirit of the law . . . and the cédula of 1765."

Such a negative recommendation did not augur well for full Cámara review of the application, for Camaristas usually agreed with the fiscal. This time, however, their first response was cautious. They acted as they often had in petitions for legitimation when the issue was unclear. They did what administrators usually do, that is, they delayed and asked for additional information. In this instance, they sent a request to the viceroy in Bogotá for more facts from the university concerning the Ayarza brothers.

When Viceroy José de Ezpeleta responded in May 1796, he forwarded a packet of even more laudatory letters of recommendation. Josef Ponciano's professors at San Bartolomé sent an unambiguous message: they hoped that his "good conduct and virtue would have its reward" given the "commendable personal characteristics of this individual." Such comments seem to have impressed the lawyer at the audiencia level in Bogotá because he recommended that the viceroy write a covering letter fully supporting Ayarza's petition. It is likely that Pedro never knew that this was one of the first, but not the last, times that various bureaucrats at different levels would support his petition, even though this favorable solution would never be carried out fully.

This time the stumbling block proved to be the viceroy in Bogotá. He agreed in his forwarding letter with the numerous witnesses who had testified to the "honor and excellent conduct" of Pedro Ayarza and of his older son. He also admitted that university officials as well as his own audiencia attorney had no problem in whitening Josef Ponciano. The viceroy was not as enthusiastic about the two younger Ayarzas, and he suggested that given their ages, it was too early to know how they would turn out.

Viceroy Ezpeleta then expanded the case beyond the personal situation of the Ayarzas, considering potential consequences on imperial policy. Specifically using the metaphor of the gatekeeper, he noted the "inconveniences" that might result from "opening the door for all others of the same quality that are in the same situation." These, if they also were of "good conduct," might apply for the "same dispensation." He also questioned the effect of the whitening cédula: if Josef Ponciano was dispensed from being a pardo, he apparently could "aspire to the offices and occupations" of whites; if he could not do so, "the gracias would be unfruitful." Since the viceroy was an accomplished bureaucrat, he only raised these issues and came down on neither side. He concluded that he had provided the requested information and left the making of higher policy decisions to his superiors.

When this letter reached Spain, the Cámara's reviewing attorney noted the favorable recommendations as well as the cautions raised by the viceroy. He came decisively down on the side of the latter and recommended yet again that the Cámara deny the Panamanian's petition. Such a repeated denial was particularly ominous. Yet, in a surprising move, the Cámara still seemed unwilling to dismiss the case, perhaps again because it was one of the first, and this was an issue they needed to resolve. And so they resorted to an uncommon tactic, one only employed when they were confused about what to do. They asked the secretaries of the viceroyalties of New Spain and Peru to comb their respective archives and look for precedents where whitening had been granted. The secretaries discovered two examples. One was from the Philippines where, in 1780, Dr. don Francisco Borla de los Santos, a racial mixture of Sangley and Indian, had successfully applied to graduate from the university in Manila even though he was a *mestizo asiático*.

Although the other example did not involve graduation from a university, it struck closer to the core issues at the heart of the Ayarza case. It concerned a 1783 petition in which Bernardo Ramírez, the fountain-keeper of Guatemala City, had asked to be treated as white given his many documented services to the crown. In his case, royal officials had wavered between the "fatal consequences" that might result when the "Spaniards and Americans of distinction" heard of his mobility and their desire to reward a subject who had shown "zeal, care, and love" that was worthy of "remuneration and recompense." They decided against whitening but suggested that he be awarded a medal or militia post.

Both the Guatemalan as well as the Ayarza cases highlighted the contesting functions of the Cámara as it represented the Spanish monarchy and state. On one hand, as agents of the king the Cámara dispensed a *gracias* with almost medieval characteristics given the monarchical function to enhance the public status of deserving vassals who had served the king and the state. On the other hand was the more contemporary, almost sociological concern of Camaristas that local elites would be alienated if the state promoted social and racial mobility for those at the margin. It is no accident that after the revolts of the 1780s (Túpac Amaru, the Comuneros), Cámara officials proved particularly solicitous of local feelings. The large majority (70 percent) of these Indies officials had served in the Americas and were keenly aware of rising social and racial tensions.[9]

In one sense the Ayarza case proved to be a benchmark precisely because Pedro and his sons were the perfect example of a new cohort that was seeking upward mobility into late eighteenth-century elite circles. The Ayarzas met two elite standards: they were legitimate, and they were rich. Only one aspect, the fact that they were pardos, legitimized the official and informal discrimination leveled against them. Added to this was the not inconsiderable variable in their favor that a flood of recommendations from elites in Panama and Colombia suggested that the Cámara's decision to whiten in this case might be a popular rather than an unpopular choice. Faced with these conflicts, the Cámara refused to make the Ayarzas "dons" or to whiten Pedro and his two youngest sons. However, they ruled that for Josef Ponciano "the quality of pardo" should be "extinguished," and they agreed that he could graduate from the university. The Ministry of Justice and the king approved the ruling in January 1797, and the royal decree was published on February 15.

It is intriguing to note that in the archival *legajo* (bundle) that contains this documentation, there was a rough draft of a cédula that not only whitened Josef Ponciano but also his two younger brothers. An attached note then commented that the privilege was only for the eldest. It is unknown whether this was a mix-up in communication or whether the Cámara had seriously considered whitening all the brothers. Pedro may again have come closer than he would ever know to attaining his goal. By 1797 he was not yet a "don," and the graduation of his remaining sons from the university remained in limbo. Josef Ponciano, however, was both a university graduate and white.

SECOND PETITION, 1799–1803

Back in Bogotá, the road was not entirely smooth for don Josef Ponciano, who, having graduated from the university, began an apprenticeship to practice as a lawyer. By 1800 a debate erupted between the two most senior lawyers in the viceregal capital as to whether the Panamanian should be admitted to the bar. One argued that many attended the university, received decrees, and yet never became lawyers; thus, don Josef Ponciano's graduation did not inevitably mean that he should be permitted to practice. The other lawyer disagreed. The fiscal of the audiencia asked the Cámara to rule on what turned out to be a most substantive issue, the one raised originally by the viceroy: What did whitenings really do?

Meanwhile, in Panama, Pedro was again collecting letters of recommendation, planning for the graduation of his two younger sons, and nurturing his own hopes to become a "don." His second application, in 1802, detailed his additional services to the king including his more than twenty-eight years as captain of the pardo militia. Twice he had subsidized Portobello troops when supplies had failed to arrive, and there was no money in the royal treasury since English pirates had held up the subsidy from Lima. He was yet to collect any salary from the state.

Pedro also argued that his younger sons were worthy, noting that he had "all the satisfaction that a father [might have] in the[ir] accomplishments." His sons, he rhapsodized, "have known how to honor the white hairs of their father" and were "worthy of [his] paternal love." He reminded officials of their "legitimacy," "good conduct, application, and literary progress," and asked that they receive "equal grace" to graduate from the university and that he and they might enjoy the "distinction of don." Pedro then tried a father-to-father approach with the monarch: "I leave to the high consideration of Your Majesty what would be the feelings of a father reproached by his two younger sons" given that "he had asked for the royal grace of Your Majesty for the eldest." He exclaimed: "What would be the heart of a father in not wanting to see his two youngest equally rewarded, for [following the] example of the eldest, they have filled the desires of their father in the attainment of such honorable inclinations."

And so, Pedro's dream entered the bureaucratic chain yet again. It rested first in the hands of the fiscal and viceroy in Bogotá who forwarded it without comment to the fiscal and Cámara of the Indies. This time, the reviewing lawyer's recommendations to the Cámara divided the Ayarza case into three parts: the two younger sons, Pedro, and the Bogotá problems of Josef Ponciano.

Although the fiscal approvingly noted the "conduct" and "progress" of students Pedro and Gaspar, he did not recommend that they receive university degrees. Instead, he concluded that they were of an "age [where] they could begin another career and the knowledge they had accumulated could serve them in whatever employment." He then expanded this decision to include all pardos, arguing that the racially mixed should not become lawyers given that occupations in agriculture and commerce were "more similar to their condition and were of the greater private and public usefullness." The question does arise, since fiscales were invariably lawyers, if at least part of his reluctance concerning the Ayarzas was to prevent pardos from entering his own legal profession.

The fiscal's negativity also encompassed Pedro de Ayarza, for the reviewing official was not impressed by his additional service to the state. Even if he deserved some accolade, the Cámara lawyer concluded that he should be "rewarded in [some] other way." The official was especially disapproving of Pedro's desire to purchase the title of "don," complaining that such requests "confused the castes with the whites." The Ayarzas were not total losers, however, for when it came to enforcing the royal cédula that granted whiteness to Josef Ponciano, the fiscal agreed that it should carry the full force of law. He recommended that the Cámara order that Josef Ponciano be permitted to practice as a lawyer and that he should be called "don."

Just as in the first application, Camaristas proved more sympathetic to the Ayarzas than the fiscal. They agreed that Josef Ponciano could be a lawyer and a "don." The Cámara, however, now seemed to be as much concerned about Ayarza family unity as about pardo mobility. Camaristas worried about the "discord that might result from brothers finding themselves in such different states of quality." And so, in July 1803, they overruled the fiscal and decided to whiten Pedro's two younger sons. Yet again, the Ayarzas may have never known how close they came to their desired goal. In a rare reversal the next month, the Ministry of Justice and the king overruled the Cámara and refused to approve the whitenings, although they agreed that Josef Ponciano could be a lawyer and a "don." So the stage was set for Ayzarza's third petition.

THIRD PETITION, 1804–1806

This time Pedro did not delay long—after all, by now his two youngest sons were twenty-two and twenty-five years old. In his 1804 repetition he asked the king to "receive with benignity the desires of these youths" to pursue a career even if "it would not be as glorious as Augustus, Demosthenes, and a thousand others equally disgraced by their [humble] birth, but useful to the public good." When in February 1805 Bogotá viceroy Antonio Amar forwarded the application, he noted "the same circumstances as the previous ones."

It was more than a year later, in August 1806, before the Cámara fiscal reviewed the application one more time. He reminded Camaristas that it had been denied in 1803 and added that it had been placed in the

Contaduría General "with the others." This was an important development: apparently, the king and Minister of the Indies had now ordered the Cámara to table any applications concerning whitening. As the fiscal explained, the state needed to decide "as a general point if it was suitable or not to dispense such gracias and distinctions to the pardos and what in the first case ought to be conceded." Such a "resolution" needed the development of "necessary rules" so as to place pardo applications in a "common system." The fiscal also reminded the Cámara of the opposition that had arisen at the University of Caracas when Lorenso María Bejarano had been whitened.

It seems unlikely that the Camaristas needed any prodding to remember the Venezuelan reaction to the Bejarano case as well as to the 1795 gracias al sacar, given the howls of protest that had erupted from local elites. Venezuelan notables had overwhelmed officials with predictions of the dire consequences that would result if local pardos could purchase whiteness.[10] Feelings had run so high that the governor of Maracaibo had issued an *obedezco pero no cumplo* (I obey, but I do not comply), the rarely issued temporary veto of an imperial action deemed too dangerous to implement. In this case he refused to publish the whitening provisions of the 1795 decree.[11]

Even given the order for administrative tabling and the Venezuelan situation, the Cámara decided to give the Ayarzas another chance. They had been sensitized by the 1803 reversal of their decision to whiten the younger sons, however, and Camaristas tended to retreat to conservatism when they had been overturned. So this time, they relinquished any decisionmaking. Instead, they simply passed the documents up the administrative chain, noting that it would be "convenient to make all known to His Majesty . . . so that he might decide what would be his royal will." The response of the monarch proved to be equally enigmatic, for in December 1806 the Cámara received a two-word reply: "Como parece," or "As it seems." Since the 1803 denial was presumably to stand, the Cámara tabled the Ayarza petition with the others.

FOURTH PETITION, 1807

Six months later the final Ayarza petition—a letter written by Pedro's Spanish apoderado, don Manuel Antonio de Echevarria—arrived at the Cámara of the Indies. He queried if the opaque monarchical decision was valid since "the resolution was not clear on what point" the decision had been based. He no longer sought to make Pedro a "don" but pleaded for the future of the two younger Ayarzas. Noting that Pedro and Gaspar had finished their university studies, he pointed out that it would be a "sad thing to see all their work lost." He again brought up the issue of family unity, reminding the Cámara of the "dissension" and "deformity" that would result from brothers in "such different states of quality." He reminded the king that he had used his "supreme authority" in granting such a gracias to don Josef Ponciano, and he begged for "equal grace" for his brothers.

This petition arrived at the Cámara in July 1807. By now the Camaristas had been rebuffed twice by their superiors, and they did not hesitate. They ordered the case to be "united with the other cédulas," and so it sat in limbo. Yet, as Napoléon marshaled his troops for the Spanish invasion that would come the next year, events not only in Spain but also in the Americas may well have opened up dramatic new options for the Ayarzas.

CONCLUSION

The case of the Ayarzas reveals how far one man willing to expend unlimited amounts of money and demonstrating enormous determination might travel to overcome popular and official racial barriers at the end of the colonial era. There were many times when Pedro came close. His quest highlights both confusions as well as contradictions of disparate players on varying levels. In his case, local elites rallied to support whitening, especially for the clearly gifted Josef Ponciano, yet the furor raised by local elites elsewhere eventually spilled over to contaminate the Ayarza case and doom a favorable outcome. Back in Spain, Camaristas also had to confront their traditional roles as dispensers of gracias to worthy petitioners altering *calidad* (social rank), with their informed understanding of the potential impact of racial alterations in the Americas. Their problems were only magnified by the indecision of the highest policymakers, at the level of the monarchy and the Ministry of Justice. What is clear in this confusion is that petitioners such as the Ayarzas, their friends and colleagues, the Cámara, and the king and his highest officers were looking at issues of quality and of race with new eyes, even as the forces of revolution and independence mobilized to change the paradigm forever.

NOTES

1. The primary sources for this paper are the years of Ayarza petitions located in the Archivo General de Indias, Panama 292, no. 2, 1803. Unless otherwise noted, quotations derive from this source and will not be further footnoted. Parts of the case have been reprinted in Rodulfo Cortés Santos, *El regimen de "las gracias al sacar"*

en Venezuela durante el periodo hispánico (Caracas, 1978), 2 vols.; and James F. King, "The Case of José Ponciano de Ayarza: A Document on *Gracias al sacar,*" *Hispanic American Historical Review* (August 1944): 440–51.

2. José Antonio Maravall, *Poder, honor y élites en el siglo XVII* (Madrid: Siglo XXI, 1989), quotes Vélez de Guevara, 84.

3. Ann Twinam, *Public Lives, Private Secrets: Gender, Honor, Sexuality, and Illegitimacy in Colonial Spanish America* (Stanford, 1999), 50–51.

4. Ibid., 50–55.

5. Archivo Histórico Nacional, Madrid, Consejos Libros 1498, n. 4, 1795 contains the original. The 1801 version that increased costs is reprinted in Richard Konetzke, *Colección de documentos para la historia de la formación social de hispanoamérica, 1493–1810*, 5 vols. (Madrid: Consejo Superior de Investigaciones Científicas, 1958–1962), 3:2, n. 354, 1801.

6. Twinam, *Public Lives, Private Secrets.*

7. Ibid., 251–61, 275–88, 291–98.

8. In contrast to the more than two hundred gracias al sacar legitimations traced in Twinam, *Public Lives, Private Secrets*, relatively few individuals had received the gracias of whiteness prior to 1795. In his monumental documentation of colonial social history Richard Konetzke reprinted several cases: in 1687 a moreno had been appointed governor of a Panamanian province in spite of his race; several Cuban pardos in the 1760s had been permitted to study and practice medicine. Konetzke, *Colección de documentos*, 2:2, n. 546, 1687; 3:1, n. 177, 1760; 3:1, n.189, 1763.

9. Twinam, *Public Lives, Private Secrets*, 13–16, 54, 335–36.

10. Rodulfo Cortés reprints thirty-five key documents in volume two.

11. Ibid., 67.

SUGGESTED READINGS

A brief commentary in English as well as some Spanish-language documents on the Ayarza case have been translated into English by James F. King, "The Case of José Ponciano de Ayarza: A Document on *Gracias al sacar,*" *Hispanic American Historical Review* (August 1944): 440–51. However, this article and document contain only a small part of the case. Background information on whitening and on the gracias al sacar appears in the works of Magnus Mörner, especially *Race Mixture in the History of Latin America* (Boston: Little, Brown, 1967). Ann Twinam, *Public Lives, Private Secrets: Gender, Honor, Sexuality, and Illegitimacy in Colonial Spanish America* (Stanford: Stanford University Press, 1999) analyses gracias al sacar purchases of legitimation, comments on the whitening legislation, and places both within the larger perspective of Bourbon reforms. Also useful is Mark A. Burkholder, *Biographical Dictionary of Councilors of the Indies, 1717–1808* (Westport, CT: Greenwood Press, 1986).

Those who read Spanish can find further cases of whitening requests in Richard Konetzke, *Colección de documentos para la historia de la formación social de hispanoamérica, 1493–1810* (Madrid: Consejo Superior de Investigaciones

Científicas, 1958–1962), 5 vols., although he usually prints selections rather than full cases. Santos Rodulfo Cortés, *El regimen de "las gracias al sacar" en Venezuela durante el periodo hispánico* (Caracas: Italgráfica, 1978), 2 vols., contains a volume of documents on the Venezuelan reaction to whitening.

CHAPTER 12

Victorina Loza

Quiteña Merchant in the Second Half
of the Eighteenth Century

CHRISTIANA BORCHART DE MORENO

Textile mills producing woolen cloth in the north-central highlands of the Audiencia of Quito served as the foundation of the regional economy. By the eighteenth century, however, a series of epidemics, natural disasters, and the introduction of large quantities of higher-quality European goods combined to erode the prosperity of cloth manufacturing. Mill owners still sold their cheaper woolens to markets in New Granada to the north, but they lost ground in the more lucrative southern markets (especially Lima) to European imports and locally produced Peruvian woolens. The declining demand for Quiteño cloth (especially higher-quality paños*) also prompted a slow agrarian decline in the north central highlands. Spanish rural enterprises had organized abundant land and labor resources to grow food, graze livestock, and produce woolen cloth for export. As the profitability of the mills declined, merchants throughout the Audiencia began to organize the production of woolen and especially cotton cloth, usually through the "putting out" system. In this system, merchants gave advances of raw wool or cotton to local producers, often Andeans, who spun thread and wove cloth in their homes and villages for the merchant suppliers. This form of cottage industry was most common in the southern highlands, near the city of Cuenca, but it also was found in scattered towns and villages throughout the highlands. Apart from financing cloth production, merchants also traded in a host of local artisan goods such as rosaries, religious paintings, and sculpture. In short, the decline of the large mills resulted in not only hardship but also a changing commercial and economic landscape.*

By the second half of the eighteenth century, Quito began to evolve from a manufacturing and commercial center to more of an administrative and service-oriented city. The Bourbon reforms led to a plethora of new government agencies and new bureaucratic jobs for the upper-class peninsular and creole populations. Most of the city's middle and lower classes, however, made more modest livings from small-scale enterprises that hardly compensated for the profits generated by the woolen textile industry in its heyday during the seventeenth century. Moreover, as the crown imposed higher taxes and administrative controls from the 1760s, even marginal economic activities suffered. When the government attempted to regulate the production and sale of aguardiente and assume direct control over the sales tax in 1765, for example, it threatened to destroy these modest urban commercial and agrarian enterprises. As a result, riots known as the "Rebellion of the Barrios" erupted in the city. A popular government took control of Quito for over one year until royal troops finally entered the city and restored the Audiencia to power. In the end, the overall economic decline of the district had serious repercussions in the city, whose population first stagnated and then began to decline by the end of the eighteenth century.

One of the merchants plying her trade in this uncertain economic climate was doña María Victorina Loza. One of four siblings from a middle-class Quiteño household, doña Victorina married an older man, Fernando Lucas de la Peña, a Popayán merchant who owned a shop in Quito. The couple both operated the business, with doña Victorina running the shop while her husband traveled frequently across the rugged Andean cordillera to sell his wares and procure merchandise for sale in Quito. When her husband died, doña Victorina married a much younger man, Francisco Xavier Sánchez de la Flor, probably to help collect debts and also to travel throughout the countryside, an activity unsuitable for a "respectable" woman. Doña Victorina was a tough, determined businesswoman, however, one of a growing group of female entrepreneurs in Quito. While her business flourished, however, her personal life did not; by 1790 her young husband had begun a sexual liaison with a woman in Quito. Doña Victorina tried to have Francisco manage her rural properties, but when he refused to leave the city and his mistress, she initiated legal action against him for squandering her assets. Throughout her life, doña Victorina remained a wily, determined, and willful merchant who operated successfully in the difficult economy of eighteenth-century Quito.

Christiana Borchart de Moreno received her doctorate in social and economic history at the University of Bonn and later took up permanent residence in Quito, Ecuador, where she has held numerous research and academic posts. After publishing her first book on merchants in late colonial Mexico, Los mercaderes y el capitalismo en México (1759–1778) *(1984), she turned her attention to Ecuadorian history. She has published a wide range of seminal articles in the field of socioeconomic history of the Audiencia of Quito, and a collection of her articles has appeared in book form:* La Audiencia de Quito: Aspectos económicos y sociales (siglos XVI–XVIII) *(1998). She has also begun working on the colonial history of gender and sexuality in the North Andes.*

The first adventure in life was survival, which was no easy task for anyone born around 1740 in the North Andes. This was especially true if a person lived in the straw hut of an Andean working on a hacienda or in an *obraje* (mill) or even an independent cotton weaver in one of the numerous highland villages. It was even true, however, if someone resided in the comfortable house of a well-established creole or mestizo family in Quito, the capital of an Audiencia district. Although there are no statistics, wills written in Quito in the second half of the eighteenth century show that parents frequently outlived one or more of their children.

Along with her four siblings, doña María Victorina, the daughter of Quito *vecinos* (citizens) don Manuel Loza and his wife, doña Tomasa Vásquez Albán, was confronted with the usual health risks of her time: frequent epidemics of smallpox, chicken pox, and measles. Moreover, Quito and the central and northern highlands of Ecuador suffered from frequent natural disasters, such as the severe earthquakes in Quito (1755), Latacunga (1757), and especially Riobamba (1797). This last quake caused the complete destruction of the town as well as extensive damage in regions as far north as Quito and its surrounding valleys. Volcanic eruptions such as that of Cotopaxi in 1740–1755 and in 1768 and nearby Tungurahua in 1773 normally caused fewer deaths, since the surrounding areas were sparsely populated. But the expulsion of ashes and the resulting landslides often destroyed large agricultural and cattle grazing areas. In 1785–86 a period of heavy rains—described in terms similar to the El Niño phenomenon of recent decades—resulted in heavy losses of both Indian workers and flocks of sheep in the central highlands and forced the closing for several months of one of the biggest textile mills in the province. The consequences were felt in villages and towns as food shortages and damage to the already depressed textile industry affected large sectors of a society that still depended on the production and trade in woolen cloth.

In addition to these recurring epidemics and natural disasters, the Audiencia of Quito also suffered from several bloody and destructive riots and rebellions touched off by the Bourbon monarchy's attempts to reform the colonial administration and raise more revenue. The impoverished population perceived every change as a new threat to their already diminished economic prospects, and they reacted violently. Most indigenous rebellions took place in the principal textile-producing centers and must have resulted in declines in production and interruptions of commerce along the royal road that linked highland textile mills and rural producers of cotton cloth to markets in Lima, Popayán, and Barbacoas. The Quito rebellion of 1765 was one of the largest urban insurrections in the eighteenth-century Spanish empire. Efforts to establish a royal *aguardiente* (cane liquor) distillery and to assume direct control over the sales tax (*alcabala*) administration triggered the bloody uprising.

There is no document, diary, or letter to show the impact of this seemingly endless list of problems and disasters on Victorina Loza's life. But, as a citizen of Quito and an active part of its merchant community, she must have felt their impact even though they did not reduce her to "critical poverty," a modern expression that applies to many members, especially women, of Quito's popular classes. Not much is known of the Loza-Vásquez Albán family. Nevertheless, the parents of the household financed two daughters' admission to the Santa Catalina convent and provided dowries for the marriages of Victorina and her sister Antonia, indicating that they were a rather well-to-do family. None of the documents related to the family gives any hint about their ethnic status. Information about ethnicity is seldom found in official documentation from the era, not even in the census data of the second half of the eighteenth century, which usually distinguishes only four rather dissimilar ethnic categories: whites, Amerindians, free (probably black and mulattos), and slaves. The 1784 census lists 17,976 "whites" from a total in the Quito population of nearly 24,000, including peninsular and creole Spaniards and *mestizos* (mixed Spanish and Amerindian). These mestizos must have formed the largest segment of this "white" category in the census, since European immigration to the Audiencia district was insignificant. Yet, within this white and mestizo segment the social and economic differences were enormous.

As in other parts of the Spanish empire, modern scholars have tended to focus their attention on the extremes of the urban society: the titled and untitled nobility on one hand, and the urban underclass or *plebe* on the other. This focus gives the erroneous impression that there was nothing in between these two extremes. According to a city council document produced in 1789, however, in Quito only about 500 persons of both sexes could claim to be members of the titled and untitled nobility, a group that included peninsular and creole Spaniards. This group represented under 3 percent of the urban population and included crown officials and large estate holders, descending from the original *encomenderos* and obraje owners, who also engaged in long-distance trade. Between this upper segment of the so-called white population and the large but not so clearly defined group at its bottom of artisans, peddlers, and unemployed, there was a small middle class. Most were merchants, who even in this critical half-century were able to accumulate capital and afford a comfortable living, but without any prospect of entering the highest ranks of society.

The Loza-Vásquez Albán family probably belonged to this middling group of merchants engaged in trade with Popayán and its gold-mining district in the northern part of the Audiencia district. To define a distinct Quito merchant class is difficult, at least in the second half of the eighteenth century, when nearly everybody from the upper class (Audiencia justices, priests, and estate owners) to lowly indigenous weavers engaged in some sort of trade. Quito never had a merchant guild that in other parts of the empire at least made clear the distinction between wholesale and retail merchants. Nevertheless, documents from the period demonstrate the existence of numerous *pulperías*, *tiendas*, and *almacenes*. Pulperías provided for everyday needs by offering basic foodstuffs and other local and regional products; tiendas and almacenes offered a wide range of higher-quality products, especially locally produced and imported textiles. Tiendas tended to serve the general public, whereas the almacenes operated largely as wholesale businesses.

A second difficulty in defining the merchant class involved the fluctuating numbers of people, especially men, engaged in trade. There were a number of reasons for this fluid merchant population. First, Quito was a rather isolated marketplace, far away from the main ports of Cartagena and Callao and also distant from the areas where the locally produced textiles were sold. Second, the Audiencia suffered from a severe lack of specie; most of the gold production in its most northern territories went directly to Popayán and Santa Fé. This difficult situation required mobility and the use of several commercial strategies for a merchant to remain in business.

The large Cartagena and Lima merchant houses, frequently owned by peninsular Spaniards, controlled the supply of European commodities. These enterprises could be contacted by mail or through local agents, who generally lived in the port of Guayaquil, not the Audiencia's highland capital. Nevertheless, most of Quito's merchants established personal contacts with these main centers of commerce. They traveled themselves, for example, to Lima, selling their locally produced woolen textiles (higher-quality *paños* and more roughly woven *bayetas*) along the way, in the viceregal capital itself, and sometimes even farther to the south. They returned with European luxury products and metal wares, Peruvian wine, and occasionally some Chinese silk. Completing this trade circuit commonly took about two years, if all went well. Another possibility was to send a hired agent to buy and sell on commission or to establish a joint venture, preferably with a family member. In these cases, one of the partners established himself for a number of years in Popayán, Lima, or Cartagena. Merchants from other parts of the Spanish empire also set up shop temporarily or permanently in Quito. Only a few came from Spain, Cartagena, and Lima. Between Quito and Popayán or Pasto, however, there was a constant coming and going of people who established ongoing commercial and family connections in the capital city.

How did women enter this rather complicated pattern of trade? For a long time scholars thought that women engaged only in small-scale commercial and productive activities, such as bread baking and street marketing. In midseventeenth-century Quito, for example, a conflict over unfair competition took place between male owners and administrators of pulperías on the one hand and the so-called *gateras* or Indian women selling in the streets on the other. The only two female owners of a pulpería recorded in the city's records of that time clearly had no active part in the day-to-day running of the businesses. By the second half of the eighteenth century this pattern had changed dramatically; city records indicate that women not only owned and ran pulperías and different kinds of artisan shops, but they were also registered as a "vecina and merchant of this city." More than one woman also owned and operated a tienda, engaging in the long-distance trade with Lima and Popayán.

Victorina Loza, who never called herself a merchant in any notarial documents from the period, fell within this emerging group of female merchants. Her commercial training may have begun at home, where she must have learned to read and write. Her first marriage was to don Fernando Lucas de la Peña, a Popayán merchant who had settled in Quito. Her parents provided the dowry—probably some cash, clothing, household silver and linen, merchandise, and perhaps a slave, which was handed over to her husband to help him in carrying the "burdens of marriage." Although the precise amount of this dowry remains unknown, it was the only capital that doña Victorina ever received from her parents. In later years her brother, don Fulgencio, whose wife was also known as a merchant in Quito, cheated Victorina and her sister Antonia of their paternal inheritance. Husbands had the right to manage but not to spend their wives' capital, which had to be returned in case of divorce or widowhood. On the other hand, even if they had not received any capital, by law husbands owed their wives support, which consisted (using the common eighteenth-century formula) of "food and an annual change of clothes" befitting her social position. In exchange the husband could expect love, obedience, and a serene life.

After marriage the couple lived quietly in Quito, although don Fernando assuredly must have spent a lot of time traveling in order to stock the almacen run by his wife in his absence. They had no children of their own but adopted a foundling left on their doorstep, whom they named Fernando de la Peña. The love that doña Victorina always expressed for this son indicates that he was probably one of the many illegitimate children (registered as foundlings) in the city. Their biological parents were sometimes one of their adoptive parents, their brother or sister, or some other relative. Since Victorina's second marriage also remained childless, it is likely that the child, Fernando, was the offspring of a close relative.

After 1767 doña Victorina appears in court records suing several dilatory debtors. The commercial and legal affairs of the couple fell completely into her hands because her husband was listed as an "invalid with a well-known ailment." Don Fernando may have been older than his wife. The lawsuits portray doña Victorina as a competent and persistent businesswoman who did not give up, even if her debtors had left Quito. One such case, for example, involved a priest who owed her money for some *efectos de Castilla* (Spanish goods) purchased before he went as a missionary to the remote province of Maynas in the Amazon region. Nevertheless, doña Victorina persisted; some sixteen years after the lawsuit began, the executor of the priest's estate finally paid the debt. Another debtor, a shop owner himself, left his tienda to a sister and supposedly fled to Lima in 1769. In 1770 the dogged doña Victorina had his shop closed to prevent him from selling any items that might have come from her almacen. Because of information she provided, the debtor was finally located in Otavalo and brought to justice in Quito. Officially she had him imprisoned, but he apparently spent only a few daytime hours in a front room, leaving the jail for his meals and overnight. Soon other creditors joined in the legal action, and the recalcitrant former shop owner had to repay the debts within five years. Doña Victorina, however, insisted on having the man post bond, signed before a notary. He probably paid his debts, because fifteen years later the man served as one of her lawyers.

Don Fernando Lucas de la Peña apparently died somewhere between the end of November 1769 and October 1771, because in October of the next year (1772) doña Victorina married for a second time. Her new husband was don Francisco Xavier Sánchez de la Flor, a Popayán merchant like don Fernando and perhaps even his former junior partner or employee. Why would a well-established widow, accustomed to managing her own business affairs, marry a penniless younger man? His motives are more understandable. A merchant without capital of his own could find employment only as a shopkeeper or as a traveling agent, with an income of about 100 pesos per year and a place at his employer's dinner table (or 2 pesos, one for the man and another for the mule, for every eight days on the road). As the husband of doña Victorina, Sánchez de la Flor could manage a considerable fortune. When he signed a receipt for the dowry in February 1776, it was worth a total of 47,850 pesos and consisted of silver coin, a house in central Quito, merchandise in the almacen, jewels, household silver, clothes, and four slaves. The sum seems high for the day and probably included debts owed to doña Victorina that she considered collectible.

A principal motive of doña Victorina's decision to marry a second time was probably her need for a man to help in collecting the debts.

Another may have been to have her young husband travel across the rugged Andean landscape to continue the trading patterns set by doña Victorina and her first husband (see Diagram). Don Fernando had not only left a house and an almacen but also some business contacts, especially with the Mosquera family, important estate holders and merchants in Popayán and its district. But contacts alone were not enough to maintain successful long-distance trade links. Quito was the point of departure for textile shipments that went north to Barbacoas, Popayán and its environs, and sometimes extended even to Santa Fé de Bogotá. The normal shipment of cloth to these northern provinces consisted of woolen bayetas and cottons, called *lienzos* or sometimes *tocuyos* (especially when they had been produced in the southern highlands near the city of Cuenca). The bundles of cloth were wrapped in coarse frieze, which was usually sold in the mining districts. Since few merchants owned textile mills, they had to purchase the cloth from manufacturers (called *obrajeros*) at the lowest possible price. Business with these obrajeros usually could be transacted in Quito, where many of the mill owners lived or at least kept part-time residences. Buying cheap bayetas, however, often involved traveling directly to the centers of production. Acquiring cottons produced by independent weavers required traveling to several Amerindian villages in the central and south sierra, even though weavers from the nearby village of Alangasí came to Quito themselves to offer their fabrics.

Going around the countryside on business was not an option for a respectable woman, and respectability was very important to doña Victorina. Women of the middle and upper classes could be seen traveling to their haciendas, escorted by servants or male relatives, or accompanying their husbands when they took up a new post within the colonial administration. But even in pulperías, business activities split along gendered lines, with the wives running the shop and their husbands on the road selling goods and getting fresh supplies. Only Amerindian women traveled "on business," such as transporting woolen fabrics from the village of Guano, near Riobamba, to the capital. As a result, the need to find a man to move around freely, maintaining business contacts and finding the best goods and prices, probably accounted for doña Victorina's decision to enter into such an unequal marriage. Moreover, having a husband gave a woman greater "respectability," which, in a general way, made matters easier in business and in the courts. Unfortunately, prospective husbands were scarce in Quito, as more and more young men were leaving the city in search of a better future in more prosperous regions. In less than twenty years the ratio in Quito went down from 75.8 men per 100 women in 1781 to 53.3 in 1797. This imbalance be-

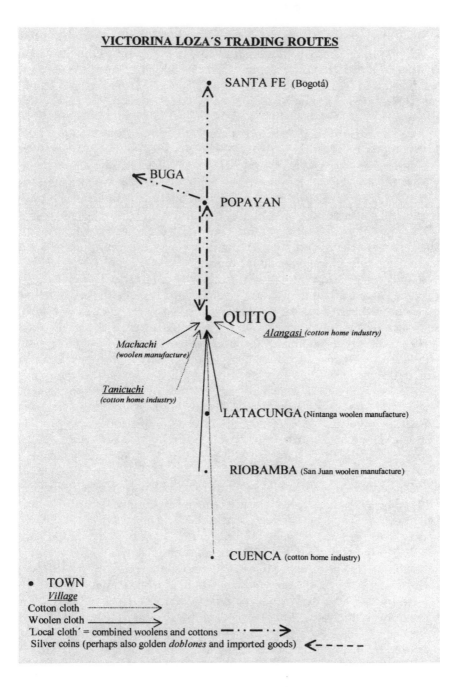

VICTORINA LOZA'S TRADING ROUTES

tween the numbers of men and women was evident in the increasing percentage of female shop owners, which grew from 29.7 percent in 1770 to 40.5 percent in 1802.

If don Francisco had cherished any dreams of gaining complete control over his wife's fortune, he must have been disappointed. Their union was apparently a marriage of convenience, and a lawyer even testified that doña Victorina and don Francisco had never shared a bed, although this assertion was never proven. Nevertheless, it was not uncommon in late eighteenth-century Quito for a wealthy widow to take a poorer husband, offering economic security to the man who entered into the marriage as a sort of junior partner. In later years, for example, one woman who could not run her fringe-making shop because of guild regulations offered "decent meals and clothing every year" to a penniless fringe master, whom she later married. As the legal documentation indicates, doña Victorina never gave up complete control of her fortune, even though she respected the formaliy of having don Fernando appear as the head and legal representative of the business.

She even had don Fernando sign a power of attorney in July 1773 so that she could control their "joint" legal affairs. Initially she acted on her own only when her husband was traveling, but when he was in Quito, she asked his permission formally to pursue legal contracts and lawsuits. Don Fernando was obviously absent, for example, in 1778–79 when she contacted obraje owners about buying bayetas and went to the alcabala office to sign documents that accompanied her shipments of these textiles to Popayán. He was also absent in 1780 when she bought a small hacienda in the southwestern outskirts of Quito. In 1788, however, her husband signed all the trade permits, and that year he appeared as a leading textile merchant in the Popayán trade.

On the other hand, no records exist of any independent business dealings of don Fernando. In 1776 he received Spanish goods from his brother-in-law don Fulgencio, but only to put them in his wife's almacen. In 1783 he sold a slave from Popayán who had escaped to Ambato, south of Quito, and who had married there under false pretenses. In this transaction, however, he was only the representative of the owner, don José María Mosquera, his wife's most important business partner. In another slave sale he acted for don Miguel Alvares del Corro (from Riobamba), the representative of a Cádiz merchant. In 1785 he delivered to don Justo Castro (from Guayaquil) 1,019 pesos from doña Victorina, asking that Castro invest the money in "showy goods" for sale in Lima. This last deal seems to have been the couple's only attempt at establishing a new, southern business route. Doña Victorina's total lack of business contacts in the viceregal capital forced her to rely on a stranger who seemed to know what highland products were "showy" enough to attract attention in Lima. Moreover, the contract included buying European goods in Lima, which Castro would sell on his return trip. Doña Victorina was to receive her money and an 8 percent commission (the usual "one-way" commission was 4 percent at that time). Only four and one-half months later, don Francisco, representing his wife's interest once again, initiated a lawsuit against Castro, who had not even started his long journey to the south. Rumors about his dishonesty must have come to his creditors' attention, because Castro had gone to jail twice before, and he was released only because of an infected leg wound. Nonetheless, he profited from the disagreements among his creditors and apparently never repaid these debts.

Although colonial lawsuits over business transactions rarely include correspondence between the litigants, in one of doña Victorina's trials, conducted by her husband, a few of her letters have survived. They offer intriguing insights into the discussions between obraje owners and merchants as well as into doña Victorina's way of doing business. Her opponent in the case was don Vicente Isidro Villavicencio y Guerrero, eldest son of the Countess del Real Agrado and administrator of her obraje of San Juan, near Riobamba. The mill was a rather destitute establishment with thirty-two native workers and another nineteen in a nearby workshop for spinning. In November 1778 doña Victorina wrote a letter to don Vicente proposing a business deal. She needed about 6,000 *varas* (one vara equals about thirty-three inches) of baize and offered to exchange European goods from her shop for the cloth. In the following March a meeting between them took place in doña Victorina's house.

At this meeting a bitter disagreement started. Don Vicente needed cash urgently, probably to repay debts or to cover some of the costs of assuming his new duties as magistrate of Trujillo. Nonetheless, his strained financial situation did not stop him from taking two pairs of English silk stockings at 16 pesos as an advance on their proposed business deal. He also wanted an additional 300 pesos in cash for himself and another 300 pesos in goods, payable to don Mariano Donoso. The 6,000 varas of baize were to be delivered the following September. Although doña Victorina had no ready cash, she offered to try and get at least half of the money within the following few days. Only a week after the supposed contract, don Vicente pressed again for the "promised" 150 pesos, and he also complained that the goods delivered to don Mariano did not amount to the promised 300 pesos. He urged her to complete the deal, terming her attitude as mere "child's play."

Doña Victorina responded that she only had promised an "attempt" to secure the money, not a hard and fast promise to deliver it. Moreover, she had never signed any contract agreeing to such terms. After all, she could not promise to pay cash (at a rate of 2 reales per vara) for baize that she would receive a full six months later. In addition, don Mariano, whose family owned estates in the nearby Machachi valley, had already made her a better offer: he could deliver the needed bayetas immediately. Moreover, doña Victorina still had contacts with the Nintanga obraje owned by the Mercedarian Order, which could also provide the merchandise. As to the price of the merchandise delivered to Donoso, she stated:

> Your Grace tells me that I have given merchandise from my shop to don Mariano Donoso [worth] 193 pesos in expensive textiles, but because of the esteem I have for the foresaid gentleman and the friendship I profess for my lady doña Rosa his wife I gave him of the most florid and at the current prices at which I am selling at this moment for silver in cash, and if all this is contemptible he will not have to go through the trouble of taking another vara of cloth . . . and I am writing the same to don Mariano Donoso so that he will not come in for more expensive textiles.

She even told don Vicente that the textiles could be returned because in her almacen "they will not rot nor will I experience any damage."

In the second half of the eighteenth century the time had long passed when wealthy obraje owners sold their woolens directly in Lima or exchanged them for European goods to be sold for high profits in the Audiencia of Quito. Don Vicente, the future Count del Real Agrado, was not the only one who had to look for commercial intermediaries. Merchants routinely offered to exchange European goods for locally produced woolens because the supply of cash was extremely limited in the Audiencia district.

Don Vicente not only failed to get the cash that he so desperately needed, but he also lost his lawsuit with doña Victorina. In November 1782 the president of the Audiencia signed an order to have don Vicente arrested. As in similar cases, the debtor fled from Quito to avoid arrest, so in March 1783 the order was extended to Latacunga, Ambato, and Riobamba. Since the documentation about the lawsuit ended with this order, the fugitive probably agreed to send some baize from his obraje to pay for the goods that don Mariano had received from doña Victorina as part of the agreement.

Most merchants in the Spanish Indies tried to invest part of their money in landed estates. This goal was true not only for wealthy upper-class merchants who traded directly with Spain but also for the more modest ones engaged in interregional trade. Doña Victorina was no exception. She bought her first estate in 1776, in Luluncoto, an agricultural area in the suburban parish of San Sebastián, located in the rural southeastern periphery of Quito. In 1780 she obtained another small hacienda, called Lloa Chiquito, on the lower slopes of Mount Pichincha, at the outskirts of the southwestern parish of San Roque. Two years later she purchased a small holding in Collacoto, close to her first investment. These properties were situated in areas of small, landed estates devoted to agriculture and cattle grazing that supplied their owners and the urban marketplace with fresh food. Together with the plain of Añaquito, north of Quito, both areas attracted investments from merchants, but the properties also changed owners frequently. Most of the buyers and sellers belonged to the merchant community.

For doña Victorina the acquisition of land represented more than just gaining access to fresh foodstuffs for her household or for sale in local markets. Her main concern was the future of her adopted son, don Fernando, who had entered the priesthood. To give him a secure, regular income (one of the conditions for being ordained) she set up a "patrimonial foundation" in 1782 to provide him with 200 pesos per year from the income generated by these rural properties. Doña Victorina also sought even better investments for her son. In August 1785, for example, she sold her Luluncoto and Collacoto properties to a fellow merchant for 6,100 pesos: 4,880 pesos in cash, or perhaps merchandise from his shop, with the rest paid out in the form of an annuity yielding a 3 percent annual return. She later sold the Lloa Chiquito estate to another Quito merchant and invested the proceeds in a hacienda, El Tintal, near the village of Perucho northwest of Quito, paying 8,400 pesos.

Although El Tintal saddled doña Victorina with a mortgage of 5,900 pesos, the estate was located in a subtropical sugarcane producing-area. During this period the sale of sugar and aguardiente still yielded considerable profits to landowners in the region, which probably justified the investment. The estate also became a refuge for doña Victorina, with a room and an oratory of her own, a formal garden with fruit trees, flower and medicinal herb beds, and a stable for her favorite riding mules. Haciendas in the Perucho region were small compared to the larger properties of Quito's nobility and the Jesuit Order (until its expulsion in 1767), which were located in the principal sugarcane-producing regions in the Chota and Mira valleys and around the villages of Urcuquí and Salinas. Instead, Quito's middle-class merchants invested in the small- and medium-sized estates near Perucho to gain status and perhaps a higher rank in colonial society.

In November 1780 the merchant, don Gregorio Betancourt, had sold El Tintal for 8,400 pesos to don Carlos Araujo. The payment should have been completed within two months, but Araujo, who only a few years later would become one of the most important owners of sugarcane and cattle haciendas in the northern highlands, cancelled the contract with the argument that he lacked sufficient cash to meet the terms of the deal. It seems likely, however, that it was not the lack of cash but the lack of a sufficient labor force that caused Araujo to withdraw. In

1780 don Gregorio affirmed that he had a great deal of sugarcane ready for grinding (worth between 4,000 and 6,000 pesos), but several witnesses stated that the area suffered from a permanent lack of native workers, which necessitated large capital outlays to attract farmhands from other regions. The estates obviously were not large enough to justify the acquisition of slave laborers.

Doña Victorina was aware of this labor problem, and so she started to "buy" the labor force needed to work on her own properties. The usual procedure was to purchase the debts of a native worker from another estate owner, offering either cash or merchandise. By this means she acquired thirteen workers over the years, one of them a mestizo. Most of the former employers were owners of small estates, perhaps in the same district. The biggest deal involved the Marquis de Villaorellana and his hacienda of Granobles in the Cayambe valley. A representative of doña Victorina's in the area somehow convinced seven laborers to leave Granobles and work on El Tintal. The Marquis, whose family had been in serious economic difficulties for years, complained to local authorities and asked for 263 pesos in compensation. In the end, he finally had to settle for only 100 pesos. The most interesting contract was signed with don Tiburcio Cabezas, the most important (or principal) cacique of Otavalo, who was paid 30 pesos in May 1799 in exchange for "the labor of his Indians" on the Tintal estate. Relying on indigenous authorities as intermediaries to secure workers was a procedure called *concertaje colectivo*, a form of labor contract in the Ecuadorian highlands, which has not yet been studied.

While her business operations ran smoothly, doña Victorina's private life suffered numerous setbacks after 1790. In early 1792, she signed a contract with her husband, leasing him El Tintal and the nearby potato-growing property of Ambuela, and promising not to interfere in their management. Although claiming that she had leased the property because of her inability to run the haciendas herself, doña Victorina's real motive was different. She had been informed of her husband's infidelity with a woman in the parish of San Roque. Putting her husband in charge of properties outside of Quito was clearly an attempt to separate him from his lover. The strategy failed, however, since don Francisco had no intention of remaining on the remote haciendas, not only because of his lover but also because he wanted to speculate in mining operations. In the late eighteenth century, the Audiencia experienced what one historian has called a "genuine mining psychosis." Local entrepreneurs such as don Francisco attempted to reverse the region's long economic depression by finding new deposits of precious metals, but most lacked both the capital and the technical expertise.

In November 1792, instead of taking direct legal action, doña Victorina wrote a secret letter to the president of the Audiencia that denounced her husband's infidelity. She probably took this more discreet and secretive procedure to avoid a scandal. Nevertheless, she eventually pressed a legal suit against don Francisco for spending 29,000 pesos of her dowry. Hoping to reconcile with her husband, however, doña Victorina suspended her suit for two months, but in January 1793 she presented her claims before the court once again. In the meantime, her husband had begun legal proceedings before the bishop to annul their marriage on the grounds of a "legal impediment." To counter this action, doña Victorina included the statements about her husband's infidelity from several witnesses sworn to secrecy. The weight of the evidence against him was sufficient to have the court sentence don Francisco to jail for some time.

Apparently, imprisonment did not sober don Francisco or make him behave more cautiously. On March 5 at 11 P.M. one of the alcaldes accompanied by a few infantry soldiers, several ministers of the law, and a clerk knocked at the door of his lover's house and

> heard quick steps from the inside until, with some delay, they opened the door. Having entered, His Grace recognized the second room which serves as a bedroom; he found on a desk before the bed a skirt and shawl from Castile and in it lying asleep, naked to his underwear, don Francisco Xavier Sánchez de la Flor to whom the judge said, "I have come after you, get up and dress yourself quickly.". . . meanwhile they looked for the accomplice who was not found in the same room but in the first one near the main door, buried in the bed under her mother's feet.

Don Francisco gave a common excuse to justify his presence in the house and in the bed of Magdalena Suárez. He claimed to have come to the house on "honorable business" but was surprised by a heavy rainstorm. Having been ill only recently, he feared for his health and stayed where he was. Despite offering this lame excuse, don Francisco went to jail, where he convinced the authorities that his lover, Magdalena, would present herself on the following day. When she did not appear, officials seized her mother and pressed both prisoners to disclose Magdalena's hiding place. Finally both were released, but don Francisco only after posting bail.

After these events, no possibility for any reconciliation between don Francisco and doña Victorina remained. Husband and wife became frequent litigants. Doña Victorina tried to recover both of her haciendas (El Tintal and Ambuela) and also sued to regain two slaves taken away by her husband, who had entered her property together with his lawyer to remove the slaves and some of his wife's belongings. Moreover, in 1796 don Francisco tried to sell two smaller properties, which, according to his own statement, were worthless without Ambuela. He assured the buyer that he would reclaim Ambuela from his wife, a procedure that he anticipated taking no more than six months. However, he lost all the suits and asked to be declared *pobre de solemnidad* (deserving poor), probably because he could not pay his debts. In 1803 his wife, certainly to avoid scandal and any additional demands by her husband, wrote her last will in the form of a "closed testament" to be opened only after her death.

In her last will doña Victorina mentioned her unhappy marriage only briefly, stating that she was "living alone for just reasons." Her beloved adopted son had died before doña Victorina, but her testament displays no bitterness or disappointment. Instead, it is an expression of her affection for the people who had accompanied her over the years and who were named in her bequests: her two slaves and two household servants, all females; her young lady of company, her cousin and clerk, and her surviving sister in the Santa Catalina convent; but most of all the two granddaughters of her sister, Antonia, and her two goddaughters, Nicolasita (the daughter of don Miguel Loza) and Regina Corral (the child of one of her lawyers). Her nephew, don Miguel Loza, inherited her estates.

The inventory of her possessions lists only 10 pesos in cash. Instead of money, there was a formidable collection of jewels, worth more than 5,000 pesos. Some of them were simple strings of pearls, which may have served as savings in case of unforeseen setbacks. The most valuable piece was a Spanish diamond necklace worth 721 pesos, and perhaps the most unusual was a rosary made of alligator teeth set in gold. Some of the jewels were given to the Santa Catalina convent, while others went to pay for Masses for the repose of her soul. The rest went to her goddaughters and her female relatives.

At the end of her life, doña Victorina's belongings totaled 38,054 pesos, which did not include the 29,000 pesos that she had been trying to claim, unsuccessfully, from her husband. In spite of all her troubles and the loss of part of her dowry, she had fared slightly better than her brother, don Fulgencio, who had left a total of 37,500 pesos to his three children. Doña Victorina died on November 25, 1805. A statement of twenty-five years earlier, very similar to some verses from the Old Testament dedicated to the "capable wife" (Proverbs 31: 10–31), best sums up her life: "a person of much sense in her conduct, prudent in her undertakings and economical in her trades to secure her advancement without ever retracting from her negotiations . . . she behaves with more prudence than the most skillful merchant to which she adds virtuous behavior . . . fearful of God."

SOURCES

All the sources are from the Archivo Nacional, Quito (AN/Q). The basic information on doña Victorina and her family comes from a document that includes her last will, the inventories of her house and estates, and copies of the concubinage trial:

Sin título (don Francisco Xavier Sánchez de la Flor sobre la testamentaria de su mujer doña María Victorina Loza). AN/Q, 3a Notaría, Juicios, 1805-XI-28.

Business Contacts

AN/Q, 3a Notaría, Juicios, 1767-X-19; 1769-IX-23; 1785-V-20.
AN/Q, Pesos, 1782-VI-28.

Don Francisco Sánchez de la Flor

AN/Q, 1a Notaría. Phelipe Santiago Navarrete, 1775–76 (vol. 408), f.283r-284r; Thomas Pazmiño, 1781–82 (vol. 419), f.361r-362r.
AN/Q, 3a Notaría. Juan Matheo Navarrete, 1772–73 (vol. 63), f.219r-219v; Juan Rodríguez, 1795–96 (vol. 73), f.172v-177v.

Landed Estates

AN/Q, 1a Notaría. Thomas Pazmiño, 1779–80 (vol. 416), f.454v-458v; Thomas Pazmiño, 1781–82 (vol. 419), f.306v-309r y f.358v-361r; Thomas Pazmiño, 1785–86 (vol. 425), f.384v-386r y f.401v-404r.
AN/Q, 3a Notaría. Juan Narciso Osorio, 1779–80 (vol. 66), f.129r-132r.
AN/Q, Tierras, 1784-VII-7.
AN/Q, Tierras, 1793-V-4.

Slaves

AN/Q, Esclavos, 1793-V-4 y 1793-X-18.

SUGGESTED READINGS

For general information on the socioeconomic situation of the Audiencia district, see Kenneth J. Andrien, *The Kingdom of Quito, 1690–1830: The State and Regional Development* (Cambridge, Eng., 1995); for details on the Bourbon reforms in the area, see Christiana Borchart de Moreno and Segundo E. Moreno Yánez, "Las reformas borbónicas en la Audiencia de Quito," *Anuario Colombiano de Historia Social y de la Cultura* 22 (1995): 35–57. An analysis of epidemic diseases may be found in Suzanne A. Alchon, *Native Society and Disease in Colonial Ecuador* (Cambridge, Eng., 1991), whereas rebellions have been studied by Segundo E. Moreno Yánez, *Sublevaciones indígenas en la Audiencia de Quito desde comienzos del siglo XVIII has finales de al colonia* (Quito, 1985). Regarding the popular reaction to Bourbon tax innovations, see Kenneth J. Andrien, "Economic Crisis, Taxes, and the Quito Insurrection of 1765," *Past and Present* 129 (November 1990): 104–31; and Anthony McFarlane, "The Rebellion of the Barrios: Urban Insurrection in Bourbon Quito," *Hispanic American Historical Review* 49 (May 1989): 282–330. Both articles together with Martin Minchom, *The People of Quito, 1690–1810: Change and Unrest in the Underclass* (Boulder, CO, 1994), offer insight into the eighteenth-century urban popular classes. Christian Büschges has studied Quito's upper classes in "Nobleza y estructura estamental entre concepto y realidad social. El caso de la ciudad de Quito y su región," *Jahrbuch fur Geschichte von Staat, Wirtschaft und Gesellschaft Lateinamerikas* 33 (1996): 166–86.

Quito's interregional trade has been studied by John C. Super, "Partnership and Profit in Early Andean Trade: The Experiences of the Quito Merchants, 1580–1610," *Journal of Latin American Studies* 2 (1979): 266–81, and by Christiana Borchart de Moreno, "Circulación y producción en Quito. De la Colonial a la República," *Siglo XIX. Revista de Historia* 14 (July–December 1993): 73–97.

CHAPTER 13

José Antonio da Silva

Marriage and Concubinage in Colonial Brazil

Muriel S. Nazzari

By the late eighteenth century, Brazil exceeded two million inhabitants, and the centers of population had shifted from the coastal sugar zones of the Northeast to the southeastern captaincies. The discovery of substantial gold deposits by the 1680s in the interior prompted a major demographic shift to the frontier captaincies or regions of Minas Gerais, Mato Grosso, and Goiás as people of all racial and class backgrounds rushed to seek their fortunes in the gold fields. New transportation networks and commercial routes developed to serve these growing settlements, but by the 1750s gold production began to decline slowly. Nevertheless, the demographic center of the colony had shifted decisively. Bolstered by the importation of large numbers of slave laborers, sugar production expanded rapidly in the southeastern captaincies by the 1790s. This expansion also spawned the cultivation of foodstuffs, grazing of livestock, and production of other exportable commodities such as tobacco, cotton, rice, and, later, coffee. The transfer in 1763 of the viceregal capital from Salvador in Bahia to Rio de Janeiro reflected the socioeconomic changes that were transforming Brazil by the eighteenth and early nineteenth centuries.

At the periphery of these changes was São Paulo, long Brazil's gateway to the interior. In the seventeenth century, this city served as the staging ground for the expeditions of bandeirantes *who roamed the interior provinces from the Amazon to Spanish Paraguay in search of indigenous slaves for coastal plantations. These bandeirantes were some of the first to discover the gold deposits later in the century. Once the gold rush began, São Paulo prospered, supplying foodstuffs and serving as a conduit for commerce to and from the coast. In 1711 it was given the official rank of city and, by 1803, São Paulo had a population of nearly 25,000. As the city's economic role expanded, the local society evolved into an urban center with well-established social hierarchies.*

Captain José Antonio da Silva was a prominent citizen in the rural parish of Santana, in the province of São Paulo, and his life and loves mirror the social realities of the city and its hinterland. The social mores of the day required José Antonio to marry someone of the same social rank as defined by ancestry, honor, and race. In keeping with this custom, he married a suitable woman, doña Clara Maria Ribeira, but the couple had no

children. His marriage and Church prohibitions against concubinage, how-
ever, did not stop him from engaging in a series of illicit relationships with
women beneath his social station and siring several illegitimate children.
By confining his sexual liaisons to women considered his "inferiors" in
class, race, and wealth, however, José Antonio's dalliances did nothing to
subvert the prevailing social hierarchies. In fact, they actually reinforced
the patriarchal societal order. Ironically, several of the women in the rak-
ish captain's life actually reaped some tangible benefits from their rela-
tionships with him. His wife, D. Clara Maria, ended her days a wealthy
woman, even marrying a much younger man. Two of his mistresses,
Gertrudes Pires and Ignacia Franca, also married well and even improved
their qualidade—census takers changed their racial categorizations from
bastarda *(meaning mestiza) or* parda *(meaning dark-skinned) to white.*
Two of his two slave mistresses also managed to secure freedom for the
children that they bore José Antonio. Despite every effort by Brazilian
elites to impose rigid social hierarchies, as the life of José Antonio da Silva
demonstrates, disorder often prevailed over colonial notions of order.

Muriel Nazzari is associate professor emeritus at Indiana University
in Bloomington. She received her doctorate at Yale University, and over
the course of her career has produced several pioneering articles on race
and gender in colonial Brazil. Professor Nazzari is the author of The
Disappearance of the Dowry: Women, Families, and Social Change
in São Paulo, Brazil (1600–1900) *(1991).*

*I*n the realm of sexual relations, order was difficult to maintain in colonial Brazilian society. The Church prescribed marriage as the only ac-
ceptable context for a sexual relationship, envisioning a society in which
most adults were married, except for religious. Although such an ideal
had never truly existed in Europe, it was especially hard to achieve in the
Americas, in part because of the difficulty in enforcing Church rules in a
colonial society. Both the Church and the civil society believed that marriage should be between equals in age, fortune, and social status. *Qualidade*
in Portuguese (or *calidad* in Spanish) was a complex term that included
issues of ancestry and honor and, in the Americas, also came to embrace
race.

Since most of the Portuguese settlers who went to Brazil in the early
years were male, they found few European women to marry who were
equals in "quality." As a result, they frequently formed liaisons with
women of other races and lower social status that were condemned by
the Church and seen as disorderly. But the resulting disorder in sexual
relations in the Spanish and Portuguese colonies ironically helped to
maintain a different sort of order in the highly hierarchical racial
system that was evolving. Brazil was no exception to this process. Both

scholars of the early colony and ordinary Brazilians of the twenty-first century well know that stable nuclear families (characterized by marital fidelity) were exceedingly rare in the early years. Scholars have found a large proportion of illegitimate children in the eighteenth and nineteenth centuries, and only a small percentage of the population was legally married.

This article describes the lives of a few residents of the municipality of São Paulo in the late eighteenth and early nineteenth centuries—in as much detail as the documents will allow—to illustrate the way in which illegitimate (disorderly) sexual relationships reinforced the racial hierarchy of the province. It will describe illicit sexual relationships, marriages characterized by differences in qualidade, and how the racial category of individuals could change in the regional censuses depending on their ownership of property, their marital status, or the sexual relationship that they maintained with an important person. The foundations of this study rest on a wide range of primary source materials: censuses, wills and settlements of estates, parish registers of baptism and marriage, Church processes for marriage and dispensations for consanguinity, the minutes of the municipal council of São Paulo, and documents in the Desembargo do Paço (the Portuguese high court that, among other things, legitimized illegitimate children).

The documents portray a colonial São Paulo where patriarchs exercised great power over women, particularly in sexual matters. The power of these patriarchs was based not only on their gender but also on their race and wealth. Yet the picture is not entirely one-sided. Colonial women made choices too and, in some cases, appear to have used their wealth and status to exert power over men. As a consequence, gender intersected with race, economic wealth, and social class, compounded by the almost absolute power that owners had over slaves.

Although much information will emerge about the lives of several individuals and their families, the main character in this tale is Captain José Antonio da Silva, commander of the militia in the rural Paulista neighborhood of Santana during the last quarter of the eighteenth century.[1] He and his wife were childless, but he had numerous illicit sexual relationships and fathered several illegitimate children. In the documents concerning the settlement of his estate, it is clear that the captain and his wife had given a small farm within their property to Gertrudes Pires, who was the mother of his eight illegitimate children.[2]

At the time there were actually two José Antonio da Silvas in São Paulo. Santana's militia captain was born in Lisbon around 1742, the legitimate son of Adrião da Silva and his wife, Joséfa Thereza, and was always known only by his name, José Antonio da Silva.[3] The other, a man almost ten years younger, was born in São Paulo and was always called José Antonio da Silva, Paulista (a resident of the city and province of São Paulo). The registration for José Antonio da Silva, Paulista's marriage indicates that he had been a foundling, baptized in 1751, and raised by Anna da Silva Pacheco. Following the custom of marriage equality, he also married a foundling.[4] He was described in an ecclesiastical document from 1800 as a businessman.[5] José Antonio da Silva, Paulista, however, was never connected to the neighborhood of Santana, and he appears in none of its censuses.

This is not the case with the Portuguese José Antonio da Silva, who already appeared in the first census of Santana (1765) as a single man, twenty-five years old, and a farmer with considerable capital for the time, 800$000 (800,000 *reis*). In that census there were eighty-three households in the rural parish of Santana, and only 31 percent of them (twenty-six households) declared any capital at all. There was only one household, headed by the widow Maria de Oliveira Furtada, which recorded more in the census than the young José Antonio da Silva; she had 1:659$000. One other single man, Domingos Gomes de Amaral, also declared capital of 800$000. Everybody else had less; the average in Santana was 264$154. This amount was slightly less than the average for the whole city of São Paulo, which was 296$154.[6] Thus, José Antonio da Silva was already a prosperous farmer in Santana in 1765. Where did he obtain this wealth? It seems unlikely that he brought it from Portugal. In that case he would probably have been a merchant, establishing himself in Rio de Janeiro or in some other coastal urban area, not in a rural parish of São Paulo. A more likely answer is that as an even younger man he joined the gold rush in Minas Gerais, Cuiabá, or Mato Grosso, making enough money to settle later as a prosperous farmer in São Paulo.

When he died thirty-two years later in 1797, he and his wife still lived in the rural neighborhood of Santana, although they owned three houses in the city of São Paulo,[7] two of two stories and one of one story. They probably lived in one of the houses whenever they were in the city and rented the other two. In Santana they owned a large agricultural property that included five different houses. The main house included an oratory with images of the Virgin Mary and several saints. Two houses were used to process sugarcane and make cane liquor (*aguardiente*), and the fourth was probably the slave quarters. The house of Gertrudes Pires was listed separately with the small farm surrounding it and a walled orchard. José Antonio and his wife owned cattle, sheep, and twenty-eight slaves. When he died, their estate was worth almost 6 *contos*, or 6:000$000, which included considerable cash, bars of gold, and bills of credit. He and his wife were undoubtedly the wealthiest family in the neighborhood, and becoming a captain of militia was always related to wealth in colonial Brazil.[8] Santana was not in itself a well-off neighborhood, however, so José Antonio da Silva probably was not one of the richest Paulistas. In addition, the extant documentation does not reveal how much of the money in his estate at the time of his death had been brought to the marriage by the dowry of his wife, dona Clara Maria Ribeira.

Moreover, José Antonio seems to have been a controversial figure, despite his wealth and important position in the militia. One of his duties as captain was to sign the yearly census of the neighborhood, but in the 1783 census an ensign signed in his place. José Antonio was in jail. In all of the thirteen censuses of Santana during this period, this is the only case of someone listed as being in jail at the time of the census. The reason for his incarceration remains unknown. It might have been for some trivial matter, such as not collaborating with a municipal council order that all neighbors contribute to the repair of the Santana bridge or to the construction of the Santana stretch of the road from São Paulo to Goiás. He might even have run afoul of the Church, which also had the power to jail persons. Furthermore, José Antonio died without making a will, because two men shot and killed him at his farm. He was clearly a man who had enemies.

On the other hand there are numerous references to José Antonio da Silva in the eighteenth-century records of São Paulo's municipal council, indicating that he was an important person in the larger community. In 1765, when he was still a young man in his twenties, José Antonio was listed as an *almotacel* (lieutenant). Ten years later he was already a captain and a justice of the peace; he presided over the municipal council of the city of São Paulo. He was clearly a man with power not only in Santana but also in São Paulo.

José Antonio had numerous sexual relationships with women over the years. One early one, mentioned in the judicial process for the settlement of his estate, produced a *filho natural* (illegitimate child), Francisco de Paula da Silva, who filed as an heir. A *filho natural* was a child of a man and woman who had no canonical impediments to marriage and thus could have married. Francisco's baptismal certificate reveals that while José Antonio da Silva was still unmarried, he became involved with a single woman, Ignacia Franca, the mother of his child and also a resident of Santana. In January 1766, when she was twenty-two or twenty-three and he was around twenty-six, they baptized Francisco together. José Antonio da Silva was named in the parish register as the father, which was unusual. Most baptismal records for illegitimate children gave the mother's name but claimed that the father was unknown. Listing a father's name was dangerous because the Church prosecuted prolonged and scandalous cases of concubinage. Having his name on the baptismal record suggests that José Antonio da Silva and Ignacia were no longer living together and that their sexual relationship had ended. As a result, a prominent person such as José Antoino could openly acknowledge the child.

Seventeenth- and eighteenth-century Paulista society was strongly endogamous; people married only their social equals. Whenever any inequality existed in a relationship, it was usually the wife who was superior to her husband in wealth and status.[9] Any liaison between a man and a woman lower in the social hierarchy, whether because of her race or her lack of property, was always carried on outside of marriage.[10] As a result, despite acknowledging his *filho natural*, José Antonio probably never intended to marry Ignacia Franca because she was not his social equal according to the criteria of the time. In fact, Ignacia was listed in the 1765 census of Santana as living with her parents, Francisco Franco and his wife, Joanna de Aguiar, and three brothers. Her father declared no capital whatsoever to the census taker, and his race is noted as *bastardo*, the term used in São Paulo to denote persons with a mixture of Indian and European blood. In two subsequent censuses (1778, 1783) her father was called a bastardo, but in two other ones (1779, 1780) he was called a *pardo* (dark skinned). Pardo was a term used then mostly for people with a mixture of white and black blood, but it was applied sometimes to individuals with any racial mixture, even to Indians. In any case, her father was not considered white. According to the standards of the day, Ignacia was inferior to José Antonio both in race and in wealth and was therefore not a suitable match for him.

The census of 1778 listed José Antonio da Silva as thirty-seven years old and already married to thirty-five-year-old dona Clara Maria Ribeira. She had not been a resident of Santana, since she did not appear in the censuses of 1765 or 1768. A much later census in 1802 indicated her birthplace as Rio de Janeiro. The parish record of their wedding is missing, however, making it impossible to know exactly when it took place. She undoubtedly must have brought the customary property to the marriage with her dowry, or it is unlikely that José Antonio would have married her. She was probably also viewed as white, because none of the censuses listing the couple records her race as different from her husband's. Nonetheless, in the 1798 census, after her husband died, she is listed as "Clara Maria parda *viúva* (widow).[11] Once again, however, in the 1802 census, after her remarriage, she was again classified as white.

In the settlement of José Antonio's estate, the documents indicate that dona Clara Maria Ribeira did not know how to sign her name. Illiteracy was not uncommon for propertied women in eighteenth-century São Paulo, even though many of the wealthier Paulista wives and daughters had learned to read and write. Dona Clara Maria may also have been older than her husband. In the first two censuses she is shown as two years younger than her husband (1778, 1779), but in the next one she is listed as a year older; in the next two censuses she is recorded as from one to four years younger. In the three censuses in the nineties (1795, 1796, 1797) she is shown as five or six years older. Given that she was probably older than her husband, illiterate, and had possible traces of Indian or African blood, it is all the more likely that she brought a substantial contribution of property, slaves, or cash to the marriage.

The next sexual partner of José Antonio da Silva was Gertrudes Pires. He was already married when he started his relationship with her by the time of the 1778 census. Gertrudes was listed there as the daughter of a white man, Salvador Pires Monteiro, and his bastarda wife, Anna de Oliveira, both residents of Santana. Gertrudes was considerably younger than Ignacia Franca, only seven by the census of 1765. According to the data, she lived with her parents up through the census of January 1779 but was no longer listed with them in 1780; neither was she listed in José Antonio's household in that year. Three years later, however, in the 1783 census Gertrudes, twenty-four years old, and her son, Damazio, appeared in José Antonio's household as white *agregados*, a census classification that means a related or unrelated person who also lives in the household of a nuclear family, though not necessarily in the same house. The fact that Damazio was Gertrudes's child was not spelled out in the census.

In the 1787 listing, Damazio and his younger sister and brother, who were born in the interim, were characterized as foundlings. Eight years later, in the census of 1795, Gertrudes and her children were again categorized as agregados without listing the relationship between the mother and her children. In the following year's census, 1796, Gertrudes was called an agregada, but her children were considered foundlings, as they also were in the 1797 census, which did not even record their mother's name. For some reason, no census taker identified the children as belonging to Gertrudes, despite the fact that in other households, a census classification exists to identify the children of agregadas even if they did not live in the same house. The details of the relationship between José Antonio da Silva and his mistress Gertrudes Pires are thereby obscured. Moreover, the baptismal records of these children gave their mother's name but listed the father as unknown.[12]

The settlement of José Antonio da Silva's estate mentions that he also had two mulatto daughters with two of his slave women. His widow made a long declaration that those young women, Maria and Thomazia, were agregadas and should not be counted as slaves. Previous censuses corroborate that their father considered them free—while they are listed as slaves through 1780, they are recorded as agregadas pardas from 1783. Despite dona Clara Maria's protestations, however, in the 1802 census, after she had remarried, Maria and Thomazia were listed as two of the couple's sixteen slaves and the only mulattos that she and her new husband owned. It is not clear whether or not they had been legally manumitted in the 1780s. Their roles may not have changed in the household, thus making it easy to list them as slaves again in 1802. In the 1807 census, Clara Maria had died and her husband had remarried; Maria and Thomazia were not among his slaves. Perhaps Clara Maria formally manumitted them in her will, or else they may have passed to her heirs as slaves.

José Antonio always carried on his extramarital relationships with women who were inferior to him by class or race: his two slaves, who probably had little say in the matter; Ignacia Franca, who was probably of mixed Indian and white ancestry and whose family had no capital; and finally, with Gertrudes Pires from a somewhat "better" family, since her father was listed as white but had no capital. The disorderly sexual life of José Antonio da Silva reinforced these women's lowly social status in the hierarchical society of São Paulo.

Did these women benefit in any way from these relationships? In all likelihood, they did, and the higher their original position, the more they benefited. The two slaves secured freedom for their children. Ignacia profited from her son's inheritance, and after she finally married, she was listed (and apparently viewed) as white in the census. Gertrudes gained the status of an agregada in José Antonio's household and in later censuses was recorded as white, even after his death. In all likelihood she was probably seen as white by the larger society. She also acquired the farm and house. In addition, Luzia, one of the slaves listed in the 1797 census as José Antonio's, appears as the property of Gertrudis in the 1798 census, together with her five children, suggesting that Luzia was also a gift. Finally, the lives of dona Clara Maria, Ignacia, and Gertrudes demonstrate that women with property in colonial Brazil could easily marry; all three of them remarried much younger men after José Antonio died.

Dona Clara Maria appears in the 1798 census, the year after her husband's death, living with a young married couple who were agregados of her household and owning sixteen slaves, her share of slaves in the community property. Four years later, in 1802, census takers recorded that she had married Francisco Xavier de Moraes, who was only twenty-nine years old. Her age is listed as sixty-two, but she was undoubtedly even older. The records indicate that they had married only eleven months after José Antonio's death. Francisco Xavier's birth certificate put his age at only twenty-three when they wed.[13] By the 1807 census dona Clara Maria had died, and her husband had remarried a woman in her twenties. By this time he held only seven slaves, his share of the community property that he had owned with Clara Maria. He had, in effect, bartered himself in exchange for the prospect of acquiring property, which later permitted him to marry a younger woman with little or no assets (since she appears not to have brought any slaves into the marriage).

Gertrudes Pires also wed a younger man, although the difference in their ages was not so great. The 1798 census recorded her as living alone with her eight children (the eldest was seventeen years old) and six slaves (Luzia and her five children). Gertrudes's offspring could not inherit from their father for they were adulterine illegitimate children. By the 1802 census, Gertrudes, who was then forty-two, had married Reginaldo Damazio da Silva, age thirty-three, and they lived with her children and nine slaves. The parish register indicates that they had married in 1800. Reginaldo apparently owned three adult slaves, which added to their joint property. Nonetheless, neither Reginaldo nor Gertrudes appears in later censuses of Santana; they must have moved away. Her eldest son, Damazio Antonio da Silva, married and continued to live in Santana, perhaps on the property originally given to Gertrudes.[14] He also married well because he and his wife were listed in the 1807 census as owning six slaves; by 1825 that number had increased to nine.

The documents for the settlement of José Antonio da Silva's estate are unclear about whether Francisco de Paula da Silva, his natural son, actually received his inheritance. The will of José Antonio's father indicates that he had a brother in Lisbon who was a collateral heir. After Francisco filed as an heir, the judge who carried out the division of the estate had the part belonging to the deceased auctioned and deposited in the Juizo dos Auzentes (court dealing with intestate goods), probably reserved for the brother in Lisbon. Francisco, however, placed an embargo on the proceeds to keep them from going abroad.

It is possible that he did inherit since there is every indication that Francisco prospered over the course of his lifetime. He first lived with his mother and grandfather until the grandfather died and then continued living with his mother. In all of this time, the family owned no slaves. In the 1798 census, however, less than a year after his father died, Francisco had acquired an adult male slave. The inheritance that he would have received from his father amounted to over 2 contos, and one slave was worth much less than that amount. Nevertheless, it is possible that Francisco, like many other rural Paulistas of that period, had not owned the land that he worked. He may have invested his inheritance in land, cattle, and one slave (that census reported no property except slaves). He did prosper thereafter; by 1802 he and his mother owned four slaves, produced and sold aguardiente, and kept fifteen horses and six pigs. By 1807, when Francisco was forty years old, these assets had increased substantially. By 1816, however, census takers recorded that he was no longer in Santana. In all likelihood he had died, because the slaves recorded as living in his mother's household were the same ones recorded as part of their joint household. In fact, she probably had inherited them from her deceased son.

Ignacia Franca had become the head of her own household by 1787 and, like her father, was sometimes labeled in the census either as a bastarda or a parda. Moreover, by the 1790s, census takers consistently reported her age as less than it really was. In 1807 they recorded it as fifty-nine when in reality she was sixty-four. By the 1816 census, when her son no longer lived in the household, Ignacia had married Manoel Barboza Bueno, a white man from Minas Gerais. Manoel's age was given as thirty-two and hers as fifty-nine when she was actually seventy-three! In the 1825 census she again appears as Manoel Barboza's wife; his age was listed as forty-two and hers as sixty-nine, even though she must have been eighty-one. In addition, after her marriage she was always labeled white in the census.

Such marriages between older women and younger men run counter to the received wisdom that younger women marry older men for their money. In colonial Brazil, however, the reverse also happened. Men needed capital to establish themselves independently of their parents, since there were few other ways to earn a good living. For their part, older women often needed a man to manage their assets, thus allowing male and female needs to coincide in some cases. It seems likely, however, that public opinion frowned on such marriages. The records in the parish register, for example, show that both dona Clara Maria Ribeira's second marriage and that of Gertrudes Pires required a special dispensation from the Church. Gertrudes and her future husband petitioned for the dispensation because "they wish to marry as quickly as possible for urgent reasons."[15] The fact that both weddings were carried out virtually in secret indicates some level of societal disapproval for the marriage of an older woman to a younger man.

Despite the illegitimate and disorderly relationship of both Ignacia Franca and Gertrudes Pires with José Antonio da Silva, both women improved their qualidade, gaining financial assets and being viewed as white. Flaunting Church notions of social order clearly advanced their wealth and social status, perhaps indicating that some women may have made a calculated choice to enter into a sexual liaison outside of wedlock.[16] Slave women, however, could not make such decisions. Although some slaves who had a sexual relationship with their masters were given clothes or preferential treatment, most slave women could only hope to benefit by the manumission of their children or even of themselves. Not all masters freed their slave children or mistresses, but when they did so, it was a wonderful gift. In a few exceptional cases, the children of slaves and their masters were legitimized, even becoming their father's heir. In a few rare cases the slave herself was manumitted and later married her master. Such cases usually occurred in regions where there were few white women, and they brought an unusual sense of order to the disorder of concubinage between masters and slaves.

The life of José Antonio da Silva and his intimate relationships with women demonstrate the tensions between colonial ideas about order and disorder and the realities of life in eighteenth-century Brazil. In his marriage, José Antonio conformed to the precepts of the Church as well as to society's requirement that he marry someone who was his equal in wealth and status. His extramarital liaisons clearly flaunted the moral order of the Church, but because his dalliances were with women considered his inferiors in property and race, they still reinforced the hierarchical racial and class order. In these relationships, men drew power not only from their gender (in a patriarchal society) but also because they were the women's superiors in class and race or, in the most extreme cases, because the female was a slave. Within this social system a woman entering into an extramarital relationship could, with luck, improve her own and her children's material circumstances and even her qualidade.

NOTES

1. Maria Beatriz Nizza da Silva, "Filhos ilegítimos no Brasil colonial," in *Sociedade Brasileira de Pesquisa Histórica, Anais da XV Reunião* (Curitiba: SPBH, 1996).

2. Arquivo do Estado de São Paulo (hereafter AESP), Inventários Não Publicados (hereafter INP), José Antonio da Silva, 1797, No. de ordem 569 c. 92.

3. I have calculated his approximate date of birth using his age as reported in the censuses of Santana for 1765, 1768, 1778, 1779, 1780, 1783, 1787, 1795, 1796, and 1797 in AESP, Maços de População, Bairro de Santana.

4. Arquivo da Cúria Metropolitana de São Paulo (hereafter ACMSP), Processos de Casamento da Sé, José Antonio da Silva, 6-57-2227.

5. ACMSP, Processos de Casamento, Reginaldo Damazo da Silva, 7-1-2511.

6. Alice P. Canabrava, "Uma economia de decadência: Os níveis de riqueza na capitania de São Paulo, 1765–1767," *Revista Brasileira de Economia* 26, no. 4 (October–December 1972): 101, 103.

7. AESP, INP, No. de ordem 569, c. 92.

8. Elizabeth Kuznesof, "Clans, the Militia, and Territorial Government: The Articulation of Kinship with Polity in Eighteenth-Century São Paulo," in David J. Robinson, ed., *Social Fabric and Spatial Structure in Colonial Latin America* (Syracuse, NY: Microfilms International, 1979).

9. Muriel Nazzari, *Disappearance of the Dowry: Women, Families, and Social Change in São Paulo, Brazil (1600–1900)* (Stanford, CA: Stanford University Press, 1991), ch. 3 and Conclusion.

10. Muriel Nazzari, "Concubinage in Colonial Brazil: The Inequalities of Class, Race, and Gender," *Journal of Family History* 21, no. 2 (April 1996).

11. This was a census in which many people were classified as pardos, but it is clearly the same Clara Maria because her age is correct and she is listed as owning sixteen slaves, which corresponds to half of the number she owned with her husband.

12. See ACMSP, Registro de Casamentos, 7-31-2815, for the marriage of Damazio Antonio da Silva in 1803, which includes a copy of his baptismal certificate of 1780.

13. ACMSP, Livro de Casamentos da Sé, 1798, Francisco Xavier de Moraes, Clara Maria Ribeira.

14. ACMSP, Livro de Casamentos da Sé, 1803, Damazio Antonio da Silva, Rita Maria do Espirito Santo.

15. ACMSP, Processos de Casamento, 1800, 7-1-2511, Reginaldo Damazo da Silva, Gertrudes Pires do Nascimento; ACMSP, Livros de Casamento da Sé, 1798, Francisco Xavier de Moraes, Clara Maria Ribeira.

16. Robert McCaa, "Marriageways in Mexico and Spain, 1500–1900," in *Continuity and Change* 9, no. 1 (1994): 11–43.

SUGGESTED READINGS

Further information on marriage and concubinage in colonial Latin America can be found in Asuncion Lavrin, ed., *Sexuality and Marriage in Colonial Latin America* (Lincoln: University of Nebraska Press, 1989); Lyman L. Johnson and Sonya Lipsett-Rivera, *The Faces of Honor: Sex, Shame, and Violence in Colonial Latin America* (Albuquerque: University of New Mexico Press, 1998).

An extensive study of race and class in marriage and concubinage is Verena Martínez-Alier, *Marriage, Class, and Colour in Nineteenth-Century Cuba: A Study of Racial Attitudes and Sexual Values in a Slave Society* (London: Cambridge University Press, 1974). Another study that considers race and class for a colonial Mexican town is Robert McCaa, *"Calidad*, Class, and Marriage in Colonial Mexico: The Case of Parral, 1788–1790," in *Hispanic American Historical Review* 64 (1984): 477–502. Information on the interaction of race with gender in Brazilian concubinage is in Muriel Nazzari, "Concubinage in Colonial Brazil: The Inequalities of Race, Class, and Gender," in *Journal of Family History* 21:2 (April 1996): 107–24.

For the infrequency of marriage in colonial Brazil, see Donald Ramos, "Marriage and the Family in Colonial Vila Rica," in *Hispanic American Historical Review* 55:2 (May 1975): 200–25. For statistics on Brazilian illegitimacy, see Elizabeth Kuznesof, "Sexual Politics, Race and Bastard-Bearing in Nineteenth-century Brazil: A Question of Culture or Power?" in *Journal of Family History* 16:3 (1991): 241–60.

CHAPTER 14

Eugenio Sinanyuca

Militant, Nonrevolutionary *Kuraka*, and Community Defender

WARD STAVIG

The Bourbon monarchy's efforts to reform trade, mining policies, military organization, and patterns of colonial administration as well as to heighten fiscal pressures exacerbated existing political and social tensions in many Andean regions. In 1772, for example, the crown increased the sales tax (alcabala) from 2 percent to 4 percent on both colonial and European goods and only four years later raised the rate once again to 6 percent. The viceregal government also established customs houses in key cities and placed suboffices along major trade routes to collect sales taxes more effectively. Moreover, the crown disturbed regional trade patterns by removing Upper Peru (now Bolivia) from the Viceroyalty of Peru in 1776, placing it instead under the control of the newly created Viceroyalty of the Río de la Plata, with its capital in Buenos Aires. During this same period colonial officials made more accurate censuses of the indigenous population to ensure that tribute and other levies were collected efficiently. The net result was a dramatic upsurge in tax revenues, often accompanied by regional economic downturns that heightened local discontent. Such regional unrest among a wide array of social groups prompted a series of revolts between 1777 and 1780, but the most serious threats to Spanish authority came from the oppressed indigenous communities of Peru and Upper Peru between 1780 and 1783.

One of the most bloody revolts broke out southeast of Cuzco in Tinta (also called Canas y Canchis) and threatened to expel Spanish authorities from the old Inca heartland. The leader of the uprising was José Gabriel Condorcanqui, who took the name Túpac Amaru II after the Inca ruler who was executed by the Spanish in 1572. The Bourbon reforms had provoked considerable economic hardship in Tinta, worsening ethnic tensions among Andean communities and also conflicts over leadership positions. The corregidor, *Antonio de Arriaga, exacerbated these problems by his heavy-handed administration of tribute and the* reparto, *the forced distribution and sale of goods by the corregidor to indigenous peoples and sometimes even to local Spaniards and mestizos. His policies led to*

241

particularly bitter conflicts with Condorcanqui, who served as kuraka *in Tinta. Túpac Amaru began his revolt by capturing Arriaga, stripping him of his position as corregidor (ostensibly on the authority of King Charles III), and executing him publicly on November 10, 1780, in Tungasuca, Tinta's capital. Within a few weeks a massive uprising had begun that spread from Tinta to Lake Titicaca and beyond.*

Túpac Amaru used a diverse set of Andean and Christian symbols to develop an ideology capable of attracting a broad-based coalition, which included some Creoles and mestizos and a large following of Andeans. He took the title of Sapa Inca and dressed in royal tunics decorated with a figure of the sun, linking him to the Inca sun god, Inti. He also invoked the image of the king of Spain, a powerful symbol of unity in the Andes, by using the rallying cry of "Long Live the King, Down with Bad Government." Apart from such symbolic efforts to recruit allies, he also relied on kin, personal, and business connections (as a prominent local merchant) to raise a rebel army that reached nearly 100,000. This massive force controlled much of the region from Tinta to Puno (near Lake Titicaca), but his failure to capture the city of Cuzco in January 1781 led his military fortunes to decline rapidly. By February, Túpac Amaru had retreated to his command center in Tinta, where he was defeated, later captured, and then brutally executed in the Cuzco's main square.

Many local kurakas joined the rebellion led by Túpac Amaru, but some, such as Eugenio Sinanyuca, the ethnic leader of Coporaque, did not. Despite the close personal relationship between Túpac Amaru and Sinanyuca, both men took very different political stances in a series of local disputes between clerical authorities and government officials. Bad blood between the bishop of Cuzco, Juan Manuel Moscoso y Peralta, and Corregidor Arriaga intensified a clash over clerical fees and Church property in Yauri, a community in Canas y Canchis. When Bishop Moscoso sent his representative, Vicente de la Puente, to resolve the problem, the local indigenous population threatened to oppose him by force, and Arriaga supported them. De la Puente was also the parish priest of Coporaque, and his relations with Sinanyuca were strained, so the kuraka and the corregidor found themselves in an uneasy alliance against the bishop and those Churchmen supporting him. Túpac Amaru, however, was a friend and supporter of Moscoso and a sworn enemy of Arriaga. When the bishop excommunicated Arriaga, Sinanyuca, and the entire community of Coporaque over the escalating disputes, the political lines hardened. The importance of such disputes and personal relationships often proved as important as larger structural socioeconomic forces or political principles in determining the allegiances of key historical actors, such as Eugenio Sinanyuca, during the rebellions of the 1780s.

Ward Stavig is associate professor of history at the University of South Florida and a secretary of the Conference on Latin American History. He has written widely on values and social relations in the colonial Andean indigenous world and on Túpac Amaru. This work culminated in his recent book-length study of the indigenous society in the eighteenth century in the region that formed the heart of the Túpac Amaru rebellion, The World of Túpac Amaru: Conflict, Community, and Identity in Colonial Peru *(Lincoln, NE, 1999).*

𝒥n November 1780, Túpac Amaru, a *kuraka* (ethnic communal leader, or *cacique*) from the Cuzco province of Canas y Canchis, who also saw himself as the "Inca," rose in rebellion against the colonial state. He and his followers threatened Spanish control of the Andes in ways that it had not been challenged since the Conquest era. Spreading out from the rural Cuzco provinces of Quispicanchis and Canas y Canchis, the rebellion resonated with many indigenous peoples as well as with some mestizos and criollos and quickly gained followers throughout much of the Andes. Not all kurakas or ordinary indigenous people, however, supported the rebellion. Some, such as the kuraka Mateo Pumacahua, also from the Cuzco region but from a different *partido* or province, even fought for the Spaniards. From the community of Chinchero, Pumacahua led his people into battle against Túpac Amaru's army and was instrumental in the royalist defense of the city of Cuzco. The depth of the differences between the two kurakas was symbolized in a painting that Pumacahua commissioned after Túpac Amaru's capture. The painting "depicted a puma (Pumacahua) defeating a snake (*amaru*) beneath the benevolent gaze of the Virgin of Monserrat, Chinchero's patron saint. In the background stood Pumacahua and his wife, both dressed in Spanish garb, affirming their territorial sovereignty. Beneath the painting was inscribed Caesar's dictum: *Veni, Vidi, Vici* (I came, I saw, I conquered), commemorating the defeat of this rival faction."[1]

There were other indigenous people, like Pumacahua and his followers, who took actions that caused them to be considered Spanish loyalists. Others, however, who were at best (or at worst) neutral in the struggle have often been lumped together under the label of "loyalists" when, in reality, their allegiances and motivations were more difficult to discern. The closer historians get to life "on the ground," the more complex the indigenous world appears. And so it was with Eugenio Sinanyuca, kuraka of Coporaque, one of the largest communities in the province of Canas y Canchis. As a result, he was well known to both the future rebel leader, Túpac Amaru, who sometimes referred to him as "cousin" in messages, and to Spanish officials. While Sinanyuca and many of the people of Coporaque did not rise up with Túpac Amaru, it would be an oversimplification to characterize this kuraka and those who followed him as loyalists. In reality, they remained largely outside the scope of combatants for most of the rebellion, although some did link up with rebel forces when they appeared in Coporaque intent on recruiting followers. The distance that Sinanyuca and many Coporaque villagers felt between themselves and their rebellious neighbors had much to do with their face-to-face, day-to-day experiences with colonial officials and other Andean people. While villagers in rural Cuzco and much of the Andes, for that matter, shared the tensions and uncertainty wrought by the changes that disturbed this world in the mideighteenth century, in other respects their particular experience created political allegiances that divided them despite their geographical proximity.

First, the similarities: both Sinanyuca and Túpac Amaru faced difficulties in being installed as kurakas. For reasons that remain unclear, colonial authorities were reluctant to give Túpac Amaru power over the communities of Tungasuca, Surimana, and Pampamarca despite the fact that his father and older brother had held the position. Moreover, Túpac Amaru had attended the prestigious Jesuit school for the children of kurakas in Cuzco. Not surprisingly, the opposition of local corregidors to his aspirations to ethnic leadership made a potential enemy of the future rebel leader. Finally, in 1766, Túpac Amaru was made kuraka; because of a political dispute he was removed from power but then later reinstalled.[2] His path to power had not been smooth, and the corregidors of Canas y Canchis were responsible.

Eugenio Sinanyuca likewise had a difficult time assuming the post of kuraka in his home community of Coporaque. When the corregidor decided to replace the former cacique, Cristóbal Sinanyuca, with Eugenio, members of the Collana *ayllu* (one of eight such Andean kinship groups that composed the community of Coporaque) opposed his elevation to leadership. Shouting and using their slings, these people disrupted the ceremony and attacked those who were preparing to offer Mass as part of Eugenio's installation. Those who participated in these actions had been drinking *chicha* (corn beer) and *aguardiente* (cane alcohol) and chewing coca at Cristóbal's house at least three days prior to the violence. The former cacique even provided his ayllu members with most of what they drank and chewed, and he incited the violent opposition to Sinanyuca's formal assumption of power as kuraka. Influenced by alcohol and coca, which often promoted group solidarity in Andean communities, and encouraged by Cristóbal, himself notorious for his "public and continual drunkenness," these ayllu members used violence to block the leadership change.

Cristóbal had previously abandoned the community and only returned a few days before Eugenio was to take office. It was because of Cristóbal's absence, his frequent inebriation, and his neglect of duty that he had been removed from his post. While the vast majority of Coporaque did not take part in the action, there were rumors that Eugenio, who was described by a member of another ayllu as having a character admirable in its "formality, honor, and good judgement," who was known never to get drunk, and who got along well with Spaniards, would try to collect the back tribute owed by the Coporaque ayllus. The commotion quickly subsided, and Eugenio was installed. Once in office, he became an effective and respected leader.[3] He not only staunchly defended community interests, working the legal system to the benefit of villagers whenever possible, but he also did not hesitate to break with the law and tradition to aid the people of Coporaque.

Both Eugenio Sinanyuca and Túpac Amaru became known for their opposition to abuses of the dreaded *mita* (forced labor) at the Potosí silver mines. Túpac Amaru had a special dislike of the mita that stemmed not only from what it did to the communities he governed but also from the harm that it had done to family members and might do to him as kuraka. His uncle, the kuraka Marcos Túpac Amaru, "was bankrupted by the seizure of a train of mules and 100 pesos' worth of goods because his mita quota was one man short."[4] The lesson was not lost on the nephew of this unfortunate man. Túpac Amaru even traveled to Lima seeking not only recognition as "Inca" but exemption from the mita for his people and for other Canas y Canchis communities. Despite the failure of his mission, villagers in his province began to view Túpac Amaru as a special leader for his efforts. A priest from Canas y Canchis later observed that "when Túpac Amaru came back from this capital [that is, Lima] to his ancient home. . . . I noted the Indians looked at him with veneration, and not only in this village but even outside the province of Tinta (Canas y Canchis); the province, proud with his protection, imagined itself free from the mita obligation."[5] Nonetheless, he saw that his mita contingents were delivered as required by colonial authorities.

Sinanyuca also disliked the mita but, like Túpac Amaru, he understood the necessity of complying with the service, both to protect himself and the community. At the same time, both kurakas protested its abuses and tried to end the system of forced labor. Thus, he too turned to the state to seek relief for his people. In 1775 some members of Coporaque's mita contingent abandoned Potosí before their term of service had ended and returned illegally to their community. Nevertheless, these were respected men with good reputations and therefore, even though detained by Sinanyuca, were treated well by the kuraka and other leaders. This lenient response had its risks, however, since fleeing from mita service was not merely resistance to the state. Rather, it put the entire community at risk because the law held both the ayllu and the kurakas responsible for such actions.

Two days before Christmas, Sinanyuca and another local kuraka wrote to the corregidor that Bartolomé García, who had been in charge of the *mitayos* (a person serving in the mita), and Gregorio Choquecota, a mita worker, had returned from Potosí illegally, without fulfilling their obligations. Although he was being held by the community, the kurakas noted that the mitayos:

> had experienced very bad whippings and affronts on the part of the head carpenter and other administrators of the refinery of don Bernardo Zenda and that it not being possible for them to endure such inhumane treatment they returned, obliged by the conservation of their lives to seek refuge, abandoning their pack llamas, their sleeping gear, and their prebend of food; that a few days earlier for the same reason two other *cédulas* [another term for mitayos] of the said mita did the same abandoning their wives and children: that when the women with their weeping [asked] said administrators not to mistreat thusly their husbands, they also mistreated them with blows, afterward locking them in a chapel, and that lately the cruelty of said administrators is so great that . . . they have forced the wives of these Indians to work in place of their husbands. The two aforementioned Indians, especially the *enterador* [person from the community responsible for overseeing mitayos] are known in these ayllus for being of very good repute, for which reason we cannot presume that they have come back fleeing, but obliged by serious motives. . . . We assure Your Majesty that we received continual complaints . . . for some years from the captain enteradores and cédulas who return from said mita, [and] they do not pay travel compensation nor justly [pay] daily wages, and that they oblige them to work more than physically possible and as a result many Indians return with chest injuries and they die here as asthmatics, for this reason everyone has the greatest horror of said mita. Although we have tried to persuade the two Indians to return to complete their mita time they absolutely resist and we do not have [the means] to send them by force a distance of more than two hundred leagues. . . . Captains have also complained on other occasions of violence. . . . We implore Your Majesty . . . for a remedy of the referred excesses that we bear and for which we ask justice.[6]

Sinanyuca placed his trust in his own "face-to-face" knowledge and experiences. Under these circumstances the kuraka and his entire community supported the assertions of their neighbors, who were citizens of good reputation. Besides, everyone knew of the abusive treatment meted out by these particular Spaniards who supervised the mitayos. Corregidor Juan Antonio Reparaz, one of the few officials in Canas y Canchis known for his fairness among the *naturales* (the colonial term for indigenous person), asked officials in Potosí to end abuses suffered by the mitayos in the refinery and ordered Bartolomé García and Gregorio Choquecota freed on bail.[7] Reparaz trusted the word of Sinanyuca, just as Sinanyuca trusted the word of people he knew to be honorable. Because their face-to-face dealings created trust, the corregidor, kurakas, and community members were able to work together to ameliorate a tense, difficult situation.

Apart from these problems regarding the mita, as kurakas in charge of their communities, Sinanyuca and Túpac Amaru shared a wide array of other concerns. In Canas y Canchis and Quispicanchis the population remained overwhelmingly indigenous throughout the colonial period; relatively few Spaniards settled in the provinces except in some rich agricultural areas or near the city of Cuzco. Although significantly altered over the course of more than two centuries of colonial rule, indigenous villages still maintained a strong set of common values over time. In the eighteenth century, however, lifeways began to change as indigenous peoples confronted increasingly difficult challenges. From the midseventeenth century the Andean population had begun to recover from the epidemic diseases introduced by the European invaders, producing acute shortages of land at a time when state demands for labor and taxes increased. Land was basic to economic and cultural survival for the indigenous peoples.

Over the course of the eighteenth century Spanish monarchs, like other rulers, gradually sought to exert greater control over their colonies. For some two centuries indigenous peoples had been subject to heavy tribute and forced labor levies, but from the mideighteenth century onward, the crown increased these responsibilities as population pressures and land scarcity made such burdens difficult to bear. Furthermore, individual colonial authorities (and even some kurakas) sought to increase their personal wealth by abusing their authority, adding their own demands to those of the state. As a result, many indigenous people increasingly questioned the legitimacy of their rulers, fearing that they could no longer maintain traditional ways of life. For many people in the southern Andes, these problems had become so severe that when confronted with a movement led by Túpac Amaru in 1780 that challenged colonial rule, they joined the rebel cause.

One of the most frequent complaints was against the *reparto*. In the 1750s the reparto, which had been functioning informally, was fully legalized. Instead of improving their situation, legalization made life for many in the indigenous communities more difficult. In Canas y Canchis, for example, the corregidor, Antonio de Arriaga, provoked tensions in the years just prior to the rebellion by distributing goods far in excess of the established quotas.[8] Reparto rates per individual for Quispicanchis and Canas y Canchis were among some of the lowest in the Andes, but the prices assessed were still often double or triple the market price for these goods. Mules were a major reparto item, and the villagers of Canas y Canchis and Quispicanchis were forced to receive 2,000 and 2,500 mules, respectively, in every reparto.[9] This trade was especially important to Coporaque because the mules brought up from northern Argentina (Río de la Plata) were grazed on their pastures, and it was here that a great fair was held. The other large regional mule fair took place in Tungasuca, a community governed by Túpac Amaru. Thus, the communities ruled by both Sinanyuca and the future rebel leader were affected in complex ways both by economic changes and by heavy reparto quotas.

With their way of life threatened, the difficulties faced by Andean villagers worsened. For the reparto, each corregidor was supposed to make only one distribution of goods with a total fixed value during his five-year term of office, but many conducted multiple repartos at values far in excess of the established schedule. A Quispicanchis priest gave this account of the reparto in his community:

> Right after the corregidors arrive in any town of their province, they send their servants to the *alcaldes* and *alguaciles* so that they will, from house to house and hacienda to hacienda, notify Spaniards and Indians (of whom they have a list) to come and present themselves in front of them to get the *repartimiento*; and their cashiers distribute to them not the items that they have asked for but whatever they want to give them, [and,] without even telling them nor negotiating the prices with them, they give them the bundles and write down the amounts owed. They [corregidors] break the tariffs set by law . . . and . . . this could not have been possible without excessively charging provincial Indians and Spaniards.[10]

In 1766, however, the priest of San Andrés de Checa also had argued that the corregidor had distributed some 300,000 pesos worth of goods even though he was legally allowed only 112,500 pesos.[11] Thus, Arriaga, accused years later by Túpac Amaru of making three repartos instead of the one permitted and of collecting a total of some 300,000 pesos instead of the assigned quota, certainly was not the first corregidor of Canas y Canchis to distribute goods far in excess of the legal limit.[12] Arriaga's repartos, however, came at a time of economic distress in the region, which probably sealed his fate once Túpac Amaru decided to rebel.

Local economic problems worsened when the crown divided the Viceroyalty of Peru in 1776, placing Upper Peru (now Bolivia) under the jurisdiction of the newly created Viceroyalty of the Río de la Plata, with its capital in Buenos Aires. This administrative change disrupted trade patterns and economic life throughout much of the southern Andes. Tensions increased further when colonial authorities in Lima increased the *alcabala* (sales tax), subjecting a number of items produced by naturales to the tax, which had previously been exempt. At the same time, customs houses were established to collect taxes with an unprecedented level of efficiency. These changes added to the burdens on indigenous communities, particularly on kurakas involved in trade, and weakened the ties binding Andean villagers to the larger colonial society. Alone, none of these factors was significant enough to incite rebellion, but taken together, they exacerbated a growing economic crisis that contributed, in turn, to an even broader crisis within Andean communities. They were "the feather that broke the camel's back."[13]

Over time, worsening economic conditions lay behind a number of violent confrontations and incidents between colonial officials and Andean communities from the mideighteenth century, reaching a crescendo in the decade before Corregidor Arriaga was hanged to initiate Túpac Amaru's rebellion. Most of these were relatively minor incidents that tended to be local in character, spontaneous, and of short duration; they were directed against individuals and sought to maintain or restore an existing order or end abusive treatment.[14] Nevertheless, these violent protests should have alerted colonial officials of the need to control abuses and rule with moderation, but this was not the case.

Perhaps colonial officials ignored the escalating levels of violence because, in reality, these incidents remained remote from the centers of regional power and were still fairly uncommon.[15] There were a total of twenty-one parishes and annexed communities in the provinces of Quispicanchis and Canas y Canchis. Most parishes, in turn, had several ayllus from which tribute or reparto payments were collected. Tribute was collected twice per year, and then added to these figures were other demands for labor and personal service together with the chance for unpleasant encounters or even confrontations that could increase local tensions. From this perspective, given the potential for unrest, violence may have increased in the 1770s, but it still remained an infrequent occurrence.

When violence broke out in Quispicanchis or Canas y Canchis, the state usually tried to contain the problem so that it would not become more dangerous. To preserve crown authority, colonial administrators did not typically inflict harsh punishments for killing or attacking officials, especially when their abusive or excessive behavior threatened the existing order and undermined the protective justice and the legitimacy of the crown. The relatively light punishment often meted out in such instances was one way that viceregal authorities tried to preserve the colonial order and, perhaps, warn lower officials indirectly to curb their excesses. Harsher conditions, however, led Andeans to perceive what had been tolerable but oppressive (and sometimes illegal) demands over time as excessive and intolerable. As changing circumstances made it more difficult for naturales to meet exactions, state officials who enforced the demands were increasingly viewed as abusive tyrants. Under these circumstances, certain abusive officials attracted attacks on their person, while other crown servants who enforced similar demands were not assaulted or otherwise harmed.

A tax collector (*cobrador*) in Cusipata (Quispicanchis), who was killed after trying to exact tribute, exemplifies these revolts. At first glance this incident appears to be a simple protest against tribute abuses, but upon closer examination it seems less a protest against colonial demands than a lashing out against a particularly hated and abusive official. In 1774, don Carlos Ochoa, a mestizo cobrador, went to collect the tribute owed by Lucas Poma Inga, the cacique of Cusipata. Ochoa, along with his brother and several associates, arrived at the house of Poma Inga and confronted him. Poma Inga could only pay 60 pesos of the tribute owed and offered the cobrador a promissory note for the remainder. Although Poma Inga was known for being reliable in meeting his obligations, this was not good enough for Ochoa, a man with a well-deserved reputation for sadistic cruelty. The cobrador and his friends hauled Poma Inga from his home, tied him up, beat him with a whip, and then took him to Ochoa's home where the cacique was again beaten and then locked in a storage room. Those who saw the cacique said that he had been severely abused, and a Spanish doctor and a scribe later testified that he was "very badly beaten over all of his body, the head, and stomach by fists, clubs, and kicks with spurs." Caciques from nearby Quiquijana also confirmed Poma's condition.

In desperation, Poma Inga's wife, whom the cobrador had also assaulted, asked the priest to intervene on her husband's behalf. The priest told her that Ochoa was "a very fearsome man and that he was not able to intervene," but after a second request from the desperate woman, the priest wrote a note to Ochoa. The cobrador not only ignored the message but verbally abused the person who delivered it. Seeing that their cacique was in bad shape and fearing for his life, the people of Poma Inga's ayllu decided to rescue him because of "the great love [they had] for their cacique." At night they broke into Ochoa's house, removed Poma Inga, and killed Ochoa for having treated their cacique badly and with "ignominy." Antonio Acuña, a tributary who served the priest, stated that at about eight in the evening there had been a great disturbance in the street and the priest had ordered the door of the church to be closed and barred. He and the priest passed a restless night in the church, and in the morning they opened a window and heard the news that Ochoa had been killed. Acuña and the priest went to the cobrador's house and found his body on the floor "amid many stones."

After the incident the priest cared for Poma Inga, who was "almost without movement," in the church and later testified both to his good character and to the cruelty of the cobrador. Other people of European descent also supported the actions of the community. Pascual Antonio de Loayza, a muleteer returning from the Coporaque livestock auction, stated that he knew Poma Inga well, considered him a friend, and knew that he was well respected by his ayllu. He had seen the kuraka being beaten and had observed his condition while locked up. Andres de Acosta, another Spanish muleteer, offered similar testimony. It was also reported that Poma Inga, even after being beaten, told his people "not to riot and to try to calm themselves."

While it is true that Ochoa was a cobrador, the people of Poma Inga's ayllu killed him not because of his post but because of his many abuses of power, which delegitimized his authority. They went beyond the bounds that governed Indian-Spanish relations in the colonial world. Neither the naturales nor the Europeans saw the killing as a challenge to colonial authority as a system. Violence was not directed at other representatives of the state nor at Europeans in general, and it did not go beyond the borders of the community. After the incident, Cusipata settled into its former routine, with normality restored for the time being.[16]

As the case of Ochoa indicates, face-to-face relations were important in determining the course of events. For instance, Juan Antonio Reparaz, a corregidor of Canas y Canchis, dealt fairly with the naturales whom he governed. He even donated 13,000 pesos of his own funds to build bridges for certain communities, including Tinta, the provincial capital of Canas y Canchis where Arriaga was later executed.[17] It does not necessarily follow that the system Reparaz was enforcing was just. Indeed, his contribution toward the bridge most likely came from illicit profits from the reparto. Nevertheless, his treatment of the people of Canas y Canchis was perceived by them as fair within the context of an increasingly exploitative system.[18] Thus, the colonial norms of behavior and understanding were maintained, making violent confrontation between naturales and Reparaz unlikely.

The majority of corregidors in Quispicanchis and Canas y Canchis were not as considerate as Reparaz. Excessive or new demands, violations of traditional arrangements, or abusive treatment strained or ruptured Indian-corregidor relations. In 1767, for example, Corregidor Pedro Muñoz de Arjona forced villagers in Pichigua and Yauri to transport dried llama dung to the silver mines of Condoroma, making it more difficult for these people to meet other state exactions. It should come as no surprise that Muñoz de Arjona had business dealings with Condoroma miners (although so did Túpac Amaru), and it was in his own interest to assure the supply of llama dung used in the refining process.[19]

Differences between colonial officials, the ways they were perceived, and the responses they evoked were apparent in the attitude of Túpac Amaru toward the last four corregidors who governed Canas y Canchis prior to his rebellion. While he grew increasingly impatient with the system that the corregidors enforced, he clearly recognized differences between individuals. Of these four men, Túpac Amaru disliked two, had mixed feelings about one, and "got along well" with the other. Corregidor Gregorio de Viana "harassed him greatly with the *repartimiento*" and treated him badly in business dealings. The next corregidor, Muñoz de Arjona, confirmed him as kuraka of Pampamarca, Surimana, and Tungasuca, something that Viana had not done. Muñoz de Arjona and the future rebel coexisted in harmony for a while, but when the corregidor jailed the kuraka over a dispute with a tax collector, the relationship soured. Túpac Amaru "got along well" with the next corregidor, Reparaz. In commenting on how the actions of Reparaz influenced him, the rebel leader informed captors that "the rebellion had been thought of for many years, but he had not determined to rebel because Corregidor Reparaz, Arriaga's predecessor, had treated him very well and looked on the Indians with compassion."[20] Túpac Amaru had been swayed by the actions of an individual corregidor to set aside the idea of rebellion against the colonial state. Personal relations and behavior had made a difference. Túpac Amaru, however, did not hold a similar opinion of the next corregidor, Antonio de Arriaga, whom he hanged to begin the rebellion of 1780.

The differences between Sinanyuca and Túpac Amaru that led them down divergent paths, despite their considerable shared realities, stemmed more from the ways they related to Church-state conflicts than from the political and economic issues that are commonly seen as central to the rebellions of the early 1780s. These struggles between the Church and state drew in the peoples of Coporaque as well as those under Túpac Amaru's control and added complexity to indigenous-Spanish relations in Coporaque and much of the rest of Canas y Canchis in the years just prior to the great rebellion. The bishop of Cuzco, Juan Manuel Moscoso y Peralta, was friendly with Túpac Amaru. Bad blood existed between the bishop and Corregidor Arriaga, however, just as it did between Arriaga and Túpac Amaru. On the other hand, Sinanyuca got along reasonably well with Corregidor Arriaga, but he and the people of Coporaque were increasingly at odds with their priest and, because of this, with the bishop.

Eventually the bishop went so far as to excommunicate Sinanyuca and the villagers of Coporaque over these differences. The bishop and corregidor had first clashed while both were serving in the distant province of Tucumán (Río de la Plata), but when they were transferred to Cuzco, their dispute became public and reached crisis proportions. Priests and civil officials as well as Sinanyuca and Túpac Amaru took one side or the other in the dispute. In this situation what should have been personal problems came to have larger meaning because of the tensions that they fostered between Church and state. These tensions, in turn, contributed significantly to local divisions such as those in the Canas y Canchis community of San Pablo de Cacha.[21]

As Epiphany approached in January 1780, the villagers of San Pablo de Cacha wanted to bring their Nativity scene from its chapel to the church to be blessed. However, they had not provided the expected "gift" for the local priests, so their request was denied. With their hopes for a religious festival dashed, the community raised not one, but two tumults against the priest. It was in this climate of acrimony that Francisco, the priest's slave, struck fear into the hearts of the villagers by fabricating a story that the corregidor was plotting to kill them in retaliation for their commotions against the priest. According to Francisco, Arriaga was sending 400 soldiers "to put them to the knife." Panic stricken, people fled to the surrounding countryside. In the flight one person fell from a bridge and was drowned. Arriaga, learning of the incident, had Francisco detained and then expelled him from the province stating that the law "prohibits that seditious and prejudicial blacks live among the naturales of these kingdoms." The rumor created an irrational fear of Arriaga, through no fault of his own, which further damaged his reputation. Writing to the priest, Arriaga, concerned about the impact of the incident, declared: "When fires are not promptly extinguished, their flames usually consume the most distant." These were especially prophetic words because only nine months later, Arriaga would become the kindling in the flames of the Túpac Amaru rebellion.[22]

The personal authority of the corregidor of Canas y Canchis eroded further when Arriaga became involved in a jurisdictional fight between parish priests and Bishop Moscoso over control of Church property. Two Yauri kurakas, Diego José de Meza and Francisco Guambo Tapa, had rented Church lands from the priest, Justo Martínez. The bishop insisted that the Yauri priest comply with his orders giving him say over the property, but neither the kurakas nor the priest wanted the bishop interfering in their affairs. Arriaga sided with Joseph and Justo Martínez, the priests of Pichigua and Yauri, respectively. Despite this opposition the bishop sent the mulatto priest of Coporaque, Vicente de la Puente, to Yauri to enforce his wishes. De la Puente, already at odds with the people of Coporaque, did not improve his reputation in Yauri. First, he embargoed the priest's goods, but then he went too far when he had an aide break down the door to Justo Martínez's house. The kuraka and community members forcibly drove the aide out of the village.

Upon receiving this news, the bishop ordered de la Puente to return to Yauri to arrest the dissenting priest, but de la Puente's arrival was preceded by rumors including, once again, one that warned that naturales would be put to the knife. Unlike the people of San Pablo de Cacha, the Yauri villagers did not flee. De la Puente arrived with armed support, but the community was prepared and a fight ensued in which several people were injured. Among those charged with responsibility for the tumult was Eugenio Sinanyuca. When representatives of the bishop injured an indigenous parishioner, Arriaga intervened in the case at the community's request and, most likely, because he was a friend of Justo Martínez. Bishop Moscoso excommunicated Arriaga "for protecting sacrilegious natives," but his bitter relationship with the prelate probably lay behind the act.[23] It was the bishop's representative, not the corregidor, who had abused the priest and people of Yauri. It was Arriaga, however, who publicly fell afoul of the Church, having sought to protect a natural and a priest from abusive Church officials.

As a result, while Arriaga is often portrayed as being alienated from the Church, he was really at odds with Bishop Moscoso and those priests who supported their superior. The corregidor was not alienated from all local priests. Those in Pichigua, Yauri, and Sicuani were his friends, and they were also generally on good terms with local parishioners. Because of personal conflicts, however, Moscoso undermined the power of these priests, which further eroded Arriaga's support in the religious circles of Canas y Canchis.

Excommunicated and portrayed as the planner of a massacre, Arriaga found that his authority was eroded by opposition from the bishop and his priestly supporters, who removed religious personnel friendly to Arriaga from their parishes. Made a scapegoat by Bishop Moscoso for abuses that in actuality rested more directly on the shoulders of the prelate, Arriaga's own well-known financial malfeasance made him increasingly vulnerable. Sinanyuca and the naturales of Coporaque, however, were increasingly at loggerheads with their parish priest, Vicente de la Puente, a close ally of the bishop. When the Coporaque priest carried out the bishop's orders in Yauri, Sinanyuca defied him. Tensions were such that the kuraka refused, during Mass, to supply a worker for the Church as tradition demanded. Sinanyuca did this on Corpus Christi of 1780, "repeating the preponderance of ritual in the most important social actions of these [Canas] communities."[24]

Although de la Puente initiated legal action against Sinanyuca, with only minor exceptions, the naturales of Coporaque allied themselves with their kuraka. Sinanyuca also served as Arriaga's tribute collector and was on good terms with the ill-fated corregidor. De la Puente, backed by Bishop Moscoso, brought ecclesiastical charges against Sinanyuca, thus avoiding the civil authority of Sinanyuca's supporter, Arriaga, while enhancing the influence of his supporter and the corregidor's enemy, Bishop Moscoso. The kuraka, on the other hand, turned to Arriaga for help.

Troubles between the priest and the community obviously had been brewing for some time. In May 1780, de la Puente filed complaints against Sinanyuca for events that had happened over a year earlier. The priest stated that after Mass at the beginning of Mardi Gras of the previous year the people of Coporaque conducted their own "pagan" rituals, including offerings to the Earth of the hearts of sacrificed animals and the smearing of corral fences with a mixture of blood and colored dirt. The Coporaque priest claimed that acts were committed against his person and the "sacred order." In the ensuing year, Coporaque, under the guidance of Sinanyuca, denied the priest traditional "gifts" and did not fill voluntary, but expected, labor services.

The charges against Sinanyuca, instead of having a "chilling effect," spread tensions to the surrounding region. When the bishop ordered de la Puente and other clerics to enforce orders against Sinanyuca, they were threatened. The priest claimed that the community was "entirely stirred up" by Sinanyuca and Arriaga's aide, Francisco Cisneros. Observing piles of rocks in the plaza that had been placed there for use in a confrontation, the religious forces retired from Coporaque. When yet another Moscoso representative sought to remove Sinanyuca from office, the kuraka appeared before the residence of the priest in the company of some 500 villagers and in a loud voice informed the official that he would not leave. Later the naturales destroyed a church jail and rooms in the priest's house, while accusing de la Puente of having stolen money from the church and *cofradía* (religious sodality or brotherhood).[25]

De la Puente, backed by armed guards, once again tried to reestablish authority in the community. Counting on the element of surprise by arriving early in the morning, he still underestimated his foe. Sinanyuca and the villagers were waiting for him. Using the church bells, Sinanyuca had summoned a thousand naturales who threatened the priest and his forces. The women were especially hostile. In the confrontation two of the priest's aides were stoned and one was "dragged from the patio of the [priest's] house to the jail, with such horrible blows that they left him for dead bathed in blood and the face like a swollen monster."[26] The tumult lasted over four hours, with community members parading in front of the priest's house carrying a coffin and singing an Inca war song: "We will drink from the skull of the traitor, we will use his teeth as a necklace, from his bones we will make flutes, from his skin a drum, afterwards we will dance."[27]

The priest, and what remained of his guard and staff, fled while the people continued to dance and sing. After this incident the entire community of Coporaque, not just Sinanyuca, was excommunicated. Corregidor Arriaga, whose excommunication had been lifted, came to the defense of Sinanyuca and Coporaque and began legal proceedings against local priests. He had promised to send their complaints to the viceroy or other high officials, but his own execution at the outset of the Túpac Amaru revolt kept him from complying.

The entire zone—Pichigua, Yauri, and Coporaque—had been upset by these conflicts between Bishop Moscoso, Corregidor Arriaga, and the priests and kurakas of these communities. In light of this struggle with the priest and bishop, it is hardly surprising that Sinanyuca and a great many of his people, who had been supported by Arriaga and excommunicated by the Church, remained aloof from Túpac Amaru, who was a friend of the bishop and who had executed the corregidor while priests friendly to the bishop watched. It was in this context that Sinanyuca made the decision not to join with Túpac Amaru when the rebellion broke out.

Sinanyuca and the people of Coporaque, and others like them, were not behaving in a manner contradictory to their interests. They made decisions based on local circumstances, their own experiences, and self-interest. They were not a generic Indian mass. They were not united with other communities or regions just because they were of the same race. They were the people of the ayllus of Coporaque and their leader was Eugenio Sinanyuca. In these personal matters they did not share Túpac Amaru's experiences or interests. Thus, out of reasons grounded in their own personal experience—their history—most people in Coporaque distanced themselves from the rebellion.

NOTES

1. Leon Campbell, "Ideology and Factionalism during the Great Rebellion, 1780–82," in *Resistance, Rebellion, and Consciousness in the Andean Peasant World, 18th to 20th Centuries*, Steve Stern, ed. (Madison: University of Wisconsin Press, 1987), 123–24.

2. Charles Walker, *Smoldering Ashes: Cuzco and the Creation of Republican Peru, 1780–1840* (Durham: Duke University Press, 1999), 27; John Rowe, "Genealogía y rebelión en el siglo XVIII," *Histórica* 6:1 (1982): 74–76.

3. Archivo Departamental de Cusco (ADC). Corrg. Prov. Crim. Leg. 79, 1745–73. 1768. Don Cristóbal Sinanyuca cacique de Collana de Coporaque . . . se ha ausentado.

4. John Rowe, "The Inca under Spanish Colonial Institutions," *HAHR* 37 (1957): 176.

5. Jan Szeminski, "Why Kill the Spaniard?" in *Resistance, Rebellion*, 173.

6. ADC. Corrg. Prov. Crim. Leg. 80, 1773–75. 1775. Coporaque. Quejas de los caciques de Coporaque por el mal tratamiento que sus indios reciben en la mita de Potosí.

7. Ibid.

8. Jurgen Golte, *Repartos y Rebeliones* (Lima, 1980), 95; Lillian Estelle Fisher, *The Last Inca Revolt, 1780–1783* (Norman: University of Oklahoma Press, 1966), 39; Ward Stavig, "Ethnic Conflict, Moral Economy, and Population in Rural Cuzco on the Eve of the Thupa Amaro II Rebellion," *HAHR* 68:4 (1988): 744.

9. Scarlett O'Phelan Godoy, *Rebellions and Revolts in Eighteenth-Century Peru and Upper Peru* (Cologne: Bohlau Verlag, 1978), 108.

10. Biblioteca Nacional del Péru. 1766. C3969. Informes de los curas de Oropesa, San Andrés de Checa y Tinta, acerca de la consulta formulada por el cabildo del Cuzco respecto a los repartimientos hechos por los corregidores.

11. Ibid. Also see Golte, *Repartos y Rebeliones*, 114–18; Fisher, *The Last Inca Revolt*, 13.

12. Golte, *Repartos y Rebeliones*, 95; Fisher, *The Last Inca Revolt*, 39; Stavig, "Ethnic Conflict," 744.

13. Scarlett O'Phelan Godoy, "Las reformas fiscales Borbónicas y su impacto en la sociedad colonial del Bajo y Alto Perú," in *The Economies of Mexico and Peru during the Late Colonial Period, 1760–1810*, Nils Jacobsen and Hans-Jurgen Puhle, eds. (Berlin, 1986), 342, 353.

14. William Taylor, *Drinking, Homicide, and Rebellion in Colonial Mexican Villages* (Stanford: Stanford University Press, 1979).

15. Golte, *Repartos y Rebeliones*, 140 (Cuadro 33).

16. ADC. Corrg. Prov. Crim. Leg. 80, 1773–75. 1774. Don Lucas Poma Inga, cacique . . . de Cusipata de Quiquijana contra don Carlos Ochoa.

17. ADC. Intend. Prov. 1786. Expediente relativo a que se verifique la fabrica de puentes en Tinta poniendo una cantidad de pesos que dejo . . . el corregidor Reparaz (a 1785 case with 1786 materials).

18. Rowe, "Genealogía y rebelión," 74–76.

19. ADC. Corrg. Prov. Leg. 67, 1766–69. [H]ucha a minas de Condoroma, 1767.

20. Rowe, "Genealogía y rebelión," 74–76; *Descargos del Obispo del Cuzco Juan Manuel Moscoso y Peralta*, vol. II of *Colección documental del bicentenario de la Revolución Emancipadora de Túpac Amaru* (Lima, 1980), 224.

21. Fisher, *The Last Inca Revolt*, 40.

22. ADC. Corrg. Prov. Leg. 81, 1776–84. 1780. Criminal contra Francisco negro livertino doméstico del cura.

23. Fisher, *The Last Inca Revolt*, 41; Luis Miguel Glave, *Vida símbolos y batallas. Creación y recreación de la comunidad indígena. Cusco, siglos XVI–XX* (Lima: Fondo de Cultura Económica, 1992), 61–63.

24. Glave, *Vida símbolos y batallas*, 137. The information on Sinanyuca comes from Glave's account and *Túpac Amaru y la Iglesia. Antología* (Lima, 1983), 165–201.

25. Ibid., 141–46.

26. Ibid., 147–48.

27. Ibid., 148. "Beberemos en el cráneo del traidor, usaremos sus dientes como un collar, de sus huesos haremos flautas, de su piel haremos un tambor, después bailaremos."

SUGGESTED READINGS

For background material on rural Cuzco and the events leading to the Túpac Amaru rebellion, there are several works in English including Ward Stavig's *The World of Túpac Amaru: Conflict, Community, and Identity in Colonial Peru* (Lincoln: University of Nebraska Press, 1999); and idem, "Ethnic Conflict, Moral Economy, and Population in Rural Cuzco on the Eve of the Thupa Amaro II Rebellion," *HAHR* 68:4 (1988). For a broader sweep one might also look at Scarlett O'Phelan-Godoy, *Rebellions and Revolts in Eighteenth-Century Peru and Upper Peru* (Cologne: Bohlau Verlag, 1985), and Steve Stern, ed., *Resistance, Rebellion, and Consciousness in the Andean Peasant World, 18th to 20th Centuries* (Madison: University of Wisconsin Press, 1987). Stern's work contains an interesting introduction and several articles, including Jan Szeminski's "Why Kill the Spaniard? New Perspectives on Andean Insurrectionary Ideology in the Eighteenth Century" and Leon Campbell's "Ideology and Factionalism during the Great Rebellion, 1780–82." The first chapters of Charles Walker's *Smoldering Ashes: Cuzco and the Creation of Republican Peru, 1780–1840* (Durham: Duke University Press, 1999) contain work on Cuzco and the rebellion and are especially good from a local political perspective. For kurakas one might begin with Karen Spalding, "Social Climbers: Changing Patterns of Mobility among the Indians of Colonial Peru," *HAHR* 50:4 (1970). On the Church and state, David Cahill's "Curas and Social Conflict in the Doctrinas of Cuzco, 1780–1814," *Journal of Latin American Studies* 16:2 (1984) sheds light on trends that were developing even before the rebellion of 1780.

CHAPTER 15

Juan Barbarín

The 1795 French Conspiracy in Buenos Aires

Lyman L. Johnson

In the late eighteenth century three great revolutions (in English North America, France, and Haiti) erupted, producing sweeping changes in the prevailing political, social, and economic order in the Atlantic world. Inspired by Enlightenment thinkers who heralded the use of reason to solve the problems of humankind, political leaders in English North America resisted efforts by the British Parliament to raise taxes and tighten political controls, ultimately culminating in a successful revolt against the mother country (1776–1783). Many of the documents promulgated by the English colonists to justify their rebellion, such as the Declaration of Independence, asserted that sovereignty resided with the people rather than with some divinely ordained monarch. After their final victory, the rebels formed the world's first large-scale democratic republic.

Although the American Revolution produced novel political changes, it did not seriously disrupt the colonial social hierarchies, leaving the old ones largely intact. In fact, the Constitution of 1787 maintained the institution of slavery. In contrast, the French Revolution of 1789 produced lasting political and social changes, as King Louis XVI, Queen Marie Antoinette, and a large number of aristocrats and commoners lost their lives in the so-called Reign of Terror engineered by Radical leaders such as Maximilian Robespierre. The revolution in Haiti beginning in 1791 also resulted in sweeping social and economic changes, as slaves on the rich sugar-producing island took power and established the hemisphere's second republic, this time run by the former slaves themselves. For elites in Europe and the Americas, traditional views about social hierarchies, economic power, and religion seemed on the verge of collapsing into disorder and chaos.

The three great Atlantic revolutions had a tremendous impact in the American colonies of Spain and Portugal, where people of different social ranks reacted with everything from enthusiasm to abhorrence. Many creole elites, members of the middle classes, the racially mixed plebeian groups, and Amerindians had chafed under the negative consequences of Bourbon political, fiscal, religious, military, and social innovations. Old colonial centers such as Lima had lost their economic primacy, but discontent simmered even in burgeoning political and commercial centers favored by the reforms, such as Buenos Aires. The crown had opened direct commerce between Spain and the port city and had also made it the capital of the new Viceroyalty of the Río de la Plata in 1776. Nevertheless, higher taxes, tighter commercial controls, and the influx of peninsular Spaniards, who dominated the viceregal bureaucracy and reaped large profits from the trade within the empire, bred resentment among many residents of the city, called porteños. *At the same time, many discontented porteños feared the consequences of revolutionary change. Independence might end loathsome Spanish policies, but it also could bring political chaos and social upheaval, especially among the growing slave population of Buenos Aires. Nevertheless, news of the revolutions in the United States, France, and Haiti provoked lively debates in the port city in the 1790s.*

By 1795 rumors of an impending slave revolt, perhaps led by radical elements of the city's French minority, swept through Buenos Aires and created a tense, highly charged atmosphere. Nevertheless, rumors of insolent behavior by slaves, secret nighttime meetings by Frenchmen, and stockpiled weapons and ammunition were difficult to substantiate. When subversive posters with only the word "Liberty" mysteriously appeared in the city, however, Viceroy Nicolás de Arredondo decided to mount an investigation. The man he chose to head the inquiry, Martín de Alzaga, was a dour, self-important member of the city council who harbored no sympathy for foreigners or revolutionaries. Alzaga's investigation soon focused on members of the French community, especially a prosperous merchant in the city, Juan Barbarín. Witnesses testified that Barbarín served as a sponsor for a black religious sodality, had Afro-Argentines visiting his house, and maintained a close and affectionate relationship with his own slave, Manuel. Barbarín allegedly even defended Robespierre and the bloody revolution in his native France. Alzaga, a staunch defender of traditional social hierarchies of the colony, considered Barbarín's behavior odious, subversive, and even revolutionary. He had the merchant jailed, along with his slave. Although later evidence apparently cleared Barbarín of complicity in any conspiracy, the merchant remained in jail and suffered financial ruin. Barbarín was later exiled in Spain, but his later life remains a mystery. In the end, Barbarín became a scapegoat for a society fearful of revolution; his belief in liberty, equality, and fraternity—the motto of the French Revolution—was his undoing.

Lyman L. Johnson is professor of history at the University of North Carolina at Charlotte as well as a leading authority on the social and economic history of Argentina in the colonial and early republican periods. He has written numerous articles and is the coauthor (with Mark A. Burkholder) of Colonial Latin America *(2001). He has also edited (with Enrique Tandeter)* Essays on the Price History of Eighteenth-Century Latin America *(1990);* The Problem of Order in Chang-

ing Societies: Essays on Crime and Policing in Argentina and Uruguay *(1990); (with Kenneth J. Andrien)* The Political Economy of
Spanish America in the Age of Revolution, 1750–1850 *(1994); and
(with Sonya Lipsett-Rivera)* The Faces of Honor: Sex, Shame, and
Violence in Colonial Latin America *(1999).*

$\mathscr{I}$t was midmorning, and already the narrow streets of Buenos Aires were
oppressed by the damp heat of the Southern Hemisphere's summer. Juan
Barbarín walked deliberately toward his shop. His slow progress was
monitored by the nervous glances of his neighbors. Barbarín's eyes sought
some sign of friendly regard in the familiar faces along his route. In place
of the greetings that had punctuated his morning walk only weeks earlier, he was now met with silence and fear. As he crossed the broad plaza
and walked past the city's unfinished cathedral, Barbarín felt exposed
and vulnerable. Suspicion lay like a heavy cloak on his shoulders. Moving carefully to avoid the horse and oxen dung that littered the plaza, he
struggled to find a solution to the problems that weighed him down.
Whom could he turn to? Whom could he trust?

In January 1795, Buenos Aires was on edge. Throughout this sprawl-
ing port city, residents of all classes and conditions talked about the great
events that were shaking the foundations of the Atlantic world. Ships
from the newly independent United States had begun to arrive in Buenos
Aires, and Spanish authorities suspected that a handful of fiercely republican Yankee sailors had circulated the Declaration of Independence in
the city. But revolutionary events in France and Saint Domingue (now
called Haiti) seemed to threaten the city even more directly than did
American republicanism.

In France the guillotine had taken the life of both the unfortunate
Louis XVI and his queen. Thousands of priests and nobles had shared
their king's terrible destiny. More troubling still to the deeply Catholic
residents of Buenos Aires (called *porteños*) was the news that revolutionaries had dared to attack the Church itself. With the execution of
Louis XVI in 1793, Spain and other European powers had been drawn
inexorably into war with the revolutionary government of Paris. The
political violence that had torn France apart for four years now spread
across the face of Europe. News arriving in Buenos Aires in late 1794
indicated that Spain's war with France was going badly. Although there
was little chance that Buenos Aires would be threatened directly by French
forces, commerce, the lifeblood of this port city, was disrupted and the
prices of imported goods seemed to rise every day.

The urban poor of Buenos Aires, however, were more immediately
concerned with the rising price of bread than with the cost of imported
cloth. After a formal investigation, city officials revealed that a powerful

group of local speculators and bakers had manipulated the effects of a poor harvest by hoarding grain, causing bread prices to rise to punishing heights. Although arrests had been made and illegal grain supplies seized, the price of bread had not fallen. As anger mounted, it was widely repeated in the streets and markets that these predatory culprits were foreigners. Some, it was said, were French. Self-interest and wartime xenophobia combined to produce a volatile political climate where the differences between distant French revolutionaries and local French residents (mostly royalists) were soon obscured.

For most porteños the most terrifying news came not from France but from Haiti, France's rich sugar colony in the Caribbean. Haiti was as notorious for the cruelty experienced by its black slaves as it was for the great wealth of its largely absentee landowners. As revolutionaries in France discussed granting political rights to free blacks and the possible abolition of slavery itself, Haiti's slaves had risen in rebellion against the colonial authorities in 1791. The plantation system had collapsed under the revolutionary onslaught, and the slaves had taken terrible revenge on their exploiters. Violence in Haiti would continue for more than a decade, leading to the creation of the Western Hemisphere's second independent republic. But in Buenos Aires and in other slaveholding colonies, public attention was narrowly focused on the violent elimination of the slaveowning class rather than on the significant political achievements of Haiti's former slaves.

In Buenos Aires popular opinion linked these two events in a seamless political narrative. It was thought that the irreligious and democratic violence of France had inevitably led to Haiti's slave rebellion and race war. In the coffee shops, neighborhood taverns, and markets of Buenos Aires men and women expressed their belief that regicide and assaults on the Church could only lead to social and political chaos and the overturning of racial hierarchy. When kings and priests were under attack, the authority of masters over their slaves was necessarily insecure. The fact that Spain was at war with Revolutionary France made these distant events more threatening.

Buenos Aires was not a plantation economy, but it was an important destination for the African slave trade in the 1790s. By 1795 it had become the primary slave port for all of Spain's South American colonies. In earlier decades the city had imported slaves from the Portuguese colony of Brazil, then sending many of them to other colonial cities in the interior. With the city's dynamic economic growth in the 1780s, a small number of merchants from Buenos Aires directly entered the African slave trade. During the war with France, other members of the Buenos Aires commercial community purchased licenses as privateers, using their vessels to attack French slave ships off the African coast and bringing captured slave cargoes to Buenos Aires. The combined effect of an expanded legal slave trade with African ports and the wartime seizure of French slave cargoes more than doubled the city's slave population in less than a decade.

Thousands of the slaves who arrived in Buenos Aires from Africa and Brazil were subsequently sent to the mining centers of Bolivia or across the Andes to Chile, where prices for blacks were higher. But, despite this secondary trade with other parts of the Spanish empire, the slave population of Buenos Aires had surpassed 10,000 (some 20 percent of the population) in 1795. Many of the city's artisan crafts were completely dependent on the labor of slaves and black freemen. The urban elite and most of the petty merchants, master artisans, and government officials who made up the middle classes all owned slaves as well. Slaves also played an important role both in agriculture and ranching across the region. Even the farms and ranches owned by the Catholic Church's convents and nunneries in surrounding rural areas were completely dependent on the forced labor of slaves. It was the growth of this racially and culturally distinct servile class that fed the fears that would overtake Juan Barbarín.

Popular fears had mounted when anonymous handwritten *pasquines* (pasquinades or lampoons in English) attacking the local authorities were pasted up around the city's central plaza. Pasquines had long been a part of Spanish colonial political life, and officials often found it difficult to identify authors and prosecute them. In the most common forms, pasquines attacked officials or other prominent residents in insulting terms for private scandals or unpopular political decisions. Despite the anger that these scurrilous or sometimes humorous posters produced among those targeted, they were grudgingly tolerated in most cases. In fact, many of those whose reputations were injured took their revenge through this same vehicle. Pasquines were, in effect, political and social siege weapons skillfully used by both the powerful and the weak. They were almost always handwritten and were seldom produced in multiple copies, the authors relying on word of mouth to multiply the effects of their insults or charges. Pasquines were almost always placed on the walls of public places, although it was not unknown for a pasquine to be thrown through the open window of a private dwelling.

The events that would sweep Juan Barbarín out of his normal routines began in 1795 with a series of inflammatory pasquines that warned of a planned insurrection and condemned Viceroy Nicolás de Arredondo for his failure to protect the public. The anonymous authors claimed that a vast conspiracy of unnamed foreigners sought to incite a slave rebellion. In the end, it was the appearance of a single word that spread fear and outrage to the center of colonial political authority. On the walls of buildings in the vicinity of the central plaza appeared tiny slips of paper broadcasting the era's revolutionary ideology reduced to a single word, "*LIBERTAD*" (Liberty). The publication of this perceived incitement to revolution was soon followed by a new round of pasquines excoriating the government for its inactivity and complicity in the face of an insurrectionary threat.

Authorities in Spain and in Buenos Aires had desperately tried to seal off Spain and its colonies from the seductive ideology of "Liberty" as celebrated by France's revolutionaries. Efforts to ban the published works of controversial Enlightenment authors had had only limited success. French social and political critics such as Jean-Jacques Rousseau and Voltaire were universally banned in the Spanish colonies before the French Revolution, but their works and those of other banned authors circulated clandestinely in Buenos Aires. Similarly, republican political tracts from the newly independent United States of America were denied circulation in the Spanish empire, but copies of the Declaration of Independence and the Constitution also filtered through the often-careless scrutiny of Spanish customs officials. With the beginnings of the French Revolution, however, Spanish officials took greater care to prevent the entrance of any publications that attacked either the monarchy or the Church. These efforts culminated in 1790 with an order to forbid all publications "that contain forms of malignant and false information."

Customs officials now began to examine more carefully the printed materials carried on American and other neutral ships calling in Buenos Aires and Montevideo, the viceroyalty's busiest ports. Any work that contained the word "Liberty" or attacked the monarchy or religion was routinely confiscated. As these restrictions took hold, everyone in the colony realized how dangerous it was to have subversive materials. Still, it was an open secret that publications sympathetic to the French Revolution were in circulation among the small circle of educated men and women in Buenos Aires. Although the number of banned books and periodicals was small and the number of readers limited, the impact of these publications was much broader since each reader tended to distill and disseminate these controversial ideas in conversations with friends and associates.

Despite these small pockets of enthusiasm for liberty and secularism, Buenos Aires remained a deeply conservative city. Most porteños, both Spanish immigrants and the native-born Creoles, reacted with horror to the events in France and Haiti. Even the largely illiterate urban underclass, which received its news informally through networks of sailors and ships' passengers, viscerally reacted to attacks on Church and king. Religious belief—indeed, religious ritual—and faith in the essential justice of the distant Spanish king were the essential props of the colonial order. Days were centered around the Catholic Mass, and months and years were organized around public celebrations of saints' days and the births, coronations, and deaths of members of the royal family.

In Buenos Aires there was no public enthusiasm for imitating the revolutions of France or Haiti. Yet one small group of residents refused to accept uncritically the strident criticism of the French Revolution. These were members of the city's small French community and their friends and associates found among other foreign residents. This population was tied together through business dealings or through informal occasions when its members met for meals and shared news from Europe. As this group fell under increased suspicion during the war with France, Juan Barbarín, among others, found that every conversation conducted in public carried the risk that a careless remark might be passed on to colonial authorities. In the superheated political climate of 1795, public opinion was in no mood to distinguish between the nostalgic reminiscence of a French merchant or baker for his homeland and the most incendiary speech made by the most radical Jacobin in Paris.

As news from Haiti circulated in late 1794, many local slave owners reported a growing insolence among their black servants. With the New Year, anger and fear had overcome reasoned discourse in Buenos Aires. Distant events had been transformed into local threats by a rising tide of secondhand information and rumor. As popular opinion focused on the perceived threat of insurrection, frustration with the apparent inactivity of Spanish colonial authorities mounted with every passing day. Unable to ignore these fears any longer, Viceroy Arredondo issued a statement in January that acknowledged reports of a conspiracy and notified the public that an official inquiry would be undertaken.

Viceroy Arredondo selected Martín de Alzaga, *alcalde ordinario* (magistrate) of the *cabildo* (city council), to head the investigation. The selection of Alzaga would prove to be a fateful decision. His powerful personality and deep prejudices gave the inquiry a relentless antiforeign character. Born in the Basque region of northern Spain, Alzaga emigrated to Buenos Aires as a young man and apprenticed with a local merchant involved in trade with Spain. Now in business for himself, Alzaga operated within the comfortable confines of the monopoly trade system. He was notoriously unsympathetic toward local merchants who profited from the liberalized commercial arrangements occasioned by the war with France or from contraband. A modestly successful businessman connected by kinship and commercial dealings to some of the wealthiest merchant families in Buenos Aires, Alzaga was among the most influential members of the cabildo. Although most found him difficult and overbearing, he had held numerous local offices in Buenos Aires. Humorless and self-important, he seemed to remember every insult and snub. His patriotism was reinforced by a passion for order and hierarchy. Once convinced of a threat to public order, Alzaga proved merciless in his efforts to track down and punish treason.

Although rumors of conspiracy churned through Buenos Aires, direct evidence was scarce. Where were these plebeian revolutionaries? Where was the local equivalent of the popular anger that had carried the Paris mob to Versailles? When announcing the inquiry, Viceroy Arredondo noted that he had received reports of unidentified individuals purchasing large quantities of powder and shot, but he had provided no real evidence of subversive acts. Alzaga knew that he was appointed in large measure to calm public fears and moved swiftly and energetically to give the appearance of purposeful action. In the dim light of proliferating fear, it was inevitable that his attention would quickly focus on the city's French immigrants. His logic was irrefutable. Was there any other segment of the city's population more likely to promote the dangerous ideal of liberty or attempt to ignite the rebelliousness of the slaves?

Alzaga first attempted to locate the authors of the pasquines, especially the writer of those inscribed with "Liberty." His agents fanned out to interview everyone with a story to tell. A priest who lived near the cathedral came forward to testify that he had seen the pasquines scattered late at night by men disguised by broad hats and capes. Unfortunately, he could not identify them. Scores of other residents eagerly came forward to offer hearsay, advice, and, sometimes, evidence. Alzaga, typically, was interested in it all. Priests seem to have been particularly eager to talk to investigators but provided few concrete leads. Father Ramón Yrazabal testified that his colleague Father Manuel Aparicio had seen conspirators placing seditious posters near the Church of Santo Domingo. Questioned soon thereafter by Alzaga, Father Manuel admitted that he had no firsthand knowledge but had merely passed on a story told to him by one of his parishioners, doña Teresa Arellano. When Alzaga tracked down doña Teresa, she testified that she had also heard this tale secondhand from her friend, doña Tadea Rivera. After two days of hard work, the story gave out, one of many dead ends chased down by Alzaga.

Despite the obvious frustrations that followed each of these false starts, there was an unbroken thread that seemed to run through the fabric of testimony, and it was this fragile thread of coherence that kept Alzaga moving forward through the clutter of hearsay and rumor. From various corners of the city, informants reported an observed forwardness and assertiveness in the city's previously passive slave population. Juan Angel Freire, for example, reported that his mother's slave, Pasquala, had defiantly announced that she would soon be "dressed in the finest garments" and would "no longer have to take orders." In separate testimony, Father Angel López claimed to have been physically threatened by a mulatto slave whom he overheard arguing about the French Revolution in front of a tavern near where pasquines with the word "Liberty" had been earlier discovered. Slaves themselves seemed equally eager to pass on information about a growing restiveness. Most typically they complained of "commotions" that were unsettling the slave community. The middle-aged slave Antonio, among others, informed the alcalde that while attending an illegal African dance held at the shop of a free black shoemaker, he had overheard two young slaves talk about a planned uprising. Other slaves reported fights and disturbances generated by disagreements over these insurrectionary plans. Alzaga redoubled his efforts.

Although unreliable at best, the first wave of testimony focused the attention of investigators on the urban neighborhood where the city's French residents were concentrated. Alzaga moved swiftly to interrogate the members of this small community. The first two French residents to fall into the alcalde's net were Juan Antonio Grimau, a baker, and the merchant Juan Barbarín. Grimau, a French immigrant, was incriminated by the testimony of his employee, the free black laborer Domingo Sandoval, who provided Alzaga with a convincing story filled with rich details. According to this employee, Grimau had thrown two books written in French into his bakery's oven after hearing news of the investigation. Alzaga then thoroughly questioned all the other employees of Grimau's bakery. He discovered one witness who claimed that after throwing the books on the fire, the baker had placed his chair in front of the oven so that he could watch while the flames consumed them. Another witness, who admitted that he could not read either Spanish or French, claimed that "Voltar" (Voltaire) wrote one of the books consigned to the flames. Alzaga had heard enough; he arrested Grimau and compiled a comprehensive list of all the prisoner's associates and friends for further investigation.

Although Juan Barbarín knew Grimau only casually, he would soon become entangled in the investigation. Pedro Muñoz, who lived near both Grimau and Barbarín, reported to the alcalde that he had overheard a heated discussion of the events in France in the barbershop of a Spanish immigrant, "Fulano Carreto," in November 1794. Since *fulano* is a Spanish word meaning "unknown person" (in English, John Doe), this use by Muñoz suggests that he was more familiar with the barbershop than with the barber, whose name was actually Juan Martín Carretero. Although Muñoz lived nearby, he was neither a client nor an acquaintance of the barber. Nevertheless, Muñoz claimed to have heard the loud argument in detail and offered the investigators what he claimed were direct quotes. As discussion of the war led to a series of angry denunciations of the French, one of the customers in the shop, the thirty-eight-year-old French merchant, Juan Barbarín, strongly objected.

According to Muñoz, Barbarín spoke provocatively, proclaiming that the French people "had good reasons to imprison and execute Louis XVI." Alone in defending the French and apparently provoked beyond endurance, Barbarín went on to suggest that "the Spanish people might have good reasons to imitate the French."

Upon hearing Barbarín's intemperate statement, one of the other visitors to the barbershop, Baltasar García, attempted to strike the Frenchman with a chair. When thwarted, he threw the chair at Barbarín's nearby shop. Cooler heads soon intervened, preventing bloodshed. The testimony of Muñoz went on to suggest to the authorities that Barbarín had potentially subversive associations, thus placing his apparently spontaneous defense of regicide in a darker political context. Muñoz told Alzaga that Barbarín "maintained a *tertulio*" (a gathering to discuss politics and literature) in his home frequented by French immigrants and other foreigners. For Alzaga, the missing elements of formal conspiracy that had eluded him as he tracked down the rumors and dead ends now seemed visible. According to this eager witness, Barbarín had not only endorsed regicide but had also held subversive meetings at his house. He had even "purchased gazettes with news of France" and then shared these periodicals freely with others. More intriguing still to Alzaga, Muñoz concluded his testimony by testifying that many of Barbarín's neighbors had remarked on the merchant's intimacy with members of the slave community—an intimacy he had maintained during his nearly ten-year residence in Buenos Aires.

The barber provided corroborating testimony that helped concentrate the alcalde's attention on Barbarín. Carretero asserted that before the war Barbarín had claimed to be from Valencia in Spain and that all his friends had been Spaniards. After news of Spain's war with France became known in Buenos Aires, Barbarín had dramatically changed his patterns and habits, seeking the friendship of other French residents and asserting his French origins. Other witnesses claimed that Barbarín now ignored the Spaniards with whom he had previously socialized. Carretero noted that among these new acquaintances, Barbarín now spent a great deal of time with the young French immigrant, Pablo Mayllos y Marcana. Barbarín's every action was now subject to intense scrutiny.

A resident of Barbarín's neighborhood, José de la Riva, offered evidence that further corroborated the damaging testimony of Muñoz. Riva stated that he had heard Barbarín praise Robespierre as "capable of making himself the owner of the world by his abilities." Riva claimed that he had challenged this remarkable belief by asking, "What did this capacity consist of given the atrocities, the abandonment of religion, and the murder of the king?" Barbarín, according to Riva, answered by saying "that if Robespierre had caused deaths he must have had a motive to do so."

Alzaga moved quickly to confirm the testimonies of Muñoz, Carretero, and Riva. Other witnesses to the argument in the barbershop were easily found, and their testimonies matched the rough outline provided in earlier interrogations. The alcalde and his assistants now sought to interview Barbarín's neighbors and business associates. Many of those questioned spoke respectfully of the suspect and noted his honesty and good habits. Some informants, however, wondered about his public interactions with the city's slave community. Barbarín, called Juan Pablo Capdepont or Capdepón when he arrived in Buenos Aires, had drawn the attention of many neighbors and customers by allowing slaves to visit him in his home and by treating his own slave, Manuel, with surprising affection and generosity.

News of the alcalde's intense inquiry into the affairs of the merchant attracted a new wave of testimony. A sergeant of the local garrison informed Alzaga that on numerous occasions he had witnessed Barbarín and his slave walking along the riverfront during the hours of siesta, a part of the day when nearly all the city's residents sought relief from the heat indoors. For this informant, the discreet timing of these walks and the pair's apparent disregard for the local siesta custom appeared suspicious. What could have been the subject of these secretive conversations between master and slave? Once asked, the question seemed to produce its own answer.

By the time Alzaga questioned Barbarín directly, the Frenchman was shaken to his core. When asked to explain his apparent intimacy with the slave community, Barbarín testified that he had served as treasurer of the black religious organization, the Archicofradía de San Benito, until recently when he had decided to resign. Why had he resigned? Barbarín claimed that his barber had warned him that rumors had linked his service to this black brotherhood to the feared slave uprising. He had resigned, therefore, to allay suspicion. He went on to remind Alzaga that his service with the group was not remarkable. Many other men of substantial means had served in similar capacities with segregated organizations of slaves and free blacks in Buenos Aires.

Barbarín's statement was undeniably true. It was the custom throughout the Spanish empire to require that white officials be appointed to supervise the fiscal affairs and the public behavior of elected black officers of black lay brotherhoods and guilds. White officers were also placed in command of segregated black militia units. San Benito in Buenos Aires was only one of many black organizations where white officials supervised the members. Like other brotherhoods, it had negotiated with a local parish church to place an altar devoted to San Benito and provide a location for meetings and religious observances. Members paid dues and collected alms in the city's streets to help pay for other members' burial costs, including special Masses for the souls of the deceased. These funds were also used to finance the celebrations associated with San Benito's feast day. Why, Barbarín wondered, was his civic service a cause of concern?

According to testimony gathered from his neighbors and associates, Barbarín's welcoming behavior toward the blacks whom he supervised pushed the limits expected of a man of property in such a role. Members of Barbarín's class universally kept all slaves and free blacks at a distance. A number of witnesses stated that Barbarín had even allowed members of the brotherhood to enter his home when they delivered alms solicited in the city's streets and markets. Although no one had thought it necessary to report these visits to authorities earlier and no one had raised objections to Barbarín, this behavior appeared more ominous, even dangerous, in retrospect, once the fear of a slave uprising had spread and Alzaga had begun to interrogate the Frenchman's neighbors. That someone of Barbarín's class and status encouraged this type of casual association with slaves seemed dangerously egalitarian to Alzaga. For him, and for most propertied porteños, black freemen and slaves could never be accepted as guests in the home of a "decent" person. Any intimacy with slaves in an era when revolutionary events in Haiti dominated porteño conversation seemed inherently subversive.

The unusual familiarity that Barbarín maintained with members of the San Benito brotherhood led inevitably to questions about his apparently warm relationship with his own slave, Manuel. Informants from the neighborhood suggested to Alzaga that the Frenchman treated his slave "with great demonstrations of affection and love." The neighbors corroborated the earlier testimony of the patrol sergeant who had observed the master and slave taking walks along the banks of the Rio de la Plata. They also told Alzaga that Barbarín seemed to treat the slave more like a friend than a servant. One informant commented in detail on the intimacy and affection that characterized their conversations. Another reported that Manuel had boasted that his owner had recently promised him his freedom. What, Alzaga wondered, was expected by Barbarín in return? Could the promise of freedom have been used to recruit Manuel into the conspiracy?

In the eyes of the alcalde, Barbarín's decision to hire the young immigrant, Pablo Mayllos, to teach Manuel to read and write was perhaps the most suspicious and damning aspect of this unusual and complex relationship between a slave and his master. It only took a few days for Alzaga to discover the background and habits of Manuel's twenty-eight-year-old tutor. After arriving in Buenos Aires, Mayllos had struggled to support himself as a private tutor and "letter writer." In addition to the income he received from a small number of students, Mayllos had set up a small table in the central plaza near the cabildo where he wrote letters for clients found among the city's largely illiterate urban underclass. For a small fee he might compose letters to distant kin or to employers or public authorities in other cities. Mayllos earned very little from these tasks. He took his meager meals at taverns and shared a rented room with another single man, Fermín Sotes. Rather too eagerly, Sotes volunteered to Alzaga that Mayllos often returned to the room very late at night. Another acquaintance noted that Mayllos was "more inclined to diversions than to work."

A French immigrant who knew of the merchant's desire to locate a tutor for Manuel had introduced the nearly destitute Mayllos to Barbarín. The young man eagerly forfeited his unpredictable earnings as a letter writer to accept Barbarín's generous wage of 4 pesos per month. As this relationship deepened, Mayllos had stayed at times in Barbarín's home as a guest and entered into the merchant's social circle. Almost from the moment that Mayllos was brought to the attention of the investigators, they wondered if he could be the author of the revolutionary pasquines that had been distributed throughout the city. Alzaga noted in a report that Mayllos's hand seemed very similar to the hand that had written "Liberty."

Barbarín's warm relations with Manuel seemed to suggest a quiet challenge to what Alzaga held to be an essential prop of the colonial social order: the power of master over slave. The alcalde took the Frenchman's highly unusual decision to provide Manuel with a tutor to be a political act. The deeply conservative Alzaga saw the bloody excesses of the French and Haitian revolutions as predictable outcomes that inevitably followed intellectual assaults on religion and monarchy and, more recently, on the hierarchy of master and slave. The bloodshed, property destruction, and sacrilege unleashed by both revolutions had their roots, for him, in the era's secularizing passions and in the dangerous erosion of what he took to be a divinely inspired order. The too-familiar mixing of white and black, of slave and free in Barbarín's house as well as Barbarín's desire to educate his slave suggested a dangerous lack of respect for this God-given order as well as a willful negligence of proprieties.

As Alzaga's interest in him grew, Barbarín became the distracted and nervous man introduced at the beginning of this essay. Repeated visits by Alzaga and his underlings to Barbarín's shop and home had provoked fears and doubts among neighbors and customers. Afraid of drawing the alcalde's attention or, alternatively, suspicious that Barbarín was in fact involved in some terrible conspiracy, once-friendly neighbors and associates now avoided him, choosing to look the other way as he passed by in the street and ignoring his greetings. Only a small circle of other French immigrants and a handful of close friends continued their social contacts with him. As the investigation increased in intensity, even these loyal associates grew increasingly nervous when they met Barbarín in public. Isolated and fearful, Barbarín now avoided his old friends because he was concerned that any meeting or contact with his fellow countrymen might appear to confirm the alcalde's xenophobic suspicions.

Having thoroughly interviewed most of Barbarín's associates, Alzaga finally turned his attention to the slave. Under questioning, Manuel freely admitted that he and his master had occasionally taken walks together. While he was treated "with love and dressed well" by his master, he insisted that this treatment and the shared moments of leisure during the siesta or early evening were completely innocent. He claimed that his master never talked about the revolutions in France or Haiti. Asked if Barbarín had promised him his freedom, Manuel stated that he had in fact been promised his freedom. However, Manuel understood that his freedom would only be granted if Barbarín returned to Spain or died in Buenos Aires. Alzaga then asked Manuel about his tutor. Why had his master paid Mayllos to teach him to read and write? Manuel replied that his master wanted his help in managing the shop's accounts. If he learned to read and write, then Barbarín would be free to leave the shop when business demanded. What, the alcalde inquired, was Manuel reading? Manuel replied that he generally only read accounts and letters relative to his master's business, but that Barbarín was willing to "read any book" to him to advance his instruction. Despite the explanations offered by Barbarín and Manuel, Alzaga clearly thought this relationship revealed dangerous egalitarian leanings. The Frenchman's willingness to compromise the expected hierarchy of master and slave was by itself a political provocation.

Having heard enough, Alzaga ordered the arrest of Juan Barbarín. For good measure, Barbarín's literate slave, Manuel, was arrested as well. A month later, Mayllos joined them in jail. With characteristic thoroughness, Alzaga then ordered the residences and shops of all those arrested to be searched and their goods seized. It was disappointing to Alzaga that despite rumors that conspirators were collecting arms and munitions, a search of Barbarín's home and shop had discovered neither.

Conditions in the Buenos Aires jail were notoriously dreadful. The cells were filthy and infested with pests. The jail's other prisoners were common delinquents or worse. When in the months preceding this inquiry officials had discovered that some prisoners were near starvation, the city fathers had responded with characteristic humanitarianism by having a barred window installed in the jail's street wall to allow prisoners to beg food from pedestrians passing by. Although Barbarín was able to pay for food for himself and Manuel, he was increasingly desperate and frightened. Fortunately for him, Alzaga's investigation was now diverted by surprising new testimony.

As Barbarín and Manuel languished in jail, don Miguel García de Bustamonte provided Alzaga with a promising new lead. He testified that a slave owned by one of his neighbors had been heard to say that the city's slaves planned to rise on Good Friday. José, placed by his master as a cook for the caulkers who worked in the Spanish naval yard, had threatened his work mates with the prospect of a slave insurrection during a lunchtime argument. José later tried to pass off his angry threats as a joke but provided more information when his master threatened him with a shotgun. Under pressure, José admitted that he had been recruited to join a conspiracy by "a man whose name I don't know and whose occupation I don't know, but who was dressed decently." After questioning the slave closely, Alzaga was able to identify the alleged insurrectionary recruiter as José Díaz, an apparently impoverished free black migrant from the interior who managed to earn a precarious living running a livery stable.

With this new conspirator in his sights, Alzaga and his agents abandoned their inquiry into the affairs of Barbarín. The alcalde turned instead to Díaz's wife, neighbors, and drinking companions. Many of these volunteered that Díaz had talked freely about a slave conspiracy. Some of his neighbors even claimed to have heard him say that the city's French residents would soon lead a slave uprising. During one drinking bout in a neighborhood tavern, Díaz stated that local French residents had offered the slaves freedom if the rebellion succeeded. Confirming Alzaga's worst fears, witnesses related that Díaz had told them that slaves were being urged to murder their masters while they slept. They were then to take the arms and money they had seized and join the French insurrectionists who planned to storm the city's fortifications on Good Friday. Some said that Díaz had openly boasted that 6,000 men waited in the interior provinces of Corrientes, Santa Fé, and Paraguay to join the rebellion once it had begun in Buenos Aires. Díaz was arrested and joined Barbarín and the others in jail.

Alzaga now began to hand over his evidence to the *audiencia* (royal court). After a preliminary examination, the chief prosecutor announced his intention to seek the execution of all the traitors. This tidy and expeditious conclusion of the investigation was soon swept aside by the appearance of a completely new conspiratorial trail. Among the scores of free blacks and slaves interviewed by Alzaga, there were very few who offered him anything other than rumor and hearsay. During one of the alcalde's visits to the foreign-owned bakeries and artisan shops spread around the city's central marketplace and nearby smaller plazas, however, a remarkable new witness had been identified—Juan Pedro, the slave of the French baker Juan Luis Dumont (or Dumonte). The testimony of this remarkable figure pushed the investigation forward in a new direction.

Juan Pedro offered detailed testimony that for the first time seemed to reveal a conspiracy large enough and well organized enough to actually threaten the colonial government. According to Juan Pedro, his master Dumont held meetings in his house that drew together many of the city's French residents. He drove home the subversive nature of these meetings with a telling anecdote. In December 1794 a particularly boisterous meeting where the conspirators had toasted "Liberty" was abruptly ended when the group's lookout brought word that a patrol of soldiers was nearby. Apparently fearing discovery, Dumont extinguished the lights and his guests dispersed. As remembered by this helpful slave, Dumont and his friends then relocated their meetings to a farm in the nearby countryside where a number of Frenchmen resided. Safely isolated from the city's armed patrols, Juan Pedro claimed that the conspirators' meeting had become larger and more animated. Convinced unambiguously of this threat, Alzaga moved quickly and arrested Dumont and all of those who had frequented his home.

There were now more than twenty "conspirators" in the jail along with Barbarín, Mayllos, and Manuel. Alzaga went to the judges of the audiencia to gain permission to question two of the prisoners under torture. These two, he assured the judges, were key to revealing the conspiracy in full. He selected the black freeman, José Díaz, who had talked openly of an uprising, and the watchmaker Santiago Antonini, one of the immigrants arrested on the testimony of Dumont's slave. In Antonini's room, Alzaga's agents had found one of the incriminating pasquines celebrating the word "Liberty." Days later, Barbarín and the other prisoners listened to the screams of the two prisoners tortured in the room above their cells. When these torments failed to produce new information about the conspiracy, Alzaga decided to torture the unfortunate Antonini a second time. Again, Barbarín and the other prisoners heard Antonini beg for mercy and scream out in pain as steel pins were driven beneath his fingernails. Despite this agony, Antonini offered Alzaga no new leads, no information on clandestine stores of arms, and no identification of the conspiracy's leadership. Desperate to bring the case to trial, Alzaga now requested permission to torture the other prisoners.

The judges of the audiencia immediately refused this request. This refusal signaled the audiencia's growing reservations about the alcalde's investigation. Thwarted by the royal court, Alzaga was forced to respond to the formal arguments offered by lawyers appointed to defend the prisoners. Although each lawyer adopted a unique strategy to deal with the evidence against his client, the combined weight of these individual attacks swept away much of Alzaga's theory of a treasonous conspiracy organized by the French. The audiencia moved slowly, however. Most of the prisoners, including Barbarín, continued to languish in prison for eight more months before the royal court made a final decision. Even then its decision left the prisoners' fate unresolved. Convinced by the arguments of the defense lawyers, the judges did not find any foreign prisoner guilty of any crime. There was simply no clear evidence of conspiracy. As one lawyer put it, "Where is this conspiracy that threatens to ruin everyone? Who are the directors of the bloody enterprise? Some poor bakers and a watchmaker."

Neither did the judges exonerate the defendants as demanded by the defense attorneys, however. Instead, the judges decided to send Barbarín and nearly all the other arrested immigrants to Spain without formal sentence. This decision to condemn the defendants to unofficial exile passed the buck to higher judicial authorities in Spain. Unlike the foreign-born prisoners, the intemperate and perhaps mentally ill José Díaz, the only free black prisoner, was condemned to suffer ten years of exile in the desolate Malvinas Islands in the South Atlantic. The royal court seemed to say that there was no convincing evidence of conspiracy or treason, but that finding the defendants innocent was both too dangerous during wartime and too offensive to the powerful Martín de Alzaga, who had led the investigation and ordered the arrests.

This clumsy decision may have been a reaction to the public scandal caused by a wave of bitter denunciations issued by one of the defense lawyers who had ridiculed Alzaga and his agents. Instead of focusing on the case against the prisoners, the court and the new viceroy, Pedro Melo de Portugal, felt compelled to defend Alzaga's reputation and, by extension, Spanish justice. This highly irregular decision acknowledged that Alzaga's long investigation had produced no convincing evidence of conspiracy. Nevertheless, Barbarín and the others would suffer severe punishment. The combination of long months of incarceration in Buenos Aires and then exile to Spain effectively ruined most of them financially and broke the health of many. The two victims of torture never fully recovered, and the surviving evidence suggests that José Díaz died as a prisoner in the Malvinas. Barbarín, who had run a profitable business before his arrest, was forced to inform the royal court from his cell that his customers had stopped paying their debts to him, thus endangering his business and draining his resources.

It is not known what happened to Barbarín after his forced exile to Spain. In August 1796 the French ambassador to Madrid wrote a formal protest to Spanish authorities over the continued incarceration of Barbarín, now called Jean Cap-de-pon, and other French citizens, despite the end of the war. The ambassador's letter imitated the angry language of the defense attorneys in Buenos Aires, excoriating Alzaga and suggesting that he had profited personally from the seizure of Barbarín's goods. There is no evidence that this strong protest led to the immediate release of Juan Barbarín and the others, but a reply to the French ambassador sent by Spanish authorities five months later claimed that there were no longer any French prisoners in the realm.

Was Juan Barbarín a party to a conspiracy? The evidence suggests his innocence. Despite an intense investigation that included a search of Barbarín's residence and shop, Alzaga was unable to discover a single compromising document or any store of weapons. After interviewing hundreds of often-eager neighbors and associates, he was also unable to link Barbarín with either José Díaz, who had drunkenly boasted of his involvement in a planned rebellion, or with Dumont's circle, who had too often and too publicly toasted "Liberty" and talked favorably of revolutionary France. In fact, there is no evidence that either Díaz or any member of the Dumont group was involved in an active conspiracy or had pursued any serious political objective. There is some evidence, however, that Mayllos, hired by Barbarín to educate the slave Manuel, was indeed the author of at least some of the pasquines. Barbarín and the others were at times indiscreet and even foolish when provoked by Spanish patriots or excited by news from France. But the xenophobic tide caused by war transformed their intemperate remarks and their habit of socializing together into a threat. There is no doubt that the violent events in France and Haiti had helped to fashion the political paranoia that fed Alzaga's investigation and led inevitably to the incarcerations and tortures.

Looking back on these events from our era, we find ourselves drawn to Juan Barbarín. He appears to be a particularly sympathetic figure, a man who embodied much of the transformative idealism of the time. He read widely and sympathized with the ideals of the French Revolution. He looked at its excesses and at its most important political symbol, Robespierre, and still saw the liberating potential of new ideas. This idealism quietly worked in his private life as well. He saw his slave Manuel as a fully human being, enjoyed his company, and planned for his future as a free man. Even in his routine responsibilities as an officer of the black brotherhood of San Benito, Barbarín recognized the humanity and dignity of its members and allowed them to enter his home as peers. Alzaga took these small acts of compassion and generosity as revolutionary. Perhaps they were. In the century that was ready to dawn, the cumulative opinion of thousands of men and women who, like Juan Barbarín, embraced the idea of "Liberty" would lead to the independence of Spanish America, the end of the African slave trade, and the abolition of slavery.

SOURCES

Research for this essay was conducted in Buenos Aires, Argentina and in Seville, Spain. The records of the legal proceedings in Buenos Aires are primarily found in three lengthy legajos found in the Archivo General de la Nación. See Criminales, Legajo 39, Expediente 14; Tribunales, Legajo 60, Expediente 6; and Interior, Legajo 38, Expediente 1. The Archivo General de Indias in Seville yielded information on the biographies of the prisoners and on the diplomatic efforts undertaken to liberate Barbarín and the others.

SUGGESTED READINGS

For intellectual life in the era of the French Revolution, see Jonathan Israel, *Radical Enlightenment, Philosophy, and the Making of Modernity, 1650–1750* (Oxford, 2001). François Furet, *Interpreting the French Revolution* (New York, 1981), breaks with earlier interpretations that emphasized class and ideology. Georges Lefebvre, *The Coming of the French Revolution*, trans. R. R. Palmer (New York, 1947), presents the classic class-based analysis. See also two newer works, Michael Keith Baker, *Inventing the French Revolution: Essays on French Political Culture in the Eighteenth Century* (New York, 1990); and Timothy Tackett, *Becoming a Revolutionary: The Deputies of the French National Assembly and the Emergence of a Revolutionary Culture* (Princeton, NJ, 1996). Lynn Hunt, *The Family Romance of the French Revolution* (Berkeley, 1992), examines the gender content of revolutionary politics.

The Haitian Revolution has received less extensive coverage than the revolutions in America and France. C. L. R. James, *The Black Jacobins*, 2d ed. (New York, 1963), is the classic study. Anna J. Cooper, *Slavery and the French Revolutionists, 1788–1805* (Lewiston, NY, 1988), also provides an overview of this important topic. See also Carolyn E. Fick, *The Making of Haiti: The Saint Domingue Revolution from Below* (Knoxville, 1990); and David Barry Gaspar and David Patrick Geggus, eds., *A Turbulent Time: The French Revolution and the Greater Caribbean* (Bloomington, 1997).

For the independence era in Spanish America, see John Lynch, *The Spanish American Revolutions, 1808–1826*, 2d ed. (New York, 1986); and Jay Kinsbruner, *Independence in Spanish America* (Albuquerque, 1994).

CHAPTER 16

Miguel García

Black Soldier in the Wars of Independence

PETER BLANCHARD

The Río de la Plata emerged as a center of resistance to Spanish authority between the establishment of a provisional government in 1810 and its formal declaration of independence in 1816. When Napoléon's troops invaded the Iberian peninsula in 1807, forced the abdication of Spain's King Charles IV and his heir Ferdinand on May 6, 1808, and placed Joseph Bonaparte on the throne, a profound constitutional crisis occurred within the Spanish empire. Many Creoles believed that without a legal monarch, sovereignty returned to the people. Consequently, from 1809 they began establishing a series of juntas in major cities in the Indies. Local Spanish colonial authorities crushed many of these provisional governments, while others fell to the armies sent by Ferdinand VII following the restoration in 1814.

One of the few juntas that survived was in Buenos Aires, capital of the Viceroyalty of the Río de la Plata. This distant viceroyalty, established in 1776, had enjoyed little support from Spain. As a result, when two British expeditionary forces in 1806 and 1807 tried to capture Buenos Aires, local citizens of the port (called porteños), *rather than the viceroy and the* audiencia, *rallied popular support to expel the invaders. When news of the Bourbon abdication arrived in 1808, local creole militia commanders in the Río de la Plata again assumed effective control and in 1810 created an autonomous junta. Spanish forces never mounted an adequate military campaign to recapture Buenos Aires and subdue the surrounding provinces, but the creole government in the capital also failed to unite all of the former provinces of the viceroyalty under its control, despite a series of military expeditions. Upper Peru (Bolivia), the Banda Oriental (Uruguay), and Paraguay remained either in royalist hands or effectively independent of the port city. Nonetheless, the ruling government in Buenos Aires and its surrounding provinces formally declared their independence as the United Provinces of Argentina in 1816.*

In the struggles between hostile armies that occurred in the Río de la Plata after 1810, military leaders faced constant difficulties in recruiting men. Despite the deep-seated fear of arming slaves, many generals ultimately turned to offering bondsmen freedom in return for military service. Colonial officials in the past had enrolled free blacks and mulattos in militia units and regular army regiments but had avoided arming any of the viceroyalty's 30,000 slaves. Faced with the challenges of the independence struggles, however, the military felt compelled to turn to this sector of the population. In time, commanders on all sides of the conflicts in the Río de la Plata actively enlisted slaves with offers of freedom. Adding to the attacks on slavery were government initiatives that included antislavery legislation. As a result, slaves who remained in bondage became more assertive; many chose to run away and enlist to try to secure their freedom. Nevertheless, slavery managed to survive the independence struggles, although in a severely weakened form.

Miguel García was one of many slaves who sought freedom through military service. He and his family belonged to a Spaniard, Pedro García, who chose to fight for the royalist army in Montevideo in 1810 and left his slaves to fend for themselves. Following his master's capture by patriot forces, Miguel decided to join the porteño army under the command of General José Rondeau in exchange for a promise of freedom. When Rondeau's army withdrew from the siege of Montevideo, Miguel and his family sought to preserve their freedom by accompanying it across the river to Buenos Aires. A new porteño invasion in 1812 brought Miguel back to the Banda Oriental with another patriot army. Once again, the porteños offered slaves freedom for joining their cause, but so too did the royalists, resulting in slaves fighting against one another under the opposing banners. Many slaves deserted, some changed sides, but they became an important component of the competing armies in the Río de la Plata. Miguel García managed to survive the fighting and eventually returned with his family to Buenos Aires. By this time, however, the urban government was trying to reestablish the old social order. When a relative of Miguel's former master claimed ownership of his wife, the courts ruled that she was still a slave despite the contribution that both had made to the independence effort. All too many veterans like García, who had fought for the cause of freedom and liberty, found that independence provided few tangible benefits.

Peter Blanchard received his doctorate from the University of London and is currently professor of history at the University of Toronto. He has written numerous articles and three books: The Origins of the Peruvian Labor Movement, 1883–1919 *(1982);* Markham in Peru: The Travels of Clements R. Markham, 1852–1853 *(1991); and* Slavery and Abolition in Early Republican Peru *(1992). He is currently working on the military participation of slaves during the Latin American independence era.*

𝒯he wars that ended Spanish rule in South America presented the area's oppressed population in general and its slaves in particular with what seemed to be an unprecedented opportunity to challenge the colonies' social realities. Countries, regions, and elites confronted one another and created a situation similar to what had occurred in Haiti, where a slave revolt destroyed both the country's colonial status and its system of bondage. In the case of Spanish America, no similar social revolution occurred, yet the lives of many slaves were profoundly altered. They participated in the fighting and raised the possibility of adding a social component to what were essentially political movements. This seemed most likely in Venezuela where free blacks and slaves rose following the declaration of the first republic in 1811 and engaged in a rebellion that threatened to become a Haitian-style conflict. No similar confrontation occurred elsewhere, but the events in Venezuela gave warning of what could happen and helped focus the attention of both royalists and patriots on the slave population. Creole leaders responded by passing antislavery legislation. At the same time, both sides turned to slaves as possible soldiers, offering them freedom in return for military service. As a result, the institution of slavery in Spanish America was seriously weakened. Thousands took advantage of the offer of freedom, thereby reducing the numbers in bondage. The appeals for slave support also led to a more assertive black population. Everywhere they protested their conditions and demanded improvements. Consequently, although slavery survived, this institution that had been a vital part of Spanish America virtually since the establishment of Spanish colonialism was at wars' end only a shadow of its former self.

The appeals for slave support, voiced throughout Spanish America, were particularly prominent in the Río de la Plata region where blacks had a long history of military participation. In the late colonial period, the viceroyalty contained a small but significant slave population of about 30,000 concentrated around the principal ports of Buenos Aires and its transriverine rival, Montevideo. These numbers had increased in the late colonial period in response to the Bourbon liberalization of trade. As a result, in 1815 over one-quarter of the population of present-day Argentina was African born; of these, 90 percent were slaves. The majority of the imports were single males between the ages of sixteen and forty—in other words, prime candidates for military recruitment—and they knew what it was like to be free. In the Río de la Plata, as elsewhere, colonial officials had at different times enrolled free blacks and mulattos in both militia units and regiments of the line. But they had consistently resisted recruiting slaves, fearful of what might happen if they armed this sector of the population. Military requirements, however, could overcome even deeply seated views, and in 1806 and 1807, in response to British attacks on the region, slaves were among those recruited. They assisted in defeating the invaders, for which a number of them were freed, thereby establishing a link between military service and emancipation.

With the declarations of self-rule throughout Spanish America after 1809, there was a renewed focus on blacks as soldiers. Warfare erupted when local elites sought to establish their authority over surrounding regions. The creole rulers in Buenos Aires claimed jurisdiction over the entire viceroyalty and organized armies to impose their will, while the royalists in Montevideo sought to crush the autonomous juntas. Blacks, including slaves, were part of this confrontation. The porteño army sent to attack Montevideo in 1811 included the Sixth Regiment, made up of dark-skinned pardos and morenos. Composed primarily of freedmen, it had within its ranks a number of slaves: runaways who had fled to join the regiment, and donations from patriotic owners. Some of the officers in the regiment were blacks, and a few were even former slaves. One was Antonio Videla, who had served in the defense of Buenos Aires in 1807 and then remained in the army. He rose to the rank of captain, serving at the siege of Montevideo and subsequent campaigns until December 1812, when he and his entire company of morenos were killed at the battle of Cerrito. Another black officer was Domingo Sosa, who had enlisted in 1808 and would be promoted to the rank of lieutenant for his service in the two sieges of Montevideo and the battles of Cerrito, Vilcohuma, and Sipe-Sipe.

As the porteños invaded the Banda Oriental, local slaves also began joining the army. It was not the presence of black units or black officers that attracted them, but rather the offer of freedom in return for military service that was announced by José Rondeau, the commander of the invading forces, and by his subordinates, including the Uruguayan leader, José Artigas. Their aims were to replace military losses and at the same time prevent the royalists from recruiting this sector of the population. Their offer proved to be extremely attractive. Perhaps as many as 1,000 slaves of both sexes flocked to their banners, coming from Montevideo, the surrounding countryside, and even Portuguese-occupied territory. Over 300 of them were organized into a battalion of *libertos*. Among the fugitives were Miguel García and his family.

Little is known about Miguel's life, but his circumstances were probably not untypical. Miguel, his wife, and two children were the property of a Spaniard named Pedro García, living outside Montevideo when the colonies began issuing their calls for self-rule. Their owner chose to remain loyal to the Spanish cause and joined the royalist army in Montevideo in 1810, leaving his slaves at Capilla de Mercedes. When Pedro was captured at the battle of Las Piedras, Miguel and his family found their status unclear. Their master's removal had seriously weakened the bonds that held them, and those bonds ruptured completely when Rondeau issued his offer of freedom. Miguel joined the army, securing his freedom and altering forever the direction of his life.

Miguel's fortunes, like those of other recruits, were now tied to the operations of the porteño army. It besieged Montevideo until Portuguese troops invaded the Banda Oriental, leading to a treaty in October 1811 between the royalists and *porteños* to forestall a Portuguese takeover. The treaty recognized the presence of runaways in the latter's army, permitting those who wished to do so to accompany the withdrawing Argentine troops. Alternatively, they could return to their owners. Miguel, like most of the others, preferred to be free, and together with his family he crossed the river to Buenos Aires. Many of the runaways who remained behind were similarly inclined. Rather than return to their owners as instructed, they continued to fight, largely under the banners of Artigas as he struggled to free his homeland. A new porteño invasion in 1812 brought Miguel back to the Banda Oriental as the Sixth Regiment went into action. Once again Montevideo was besieged, once again the invaders offered freedom to slaves who volunteered, and once again runaways flocked to the invading army.

Slaves thus fought, but they were not fighting for a common goal. Indeed, they were often fighting against one another as the royalists, like the patriots, began recruiting slaves. Some ended up fighting for both as they changed sides or were drafted consecutively into the opposing armies, as Artigas and other provincial leaders challenged the aims of Buenos Aires's centralizing rulers. Blacks remained an important part of Artigas's army, and at one point he even offered to abolish slavery. Military defeat prevented the implementation of his offer, but the policy of freedom in return for military service became widely accepted in the Banda Oriental. Even the Portuguese, who had opposed Artigas, in part because of fears that he might promote slave uprisings in Brazil, and who invaded the neighboring country again in 1816, used the offer of freedom to attract recruits. The dispersion of slaves among the contending armies as they fought for political goals, however, ensured that their particular interests were not central to the struggles.

Nevertheless, because of military demands attention remained focused on slaves and slave issues throughout the Río de la Plata region during these years. Compelled to fight on a growing number of fronts, the Buenos Aires government turned to its slaves as possible recruits. First, it made efforts to win over the black population by passing the Free Womb Law and by ending the African slave trade in 1812. Subsequently, it began recruiting slaves, perhaps influenced by what had taken place in the Banda Oriental. The resulting program satisfied both the blacks' desire for freedom and the government's determination to obtain troops while protecting property rights and avoiding an anarchic flight of slaves similar to what had occurred across the river. On June 1, 1813, it issued the first of a series of laws that recruited slaves to serve in a regiment of *libertos*. In return for their freedom, the slaves had to serve for five years; they were evaluated and their owners compensated by the state. Over the next few years further laws recruited more slaves, particularly those of Spaniards whose property became an obvious target once independence was declared in 1816. The period of service changed slightly but the right to freedom remained clearly stated.

As a result, between 1813 and 1818, some 2,000 blacks were recruited from the province of Buenos Aires, with additional ones coming from the other provinces, such as Mendoza, San Juan, and Córdoba. Far more were recruited than served, as all had to be examined first by a surgeon, and many were returned to their owners as unfit for service. The records show that a high percentage were African-born, listing themselves as natives of the Congo, Mozambique, Benguela, Mina, and other nations. Most ranged in age between eighteen and thirty, but it was not uncommon to find much older and even younger soldiers, as black children as young as eight served as regimental drummers and flautists. Joining them were slaves drawn from other quarters. Criminals were taken from jails and vagabonds off the streets, while some slaves were simply abducted or pressed into service. One particular group comprised men taken from slave ships that had been captured by government-commissioned privateers. If the owners of any of these men appeared and claimed their property, they were usually compensated according to the provisions of the recruiting laws. Most of the recruits were initially assigned to the black Seventh and Eighth Battalions and the integrated Tenth Battalion, but other units also came to have former slaves within their ranks. The majority went into the infantry, with smaller numbers in the artillery, the cavalry, and even the navy, including duty on privateers. As a result, they came to constitute a significant percentage of the Argentine forces. For example, as early as 1813, two-thirds of the Army of the North, operating in the northern provinces of the viceroyalty, were said to be composed of libertos.

The recruiting took place despite differing opinions about blacks as soldiers. General Manuel Belgrano was one of those who were opposed to their recruitment. In a letter to General José de San Martín, he made the rather contradictory charge that "the blacks and mulattos are a rabble who are as cowardly as they are bloodthirsty. In the five engagements that I have had with them, they have been the first to break ranks and to search for walls of bodies [against which to hide]." Others, like Rondeau, were more favorably disposed. After the battle of Cordón of June 4, 1811, he commented that "the boldness and valor of the pardos and morenos and of their intrepid leader make them worthy of the most profound elegies." San Martín seemed to be of the same view, noting that "slaves make the best troops of the line, as a result of their undeniable subordination and natural readiness for hard work."[1] In 1816, when he began collecting and training an army to invade Chile and Peru, he made a special effort to recruit slaves.

Regardless of the differences of opinion, recruiting proceeded. The program proved as attractive to Argentina's slaves as it had been to those in the Banda Oriental. While the laws compelled owners to supply a specified number of their slaves to a pool from which the recruits were drawn, and numerous owners began donating theirs in response to the legislation, many slaves pressured their owners to be permitted to serve. Often they couched their requests in patriotic terms. Twenty-year-old Manuel was described by his owner as "healthy and without vices and with an inclination to military service." Another owner claimed that his slave had the "strongest desire to follow a military career," while Antonio Castro was reported to have expressed the wish "to sacrifice himself for the just cause of the homeland."[2] Some even sought to pay their owners to join, offering their army wages for this purpose.

While statements supposedly made by slaves have to be treated with caution, as owners may have been using the recruiting laws to unload unwanted property, nevertheless, there is no question that many slaves wanted to serve. They were attracted in large part because few other routes existed for them to obtain their freedom. Complete abolition was out of the question because of the authorities' commitment to property rights and their fear of a large contingent of suddenly released blacks. Each year owners freed a few, but they tended to be females and the aged. A few more managed to buy their own freedom, but the number was still very small. Other factors may also have played a role in the slaves' decision. Their feelings of patriotism may have been as strong as their words suggest. In addition, service in the military provided them with an opportunity to release the pent-up resentment and frustration of years of servitude. They could be as bloodthirsty as they wished without fear of retribution or punishment.

Army service had its obvious dangers, but they may have appeared no worse than the degrading and unhealthy tasks that many slaves had to perform already. Moreover, the uniforms, weapons, and military pageantry must have served as a lure, particularly since it meant association with an institution that was emerging as one of the most important in the new nation. And within that institution they were not forced to remain at the bottom of the ladder. Promotion through the ranks was possible. Already there were black officers and noncommissioned officers, and the practice continued despite pressures to end black promotions when the recruiting program began. Among those promoted was Lorenzo Barcala, a slave from Mendoza who joined the Battalion of Civic Pardos of Mendoza in 1815 under San Martín and rose through the ranks to sergeant, second lieutenant, and eventually captain. One of the black noncommissioned officers was Miguel Bonifacio Otárola, who was recruited under the June 1813 law and served first in the Seventh Battalion in Upper Peru and later in the Ninth Regiment, becoming a sergeant in the process. In 1819, when he asked for his discharge papers, his request was granted, but he was told to reconsider reenlisting because the army "did not want to lose a good soldier."[3]

Another lure of military service was the wage that it offered and what could be done with that money. Soldiers received 6 pesos per month that had to cover many of their daily expenses. Whatever was left over was often spent to satisfy immediate desires and whims or gambled away. Some soldiers, however, assigned a specified portion to family members for their sustenance or for assistance in paying for their freedom. Felipe Malaver, a black officer in the Sixth Regiment, assigned part of his wages to secure the freedom of his wife, Francisca. His daughter or stepdaughter, who had the same owner as his wife, sought the wages of her soldier-husband for the same end. Domingo Sosa in 1815, when a lieutenant in the Sixth Regiment, directed that money he had saved be used to purchase his wife's freedom.

The attractions were sufficiently great for many slaves to take the path that Miguel had followed. They fled their owners to join the military in expectation of their freedom. Slaves from various parts of the United Provinces of the Río de la Plata ran away to Rondeau's forces during the sieges of Montevideo. In some cases they remained and fought under Artigas. Others followed the black regiments as they headed out of Buenos Aires on their campaigns. To remain in service the runaways had to develop strategies to avoid being returned to their owners. Many changed their names. They had no particular commitment to their given names, especially those who had been born in Africa, and switching seems to have been common. Thus, José Sánchez became José Mosqueira, José Pérez became José Antonio Moreno, and Dolores Salgados's Mina-born slave Francisco became José Ferreyra. They then disappeared into the growing number of regiments that contained black soldiers. Who could tell the difference between a free black volunteer and a runaway slave? Who was going to check? Commanders, desperate to fill their ranks, showed little interest in doing so. Moreover, even when the volunteers' true legal status was revealed, their superiors were reluctant to arrest them, considering it unfair to reenslave those men who had risked their lives for the homeland. One such case involved Antonio Lama, a slave who fled his owner early in 1813 and joined the Tenth Regiment, where he served for over two years. He fought in a number of battles, in one instance carrying his captain to safety despite being shot in the knee. Described by his sergeant as "one of the best soldiers in his corps," he was subsequently captured but escaped and returned to his unit. When he was eventually apprehended as a runaway, his commander testified on his behalf, commenting that a return to slavery would be "unjust." He recommended instead that the state compensate his owner, a common response of officers. The courts expressed similar reservations about re-enslaving men who had defended the country. One court decided that having fought at all, even though not for the required time, was sufficient for a slave to secure his freedom. It declared that "it would be tyrannical and monstrous to reduce him" once again to slavery.[4] Responses such as these gave a clear signal that military service could lead to freedom and probably prompted more slaves to run away.

Faced with the realities of army life, however, many of these runaways must have wondered whether they had made the right decision. The initial euphoria of joining the ranks with the promise of freedom followed by the distribution of colorful uniforms, the payment of a monthly wage, and the assignment of weapons probably carried them through the first weeks of training. Questions may have begun with the actual campaigning. Long days of marching through inhospitable terrain and contending with insects, rain, and cold, with poor food, little protection, numerous diseases, and limited if any medical treatment must have raised doubts, especially when no apparent military objective was attained. The company of their families, as occurred in Miguel's case, may have provided some relief. His wife, Juliana, and two children, Ventura and Mateo, were with him in the two sieges of Montevideo and the subsequent invasion of Upper Peru, until the battle of Sipe-Sipe where much of the Argentine army was destroyed.

Miguel managed to survive the disaster and return to Buenos Aires, but others were not so lucky. Many men were captured and shot. Some were held prisoner for several years. Former slaves captured at Sipe-Sipe were sold to plantations on the Peruvian coast where they remained until 1821, when forces under the command of General William Miller freed them. Miller described these survivors as "broken."[5] This was true as well of other veterans, who returned home with injuries so severe that they were incapable of further military service or any other activity. Some were blinded; others were lame. One soldier recounted how a rifle ball had smashed his jaw and teeth and made it impossible for him to eat solid foods. What were they to do? Who would care for them? What was the status of those who had not completed their required years of service?

The authorities in Buenos Aires addressed the latter issue by assigning returnees to a corps of invalids, a battalion of veterans, and various militia units. This provided the necessary military service, although it also meant that they could be returned to active duty. Service in regiments of the line, however, had come to an end for most of them, and assignment to the more ceremonial and defensive units became a frequent request. As for those whose injuries and circumstances left them, in their own words, "naked" and "useless," their appeals for financial assistance over the next decade attest to their large number and to their pitiful state. The small amount of money that the state allotted was hardly sufficient to meet their needs. Many men probably ended their days begging in the streets of Buenos Aires.

Because of the conditions, recruits soon lost their enthusiasm for army life and sought ways to bring an end to their military careers. This was true of soldiers regardless of race or background, although the former slaves had their own particular reason for trying to avoid hazardous duty. The majority of them had been attracted into the military by the offer of freedom. They had no desire to suffer injury or death. Therefore, they sought to avoid fighting. One strategy was to claim an illness or physical problem that made further service impossible. Some made their claims almost immediately on being recruited, while many more raised their voices after they had trained, served, and fought. The majority of claims may have been genuine, but some obviously were not. Antonio Sinen, who had fought in the Banda Oriental with the Sixth Regiment for several years, cited a ruptured groin as his reason for asking to be relieved of duty. A medical examination, however, found him still fit for service.

Many slave recruits also resorted to another common response of disaffected soldiers throughout Spanish America: they deserted. Some, taking advantage of their separation from their owners, fled almost as soon as they were recruited. Others waited until after they had tried military service. From the complaints of their commanders, it appears that desertions occurred constantly, but they were particularly prevalent during the confusion before and after battles. The authorities tried to stop the flow by hiring bounty hunters and imposing harsh penalties that ranged from a whipping and extra years of service to being shot. But nothing seemed to work, as desertion remained a constant problem during the wars.

Like other soldiers, black soldiers also resorted to more dangerous forms of resistance. Outright mutiny was extremely rare but not unknown. In November 1813 the Company of Pardos of Punta Gorda, a unit that included former slaves, was reported to be in a state of insubordination, with troops deserting, weapons being stolen, and officers being insulted and even assaulted. There were fears that the company would desert to the enemy in battle and take other units with them. As a result, the company was disbanded and its members reassigned. A more serious incident occurred in Peru in February 1824 when Argentine and Chilean troops, including blacks from the Seventh and Eighth Battalions, antagonized by a lack of pay and orders to move north, mutinied and handed over control of the fortresses in Callao to the royalists. Many of the mutineers then began looting Lima, Callao, and other towns until royalist forces intervened to restore order. Fortunately for the independence forces, the mutineers' treason had no long-term repercussions as the royalists were soon compelled to retreat into the fortresses, the mutineers among them. Many died in the subsequent siege, primarily from disease and starvation, but also at the hands of the fortresses' authoritarian commander, José Ramón Rodil. The few who survived emerged in January 1826, when Rodil finally accepted the reality that Spanish power in South America had come to an end.

The instances of this sort, however, were few, and there is no question that the slave recruits from the Río de la Plata made a substantial and positive contribution to the war effort. Many of them helped to defend the Argentine provinces against royalist incursions from Upper Peru. Others, like Miguel, took part in expeditions into neighboring regions. Their aim was to suppress opposition governments, establish control over the area, and, following Buenos Aires's declaration of independence in 1816, to protect that independence by destroying the remaining royalist armies. Many served in the second siege of Montevideo and the unsuccessful invasions of Upper Peru that ended with the defeats at Ayohuma (1813) and Sipe-Sipe (1815). The latter was so decisive that the Sixth Regiment had to be disbanded and its survivors redistributed among other units. In Miguel's case, he was eventually transferred to the Third Regiment of the Army of Peru. Other former slaves participated in one of the most brilliant campaigns of the war. They were part of the army that José de San Martín organized in Mendoza to invade Chile and Peru. An existing pardo militia provided a base for black recruitment, local slaveholders added 710 slaves, and a further 840 were drawn from other parts of the country.

As a result, one-half of San Martín's Army of the Andes was composed of free blacks and former slaves. They crossed the Andes in January 1817, surprising the royalists and defeating them at the battle of Chacabuco. The following year the black soldiers fought at the battle of Maipo that ensured Chile's independence, drawing comments for the "savage fury" that they displayed in the fighting.[6] San Martín added new slave recruits to his army in Chile and even more in Peru after his invasion of September 1820, so that by January 1822 the majority of his army may have been composed of former slaves. After the transfer of command of the army in 1823 to the Venezuelan liberator, Simón Bolívar, a new black component was added. Bolívar's northern army included a large number of slaves recruited in Venezuela, Colombia, and Ecuador. Together with the Argentines, Chileans, and Peruvians, they destroyed the remaining royalist armies at the battles of Junín and Ayacucho in 1824, thereby confirming once and for all the independence of the continent.

Blacks were thus a prominent part of the liberating armies of South America, but despite their numbers and their common background they remained disunited and unable to impose a black agenda on the struggles. The same division into patriot and royalist forces that had occurred in the Río de la Plata was also evident in Peru, where the viceroy recruited slaves to confront San Martín. Moreover, splits developed along national lines, with differences evident between the Chilean and Argentine troops in Chile, and similar divisions in Peru between those from the north and those from the south. The differences continued after independence had been won, as national allegiance assumed far greater importance than racial identity in determining the actions of black soldiers.

While they could not impose their wishes on the independence struggles, the slaves managed to affect the nature of the institution in their countries in other ways. A more assertive and aggressive slave population was evident by the time independence was secured. The soldiers' demands for their discharge papers, their appeals for benefits, their requests for permission to serve in militia units or in the battalions of veterans and invalids, and their claims of infirmities were indicative of this change. They also used the fact of their military ties to make other demands, such as the freeing of loved ones, reducing the sale values of family members, and securing custody of their freed children.

This new assertiveness was evident not only among male slaves but also among females. The nature of military service had prevented most female slaves from taking advantage of the offer of freedom. A few, such as those who served as spies, were among a small number of exceptions. Nevertheless, the recruitment of slaves provided an opportunity for them to challenge the system in other ways. At least one slave claimed her freedom on the basis of having married a black soldier. Others asked for it for having accompanied their spouses on campaign. They also pressured the state to secure the release of husbands who had stayed their required terms. The reasons were obvious. Beyond the issue of emotional ties, there was the practical fact that a free partner could assist them in securing their own freedom. Some managed to achieve it by using the wages assigned by their soldier-relative. Others claimed the back pay of dead husbands for the same end. María Antonia Gauna, a

Mozambique-born slave and the widow of José Bernardino Gauna, a Congo nation slave who had served for six years in various units and campaigns until his death in January 1820, asked for three years of his assigned wages to free herself. In many cases, however, the husband returned injured and incapable of any work, leaving him dependent on his family. Numerous others never came home, and their families spent years without knowing their fate, writing forlorn letters asking for information, back pay, pensions, and charity.

Thus, slavery may have survived the wars, but it was not the institution it had been fifteen years earlier. The sacrifice of blacks like Miguel, who had fought for the region's political freedom and had won their own freedom as their reward, had seriously weakened slavery. Moreover, slaves were now more assertive than they had been in the past, and their voices were still being heard as the new, independent governments began to organize themselves.

Nonetheless, the context and the circumstances had changed for the slaves. Soldiers like Miguel, who had fought and obtained their freedom, could offer little as a united group for families and friends who remained enslaved. Many of the black soldiers had died or disappeared. Only 150 of the 1,500 who had accompanied San Martín across the Andes returned to their homes. As a result of the freeing of recruits and the end of the slave trade, areas of postwar Argentina now had a larger percentage of adult female slaves, which meant fewer male-headed black households. And the military recruiting had not ended. Conflicts among the regions of the United Provinces of Río de la Plata broke out even before independence had been secured, and war with Brazil over the status of the Banda Oriental soon followed. Slaves, recruited into the contending armies, were once again part of these conflicts, but freedom was no longer offered as an inducement. Slaveholders were a political and economic force whose interests had to be respected, and slavery remained too important an institution for emancipation to be granted as liberally as it had been in the past. Many of the slaves who had fought now found themselves in the courts defending themselves against former owners who claimed them back.

The courts in general continued to recognize the contribution of those who had served, but not in every case. After Francisco Silva fled his owner in 1812, he had an intense and varied military career. He served first in the Regiment of Mounted Grenadiers until being wounded. After recuperating, he was assigned to the militia where he served for a year without pay. There followed nine months of helping to train soldiers before returning to active duty with the Second Regiment in Buenos Aires. His career now shifted as he volunteered for the naval squadron sent to besiege Montevideo, remaining on board the schooner *Fortuna* for the duration of the siege. He subsequently transferred to a new ship, only to be wounded again in an attack on the Arroyo de la China. Nevertheless, he remained in service for a time before retiring to Buenos Aires. Released largely because of his physical infirmities, he soon found himself under arrest on the orders of his old owner. His subsequent treatment is almost incomprehensible: he was taken to jail and then over two days given fifty lashes. Ordered held until a new owner could be found, Francisco considered this unlikely because in his own eyes he was "useless," owing to his various wounds. He asked for help, for his freedom for the "thousand sacrifices" that he had made, but the environment was obviously less favorable than it had been a few years earlier.[7]

For those who had not served in the military, the situation was even less promising. Among them was Miguel's wife, Juliana. Returning to Buenos Aires with her husband after four years of trials and tribulations, she suffered a period without food or clothing before eventually being apprehended by a relative of her former owner. Before the courts she sought freedom for herself and her now four children. "I consider myself worthy of being free together with my children," she said, basing her claim on the grounds that her owner, a Spaniard, had lost all his property rights and that the government had an obligation to her for the "fatigues" she had suffered while she had accompanied her husband. Her appeal failed, however, as the court interpreted Rondeau's offer of freedom very narrowly, finding that it applied only to those who had fought and to those who had fled from Montevideo. She had not been living in the city, nor was her contribution considered equal to fighting. Thus, like others, she returned to bondage. Slavery may have been weakened, but it was not yet dead. It would take several more years of struggle and sacrifice by the Argentine slaves before it was ended once and for all.

NOTES

1. George Reid Andrews, *The Afro-Argentines of Buenos Aires, 1800–1900* (Madison, 1980), 126–27; *Gazeta de Buenos Aires*, June 13, 1811; José Luis Masini, *La esclavitud negra en Méndoza: época independiente* (Mendoza, 1962), 18.

2. Archivo General de la Nación, Buenos Aires (hereafter cited as AGN), Contribución Directa, 1813–1817, "Contribución de fincas, comprobantes de pago," III-35-4-5, Solicitudes Militares, 1815, X-8-7-4, Solicitudes Civiles y Militares, 1816, X-9-2-4.

3. AGN, Solicitudes Militares, 1819, X-11-1-7.

4. AGN, Solicitudes Militares, 1815, X-8-7-5, Administrativos, 1816–1817, Legajo 32, Expediente 1123, "Doña Manuela Tadea Pinazo solicitando la entrega de los esclavos europeos, 1815," IX-23-8-6.

5. John Miller, ed., *Memoirs of General Miller in the Service of the Republic of Peru*, 2d ed., 2 vols. (London, 1829), 1:335.

6. Samuel Haigh, *Sketches of Buenos Ayres, Chile, and Peru* (London, 1831), 235.

7. AGN, Solicitudes, Protección de esclavos, 1816, X-22-1-2.

SUGGESTED READINGS

The few details about the life of Miguel García can be found in the file "La morena Juliana García, esclava que fué de don Pedro García, reclamando su libertad, 1818," located in the Archivo General de la Nación, Buenos Aires, Argentina, Administrativos, Legajo 33, Expediente 1179, Sala IX-23-8-7. Information about the slave soldiers comes principally from George Reid Andrews, *The Afro-Argentines of Buenos Aires, 1800–1900* (Madison, 1980), and José Oscar Frigerio, "Con sangre de negros se edificó nuestra independencia," *Todo es historia* 250 (April 1988): 48–69, as well as the AGN documents entitled Solicitudes Militares, Solicitudes Civiles y Militares, Guerra, Rescate de esclavos, 1813–1817, X-43-6-7, Rescate de esclavos certificados, 1813–1817, X-43-6-8, and Ejército de los Andes, 1816, X-4-2-5 and X-4-2-6. Marta B. Goldberg, "La población negra y mulata de la ciudad de Buenos Aires, 1810–1840," *Desarrollo Económico, Revista de Ciencias Sociales* 16 (April–June 1976): 74–99, and Marta B. Goldberg and Silvia C. Mallo, "La población africana en Buenos Aires y su campaña. Formas de vida y de subsistencia (1750–1850)," *Temas de África y Asia* 2 (1993): 15–69 provide statistics and general background on the slave population in Buenos Aires, while the events of the independence period are the focus of Tulio Halperín-Donghi, *Politics, Economics, and Society in Argentina in the Revolutionary Period*, translated by Richard Southern (Cambridge, 1975). José de San Martín's recruiting in Mendoza has been examined by José Luis Masini, *La esclavitud negra en Méndoza: época independiente* (Mendoza, 1962), and Irene S. Ricoy, "San Martín y la formación de batallones de negros en el Ejército de los Andes," *Boletín Informativo. Dirección de Estudios Históricos. Comando General del Ejército* (Buenos Aires) 7–8 (1973): 115–29. Timothy E. Anna, *The Fall of the Royal Government in Peru* (Lincoln, 1979), describes the actions of the Argentine troops in Peru.

CHAPTER 17

Angela Batallas

A Fight for Freedom in Guayaquil*

CAMILLA TOWNSEND

The city of Quito formed one of the first ruling juntas in 1809, following the forced abdications of Spain's Charles IV and Prince Ferdinand. The head of this new government was Juan Pío de Montufar (Marqués de Selva Alegre), scion of a distinguished noble family, and members of this relatively conservative junta initially sought to rule only until the restoration of the monarchy. Dissension among them and their failure to garner widespread support in other regions of the audiencia *district led to the junta's collapse a mere three months later. When royalist troops occupying the city feared a popular uprising in 1810, however, the soldiers brutally executed most of the rebel leaders in their jail cells. Popular outrage at this massacre contributed to the formation of another provisional government in 1810. This junta ruled for two years, until a royalist army under the command of the newly appointed Audiencia president, Toribio Montes, forced them from power and reestablished royal authority.*

The defeat of these provisional governments in Quito discouraged any new creole autonomy movements anywhere in the Audiencia district (what is today Ecuador), until discontent in the port city of Guayaquil led coastal elites to rise up and form the so-called Republic of Guayas, which proclaimed independence for the city and its hinterland. The new regime embraced many prevailing liberal sentiments, which were reflected in its proclamations and legislation. Two laws, for example, prohibited any future residents of the region from being enslaved and also ended the importation of slaves into the Republic. Moreover, as of July 21, 1821, all children born to slaves were declared free upon their eighteenth birthday. Some legislators even pushed for a decree freeing all of the Republic's slaves. Support for the Liberal Republic did not extend beyond the coast, however, and formal independence for the entire Audiencia district of Quito did not come until the northern insurgent armies of Simón Bolívar's lieutenant, José Antonio de Sucre, won the Battle of Pichincha in 1822. After this victory, Bolívar set up his headquarters in Guayaquil, where he met with the leader of the southern rebel armies of José de San Martín. After that

*An earlier version of this article originally appeared in *Colonial Latin American Review* 7, no. 1 (1998): 105–28.

fateful meeting in Guayaquil, San Martín resigned his command, effectively placing all of the major independence forces under Bolívar.

At this crucial juncture of the independence movements in South America, the young slave woman, Angela Batallas, demanded and received an audience with Bolívar the Liberator. She told an all-too-familiar story. A young slave, she had fallen into a relationship with her owner, Ildefonso Coronel, after he had promised her freedom in return for sexual intimacy. Coronel was in some ways an idealistic and liberal young merchant who gave generously of his time and money to support the independence effort. He also shared his ideas about liberty and freedom with his slave mistress. Problems in the relationship began when Angela became pregnant and later gave birth to a baby girl. Coronel and his family feared that his fathering a child with a slave woman would result in a public scandal and impugn his honor. Nevertheless, Coronel acknowledged the infant as his own on the baptismal certificate, making her legally free, and also sent a regular allowance for his mistress and child.

Angela Batallas, however, wanted more—the freedom that Coronel had promised. This determined young woman filed a legal complaint, secured the services of a lawyer, gathered witnesses, and made an eloquent case. For his part, Ildefonso Coronel (who, in the meantime, had taken a new mistress and also had become engaged to an eligible young woman from a leading Guayaquil family) denied having any sexual relationship with Angela. While pressing her case in court, Angela decided to meet with Bolívar and seek his intervention. Afterward the Liberator wrote a letter to the court supporting her cause, and the determined young slave woman finally secured her freedom.

Camilla Townsend received her doctorate from Rutgers University and is associate professor of history at Colgate University. She has produced several articles as well as written a book comparing social and economic life in two distinct cities, A Tale of Two Cities: Race and Economic Culture in Early Republican North and South America: Baltimore, Maryland, and Guayaquil, Ecuador *(2000).*

*I*n March 1823, Angela Batallas, a slave, demanded to see Simón Bolívar, known as the Liberator, who was leading the war for independence against Spain. The young woman had not chosen the best of moments from the general's perspective. He was camped in the military barracks of the Ecuadorian city of Guayaquil as he tried to organize a southern campaign to expel the Royalists remaining in Peru. "A large number of troops is not being sent because it is impossible," he agonized. "I have no ships, no provisions, and no troops here. We have already spent a hundred thousand pesos and we are just beginning the enterprise. In order to send the next 3,000 [men] God knows what we shall have to do."[1] Angela

Batallas, however, the legal property of a wealthy merchant in the city, would not be dissuaded and insisted that he make time for her. Her dark hair curled around her face in the steamy heat of the rainy season; her skirts were spattered with the mud of the road, for slaves traveled on foot, not on horseback. Whatever the sentries may have thought, given the general's reputation as a ladies' man, this woman had come there neither to engage in any kind of sexual relations with the Liberator nor to accuse him of being the father of her child. Instead, she had come to make a plea and a statement: she wanted her freedom. She believed that justice and the politics of the Liberator were on her side, and she demanded that he hear her out.[2]

There were numerous tensions embedded in the scene that Angela Batallas was about to make. In the hierarchy of the colonial world that Bolívar and Batallas both knew well, he was at the top and she was at the very bottom. The son of a wealthy sugar planter, he was educated in Europe and was now a military general. As a female slave, many would have said that she had even less power than an indigenous peon. Batallas was expected to be docile in her role—grateful to both her master and the general for sharing with her their civilization and religion, for planning the economy that provided her with food, and for protecting her in a world they assumed she could not understand. Yet both Bolívar and Batallas had experienced the different realities of the dynamic between slave owners and the enslaved. Real people of all colors and classes interacted with each other every day. Masters regularly abused their power even by the standards of their own era, and slaves asserted themselves when and wherever they could, in a long continuum of possibilities ranging from completing a task more slowly than a master desired to outright rebellion. Furthermore, Spanish law issued by the crown had always allowed slaves some legal rights vis-à-vis their masters: they could, for example, testify in court, or keep their own gardens and retain the proceeds. In an urban environment, the enslaved were especially knowledgeable about their rights and active in defending them, because most households consisted not only of masters and slaves but also of free black and *mestizo* (mixed European and Amerindian) servants with widely varying life experiences.

The present moment brought a new twist on the old theme. In the early years of the nineteenth century, many of the gentlemen of the Enlightenment who believed that the colonies should be free of control by Spain also considered the possibility that slaves should be free of their masters. Bolívar himself had complex thoughts on this subject. But true to their notion of the natural social hierarchy, all such liberal gentlemen assumed that the slaves would eventually be released by enlightened champions. The reality, however, as Angela Batallas was shortly to remind the general, was that the slaves themselves in many cases took an active interest in politics. They could listen to stories of current events and speak their minds; they could also adroitly turn events to their own advantage.[3] Despite the whites' expectations to the contrary, the enslaved blacks were not waiting passively for their patriotically minded masters to turn their attention to the slavery question.

In the story that Batallas recounted to Bolívar in the Guayaquil barracks, both the traditional and the then-current social tensions surrounding the realities of slavery were exquisitely illustrated. On one hand, she presented the age-old narrative of a man of the master class selecting the mistress of his choice from among his human chattel and then leaving her to face the consequences; on the other hand, that man was forced to learn that control over the woman he thought to dominate was actually impossible. On another level, the drama unfolded at the exact eye of the hurricane of the independence movement. While battles raged around them, the patriot-master who considered himself enlightened on the issue of slavery (among others) was himself effectively attacked by a woman slave, and even Bolívar the Liberator was chastened.

It is difficult to learn about the slaves' part in the dynamic interactions with their owners or to catch glimpses of their political views. They were discouraged even from speaking and certainly were not taught to write or leave diaries. Depending on their own political perspectives, historians have often assumed increasing radicalism or conservatism on the part of the enslaved during the late colonial era and struggle for independence. Neither view is illogical. It is true, for example, that slaves were busy washing floors and plucking chickens and might easily have felt some impatience with their young masters' heady talk of independence, believing that nothing would ever really change for them. On the other hand, the enslaved heard news of uprisings up and down the continent from sailors, many of them black, and from priests sympathetic to their cause; they might have perceived that a new day was coming if they seized their opportunities. Actual evidence as to their views is thin; the best comes from court cases brought by slaves suing for freedom at this time. Such testimony must be used with caution because it comes to us filtered through the Spanish legal apparatus and can hardly be seen as a direct transcription of a slave's first thoughts.

Angela Batallas was one of the many who brought suit against their masters, and it is her case that will be explored here. Indeed, she went to see the Liberator specifically to gain his support. Due to the nature of the court proceedings, the historian can hear only snippets of her own voice, which might be meaningless to the modern ear if quoted out of context or considered from only one angle. For that reason, an effort is made to describe in some depth what was going on in the world in which she made her utterances. The disjunction between her experiences and the political conversations of the day struck her forcibly.

SLAVERY AND GUAYAQUIL

In July 1822 the two great patriot generals, Simón Bolívar and José de San Martín, met for the first time in the city of Guayaquil. Over the course of ten years, Bolívar had successfully fought his way south and westward from his native Venezuela, while San Martín had crossed the Andes from Argentina into Chile and then made his way northward. Now the two men organized the final campaign against the Royalists still left in Peru. Yet despite these momentous events in their own backyard, daily life for the region's ordinary folk in many ways remained unaltered. Change came especially slowly to the countryside surrounding the city. Near the ocean's shore the province of Guayas was dry and sandy: Indians dove for pearls and for the shells used to make purple dye, but there was little vegetation. Not far inland, however, around a network of creeks and rivers, the land turned lush and green, rising gently to peak ultimately in the Andean Mountains.

Plantains, rice, and other food crops grew well in the littoral, making agriculture important. African slaves traditionally worked on the larger plantations. Over the course of the last generation, however, landowners had turned increasingly to hired help. Migrant workers had been coming down from the highlands in large numbers in flight from the depression in their weaving industry, caused by an influx of British textiles under recent government trade reforms. And planters had learned that cacao, which was used for making chocolate and was growing in importance as a cash crop, did not require year-round attention. It was often more cost-effective to hire temporary laborers than to buy slaves. The plantation owners could sell superfluous bondsmen to passing traders or send them to Guayaquil to work for wages as domestic servants, artisans' assistants, or laborers.

In the pre-independence era, slaves thus constituted about 8 percent of the population of the city of Guayaquil, which was home to roughly 20,000 people. The proportion was higher, however, in the town center, on the bank of the Río Guayas where the wealthy lived. Even after the war, on the most fashionable blocks, 24 percent of the residents were enslaved, but toward the outskirts of the city only 4 percent were held in bondage. Life experiences varied considerably for the slaves in the different sections of town. In the most elegant area, one out of every four people was enslaved, and in this sense they could not have felt isolated. Yet they were a people apart within their own neighborhood—darker than the majority and of a clearly lower status. Courtroom evidence indicates that white neighbors knew to whom they belonged, for example, but did not necessarily know their names. On the other hand, further inland from the wealthy riverwalk lived a greater number of people of color, of both Indian and African descent, and most of these, although relatively poor, were not enslaved. The bondsmen among them were not necessarily marked as slaves in their daily workaday lives, and their neighbors probably knew their names. Yet for them, life was filled with its own trials; a slave here was usually the sole servant of his or her owner and thus carried a heavy workload. Such slaves were aware that they comprised by far the largest share of their masters' wealth. One white man who died in 1823 left 600 pesos worth of property, of which 550 came from the value of his slave and her two children.[4]

Besides working almost ceaselessly, enslaved women also had to endure unwanted sexual advances and then live with the repercussions. Their vulnerability to sexual overtures on the part of a series of owners and sometimes other men in the household is demonstrated not only by the high incidence of sexually transmitted diseases among them but also, more tellingly, by the high incidence of the discovery of such diseases by their masters, who often then sued the sellers of the female slaves.[5]

In 1820, two years before the arrival of the famous generals, the province of Guayas had declared itself independent, and the few Spanish soldiers in the area, unable to obtain reinforcements, put up only token resistance. The change in local government may not have made dramatic changes in most people's lives, but from that moment it was clear that in this part of the world, at least, the patriot cause was in the ascendance. The passing battalions of freedmen fighting in the armies of Colombia and Venezuela told their stories. Men who enrolled in the Republican army in exchange for freedom had reason to believe that they would be on the winning side. Some joined the army only to desert later; their women might help them hide. A documented rise in the number of runaways indicates that some took advantage of the atmosphere of chaos caused by the militarization to flee.

In the current political climate, a popular language of "liberty" and "independence" reigned. Thus, there arose among enthusiastic white patriots a certain degree of discomfort with slavery. Did people fighting "tyranny" have the right to tyrannize others? Here the elites could not create a simple dichotomy between white and black as their rebellious North American counterparts had done not long ago, for in this southern world people came in a more varied range of colors and shades and free and slave were not always visually distinguishable. Only two months before Angela Batallas visited the Liberator, the Public Defender who had represented slaves in their legal cases under the colonial regime was pleased to remind the court that it was the Spaniards who had introduced slavery into the New World. He spoke of the "unhappy people . . . whose liberty was snatched away so barbarously by the Spanish."[6] Throughout South America, white enthusiasts for liberty were susceptible to this kind of argument. They remained concerned about protecting their property and their privileged position in the social hierarchy, but at the same time they proudly defined themselves as the creators of a new and more just world.

In the heady days of Republican triumph, the young radicals who governed the independent Republic of Guayas from 1820 to 1822 passed two new laws that directly impacted the slaves: the latter were not themselves freed, but it was made impossible for future Guayaquileños to be enslaved. Further importation of slaves in Republican territory was prohibited—current prices were frozen to prevent speculation—and, as of July 1821, all children born to slaves henceforth were to be freed on their eighteenth birthday. Later a manumission fund was established of monies collected through a small tax on inheritances and deposits made by participating slaves who were hoping to buy their freedom with the aid of the fund. There was even talk of a possible "Decree of Liberty." Many slaves did not waste time waiting to see if such a decree would ever be issued. Instead they set about working in their off hours and depositing weekly sums in the manumission fund. In record numbers they argued with or sued their owners to lower the prices for self-purchase. If liberty was within their grasp, they would reach for it.[7]

THE SUIT OF ANGELA BATALLAS

Angela's childhood remains unknown, even the exact year of her birth, although it was certainly not long after 1800. This utter blank in her story is all too typical. Slave children, except in their occasional church-recorded baptisms, do not exist in the written record of the period. They may appear in the margins of portraits of their masters or as unnamed messengers referred to indirectly in letters, but that is all. Angela Batallas appears in the historical record for the first time only at the moment when her life intersected with that of a leading proponent of the patriot cause. She was still a very young woman when Ildefonso Coronel noticed her and decided to buy her from her old master. It was November 1821 and Guayaquil was in a storm of excitement. The armies of the independence wars were on the move, and the new gradualist emancipatory laws had just been passed. Twenty-seven-year-old Coronel was a wealthy young man actively involved in the patriot movement that was brewing in elite homes like his own, where young people's clubs met to read the works of men such as Thomas Jefferson and Abbé Raynal. Although he had been born in the mountain town of Cuenca to a plantation-owning family, he had lived in this city with his widowed mother since the age of sixteen and was accepted there as a leading citizen. Coronel was a merchant trader, and he hoped that his city's new freedom from Spanish control would allow him to negotiate profitably with British businessmen. He would soon forge a solid relationship with the firm of Gibbs, Crawley & Co. In the meantime, he gave generously of his time and resources for "the cause," so that his name appeared with some frequency in the city's new paper, *El Patriota de Guayaquil.*

Ildefonso paid 350 pesos for Angela, slightly higher than the average price of 325 pesos for a young woman. What her former owner thought we do not know: perhaps he was one of the many who were eager to sell at this time, fearing a general emancipation edict from the new government. Ildefonso did not rape Angela. In fact, he was kind to her. Over the course of the next two months, he did not make direct sexual overtures. When he saw her, he talked to her. They may have spoken about the dramatic current events that everyone was discussing and that influenced them both directly, although in different ways. On the day he approached her to initiate a sexual relationship, he did not threaten her, nor did he promise her the usual pretty clothes or offer her the carrot then most popular—a lowered self-purchase price. Instead, Ildefonso promised Angela her liberty. In the glory of the new Republic that he and his peers were creating, he told her that his love for her would set her free.

In those early months of 1822, Angela apparently was happy, or at least she complained to no one. Her circumstances were not unenviable. She was living in an exciting time. The world around her was unshackling itself, and so was she. A wealthy and powerful man had told her that he loved her. He set her up in a little house by a bridge over a stream that cut into the city from the river, and he came to visit her there, in what she felt was her own home. (He lived with his mother in a fine house on the riverwalk.) Angela later claimed that Coronel treated her as an equal in their private dealings. Master or not, it was the only way he could treat her if he wanted to continue to see genuine joy in her face when he went to her. When she presented herself to the court, she knew how to write her name beautifully, ending her signature with a distinctive flourish. Although this did not prove that she actually knew how to read, even signing her name was more than many free deponents knew how to do. Probably Ildefonso had taught her, or if not, then she had come to him with an unusual degree of sophistication. In either case, it seems likely that they were enjoying together the great days of 1821 and 1822, when the elites of Guayaquil governed their world themselves for the first time, when slavery met the beginning of its end, and when Bolívar purposefully wended his way toward their suddenly important city and then arrived with pomp and met with San Martín.

There were, however, problems. Angela became pregnant almost immediately. At first this did not seem to distress Ildefonso, but eventually he became very upset. It became clear to him that the choices he was making were more complicated than he had thought. He simply could not keep his position in society and at the same time have Angela as the equivalent of a wife or even recognize their child. The radical patriots had not intended this kind of change. He tried to persuade Angela to go to his family's plantation near Cuenca for the birth, in order to keep the child a secret. She refused to go and indeed may have threatened to make the issue public if he attempted to force her, for he did not insist. There in the city, with the help of a free black midwife, Angela gave birth to a daughter, María del Carmen. Ildefonso handed the midwife a note to take to the priest for baptism, indicating that the child was his. He did not mention the slave status of the mother, so that the child was implicitly free now rather than having to wait for her eighteenth birthday, according to the recent law. He did not continue to visit often, but he sent a servant every week with an allowance for the baby's support.

Either late in the pregnancy or right after the birth, Ildefonso chose to distance himself by beginning a relationship with another woman. This time he tried to avoid complications. Melchora Sánchez was free, and she would not press him for marriage or even support: she was already married. She knew about Angela and María del Carmen and was angry that Ildefonso continued to visit them. At the same time, Ildefonso's mother complained bitterly about his scandalous relationship with a slave. She was probably concerned that it would be difficult to arrange a good marriage for him while he was engaged in such an affair. The young man conceived a plan that would satisfy both his mother and Melchora: he moved Angela to the house of his mistress so that the latter could supervise her movements, and he told his mother that he had sold the slave. Then he chose to make himself scarce and went to Lima on a business trip.

While Ildefonso was away, Melchora taunted Angela that she really was to be sold. Angela struck her. She later recounted the incident to her lawyer, apparently without any embarrassment and perhaps even with pride, patiently explaining why Melchora was particularly angry with her. More important, it was after this turn of events that Angela decided to sue for her freedom. She paid the money necessary for the official paper and the cost of a scribe—she could have earned it doing laundry or other chores—and she dictated her complaint. She signed it herself and presented it at the Casa de Gobierno.

The next day she appeared again as she had been told to do, this time with her evidence. She had the baptismal certificate and a list of five women who could serve as witnesses, including the midwife, the servant who had brought the weekly allowance, and the respectable free woman who had served as the child's godmother. Angela must have been beloved by her friends—or else they loathed Ildefonso—for they risked his wrath to testify for her. The servant actually worked in his mother's household, and yet she spoke up as bluntly as the others. Perhaps her age gave her confidence—she was nearly fifty—and certainly she had been charmed by the baby.

Ildefonso denied everything, but Angela clearly had other supporters as well, for she then found a lawyer to present her case. Whether she had saved some money or he volunteered his time or friends helped to secure him is not clear. Later the judge, who was also the governor, ruled that as a slave she was entitled to free representation by the Public Defender. She would need his services, for Ildefonso went to great lengths to account for the misinterpretation that he claimed all the witnesses were maliciously promoting. He clearly felt a great need to do this, and in fact seems to have made a definite decision as to the form he wanted his life to take. By now he must have been courting Mercedes Mateus, a young girl of about sixteen years from one of Guayaquil's leading families, whom he married in February 1824.[8] Coronel argued that the child in question was not his but rather that of a free black man who had befriended Angela. Or perhaps, he said, it had actually been sired by the lawyer, because a slave woman clearly could not have paid him in cash and likely paid with sex. If that were the case, she had probably been his lover for a long time.

It is small wonder that Ildefonso wanted to discredit the lawyer, for with that same lawyer, Angela had presented the most eloquent version of her case. In their statement, the two tied the rhetoric of independence and liberal democracy to Angela's situation as a slave and a woman. They argued that one could not free the colony without freeing all the people. They began by approaching the case from a woman's perspective, arguing that a patriot such as Coronel who had declared himself free of colonial shackles could not become intimate with a person who was unfree. He had become one with her, through intercourse and through their child. Therefore she, too, must be free: "The union of two people of opposite sex renders them one, for from this act regularly results issue: *et erum duo in carne una.* And is it possible to believe, using good judgment, that Ildefonso Coronel, when he proposed such a union to me, wanted half his body to be free, the other half enslaved, subject to servitude, sale and other hatefulness, which some disgraced people cling to as relics of the feudal system that has enveloped us for nearly three centuries?"

The united bodies of the one couple in many ways symbolized the larger body politic: for the whole to be free, all its parts would have to be liberated. In case they had not yet made their point, Angela and the attorney went on to say specifically that a government promoting itself as Republican and demanding popular loyalty on those grounds was going to have to side with Liberty in order to retain its internal logic and widespread support. In European thinking there had, of course, been tension between the principle of slavery and the principle of republicanism since the first appearance of the latter. The lawyer, the judge, and probably Ildefonso were familiar with attempts at reconciliation between the two ideas going back as far as Aristotle and Plato. But the Enlightenment era that had culminated in the independence movement had poked holes in the traditional logic. In Angela's voice she and her lawyer were confident that this new government would not accept her enslavement: "I do not believe that this tribunal will justify it, nor that meritorious members of a Republic that, full of philanthropic and liberal sentiments, has given all necessary proofs of liberalism, employing their arms and heroically risking their lives to liberate us from the Spanish Yoke, would want to promise to keep me in servitude, even against the promise that Coronel made to me the first time he united himself with me."

The language of the presentation is clearly filled with the expressions of the lawyer, Rufino Mora. Whether Angela Batallas could read or not we will never know, but she certainly could not quote Latin. It might be tempting to conclude that a well-educated abolitionist and patriot simply used Angela's pathetic story to make his own points in a public forum. A closer examination of the case, however, indicates that such a conclusion would not be fair. The evidence suggests that Angela herself was actively involved in the construction of the discourse.

At the heart of the argument presented there are two ideas: first, that the joining of the bodies is socially significant; and second, that the patriots are not defending their honor in a consistent manner. Both of these ideas were Angela's. They may have occurred independently to her lawyer, or they may have been in common parlance. The relevant fact here is that she did not owe the ideas to him. She expressed them on her own in her dictated complaint and also verbally in court in a transcribed deposition before Ildefonso denied the charges and before she hired a lawyer. (Ildefonso's charge that she had probably been sexually involved with the lawyer for many months was ignored by the court and still seems dismissable now.) Before the lawyer took over the presentation of the case, Angela talked graphically and without any Latin about the importance of the union of bodies. She emphasized the resulting child who was literally the embodiment of both parents. Of Ildefonso she said: "He is trying to torment a slave woman with whom he has united his blood." Instead of simply referring to her pregnancy, the midwife quoted her as speaking of "the child of his that she carried in her belly."

The idea of the patriots losing their honor through inconsistency may have loomed even larger for Angela than did the concept of the joining of two bodies. The focus of her argument lay in the fact that Ildefonso, a good patriot, had "promised" her liberty. She repeated several times that she had only responded to his advances in the first place because he had given her his word. Once, in her oral testimony, she lost her temper, forgot her social station in relation to those around her, and spoke sarcastically: "Coronel tried to send me to Cuenca to give birth, for the ridiculous reason of not losing his honor—which he values so highly."

Angela touched on a sore point here. Honor had always been a subject of concern to those descended from the Spanish *hidalgos* (noblemen), but it had taken on new resonance in the independence era. The patriots' language was full of references to it. Indeed, they were risking their property and their very lives for their honor: as they saw it, they were asserting their manliness and independence to fight on the side of justice and to defend a savagely abused land and people. They were self-declared heroes. And heroes do not break promises, nor are they hypocrites. Angela implied that if Guayaquil's elite wanted to govern as heroes in a free land, there was only one course open to them.

There is other less direct evidence that Angela had a hand in forming the argument of Rufino Mora's legal brief. First, she obviously had a strong personality and was unlikely to let herself be pushed aside by a man whom she had herself hired or at least agreed to work with. Second, in the next deposition, the one prepared by the assigned Public Defender over whom she would have had no control, the arguments are dry in tone as well as being substantively different. Rather than follow the political lines of argument she had set in her earlier oral testimony, as did Rufino Mora, the new lawyer concentrated instead on a legal technicality: the baptismal certificate proved that Coronel had treated Angela as if she were free and that he had recognized the child as his own. Finally, Rufino Mora wrote erratically, sometimes using flowery rhetoric and foreign words and sometimes speaking like anyone on the street. There are times when he apparently quoted Angela directly. Before launching into one of the polished speeches cited earlier, he wrote the following convoluted—almost chatty and conversational—sentence: "The baptismal certificate is convincing that he considered me free, and that is why he did not mention the character of my servitude, which Coronel certainly had not forgotten about, rather he had already promised me my freedom."

It was certainly Angela Batallas alone who chose to visit Bolívar. Anyone could have thought of it; she did it. Two months after meeting with San Martín, the Liberator had left to tour the highlands, traveling to Cuenca and Quito. He was away when most of the case unfolded, during which time Angela was lodged by the court with a temporary master who volunteered to buy her from Coronel in a lease-like arrangement while the case was being settled. Not long after Bolívar returned to Guayaquil to prepare for the Peruvian campaign, Angela went to see him. No one recorded their conversation, but shortly afterward Bolívar ordered his assistant to write to the court of Guayaquil. He did not try to protect her master's name, despite his high station. "The slave woman Angela Batallas has presented herself to His Excellency the Liberator, complaining of her former master Ildefonso Coronel. His Excellency orders me to recommend to you justice for this unhappy slave."

The note was effective: the Public Defender who received it submitted it that same day to the court, where it became part of the permanent record. Even though Ildefonso responded that there was no new proof of wrongdoing on his part, the Public Defender for the first time felt strong enough to say that it did not matter if some of the witnesses were slaves speaking without their owners' permission, or even if Angela was immoral and the child was actually another man's. The point was that Ildefonso's note to the priest for the baptismal certificate proved that he had promised freedom to the woman: the "integrity" of the new government demanded that Coronel be forced to pay the temporary master for her freedom so that she might be released. The usually dry-toned Public Defender went so far as to say that Coronel was a "miserable man without principles."

It is possible to interpret Angela's visit to Bolívar not as a political statement, or even a savvy effort to intervene in a judicial process stacked against her, but simply as the traditional act of a supplicant appearing before a lord. For generations, the powerless had dreamed of bypassing their overseers to speak to the master or of bypassing their masters to speak to the king. There is something different in this instance, however. Bolívar was hardly a king. He was not ultimately all-powerful in Angela's world: he was the head of one army, still fighting another, not necessarily victorious, and certainly moving on, probably never to return. She knew that he could not simply free her. It is more likely that she saw him as a great and articulate spokesman for ideas she believed in, as someone who would be able to convince others where she had failed. The evidence suggests that Angela Batallas did not visit the Liberator merely to beg a favor, but rather to ask him to publicly side with her on an issue of sweeping importance. In so doing she forced the slaveholding landowner and patriot, Ildefonso Coronel, to reckon with her in a way that he had never intended.

The importance of Angela Batallas lies in the fact that she not only heard everything that was going on around her, thought about it, analyzed it, and perceived the master class with her own eyes, but that she also spoke out about the issues. Despite their best efforts and their wishful assumptions, owners could not keep their slaves from reacting to events. It had to have happened on a daily basis in the colonial era: it took on new significance in the independence era. When political chasms loomed visibly among the elites at the dawn of the nineteenth century and political debate became commonplace, owners could not prevent slaves from participating in their own way. Angela Batallas, like other slaves, used her knowledge of republicanism to further her own case, and she vocalized connections between her own plight and the plight of others who were unfree. Once the enslaved had done that, nothing in the former colonial kingdom could ever be the same again. Now they were engaging in more than psychological struggles with individual owners: they were taking sides in a political battle.

NOTES

1. Harold A. Bierk, ed., *Selected Writings of Bolívar* (New York: Colonial Press, 1951), 359.

2. Archivo Histórico del Guayas, Guayaquil (henceforth AHG), document 698, "Angela Batallas contra su amo, sobre su libertad" (1823). All quotations from the Batallas case come from this document.

3. For example, see Peter Blanchard's article in this volume (Chapter 16) on a typical male slave who joined the army to escape his bondage.

4. Archivo de la Biblioteca Municipal de Guayaquil, Volume 136, Padrones of 1832. AHG document 608, "Inventarios de los bienes quedados por la muerte de Pedro Gonzales" (1823).

5. The *Cuaderno de Conciliaciones* for 1822–23 (AHG document 1546) contains more cases of this kind than of any other type.

6. AHG document 1546 (1822).

7. Camilla Townsend, "En Busca de la Libertad: los esfuerzos de los esclavos guayaquileños por garantizar su independencia despues de la Independencia," *Procesos: Revista Ecuatoriana de Historia* 4 (1999): 73–86.

8. Over the course of the next twenty-eight years, Mercedes went on to bear eighteen children, a number of whom died young. Pedro Robles Chambers, "Genealogía de los Mateus," *Contribución para el estudio de la sociedad colonial de Guayaquil* (Guayaquil: Imprenta de la Reforma, 1938).

SUGGESTED READINGS

Information on Angela Batallas is confined to the records of the Archivo Histórico del Guayas in Guayaquil. However, her life can be compared with that of another female slave: *María Chiquinquirá Díaz, una esclava del siglo XVIII: Acerca de las identidades de amo y esclavo en el puerto colonial de Guayaquil*, by María Eugenia Chaves (Guayaquil, 1998). More information on Batallas's master is available in Guillermo Arosemena, "Los Coronel: grandes comerciantes guayaquileños del siglo XIX," *Revista Ecuatoriana de Historia Económica* 12 (1995): 91–147. A journal kept by a foreign visitor to Guayaquil during the exact period of this narrative makes interesting reading: Basil Hall's *Extracts from a Journal Written on the Coasts of Chili, Peru and Mexico* (Edinburgh, 1824). To place these events in the context of larger changes in the nation, see Kenneth Andrien, *The Kingdom of Quito, 1690–1830: The State and Regional Development* (Cambridge, MA, 1995). For more on the historical struggles between masters and slaves in the area, see David Chandler, "Slave over Master in Colonial Colombia and Ecuador," *The Americas* 38 (1982): 315–26. For the larger Afro-Latino experience, see Herbert Klein, *African Slavery in Latin America and the Caribbean* (New York, 1986). For the theoretical debate on slaves' assertion of power while in their relatively weak position, start with Orlando Patterson, *Slavery and Social Death: A Comparative Story* (Cambridge, MA, 1982), and the more recent collection of essays edited by Stephen Palmié, *Slave Cultures and the Cultures of Slavery* (Knoxville, TN, 1996). For the tensions between slavery and freedom born at the end of the colonial era, see the classic by David Brion Davis, *The Problem of Slavery in the Age of Revolution, 1770–1823* (Ithaca, NY, 1975).

Index

Acosta, Andres de, 251
Acosta, José de, 150
Acuña, Angelina, 44
Acuña, Antonio, 250
Acuña, Juana de, 38, 44
Acuña, Juan de, 36, 43, 44, 47
Acuña, Mariana de, 44
Acuña, Pedro de, 68, 74, 75
Africa, slaves from, 4, 106, 110, 111; religious practices in, 111
Agregadas/agregados (household members), 235
Aguardiente (white rum), 104, 213, 232, 244
Aguiar, Joanna de, 234
Ahaw Kan Ek', negotiations with Spaniards, 164–88
AhChan, 87, 164–88; birth of, 168; brothers of, 174; baptized as Martín Francisco Chan, 179–80, 183, 185; parents of, 168, 169; as mediator between Itza and Spaniards, 168; first mission to Mérida, 172–76; Itza system of governance, 169; marriage into Kowoh ruling family, 168, 169; return to Itza territory, 180–83; role as cacique and king in exile, 184–86; second mission to Mérida, 176–79; escape from Spaniards, 180–84
AhChant'an, 174
AhK'u, 174
AhPana, 181
AhTek, 174, 180
Albornoz, Cristóbal de, 147, 150
Alcabala (sales tax), 213, 241, 248
Alcalde mayor (mayor), 14
Alcalde ordinario (magistrate), 265
Alguacil (constable), 66
Almeida, Paula d', 56
Alvares del Corro, Miguel, 220
Alzaga, Martín de, investigation of Barbarín, 259–77

Ama (owner), 93
Amar, Antonio, 206
Amaral, Domingos Gomes de, 232
Amaro *mocambo*, 112
Amerindians: Catholic evangelizing of, 4, 60–61, 121; enslavement in Portuguese Brazil, 4, 51–52, 86; impact of European disease epidemics, 1, 19, 54, 64, 127, 171, 247; impact of European settlements, 64; prohibited transport to Europe, 66
Anama, Ana, 40
Andaca, Domingo, 40
Andean peoples: after Spanish invasion, 24–26; Aymara language, 140; Chachapoyas, 87; *forasteros advenedizos*, 144; *forasteros revisitados*, 144; migration practices, 45; *originarios*, 144; pre- and post-Conquest property customs, 45, 46; Quechua language, 140, 141; *quipu*, 140; *quipucamayocs*, 140; religious and cultural traditions, 35; Taki Unquy, 150; worship of Catequil, 30; *yanaconas*, 144; Yarovilca dynasty, 159, 160. *See also* Inca empire; Itza Maya kingdom; Maya kingdom; Peru
Angasnapon, Francisco, 27–28
Angasnapon, Pedro, 27
Ánimas solas (orphaned souls), 99
Antonini, Santiago, 274
Aparicio, Manuel, 266
Apoderado (legal representative of Spain), 197
Arancel (price list of favors), 196
Arataca, 53, 54, 57
Araujo, Carlos, 223
Archivo General de Indias, 66, 80
Arellano, Teresa, 266

Argentina: Buenos Aires, 259–77; Corrientes province, 273; in Inca empire, 24; military companies, battalions, and regiments, 283, 285, 287, 288, 290; Paraguay province, 273; Rio de la Plata, 270; Santa Fé province, 273; slaves in military forces, 278–92; United Provinces, 278. *See also* Barbarín, Juan; García, Miguel

Argüello, Bernardo de, 66

Aricoma, Diego, 43

Arredondo, Nicolás de, 260, 263, 265, 266

Arriaga, Antonio de, 241, 242, 252–54, 256

Artigas, José, 281, 282, 285

Atahualpa Capac, 24, 26

Augustinians, 30, 122, 127–28

Autos-da-fé, 14, 15

Avendaño y Loyola, Andrés de, 170, 171, 173, 174, 176, 178, 180

Avila, Francisco de, 141, 177

Ayacucho, battle of, 289

Ayala, Martín de, 146, 156

Ayarza, Gaspar de, 196, 205

Ayarza, Pedro de, 194–210; purchasing *gracias al sacar,* 196–210; wealth and legitimacy, 204; first petition, 199–204; second petition, 204–6; third petition, 206–7; title of "don" granted to son Josef, 206; fourth petition, 207–8. *See also* Ponciano, Josef

Ayllu (kin group), 47

Ayohuma, battle of, 288

Aztec empire, 1

Báez, Francisco, 66, 67, 68, 69, 70, 73, 76

Banda Oriental (Uruguay), 278, 279, 281–82, 284, 287, 290

Bandeirantes (expeditions for indigenous slaves), 229

Bandera, Damián de la, 147

Barbarín, Juan, 193, 259–77; activity with slave community, 269–70; relationship with slave Manuel, 260, 270–72; suspected conspiracy in Buenos Aires, 259–77; arrest and

incarceration of, 272–75; exiled to Spain, 260, 275, 276

Barboza Bueno, Manoel, 238

Barcala, Lorenzo, 285

Basques, Leonor, 101

Bastarda/bastardo (category of mestiza), 230, 234

Batallas, Angela, 193, 293–307; sexual favors for freedom, 300–301; birth of illegitimate child, 294, 301; lawsuit against owner for freedom, 296, 302–4; meeting with Bolívar for intervention, 294–97, 305; freedom won in Guayaquil court, 305

Bautista, Juan, 31

Beata (pious laywoman), 90, 91, 92, 98

Bejarano, Lorenso María, 207

Belgrano, Manuel, 283

Beliaga, Isabel, 58

Belize: Belize River, 166, 173, 185; Chetumal (Chaktemal), 166; and fugitive Maya, 87; Indian Law Resource Center, 186–87; Itza Maya kingdom, 165, 166, 168, 169, 185, 186; San Antonio, 186; San Ignacio, 169; San Luis, 186; Tipuh, 166, 168, 169, 174, 180, 181; Toledo district, 186; Toledo Maya Cultural Council (TMCC), 187; Tz'ul Winikob' province, 166; Waymil, 166

Betancourt, Gregorio, 223–24

Bolio, Manuel, 180

Bolívar, Simón, 289; meeting with slave Angela Batallas, 193, 294–97, 305; views about slavery, 296, 299

Bolivia: Audiencia of Charcas, 35; Cuzco, 41; in Inca empire, 24; Lake Titicaca, 121; La Plata, 35, 36, 38, 40, 42, 46; mining in, 263; Potosí, 45, 88, 126; Santiago de Curi, 35, 36, 38, 40, 42, 44–48; Sucre, 35, 36; Toropalca, 42, 45, 46

Bonaparte, Joseph, 191–92, 278

Borla de los Santos, Francisco, 203

Bran, María, 100

Brazil: African slaves in, 57, 61, 104; Alagoas, 104, 106, 107, 113; Bahia, 52, 53, 57, 58, 61, 116, 229; Bay of All Saints, 52, 57; brazilwood trade, 51; Candomblé, 111; Cubiabá, 232;

Cucaú, 115; Dutch invasion of, 85, 86, 112; enslavement of Amerindians, 51–52; Goiás, 86, 229; Jaguaripe, 57; Kalunga, 106; Luso-Brazilian troops, 104, 113–14, 116–19; Macaco *mocambo*, 104, 105; Mato Grosso, 86, 106, 229, 232; Minas Gerais, 86, 229, 232, 238; *mocambos* in, 104–20; Olinda, 4, 51; Palmares settlement, 86, 104–20; Penedo, 117; Pernambuco, 51, 53, 58, 61, 85, 86, 104, 106, 107, 116; Porto Calvo, 105, 112, 113, 116, 117, 118; Portuguese settlement of, 4, 51–63; *quilombolas/mocambos* in, 106–20, 109; Recife, 104, 105, 107, 114, 116, 117; Recôncavo, 52, 56, 57, 59; Rio de Janeiro, 51, 104, 229, 234; Salvador, 55, 56, 57, 104, 229; Salvador da Bahia, 4, 51, 52, 57; Santana, 192, 232–33, 234, 237; São Paulo, 4, 116, 192, 229; São Vicente, 51, 53; Serra da Barriga, 107, 109, 112, 116; Serra Dois Irmãos, 118; settlement of New Christians, 56, 58; sugar production in, 61, 232; Tall Palms, 59; Tupi-Guarani peoples, 51, 52. *See also* Fernandes Nobre, Domingos; Silva, José Antonio da; Zumbi of Palmares
Brito Freire, Francisco de, 110

Cabello Balboa, Miguel, 150
Cabezas, Tiburcio, 224
Cabildo (city council), 4, 265
Cabral, Pedro Alvares, 4, 51
Cacica (female ethnic leader), 92
Cacicazgo (chieftaincy), 40
Cacique principal (paramount lord), 25, 27, 35, 38
Caciques (indigenous leaders), 23, 25
Calidad (social rank), 208, 230
Camacho, Juan, 77
Cámara, granting "whiteness," 194, 195–98, 200, 202–5, 207–8
Canary Islands, 71
Cano, Isabel de, 92
Caramurú, Diogo Alvares, 53
Cardoso, Brás da Rocha, 112
Carlos II, 178, 179

Carmen, María del, 301
Carmen, Virgin (Our Lady) of, 90, 94, 97, 101
Caro, Rodrigo, 71, 72
Caro, Ysabel, 71, 72
Carretero, Juan Martín, 267, 268, 269
Carrilho, Fernão, 114
Carua, Juana, 44
Caruarayco, Felipe, 27. *See also* Caruarayco Capac
Caruarayco, Luis, 32
Caruarayco, Melchior, 4–5, 22–34; as *kuraka* of Cajamarca, 22–34; religious changes, 30–33; last will and testament, 27–29
Caruarayco Capac, 26–27
Caruatongo Capac, 26
Carvalho e Melo, Sebastião José de, 189, 191
Casa de la Contratación (Board of Trade), 66, 76, 78, 79, 80
Castas (mixed racial ancestry), 88
Caste: colonial descriptions of, 81; Indian, 68. *See also* Catalina
Castilian law: about kinship and legitimate heirs, 41; governing inheritance, 35–50; *imbecilitus sexus*, 39; parental assets to legitimate heirs, 42; patterns of inheritance, 37
Castilla, Francisco de, 69, 70, 73
Castillo, Gaspar Antonio del, 8
Castro, Antonio, 284
Castro, Justo, 220–21
Catalina, 5, 64–83; feature of *pequeña de cuerpo*, 80; Indian caste, 68; and *limpieza de sangre*, 65; as *mestiza*, 68; as *morena*, 73; parents of, 67, 72; "passing," 65; as *perra india*, 69; with physical markers of an Indian, 69, 70; sister María, 67; as *soltera*, 80
Catholic Church: Brotherhood of Our Lady of Copacabana, 40, 44; Church of Our Lady of Ajuda, 55; on concubinage, 233; Convent of Santa Clara, 86; converting Andeans, 140; Council of Trent, 126; evangelizing Amerindians, 4, 60–61, 121; Our Lady of Guadalupe, 38, 87; presence in Peru, 25, 32; Third Order of the Regular clergy in Peru, 92

Caxal, Juan, 77
Cédula de gracias al sacar (edict of legitimation), 192, 194, 196
Central America, independence of, 192
Cercado (urban indigenous sector), 88
Cerrito, battle of, 281
Chab'in, Juan, 185
Chacabuco, battle of, 288
Chachapoyas, 27, 87, 141, 154–56
Chamach Xulu, 183
Chan, Pedro Miguel, 179–80
Charles II, 189
Charles III, 242
Charles IV, 191, 196, 278, 293
Chayax, Manuel Joseph, 180, 182, 183
Chi, Ah Kulel: birth of son, 20; murder of, 11, 18–19
Chi, Gaspar Antonio, 4, 6–21; birth of, 7, 19–20; baptism of, 18; childhood and youth, 16–20; Franciscan schooling of, 6; murder of father, 10; adult years, 12–16; as Interpreter General, 9–10, 13, 17; Otzmal massacre, 19; singing plainsong, 17; at summit at Uxmal, 17–18; senior years, 9–12; on Yucatán before Conquest, 11; death of, 7, 8–9
Chicha (maize beer), 29, 39, 244
Chile: and Inca empire, 24; independence of, 288; slaves sent to, 263. *See also* García, Miguel
Chinori Guarachi, Martín, 40
Chocoboto, María, 40
Chols, 185
Choquecota, Gregorio, 246–47
Christianity: activities in Peru, 30–33; Portuguese efforts in Brazil, 54. *See also* Catholic Church
Chuplingón, Alonso, 26, 31–32
Chuptongo, 26, 32
Chuquichambi, Hernando, 38
Cinchon, Conde de, 32
Cisneros, Francisco, 255
Ciudad Rodrigo, Pedro de, 13–14
Clare of Assisi, Saint, 93, 96
Cloth manufacturing, impact of European goods, 211–12
Cobo, Bernabé, 91
Cobrador (tax collector), 250
Coca (coca leaves), 39

Cofradía (religious brotherhood), 38, 88, 125, 255
Colombia: Barbacoas, 213; Cartagena de Indias, 4, 64, 66, 70, 71, 74, 78, 81; in Inca empire, 24; Popayán, 213, 214, 215, 218; Santa Fé de Bogotá, 215, 218; Santa Marta, 68; Xagueyes del Rey, 68, 69, 70
Columbus, Christopher, 1, 64
Comentarios reales de los Incas (Vega), 141
Comunero Revolt, New Granada (1781), 191, 204
Concacax, 26
Concepción, Francisco de la, 92
Concertaje colectivo (labor contract), 224
Condorcanqui, José Gabriel, 193, 241, 242
Conversos (converted Jews), 56, 66, 197
Copacabana, Virgin of, 121
Corbacho de Espinosa y Albares, Lorenzo, 200
Cordón, battle of, 283
Córdova y Salinas, Diego de, 92
Coronel, Ildefonso, 293–306; sexual relationship with female slave, 294–306; birth of illegitimate child, 294, 301; and Gibbs, Crawley & Co., 300; marriage of, 302. *See also* Batallas, Angela
Corral, Francisco del, 67, 68, 78
Corral, Regina, 226
Corregidores de españoles (magistrates), 1
Corregidores de indios (rural magistrates), 1, 22, 27, 38
Cortés, Hernán, 1, 20, 167
Corvée (forced labor service), 1
Cosatongo, 26
Couto, Loreto de, 117
Creoles, 85, 147
Criada (servant), 95
Cristo, Catalina de, 92
Cristo, Juan de, 92–93
Cruz, Francisca de la, 101
Cuba: Havana, 64–83. *See also* Catalina
Cueva, Luis de la, 72

Delgado, Juan, 67, 74
Demandadores (agents), 122, 124, 125, 129
Diamond mining, 86

Dias, Diogo, 56, 57
Díaz, José, 273, 274, 275, 276
Díaz, María, 69
Diseases. *See* Epidemics/diseases
"Don," purchase of title, 194–210
Donadas/donados (servants recognized for spiritual contributions), 89, 92
Donoso, Mariano, 221–22
Duarte, Ana, 71
Dueños de indios (ethnic lords), 23, 31
Duho (stool of office), 31
Dumont, Juan Luis, 274, 276
Durán, Bartolomé, 182

Echevarria, Manuel Antonio de, 207
Ecuador: Barbacoas, 218; Collacoto, 223; Cotopaxi, 213; Cuenca, 211; Guayaquil, 215, 220, 293–307; Latacunga, 213; Luluncoto, 222, 223; Mount Pichincha, 222; Otavalo, 217, 224; Quito, 26, 155, 211–28; Riobamba, 213; Río Guayas, 297; San Sebastián, 222; Tungurahua, 213. *See also* Batallas, Angela; Loza, Victorina
El Patriota de Guayaquil, 300
El primer nueva corónica y buen gobierno (Guaman Poma de Ayala), 140, 141, 144, 145, 148–49, 152–53, 157–61
Encomenderos (grant recipients), 1, 11, 17, 75; in Ecuador, 214; tax and labor assignments in Andes, 22
Encomiendas (grants), 1, 6, 22
Engenhos (large plantations), 86, 105
Enlightenment thinking, 259, 264, 295, 303
Enríquez, Diego, 71, 72
Enterador (overseer), 246
Entradas (expeditions), 53
Epidemics/diseases: impact on Amerindians in Brazil, 54, 64; impact on Andean peoples, 25; impact on native populations in Peru, 127, 247; impact on Spaniards and native population in Yucatán, 171; of yellow fever in Brazil, 116
Escribano del rey (royal notary), 66
Esquivel, Rafaela de, 94–95, 98
"Expediente Prado Tello," 144, 145
Ezpeleta, José de, 202, 203
Ezterripa, Francisco Xavier de, 201

Familiares (privileged group serving Inquisition), 56
Ferdinand V, 55, 56
Ferdinand VII, 191, 192, 278, 293
Fernandes Nobre, Domingos, 5, 51–63; as *mameluco* go-between, 52; dual identity of, 54–55; identity of "Tomacauna," 55, 58, 59, 60, 61; wife of, 55, 58; practicing Santidade, 52, 56, 57, 58, 59; denouncement of, 56; confession of, 58–60
Fernández Farias, Antonio, 75
Fernández Jaramillo, Juan, 66–67, 69–70, 73–75
Ferrera, Alonso, 74, 75
Filho natural (illegitimate child), 233, 234
Fiscales (attorneys), 197
Florida, 64
Forasteros (migrants), 45, 144, 154
Forasteros advenedizos (recent arrivals in *ayllus*), 144
Forasteros revisitados (living in their respective *ayllus*), 144
Fortuna (ship), 290
Franca, Ignacia, 230, 233–34, 236, 238
Franciscans, 92, 167; activity in Peru, 30; education of local boys in Yucatán, 16; La Mejorada convent, 174, 177
Franco, Francisco, 234
Free Womb Law, 282–83
Freire, Angel, 266
Freitas, Décio, 107, 108
French Revolution, 259, 261, 264, 265, 267
Fuentes, Juan de, 31

Galeota (heavily armed attack boat), 171, 182
Gananciales (community property), 39
Ganga Muiça, 114
Ganga Zumba, 105, 111; Ardra origin, 111; chief of confederation of *mocambos*, 114; growth of Palmares, 112; *nganga* (religious specialist), 111; Portuguese suppression of, 115, 116; as *rei*, 114; retreat to Cucaú, 115. *See also* Zumbi of Palmares

García, Baltasar, 268
García, Bartolomé, 246
García, Juliana, 286, 291
García, Mateo, 286
García, Miguel, 193, 278–92; fighting at Montevideo, 279, 280–82, 285, 286, 288, 291; realities of army life, 286–87; seeking freedom through military service, 278–92; spouses of black soldiers and compensation, 286, 289; wife kept at slave status, 279, 291
García, Pedro, 279, 281
García, Ventura, 286
García de Bustamonte, Miguel, 273
Garcilán, Lucas, 68, 80
Garrástegui Oleada, Pedro de, 179
Gauna, José Bernardino, 290
Gauna, María Antonia, 289–90
Gendias, Lieutenant, 75
Gil de Azamar, Pablo, 174, 175, 176
Gold mining, 86, 229
Gómez, Cristóbal, 67–68
González, Juan, 182
González, Luis, 68
González de Cuenca, Gregorio, 30, 31
Gracias al sacar (price list of favors), 194
Graham, Richard, 52
Grimau, Antonio, 267
Groot, Pedro, 201
Guadalupe, Virgin (Our Lady) of, cult in Peru, 38, 87, 122, 125–28, 131, 134–36
Guaman Poma de Ayala, Felipe, 28, 87, 140–63; as mitmaq descendant, 142; birth in Huamanga, 145; education and assimilation of European ways, 145–46; as cacique principal, 144; serving church and state, 147–54; as indio ladino, 144, 145; discrediting and punishment of, 141, 154–57; expulsion from Huamanga, 146; Tingo-Guaman claims to land, 141, 155–56; identified as Lázaro, 156; kinsmen's dispute with Chachapoyas, 141; contribution to Black Legend, 160
Guambo Tapa, Francisco, 253
Guarangas (unit of 1,000 households), 27

Guatemala: Baja Verapaz, 166; Ch'ich', 181; Chich'en Itza, 166, 168; Lake Petén Itzá, 164, 170–71, 175, 180, 181; Los Dolores, 185; Motskal, 181; Nohpeten, 167, 169, 170, 171, 173–75, 178, 180, 181, 183; Petén, 87, 164, 166, 167, 168, 172; Santiago de Guatemala, 171, 185; Spanish conquest of Itza kingdom, 164–88
Guayas, Republic of, 293, 299
Guayna Capac, 24, 26
Gutiérrez, Magdalena, 44
Gutiérrez, Ysabel, 72
Guzmango Capac title, 26

Haiti, slave uprising and revolution, 260, 261, 262, 265
Hamamani, Domingo, 40, 42
Hariza y Arruyo, Francisco, 173–76
Hernández Portocarrero, Martín, 76
Herrera, Beatriz de, 18
Hidalgos (noblemen), 304
Historia general del Perú (Vega), 141
Honduras, 166, 167
Huanca, Catalina, 92
Huascar Capac, 24, 26
Huayna Capac, 155

Illanez, Pedro Juáres de, 27
Inca empire: aclla, 35; after Spanish invasion, 24–26; ayllu, 22; Cajamarca region, 23; Chuptongo, 26; City of the Sun, 24; Concacax, 26; Cosatongo, 26; cults of, 22; founding of, 140–41; guaranga curaca, 28; Guayna Capac, 24; Guzmango Capac, 26; hatun curaca/huno apo, 28; huacas, 22; Huayna Capac, 155; impact of epidemic diseases, 25; Inca's seat (usnu), 151; kurakas, 22, 23–24; pachaca camachicoc, 28; Quechua language, 140, 141, 142; Sapa Inca (unique or supreme ruler), 35; Sun god (Inti), 35; Tawantinsuyu, 25, 35, 140–41, 160; Túpac Inca Yupanqui, 26; Vilcabamba, 150; Vilcashuaman, 151. See also Chi, Gaspar Antonio; Guaman Poma de Ayala, Felipe; Túpac Amaru

Inconfidencia Mineira, Minas Gerais (1788), 191
Inquilla, Domingo, 5
Inquisition: history of Portuguese, 55–56; history of Spanish, 55–56; Holy Office in Lima, 88; torture of Cocom nobles, 10
Inter-American Commission on Human Rights, 187
Isabella, and Spanish Inquisition, 55–56
Itquilla, Alonso, 41, 42, 43
Itquilla, Diego, 41, 43
Itquilla, Domingo: joint assets in marriage, 35–50; *cacique principal* in Bolivia, 35, 36; *chacra* of Chilcane, 40, 41, 42, 44; first will and testament, 40–41; gaining office of *cacique*, 47; illegitimate/bastard sons, 41, 43; Vilcaparo and Otavi properties, 41, 42, 44; last will and testament, 42–44; death of, 44. *See also* Sisa, Isabel
Itza Maya kingdom: impact of disease epidemics, 171; Spanish conquest of, 164–88; Tipuh, 166, 168, 169, 174, 180, 181; Tz'ul Winikob', 168. *See also* AhChan
IxKante, 168, 169

Jácome Bezerra, Antônio, 113
Jaga, 106
Jauli, Domingo, 156, 157
Jefferson, Thomas, 300
Jerome, Saint, 123, 124
Jeronymites, 86. *See also* Ocaña, Diego de
Jesuits, 91, 177, 185, 223; activities in Brazil, 54
Jews: as *conversos*, 56, 197; as New Christians in Portugal, 56; as Old Christians in Spain, 197
João VI, 191
Junín, battle of, 289
Juntas (provisional governments), 192

K'eb', Andrés, 175
Kehaches, 167, 173
Kowohs, 166, 167, 168, 169, 171, 172, 184

Ladino (Hispanized, cultured), 12, 17
Lama, Antonio, 285–86
Landa, Diego de, 7, 10, 11; as province bishop, 12–13; jailing and torture of Mayas, 14; burning of pre-Conquest Maya literature, 14–15; investigation of, 14–15; return to Yucatán as bishop, 16. *See also* Chi, Gaspar Antonio
Las Piedras, battle of, 281
Levia, Damián de, 72
Lima, Peru: Barrios Altos, 89; Convent of Santa Clara, 89, 92, 101; cult of Señor de los Milagros, 92; enshrined image of Our Lady of Guadalupe, 125, 134; *limeño* (resident of Lima), 90, 92; obsession with Purgatory, 97; Saint Rose of Lima, 101; Third Order of the Regular clergy, 92
Limpieza de sangre (purity of blood), 65
Lizarraga, Nicolás de, 185
Loayza, Pascual Antonio de, 251
Lockhart, James, 7
Lopes, Manuel, 113–14
López, Angel, 266
López de Aguila, Juan, 77
López de Cogolludo, Diego, 17
Losar, Diego del, 130
Louis XVI, 259, 261, 268
Loza, Manuel, 213
Loza, Miguel, 226
Loza, Nicolasita, 226
Loza, Victorina, 192, 211–28; early life in Quito, 213, 214; conducting business, 220–25; death of first husband, 217; estate of El Tintal, 223, 224; estate of Lloa Chiquito, 222, 223; hacienda of Ambuela, 224, 225; keeping established trading routes, 218–20; marriage to second husband, 212, 217, 220, 225–26; purchasing land, 222–24; second husband's infidelity, 225–26; last will and testament, 226
Ludeña, Francisco de, transporting *india* to Europe, 64–83. *See also* Catalina
Ludeña, Gerónimo de, 71, 77, 79

Ludeña, María de, 77
Ludeña Valdes, Mateo de, 71, 77

Macaco *mocambo*, 104, 105, 107, 112, 114, 117
Maiorais (chiefs), 111, 112
Mairena, Anton de, 67, 72, 73
Mairena, Catalina de, 79
Malaver, Felipe, 285
Malaver, Francisca, 285
Malcaden, Pablo, 31, 32
Maldonado, Melchor, 76, 78
Malvinas Islands, 275
Mamelucos (mixed-blood offspring), 51, 53, 60, 61–62, 116
Mandoncillos (lesser lords), 28
Mandones (overseers), 28
Marie Antoinette, 259, 261
Martínez, Joseph, 253
Martínez, Justo, 253, 254
Martínez de Murgia, Juan, 78
Mata, Juan de, 27
Mateus, Mercedes, 302
Maya kingdom, 1; AhChan, 87, 164–88; *ah kin*, 13; alphabet adapted from Spanish, 10; *batab*, 7, 8; *batabob*, 10; *cah/cahob*, 6, 9, 10; *chibal/chibalbob*, 6; Cholan Maya languages, 165; Cocom, 10, 18–19; Cocom *chibal*, 6; impact of disease epidemics, 19; *k'atun* calendar, 170; K'ekchi' Mayas, 186, 187; Maya language, 12; Mopan Mayas (Muzuls), 167, 173, 176, 177, 185, 186, 187; Nachi Cocom, 10, 11, 16, 19; Otzmal massacre, 19; Spanish conquest of Itza kingdom, 164–88; Tekax, 8, 9, 10; Tiho, 19; Tizimin *cah*, 7; Xiu clan, 4, 6, 7, 8, 10, 12; Xiu Family Tree, 18; Yucatec Mayan dialect, 166. *See also* Ahaw Kan Ek'; Chi, Gaspar Antonio; Landa, Diego de
Mayllos y Marcana, Pablo, 268, 269–70, 272, 274, 276
Mayordomos (stewards), 125, 129
Mejora (supplementary bequest), 42
Melgarejo Sotomayor, Luisa de, 90, 91, 98
Melo, Antônio, 105, 112, 113, 114
Melo de Portugal, Pedro, 275

Mencos, Melchor de, 184
Mendoza, Juan de, 77
Mercedarian Order, 222
Mesa, Francisco de, 78, 79
Mestizaje (racial mixture), 66, 146
Mestizo/mestiza (racial mixture of European and Indian), 33, 47–48, 68, 146, 214, 295
Mexia, Andrés, 11
Mexia, Jordana, 29
Mexico: Cortés in, 167; independence of, 192
Meza, Diego José, 253
Miller, William, 286
Mita (forced labor draft), 46, 147, 151, 245–46
Mitimaes (fixed permanent residences), 143
Mitmaqkuna (Inca settlers of newly conquered areas), 45, 142
Montejo, Francisco de, and invasion of Yucatán peninsula, 6, 18, 20, 164, 167
Montes, Toribio, 293
Montufar, Juan Pío de, 293
Mora, Rufino, 303
Moraes, Francisco Xavier de, 236
Moreno/morena (dark complexion), 73
Moriscos (converted Muslims), 66, 74
Moscoso y Peralta, Juan Manuel, 242, 252, 253, 254–56
Mosquera, José María, 218, 220
Mulatas (women of mixed African and European ancestry), 69, 92, 107
Mules, trade in, 248
Muñoz, Pedro, 267–68, 269
Muñoz de Arjona, Pedro, 251, 252
Murúa, Martín de, 146

Nachi Cocom, 10, 11, 16, 19
Nahuatl, 12, 15, 17
Napoléon, invasion of Iberian peninsula, 191, 278
Navarro, Diego Lorenzo, 78
Nesado, Anton, 69
New Christians: Jews as, 56; settlement in Brazil, 56, 58
New Granada, Viceroyalty of, 189, 190, 197, 200
Nikte Chan, 174
Ninalingón, Sebastián, 32

Obregón, Antonio de, 76, 79
Ocaña, Diego de, 86, 87, 121–39; as
    Guadalupan *demandador* in Peru,
    125–27; as creator and dispenser of
    holy images, 129; and death of
    Martín de Posada, 127; *libros de*
    cabellerías a lo divino, 135; narrative
    of visit to New World, 126, 127–36;
    paintings of Virgin of Guadalupe,
    122; temptation of, 130–34
Ochoa, Carlos, 250
Oliveira, Anna de, 235
Oliveira Furtada, Maria de, 232
Olmedo, Martín de, 41–42
Oré, Luis Jerónimo de, 150
Originarios (native-born members of
    Andean settlements), 144
Orixás (Afro-Brazilian religion), 111
Osenga *mocambo*, 113
Otárola, Miguel Bonifacio, 285

Pachacuti (inversion of world), 25
Padilla, Simón de, 68–69, 73, 74
Palmares: Catholic influences, 111;
    central position of women, 110;
    communal principles, 108; creole
    language, 110; Luso-Brazilian
    attacks of, 114, 115, 116; members
    and inhabitants of, 108; polyandrous
    marriages in, 110–11; religious
    practices, 111; religious "temple" or
    council house, 109; slash-and-burn
    agriculture, 108; trading or raiding
    practices, 108, 109–10. *See also*
    Zumbi of Palmares
Panama, 64
Paraguay, 278
Parcialidades (lineages of larger
    community), 27
Parda/pardo (dark-skinned), 195, 230,
    234
Pasquines (handwritten lampoons), 263
"Passing" as white, 65, 194
Pax colonial, in Yucatán, 17
Pedro I, 191
Peña, Fernando Lucas de la, 212, 216–
    17
Peru: after Spanish invasion, 24–26;
    Army of, 288; Aymaraes province,
    146, 151; Bambamarca, 29;
    Cajamarca, 23, 26, 27, 28, 29;

Callao, 288; Canas y Canchis, 241–
    43, 245, 247–48, 249, 251–52, 254;
    Cascas, 28; Chachapoyas, 154–56;
    Chiara, 155; Chilete, 27, 28;
    Chinchero, 243; Chulaquys, 28;
    Chupas, 141; Chuquisaca, 125, 134;
    Churcan de Cayanbi, 28;
    Colquemarca, 27; Condoroma, 251;
    Contumasá, 28; Coporaque, 193,
    242–44, 248, 251–52, 254–56;
    Cuenca, 30; Cunchamalca, 28;
    Cusipata, 251; Cuzco, 125, 134, 151,
    241, 242, 243, 244; earthquake
    disaster in 1687, 88; Espiritu Santo
    de Chuquimango, 27; Gironbi, 28;
    Guadalupe, cult of Virgin of, 122,
    126–28, 131, 134–36; Guaento, 28;
    Guamachuco, 30; Guzmango, 26,
    27, 28, 29; Guzmango Capac, 26;
    Huamanga, 142, 144, 145, 151, 154;
    Huancayo, 157; Huánuco, 142; Ica,
    125, 134, 157; Inquisition, Holy
    Office of the, 88; Junba, 28; Lake
    Titicaca, 242; Lima, *see* Lima, Peru;
    Lucanas province, 145, 147, 150,
    151; Malcaden, 27; Nazca, 157;
    Olmos, 130; Pacasmayo, 127;
    Pampamarca, 244, 252; Pichigua,
    251, 253, 254, 256; Piura, 130;
    Potosí, 125, 126, 134, 245–46;
    pueblos, clusters of, 146;
    Pumacahua, 243; Puno, 242;
    Quiquijana, 250; Quispicanchis,
    243, 247–48, 249, 250; Rose of
    Lima, Saint, 89, 91, 92; Saña, 87,
    121, 127, 134; San Andrés de Checa,
    248; San Lorenzo de Malcadan, 27;
    San Pablo de Cacha, 253; Santa Ana
    de Cimba, 28; Soras province, 147,
    150, 151; Sucre, 125; Surimana, 244,
    252; Tinta, 242, 245; Trujillo, 27,
    29, 121; Tucumán, 252; Tungasuca,
    244, 248, 252; Viceroyalty of, 241,
    248; Yauri, 251, 253, 254, 256. *See*
    also Guaman Poma de Ayala, Felipe;
    Ocaña, Diego de; Sinanyuca,
    Eugenio
Philip II, 56, 77, 124
Philip III, 157, 160, 161
Philip V, 189
Philippine Islands, 85

Pichincha, battle of, 293
Pires, Gertrudes, 230, 231, 232, 235–36, 237, 238
Pires Monteiro, Salvador, 235
Pius V, 55
Pizarro, Francisco, 1, 26, 27
Polo, Cristóbal, 198
Poma Inga, Lucas, 250–51
Pombal, Sebastião José de Carvalho e Melo, Marquis of, 189, 191
Ponciano, Josef: father's attempts to purchase whiteness, 195, 196, 200–208; permission to receive university degree, 196, 204; granted title of "don," 206. *See also* Ayarza, Pedro de
Popoloca, 15
Porras, Martín de, 92, 100
Porteños (residents of Buenos Aires), 260, 261, 265, 270, 278
Portobelo trade fairs, 4
Portugal: Cape San Vicente, 76; exploration and settlement of Brazil, 4, 51–63; high court in Brazil, 84–85; Inquisition, 52; Pombol reforms, 189, 191; sugar production in Africa, 53–54
Posada, Martín de, 122
Prica, Juan, 40
Probanza de mérito (proof of merit), 9
Procurador (solicitor), 78
Puente, Vicente de la, 242, 253–55
Puerto Rico, 64
Pulgar, Inés de, 90
Pumacahua, Mateo, 243

Qualidade (ancestry and honor), 230
Quechua language, 140, 141, 142
Quijada, Diego de, 14
Quilombos or *mocambos* (settlements of fugitive slaves), 104, 105, 106–20
Quimbundo language, 106
Quinterones (persons of one-fifth mixed race), 197
Quipu (system of knotted cords), 140
Quiteño cloth, 211

Race: *mestizaje* (race mixture), 66; "passing," 65. *See also* Catalina
Racial hierarchy, 231–40
Ramalho, João, 53
Ramírez, Bernardo, 203

Rappaport, Joanne, 48
Raynal, Abbé, 300
Rebellion of the Barrios, Quito (1765), 191, 212, 213
Recôncavo, 52
Reducciones (consolidation of settlements), 33, 46, 151, 154
Relación (Landa), 15, 16
Relación de antigüedades de este reyno del Pirú (Salcamaygua), 141
Reparaz, Juan Antonio, 246–47, 251–52
Reparto (forced distribution and sale of goods), 241, 247
Rey, Josef, 201
Ribeira, Clara Maria, 229, 230, 233, 234, 236, 238
Río de la Plata, Viceroyalty of, 189, 190, 241, 248, 260; battles for independence in, 279, 280, 282, 285, 288, 289, 290; resistance to Spanish authority, 278–92
Ríos, Gerónima de los, 90
Ritos y tradiciones de Huarochirí (Avila), 141
Riva, José de la, 268–69
Rivera, Pedro de, 156
Rivera, Tadea, 266
Robespierre, Maximilian, 259, 260, 268, 276
Rodil, José Ramón, 288
Rodríguez, Bartolomé, 72–73
Rodríguez, Catalina, 67, 72
Rodríguez, María, 74
Rodríguez Sierra, Diego, 79
Rondeau, José, 281–82, 283, 285, 291
Rose of Lima, Saint, 89, 91, 92, 101
Rousseau, Jean-Jacques, 264
Roxas, Gómez de, 67, 68

Saint Domingue. *See* Haiti
Salazar, Diego de, 31
Salcamaygua, Joan de Santa Cruz Pachacuti Yamqui, 141
Sánchez, Melchora, 301
Sánchez, Pedro, 67
Sánchez de Aguilar, Pedro, 16, 18
Sánchez de la Flor, Francisco Xavier, 192, 212, 217, 220, 225–26
Sandoval, Domingo, 267
San Francisco, Agustina de, 92
San Joseph, Estephanía de, 92

San Martín, José de: campaign against
    Royalists, 283, 284, 285, 288–89,
    290, 297; resignation of, 293–94
San Pedro (ship), 77
Santa María la Rosa (ship), 78
Santidade cult, 52, 56, 57, 58, 59
Santillana, Pedro de, 12
Santo Domingo, Royal Audiencia of,
    76
Sapa Inca, 242
Selva Alegre, Marqués de, 293
Señor de los Milagros, cult of, 92
Senzalas (slave barracks), 105
Sequera, Juan de, 68, 70, 73, 75
Sertão (wilderness interior), 51, 53
Silva, Adrião da, 231
Silva, Damazio Antonio da, 235, 237
Silva, Francisco, 290
Silva, Francisco de Paula da, 237
Silva, José Antonio da, 192, 229–40;
    extramarital liaisons, 230, 231, 233–
    34, 235, 236, 239; illegitimate
    children of, 230, 231, 233–34, 235,
    236; mulatto daughters by his slave
    women, 235–36; wife of, 229, 230,
    233, 234, 236, 238
Silva, José Antonio da (Paulista), 231–
    32
Silva, Joséfa Thereza, 231
Silva, Nicolás de, 68
Silva, Reginaldo Damazio da, 237
Silva Pacheco, Anna da, 232
Silver mining, 85, 88
Sinanyuca, Cristóbal, 244–45
Sinanyuca, Eugenio, 193, 241–58;
    Collana *ayllu*, 244; as *kuraka* of
    Coporaque, 243–44; effects of
    reparto rates, 248; opposition to
    mita, 245–47; relationship with
    Arriaga, 252; struggle between
    church and state, 252–53; excom-
    munication of, 252–53
Sinen, Antonio, 287
Sipe-Sipe, battle of, 281, 286, 288
Sisa, Isabel, 5, 35–50; shared assets in
    marriage, 44; and *imbecilitus sexus*,
    39; *chacra* of Chilcane, 39, 44, 47,
    48; Vilcaparo and Otavi properties,
    47; legitimate son and sole heir, 39,
    41; last will and testament, 36–40,
    48

Slaves/slavery: abolition of, 106; from
    Africa, 64, 111; African freedmen,
    88; African slaves in Brazil, 57, 61,
    86, 104; Amerindians as slaves, 51–
    52, 86; Archicofradía de San Benito,
    269, 276; and black soldiers in
    service for freedom, 278–92; Buenos
    Aires as slave port, 262–63; deposits
    in manumission fund, 299; end of
    African slave trade in 1812, 282;
    Free Womb Law, 282–83; Portu-
    guese slave trade in Africa, 54;
    quilombolas or *mocambos*, 104; revolt
    of slaves in Haiti, 259, 260, 261,
    262, 265; sexual advances by
    masters, 298, 300. *See also* García,
    Miguel; Ursula de Jesús; Zumbi of
    Palmares
Soares, Antônio, 117
Society of Jesus, 54. *See also* Jesuits
Solsol, Baltazar, 155
Sosa, Domingo, 281, 285
Sota, Juan, 156
Sotes, Fermín, 271
South America, independence of, 192
Spain: Alcalá de la Guadaira, 67, 71,
    72, 79, 80, 81; *arancel*, 196; *cédula de
    gracias al sacar*, 194; Córdoba, 75;
    Extremadura, 122, 123, 126; Gandil,
    72; Guadalquivir River, 76;
    Guadalupe, Our Lady of, 121, 123;
    Jerez de la Frontera, 47; Royal
    Pragmatic on Marriages, 194, 195;
    San Lorenzo, 77; Sanlúcar de
    Barrameda, 76, 78; San Pedro, 80;
    Seville, 4, 71, 72, 76, 77, 78, 80;
    "The king counts more than blood,"
    197; Toledo, 124; war with France,
    261, 262. *See also* Inquisition
Suárez, Magdalena, 225
Suárez, Pedro, 80
Suárez de Poago, Ana María, 68
Suárez de Poago, Melchior, 68, 75,
    76
Sucre, José Antonio, 293
Sugar production, 51–52, 53, 61, 64,
    86, 104
Sumkal, Francisco, 186

Tabasco, 166, 167
Taki Unquy, 150

Talavera, Gabriel de, 124, 125
Tawantinsuyu, 22, 35, 140–41, 160
Tek, Juan Francisco, 180
Tekax, 8, 9, 10
Tenochtitlan, 167
Tingo, Juan, 155
Tipuh, 166, 168, 169, 174, 180, 181
Toledo, Francisco de, 46, 143, 151, 152, 154
Toledo Maya Cultural Council (TMCC), 187
Tomacauna. *See* Fernandes Nobre, Domingos
Toral, Francisco, 7, 12–13, 15
Torres, Tomás Andrés, 200
Torres y Portugal, Fernando de, 155
Tudela, Juan de, 38
Tupa, Hernando, 44
Túpac Amaru, 151, 153; as *kuraka* of Canas y Canchis, 243, 244; opposition to *mita*, 245; opinion of system of *corregidores*, 251–52; rebellion against *reparto*, 247–49; revolts in Andes, 191, 204; stripping Arriaga of *corregidor* status, 242, 252, 256; title of Sapa Inca, 242; capture of, 243
Túpac Amaru, Marcos, 245
Túpac Amaru II, 193, 241
Túpac Inca Yupanqui, 26
Túpac Katari, 191
Tupi-Guarani, 4, 51, 52
Tz'ul Winikob', 168

United States: Constitution, 264; Declaration of Independence, 259, 261, 264; independence of, 261
Upper Peru, 278, 285, 288
Ursúa y Arizmendi, Martín de, 164, 168, 170–82
Ursula de Jesús, 86, 88–103; as *donada* in Convent of Santa Clara, 89, 95; influence of Melgarejo Sotomayor, 90, 91; brush with death, 94; devotion to Virgin of Carmen, 90, 94, 97, 101; diary of, 90–91; entrance to Convent of Santa Clara, 90; familiarity with dead souls in Purgatory, 96–97; as spiritual authority, 98; death of, 101

Uruguay: as Banda Oriental, 279, 281–82, 284, 287, 290; Montevideo, 279, 280–82, 285, 286, 288, 291
Uz, Fernando, 8

Valdes, Gerónimo de, 68, 70, 73
Valdes, Leonor de, 77, 78
Valtierra, Antonio, 185
Vásquez, Diego, 47
Vásquez Albán, Tomasa, 213
Vecinos (citizens), 42, 68, 213
Vega, Garcilaso la, 141
Velho, Domingos Jorge, 116–17
Venezuela, 289; Caracas, 71; Santiago de León, 71
Veracruz, 4, 167
Verdugo, Melchior, 27, 29
Viana, Gregorio de, 252
Videla, Antonio, 281
Vieira de Melo, Bernardo, 117
Vilcohuma, battle of, 281
Villacis, Catalina de, 77, 80
Villaorellana, Marquis de, 224
Villavicencio y Guerrero, Vicente Isidro, 221, 222
Virgin Mary, devotion to. *See* Carmen; Copacabana; Guadalupe
Visitador (ecclesiastical inspector), 147, 189
Visita general (general inspector), 46

"Whiteness," purchase of, 194–210
Wikab', Mateo, 174, 175, 176, 179
Women and gender inequalities, 35–50; *imbecilitus sexus*, 39

Xiu, Ix Kukil, 18, 19
Xiu, Pedro, 8
Xiu Family Tree, 18
Xulcapoma, Cristóbal, 31
Xulcapoma, Sancho, 31

Yalain, 174, 183
Yanaconas (Andeans in service of Europeans), 144, 156
Yarovilca dynasty, 159, 160
Yrazabal, Ramón, 266
Yucatán: AhChan's missions to Mérida, 172–81; Bacalar-at-Chunhuhub', 173, 176; Campeche, 166; Chich'en Itza, 18, 19, 164; Cocom clan, 17;

Hocaba region, 14; Homun region, 14; Izamal, 17; Mani, 7, 8, 13, 18; Mérida, 6, 7, 8, 13, 16, 17, 19, 164; *pax colonial*, 17; Quintana Roo, 166, 173; Saksuus, 173; Salamanca de Bacalar, 167; Sotuta, 10, 14, 17; Spanish conquest of Itza kingdom, 164–88; Tizimin, 13, 17; Uxmal, 17; Xiu clan, 17

Zenda, Bernardo, 246
Zorrilla, Juan A., 144
Zublián, Diego, 27

Zumbi of Palmares, 86, 104–20; birth in Palmares, 105; stolen at young age, 111; baptized as Francisco, 112–13; Catholic upbringing, 111–12; education of, 112; teenage years in Palmares, 113; as *cabo de guerra*, 113, 114; changing name to Zumbi, 113; *mestre de campo* (general of arms), 114; predecessor of, 105, 111; support by communal surplus, 110; wife of, 105, 113; defeat and death of, 117–18. *See also* Palmares